Power, Legal Education, and Law School Cultures

There is a myth that lingers around legal education in many democracies. That myth would have us believe that law students are admitted and then succeed based on raw merit, and that law schools are neutral settings in which professors (also selected and promoted based on merit) use their expertise to train those students to become lawyers. Based on original, empirical research, this book investigates this myth from myriad perspectives, diverse settings, and in different nations, revealing that hierarchies of power and cultural norms shape and maintain inequities in legal education.

Embedded within law school cultures are assumptions that also stymie efforts at reform. The book examines hidden pedagogical messages, showing how presumptions about theory's relation to practice are refracted through the obfuscating lens of curricula. The contributors also tackle questions of class and market as they affect law training.

Finally, this collection examines how structural barriers replicate injustice even within institutions representing themselves as democratic and open, revealing common dynamics across cultural and institutional forms. The chapters speak to similar issues and to one another about the influence of context, images of law and lawyers, the political economy of legal education, and the agency of students and faculty.

Meera E. Deo, JD, PhD, is Director of the Law School Survey of Student Engagement (LSSSE) and Professor of Law at Thomas Jefferson School of Law. Her research merges jurisprudence with empirical methods to interrogate institutional diversity, affirmative action, and racial representation. Her book, *Unequal Profession: Race and Gender in Legal Academia* (Stanford University Press, 2019) examines how raceXgender affects workplace interactions, tenure, work/life balance, and more. Professor Deo has been a member of the California Commission on Access to Justice, consultant to the ACLU of Southern California, and Chair of the AALS Law and the Social Sciences Section.

Mindie Lazarus-Black is Professor Emerita of Anthropology, Temple University. She has conducted fieldwork in Antigua, Trinidad, and the U.S. to understand how, when, and why law operates as a discourse and practice of rights and repression. She is the author of *Everyday Harm: Domestic Violence, Court Rites, and Cultures of Reconciliation* (2007), *Legitimate Acts and Illegal Encounters: Law and Society in Antigua and Barbuda* (1994), and is co-editor (with Susan F. Hirsch) of *Contested States: Law, Hegemony, and Resistance* (1994). She has also published in, among others, *American Ethnologist, Caribbean Studies, Law & Social Inquiry*, and *Indiana Journal of Global Legal Studies.*

Elizabeth Mertz is an anthropologist and law professor; her research focuses on legal language and law school education. Her book, *The Language of Law School: Learning to "Think Like a Lawyer"*, won the Law & Society Association's Herbert Jacob Book Prize; it also provided empirical support for the 2007 Carnegie Report on legal education. She is a Fellow of the American Anthropological Association; Research Professor at the American Bar Foundation; and John and Rylla Bosshard Professor Emerita at the University of Wisconsin Law School. Her current research focuses on U.S. law professors and the "new legal realism" project.

Emerging Legal Education

Series Editors:
Paul Maharg, *Osgoode Hall Law School, North York, ON, Canada*,
Elizabeth Mertz, *University of Wisconsin-Madison/American Bar Foundation, USA* and
Meera Deo, *Thomas Jefferson School of Law, San Diego, CA, USA.*

Emerging Legal Education is a forum for analysing the discourse of legal education and creating innovative ways of learning the law. The series focuses on research, theory and practice within legal education, drawing attention to historical, interdisciplinary and international characteristics, and is based upon imaginative and sophisticated educational thinking. The series takes a broad view of theory and practice. Series books are written for an international audience and are sensitive to the diversity of contexts in which law is taught, learned and practised.

Other titles in this series:

Law and Leadership
Integrating Leadership Studies into the Law School Curriculum
Edited by Paula Monopoli and Susan McCarty

The Moral Imagination and the Legal Life
Beyond Text in Legal Education
Edited by Zenon Bankowski and Maksymilian Del Mar

The Arts and the Legal Academy
Beyond Text in Legal Education
Edited by Zenon Bańkowski, Maksymilian Del Mar and Paul Maharg

Affect and Legal Education
Emotion in Learning and Teaching the Law
Edited by Paul Maharg and Caroline Maughan

Imperatives for Legal Education Research
Then, Now and Tomorrow
Edited by Ben Golder, Marina Nehme, Alex Steel and Prue Vines

https://www.routledge.com/Emerging-Legal-Education/book-series/ELE

Power, Legal Education, and Law School Cultures

Edited by
Meera E. Deo, Mindie Lazarus-Black
and Elizabeth Mertz

Routledge
Taylor & Francis Group
LONDON AND NEW YORK

First published 2020
by Routledge
2 Park Square, Milton Park, Abingdon, Oxon OX14 4RN

and by Routledge
605 Third Avenue, New York, NY 10017

First issued in paperback 2021

Routledge is an imprint of the Taylor & Francis Group, an informa business

Publisher's Note
The publisher has gone to great lengths to ensure the quality of this reprint but points out that some imperfections in the original copies may be apparent.

British Library Cataloguing-in-Publication Data
A catalogue record for this book is available from the British Library

Library of Congress Cataloging-in-Publication Data
Names: Deo, Meera E. (Meera Eknath), 1975- editor. | Lazarus-Black, Mindie, editor. | Mertz, Elizabeth, editor.
Title: Power, legal education, and law school cultures / Meera E Deo, Mindie Lazarus-Black, Elizabeth Mertz.
Identifiers: LCCN 2019041892 (print) | LCCN 2019041893 (ebook) | ISBN 9780367199401 (hardback) | ISBN 9780367199432 (ebook)
Subjects: LCSH: Law--Study and teaching--Social aspects. | Law--Study and teaching--Social aspects--United States.
Classification: LCC K100 .P69 2019 (print) | LCC K100 (ebook) | DDC 340.071/1--dc23
LC record available at https://lccn.loc.gov/2019041892
LC ebook record available at https://lccn.loc.gov/2019041893

ISBN 13: 978-1-03-224012-1 (pbk)
ISBN 13: 978-0-367-19940-1 (hbk)

Typeset in Galliard
by Taylor & Francis Books

We dedicate this volume to Manoj Kulkarni, Bill Black, and Chas Camic, with deep thanks for your support in this and so many other projects important to us.

Contents

Illustrations

Figures

Tables

Boxes

Author Biographies

Swethaa Ballakrishnen is an Assistant Professor of Law at the University of California Irvine School of Law and Affiliated Faculty at the Center of the Legal Profession, Harvard Law School. Ballakrishnen's research broadly examines the intersections between law, globalization, and stratification from a global south, critical feminist perspective. Particularly, across a range of sites and levels of analysis, their work interrogates how law and legal institutions create, continue, and counter different kinds of socio-economic inequalities. Together, these motivations have resulted in three main areas of empirical inquiry – gendered inequalities across comparative legal institutions, diversity and the reproduction of hierarchy within legal education and the profession, and the socio-legal ramifications of transnational migrant families. Scholarship from these projects has appeared in, among other journals, *Law and Society Review*, *Law and Social Inquiry*, *International Journal of the Legal Profession*, and *Fordham Law Review*. A forthcoming book that explores the case of unexpected gender parity in elite Indian law firms is under contract with Princeton University Press.

Émilie Biland is a Full Professor of Sociology at Sciences Po (France). She is a member of the Centre de Sociologie des Organisations in Paris and of the Institut Universitaire de France. She has worked on several areas of socio-legal studies, such as legal education, public law, and family law. She is interested in the role of law and lawyers in public policies, since they contribute to the shaping of gender and class relations. She has published articles in this field of study in several journals. Articles published in English include: "Government Lawyers and the Training of Senior Civil Servants: Maintaining Law at the Heart of the French State" (with Rachel Vanneuville), *International Journal of the Legal Profession* (2012); "National Paths Towards Private Ordering: Professional's Jurisdictions and Separating Couples' Privacy in the French and Canadian Family Justice Systems" (with M. Mille and H. Steinmetz), in *Delivering Family Justice in the 21st Century* (2015); and "Are Judges Street-Level Bureaucrats? Evidence from French and Canadian Family Courts" (with Hélène Steinmetz), *Law and Social Inquiry* (2017).

Stephen Daniels is a Research Professor at the American Bar Foundation. He holds a PhD in political science from the University of Wisconsin-Madison. His research focuses on law and public policy, legal education, and the various aspects of the American civil justice system. He has written on law school curriculum and financing, trial courts, juries, plaintiffs' lawyers, and the politics of civil justice reform – including the areas of medical malpractice, products liability, and punitive damages. He is co-author (with Joanne Martin) of *Tort Reform, Plaintiffs' Lawyers, and Access to Justice* (2015). Professor Daniels is now working on two projects. The first examines questions surrounding affordability and the financing of legal education. Supported in part by a grant from AccessLex Institute, this research builds on his work as the reporter/consultant to the 2014–15 American Bar Association Task Force on the Financing of Legal Education. The second examines questions surrounding the increasing interest in licensed legal professionals as means of promoting greater access to justice.

Meera E. Deo, JD, PhD, is Director of the Law School Survey of Student Engagement (LSSSE) and Professor of Law at Thomas Jefferson School of Law. She has held visiting positions at the law schools at UC Davis, UC Irvine, UCLA, and UC Berkeley. Her research utilizes empirical methods to interrogate institutional diversity, affirmative action, and racial representation. Professor Deo's scholarship has been published in leading law journals and cited in numerous amicus briefs filed in the U.S. Supreme Court. Her forthcoming book, *Unequal Profession: Race and Gender in Legal Academia* (Stanford University Press, 2019), draws from her landmark Diversity in Legal Academia project, a study that examines how the intersectionality of race and gender affect interactions with faculty and students, tenure and promotion, work/life balance, institutional support, and other aspects of the personal and professional lives of American law faculty. While a law student at the University of Michigan, Professor Deo was an Intervening-Defendant and member of the legal team supporting integration/affirmative action in *Grutter v. Bollinger*. She later practiced civil rights law with the ACLU National Legal Department in New York City and the California Women's Law Center in Los Angeles. The National Science Foundation (NSF), the Paul & Daisy Soros Fellowship, and numerous internal grants and awards supported her at UCLA, where she earned her doctorate in Sociology. Professor Deo serves on the Executive Committee for the AALS Section on Law and the Social Sciences and was an appointee to the California Commission on Access to Justice. She also has been an empirical research consultant to the South Asian Network (SAN) and the ACLU of Southern California.

Liora Israël is Professor of Sociology at L'École des Hautes Études en Sciences Sociales (Paris), Centre Maurice Halbwachs. Her scholarship focuses on several topics, including political mobilization of law during the twentieth century, legal education, and anti-discrimination law. Professor Israël is the author of two books and has edited several volumes including *Dealing with Wars and Dictatorships: Legal Concepts and Categories in Action* (with Mouralis

Guillaume, 2014). She was awarded the Adam Podgorecki Prize by the Research Committee on Sociology of Law of the International Sociological Association in 2008. She has served as a member on the Editorial Board of the *Law and Society Review*, *Canadian Journal of Law and Society*, and *Droit et Société*. She was also elected trustee of the Law and Society Association (2014–2016).

Mindie Lazarus-Black is Professor Emerita of Anthropology, Temple University. Previously she served as Professor of Criminology, Law, and Justice, and Affiliate Professor of Anthropology, at the University of Illinois at Chicago. She received her PhD in Anthropology from the University of Chicago. Professor Lazarus-Black's scholarship focuses on anthropology and law, domestic violence, and the history and ethnography of class, kinship, gender, and the state in the English-speaking Caribbean. She is the author of *Everyday Harm: Domestic Violence, Court Rites, and Cultures of Reconciliation* (2007), *Legitimate Acts and Illegal Encounters: Law and Society in Antigua and Barbuda* (1994), and co-editor (with Susan F. Hirsch) of *Contested States: Law, Hegemony, and Resistance* (1994). She has published in, among others, *American Ethnologist, Caribbean Studies, Law & Social Inquiry*, and *Indiana Journal of Global Legal Studies*. Her fieldwork in Antigua and Barbuda, Trinidad and Tobago, and in the U.S. explores how, when, and why law operates as a discourse and practice of rights and repression. Currently she is focusing on "Lawyers Beyond Borders," a study that interrogates the internationalization of legal education. Her research investigates the experiences of transnational lawyers who have come to the U.S. to pursue a LL.M. degree, the faculty who teach them, and the administrators who admit and advise the students during their studies. Recent publications examine who seeks a U.S. law degree and why, and what these students observe about the U.S. ("us").

Elizabeth Mertz is Research Professor at the American Bar Foundation and John and Rylla Bosshard Emerita Professor of Law at the University of Wisconsin Law School, where she is also Affiliated Faculty in the Department of Anthropology. Her scholarship focuses on legal education, on translating social science for law, and on the intersection of law and language, analyzed from an anthropological perspective. Professor Mertz's study of first-year law school education, *The Language of Law School: Learning to "Think Like a Lawyer"* (2007) was co-winner of the Law & Society Association's Herbert Jacob Book Prize. She holds a PhD in Anthropology as well as a JD, and was elected a Fellow of the American Anthropological Association. She was Editor of the *Political and Legal Anthropology Review* from 2007 to 2011, and for many years served as an Editor of *Law & Social Inquiry*. Professor Mertz was elected Treasurer of the Law & Society Association, a Trustee on the LSA Board, and class representative to the Executive Board of LSA. Her current empirical research projects focus on law professors in the U.S., and on the process by which social science is translated for use in legal settings. Her writings have appeared in such publications as the *Harvard Law Review, Law & Society*

Review, and the *Annual Review of Anthropology*. She is co-editor of *Law in Action: A Socio-Legal Reader* (2007) and *The New Legal Realism* (2016); she is editor of *The Role of Social Science in Law* (2008).

David Sandomierski is an Assistant Professor in the Faculty of Law at Western University. He holds an SJD from the University of Toronto, where his doctoral dissertation received the Governor General's Academic Gold Medal. He has served as Editor-in-Chief of the McGill Law Journal and as law clerk to the Chief Justice of Canada, the Rt. Hon. Beverley McLachlin.

Carole Silver is Professor of Global Law and Practice at Northwestern University Pritzker School of Law and Affiliated Scholar at the American Bar Foundation. Her research explores the ways in which global forces interact with legal education and the legal profession, including its regulation. She conducted the first empirical study of the careers of international LL.M. graduates, and has written about the ways in which U.S.-based elite law firms respond to globalization's influences, focusing on hiring preferences, growth and organizational approaches. Additionally, her scholarship has explored diversity in law school and in global law firms. Publications of her work have appeared in law reviews and peer-reviewed journals. Prior to joining Northwestern, Silver was Professor of Law at Indiana University Maurer School of Law and Director of the Law School Survey of Student Engagement; earlier, she served as the first Executive Director of Georgetown's Center for the Study of the Legal Profession.

Aaron N. Taylor is the Executive Director of the AccessLex Institute Center for Legal Education Excellence and a Professor at Saint Louis University School of Law. He joined AccessLex and before that SLU LAW, after a career as a higher education administrator. Professor Taylor's primary research interests are in the area of higher education law and policy. From 2014 to 2017, Professor Taylor was director of the Law School Survey of Student Engagement (LSSSE), a national study that seeks to measure the effects of legal education on students. Professor Taylor's articles have appeared in journals published by American University, Howard University, Stanford University, University of Notre Dame, and University of New Mexico. His commentaries have appeared in numerous publications, including *The Chronicle of Higher Education* and *The New York Times*. He is a frequent media commentator on education and diversity topics. Professor Taylor received a bachelor of arts in political science from North Carolina A&T State University, a juris doctor from Howard University, and a doctorate in higher education leadership and policy from Vanderbilt University. He is also an alumnus of the Harvard University Administrative Fellowship Program. He is a member of the Florida Bar.

Riaz Tejani is Associate Professor of Business Ethics in the School of Business at the University of Redlands. His research into law school marketization addresses problems of race and class inequality, access to justice, finance and globalization, and organizational culture. Professor Tejani's first book, *Law Mart: Justice, Access, and For-Profit Law Schools* (2017), is an ethnographic account of proprietary legal education during and after the global financial crisis. His second, *Law and Society Today* (forthcoming 2019), critically surveys contemporary themes in socio-legal studies after "law and economics." Professor Tejani serves on the National Advisory Council of the non-profit research center Law School Transparency, and his recent articles have appeared in *American Ethnologist, U.C. Irvine Law Review*, and *Political and Legal Anthropology Review*. His work has been cited in outlets ranging from the *Yale Law Journal Forum* and *Annual Review of Law and Social Science* to *Inside Higher Ed* and *NPR Illinois*. Professor Tejani holds a PhD in social anthropology from Princeton University and a JD from the USC Gould School of Law, where he was a Fellow at the Center for Law, History, and Culture. His past research affiliations include the École Normale Supérieure-Ulm and the United Nations Education, Scientific, and Cultural Organization in Paris, France.

Rachel Vanneuville holds a PhD in political science and is a research fellow at the French National Center for Scientific Research. She works at "Triangle," a research center based in Lyon. Her primary interests center on relationships between law and politics. Her current research focuses on the French highest administrative court (Council of State), and on legal education. Together with Liora Israël, she directed a research project on the legal training of French elites (Elidroit, 2009–2012). Related publications include: Émilie Biland and Rachel Vanneuville, "Government Lawyers and the Training of Senior Civil Servants: Maintaining Law at the Heart of the French State," *International Journal of the Legal Profession* (2012); Liora Israël and Rachel Vanneuville, "Legal Training and the Reshaping of French Elite: Lessons from an Ethnography of Law Classes in Two French Elite Higher Education Institutions," *Journal of Education and Work* (2017).

Introduction

Mindie Lazarus-Black, Elizabeth Mertz and Meera Deo

A pervasive assumption lingers around legal education in many democratic states. That assumption would have us believe that law schools are neutral settings in which professors use their expertise to train meritorious law students to become lawyers. Those lawyers will in turn take rules and laws, and the technical mode of analysis taught by law schools, and apply these in concrete situations to support a legal system that takes formal law seriously. Over time lawyers, judges, and administrators shape a legal system that treats most people equitably and fairly. The stated principles and rules, then, hold the key to understanding and practicing law.

Of course, many would acknowledge that this assumption is flawed – that it is overly idealistic, at the very least. But even a cursory glance into the cultures of otherwise diverse law schools will reveal how central the story remains to justifying those schools' educational practices and institutional legitimacy. Like many cultural beliefs, these ideas remain resistant to contrary evidence, to findings from empirical research, and to repeated efforts at reform. Beneath the surface are dynamics that continue to deliver results contradicting the stated goals of law schools – at the same time making those results seem inevitable and natural. Indeed, any unfairness or unevenness in process or outcome will disappear within a story that attributes the results to merit – while any cultural skewing in the content of legal pedagogy will become invisible within a set of values viewing legal principles as neutral. Similarly, efforts to address the professed division between theory and practice can run afoul of hidden dynamics buried in professors' conceptualization of professional identity. In all of these cases, deeper structural and power dynamics are at work within and beneath law school cultures.

The chapters in this volume demonstrate that reform efforts within legal education will need a strong foundation in social science studies in order to address those deeper dynamics, if those efforts are to succeed. Research on legal education is burgeoning across many social science and legal communities. However, much of the academic and media discussion of how best to reform legal education rests upon inadequate empirical research – a gap these chapters seek to help remedy. This volume originated in a process of creating networks and dialogue that could draw empirical scholars working on legal education together across many silos and boundaries, building from a National

Science Foundation funded conference held at the American Bar Foundation in Chicago.[1] Among the silos that have prevented collaborative knowledge-building are boundaries between scholars espousing different methods (quantitative versus qualitative, for example), between experts concerned with structural barriers in legal education and those concerned with curricular reform, and among scholars from different parts of the world. In coming together, we challenge assumptions about the neutrality, equity, and fairness of legal pedagogy.

The Power in Hidden Messages: Law School Cultures in the Process of Reform

The contributions to this volume track the way power operates within legal training – and the way law school cultures harbor hidden dynamics that are not easily accessible to researchers, but rather require deeper analysis and investigation. Together these chapters document processes that operate at multiple levels. Instead of creating equal playing fields for law students and professors of all backgrounds, these invisible processes contribute in unrecognized ways to hierarchy and exclusion. They accomplish this, in part, by making particular ideas about law seem natural or inevitable, while blocking consideration of alternative conceptualizations. Those quiet processes also create unacknowledged barriers for students from traditionally excluded groups (and even when those students are able to surmount those barriers, they do so surrounded by subtle messages that continually enforce dominant norms and values which differentially discourage "outsiders"). For example, drawing on W.E.B. Du Bois's conceptualization of "marginality," Aaron Taylor provides stunning empirical evidence of how U.S. law schools have perpetuated black students' "adverse incorporation into dominant cultures or centers of power, resulting in deficient power" in these contexts, from admissions practices through funding to the content of curriculum (and see Du Bois, 1903). Stephen Daniels details how continuing financial barriers contribute to unequal access to legal education. An apparently equal playing field is anything but equal, but the struggles caused by inequality can only be seen through a deeper look at the facts.

In these studies of students learning about law as text and as empirical practice, structural processes of quiet marginalization, alongside cultural beliefs that imbed bias in institutions, turn out to be core aspects of legal education (not the exceptions we would prefer to think they are). Deeply embedded in the curricula of law

1 The NSF conference took place at the American Bar Foundation in March 2017, which under PI Elizabeth Mertz spearheaded the effort to organize a workshop to forge connections among the varied social science researchers currently undertaking studies both of legal education in the U.S.A., and of global connections between U.S. law schools and legal training in other parts of the world. It was designed to form the basis of ongoing cooperation and networking among scholars working on legal education, as well as to lay foundations for this book. More information on the conference, as well as preliminary versions of papers and powerpoints, can be found at www.americanbarfoundation.org/research/summary/1043 (last visited 6/12/2019).

schools are invitations to accept hierarchies in the worlds governed by law, as Émilie Biland and Liora Israël, and Rachel Vanneuville demonstrate with regard to cultures of law and of capitalism in France. Analyzing law schools' own rhetoric in U.S. legal discourse, Riaz Tejani finds that a market logic substitutes for concerns about justice and morality, while David Sandomierski demonstrates that U.S. law schools have much to learn from an empirical account of the Canadian experience regarding faculty members' professed theory about law and its relationship to practice. Among law students, international students struggle uniquely with the language and experiences of legal education. As Swethaa Ballakrishnen and Carole Silver show, being international is a fluid, not a rigid state; power within and between students, faculty, and administrators circulates in oftentimes unpredictable ways. In addition, Meera Deo's study of the remarkably complex experiences of women of color demonstrates the great importance of using an intersectional (raceXgender) lens to understand how law schools continue to emphasize powerful entrenched norms that assume the ineptitude of such faculty, at the same time that they encourage service activities that undermine those professors' professional success. Drawing upon her own and Deo's research on the difficulties faced by "traditional outsiders" within law school faculties, Elizabeth Mertz explores why these institutions fail to shift their culture and rhetoric, pointing our attention especially to the issue of implicit bias. Even conscious efforts to challenge the status quo can be diverted – in ways that are difficult to detect but nonetheless extremely powerful. Building from the Bourdieu-inspired work of law professor Bryant Garth (2015) on global flows of power through legal education and from anthropologist Michael Herzfeld (2015), Mindie Lazarus-Black's contribution cogently analyzes this as "inchoate power," a phenomenon that is explored throughout the volume.

Each of the sections in the book highlights different aspects of inchoate power in legal education – but, as noted above, threads of the collection's central themes run throughout. In Part I, the volume begins with a consideration of hidden messages in law school pedagogies, showing how power is refracted through the obfuscating lens of legal curricula. In Part II, authors directly tackle questions of class and market as they affect law training in subtle ways. Finally, Part III asks how structural and cultural barriers continue to operate to replicate forms of power within institutions (law schools) that represent themselves as democratic and open. The chapters within each section speak to similar issues and to one another, although they also span different countries and settings. Throughout we see that context matters, but at the same time we also see that inchoate power is at work across all contexts. The book as a whole allows us to think about the dynamics of legal training within capitalist settings across a variety of cultural and institutional forms.

Volume Outline

In Part I, *Legal Pedagogies in Context(s)*, studies of the law school curriculum and modes of instruction provide clear examples of seemingly objective and unproblematic facets of legal education that are actually part of how academic culture both reflects and perpetuates an unequal power structure. Interestingly, it is at that level that some real opportunities for change may lie. Beginning with interview and textual analysis findings from David Sandomierski, we recognize that the tension between theory and practice evident in Canadian law schools (and perhaps worldwide) may be both more nuanced and less antagonistic than originally perceived. We also see that qualitative empirical research can uncover patterns that have unrecognized effects on issues that are central to reform efforts, as law schools struggle to incorporate practice into teaching. Mindie Lazarus-Black provides additional clarity with an insightful ethnographic examination of how inchoate power affects the ongoing globalization of legal education (both at home and abroad), invoking questions about academic culture, the imperial process, and pedagogical style. Here again, detailed contextual analysis points out hidden patterns with important effects on pedagogy and student experience. This part ends with Émilie Biland and Liora Israël's painstaking observation-based research at two elite French institutions, revealing that in spite of underlying differences, there are theoretical, practical, and pedagogical similarities in how both schools acculturate students into capitalist ideology. These patterns go unrecognized in the absence of in-depth observational research.

Part II explores *Class and Market in Legal Education*, examining how debt, financing, and recruiting not only contributed to the current crisis in legal education but also continue to maintain inequities with regard to race, class, and social status. Rachel Vanneuville's observational study of training for French civil servants reveals the political stakes related to legal education, including ways in which students are socialized into their future government positions as the law alternately creates and bars entry to powerful positions. In the next chapter, Stephen Daniels builds a fascinating historical timeline of broader structural patterns affecting legal education, including how cost, affordability, and access have been eroded by challenges associated with tuition, enrollment, and student debt. Riaz Tejani concludes this part discussing "market creep," utilizing discourse analysis to investigate how the actual language of law-and-economics has infiltrated legal education and now affects law school recruitment, curriculum, and financing. In all of these cases, aspects of legal education reproduce hierarchy in ways that often go under the radar in public and professional discussions of current dilemmas in law schools.

The final part, *Invisible Processes and Images in Legal Education*, demonstrates that while academic culture purports to facilitate fairness, it instead often perpetuates unequal hierarchies. Swethaa Ballakrishnen and Carole Silver have been among the first scholars to empirically investigate the experience of international students, studying their interactions with peers and general sense of belonging. In their chapter, they report findings on the impact for these students not only of language differences, but of quiet messages conveyed in the *cultures surrounding language* in the classroom – both on students' self-perception as well as on their sense of fitting in while identified as "international." Aaron Taylor delves into race, class, and accessibility by relying on quantitative data to reveal that racial and ethnic disparities in testing merge with supposedly "merit-based" scholarship policies to funnel Black students into schools with the least favorable outcomes and yet leave them with the highest debt loads. In her chapter, Meera E. Deo contributes to theory in the emerging field of "empirical Critical Race Theory" (eCRT) with findings from her mixed-method study of legal academics, exploring not only how academic culture and existing power structures thwart the success of women of color professors who are both presumed incompetent and expected to be academic caretakers but also sharing individual strategies and structural solutions to overcome these barriers. The book concludes with a chapter from Elizabeth Mertz, who identifies traditionally underrepresented faculty as "canaries in the mines" of legal education – reviewing interdisciplinary literature from anthropology, sociology, education, and law pointing to the precarious position of women and people of color in legal academia and drawing from her "After Tenure" study to critique the stubborn inequalities and slow process of improvement in legal education.

Thus the volume draws together work on legal education across fields that often do not touch or speak with one another. In the process, it shows how this kind of interdisciplinary cooperation can be vital in providing a theoretically and empirically sound foundation for understanding what is happening in legal education today. Without quantitative data, we would have no way of capturing the economic inequities that disproportionately impact students of color and students from less wealthy backgrounds on the path to and through law school. Without qualitative research, we would be unable to track with any specificity the hidden processes that perpetuate inequalities through and after law school. The kind of foundation provided by connecting what we know from a variety of studies of legal education will be vital to any realistic process of reform.

Cross-Cutting Themes

The chapters in this volume also speak to each other across the three sections outlined above, so that some very intriguing resonances emerge from themes that echo through different parts of the book. Here we focus on (1) the role of context in legal education; (2) the way legal education inculcates subtle images of law, lawyers, and norms; (3) the effects of the complicated political economy of legal education; and (4) how to conceptualize the agency of professors and students given what we have learned about inequality, forms of resistance, and the possibility of training law students in ways that are true to law's stated aims in democratic states. By cross-referencing the chapters, we discern the depth of inquiry required to obtain an accurate picture of power and implicit messages in the culture of legal education. We also see the importance of combining different kinds of social science methods if we want a full picture of the core dynamics at work.

Context Matters

We offer three examples of the power of multiple methods in an examination of how context matters to the study of legal education. Using in-class observations, interviews, and textual analyses, these chapters uncover many critical components of context: the content of classes, the speed at which materials are presented, styles of pedagogy, the locations in which training is done, the composition of the student body, and the relationship between legal training and the state.

We see quite clearly the influence of context in Mindie Lazarus-Black's comparative study of LL.M. classes taught abroad, classes taught in the U.S. designed specifically for international LL.M. students, and classes taught primarily for U.S. JD students. For administrators, faculty, and students, hierarchical relations of power, patterns of contestation, and an underlying imperial process operate differently in each setting. Lazarus-Black demonstrates that administrators and faculty can partner with law schools in other nations – but only in certain cultural terrains and under certain strictures. She explores the ways in which context causes faculty to redesign the content of their courses, their pedagogical and linguistic styles, references to history and popular culture, how they evaluate their students, and sometimes their sense of humor. Moreover, notions about what law is, who lawyers are and what they do, and the relationship of the U.S. legal system to that of its global neighbors are portrayed and challenged differently in each context. A great complexity characterizes teaching and learning law across borders.

Émilie Biland and Liora Israël demonstrate the complexity of context for legal education within the confines of a single state, France, but in two non-traditional locales. Biland and Israël investigate legal programs at two elite institutions, Sciences Po and HEC business school. They trace historically the schools' conflicted relationships to formal law schools, as well as between these two non-traditional programs. Sciences Po and HEC serve different markets. The schools differ in the backgrounds of their faculty, styles of pedagogy, the curricula, and the lengths of the programs. We are fascinated to learn, nevertheless, that the two sites share at least one underlying pedagogical message: there is socialization to accept a capitalist ideology through emphasis on business law and business lawyers.

David Sandomierski speaks to a social context framed by fellow scholars whose research on legal education has (mostly) focused on the "macro" (top-down) scale of curricula, institutions, and the market for legal services, accompanied by a trope in the professional legal community that holds that law schools train lawyers (as theoreticians) who are mostly unable to do what lawyers do (as practitioners). In teaching contracts, Canadian professors talk about the relationship between theory and practice as mutually reinforcing, that this relationship is essential to making "better lawyers" who can think and read critically, argue persuasively, and practice law ethically and morally. But when professors discuss their roles more generally, or the mission of the law school, theory and practice are described in oppositional terms. Sandomierski suggests empirical research into legal education from the perspective of the professorate, coupled with insights generated from qualitative analyses of course materials and texts, engenders new questions and new frameworks of discourse imperative for designing the future education of law students.

In short, these chapters challenge us to reflect upon the ways in which social context matters and to attend to which contexts we study. Social contexts change the dynamics of the relationships among administrators, faculty, and students. Attention to social context also offers a methodological advantage by alerting us to why the position of the researcher is so critical. Without research that explores these kinds of details, we might not be able to understand the different kinds of behaviors, and the messages taken by students that result from variations in the contexts of legal training.

Power in Implicit Messages

Similarly, there are subtle messages conveyed tacitly in legal education, as the studies in this volume show. As noted above, subtle variations in *context* can shape the training of students, even in the absence of any overt or explicit messaging – sending strong implicit messages. Another example of hidden messages can be found in the *content* of how professors and law schools describe what they do, what lawyers do, and what law is about. This kind of message is all the more effective because it is never openly acknowledged. In fact, the subtle messaging may be covered over by explicit aspirations found in law schools' mission statements or overt curricula. As Biland and Israël explain:

> observation allows us to grasp what is in play in the concrete teaching of legal subjects, above and beyond the announced program and orientations declared by institutions and their representatives (what the sociology of education calls a "formal curriculum"), in order to get through to the hidden … curriculum. (p. 74)

There is a special power in this hidden curriculum, because it rules out whole domains of thought and experience while forefronting others – and all without any explicit debate or conscious reflection.

Vanneauville documents this process in the legal training of civil servants in France. On the one hand, students are encouraged to focus on formal law, and to understand themselves as technicians; on the other hand, a hidden curriculum encourages a more instrumental and utilitarian vision that feeds "the process of rapprochement between the French administrative and economic elites" (p. 123). Tejani similarly demonstrates how subtle aspects of phrasing in describing the goals of legal education can help make an orientation to the market and economic maximization, as opposed to questions of justice, seem natural. Deo and Mertz point to myriad quiet messages that signal presumptions of incompetence or marginality to faculty of color in U.S. law schools. These are all examples of how inchoate power makes itself felt within legal education, under the radar but still highly influential.

The Political Economy of Legal Education

Another tacit structure shaping legal education is the political economy that makes access to law schools dependent on financial issues that undermine any claim that merit is primary to the admission or matriculation process. Stephen Daniels provides a rich history of debt and financing in legal education, providing necessary context to the changing investment of law schools over time. Daniels not only introduces the value proposition business model – positing that even significant debt in pursuit of legal education will pay off with eventual high status and lucrative employment opportunities – but also questions whether the shifting role of government financing and the changing economy render the model ineffective. Who then has access to legal education and the expected spoils of a successful legal career? Aaron Taylor addresses these questions directly, drawing from theoretical discussions of marginalization. Taylor's powerful empirical analysis of admissions reveals the troubling exclusion of African American students from legal education, which is compounded by both a lack of scholarship support and increasing debt. Again, though built on a myth of merit, legal education relies on exclusive admissions and problematic scholarship and debt processes that result in profound racial effects. Legal education relies on myths of meritocracy and fairness in other ways too; Riaz Tejani draws on his skills as an anthropologist to discuss how economic theories are interwoven into legal education, perpetuating and naturalizing the use of law in service of global marketization. By examining discourses of law school inequality, governance, and reform, Tejani reviews how commentators discussing recruitment, curriculum, and financing push an understanding of legal education as a product – with underlying market tensions and moral impacts.

Agency, Inequality, Resistance, and the Possibilities for Change

Finally, the chapters in this book raise substantial questions about law schools as sites for the reproduction of inequality, while also squarely focusing our gaze on questions of where and whether there are opportunities for resistance and change. Can professors, students, administrators, or others concerned about reforming law and legal education exert any agency in the face of the deeply rooted structures that continue to hold sway? And what is the impact on our ability to answer those questions of the increasingly transnational levels at which law and legal training operate?

On the one hand, the message of many of these studies is somewhat discouraging: inchoate forms of power and inequality encoded in the cultures and structures of law schools can be very resistant to change. This message is all the more depressing when viewed in international perspective, when we find evidence supporting Garth's theory of U.S. global success in exporting its model of legal expertise and socialization. On the other hand, some of these studies provide windows on places where marginalized students and faculty can exert some agency, can resist, can push for change. Those pockets of actual or possible resistance may seem small in the face of larger forces, and indeed they are. But to ignore them is, we would argue, to further enforce a vision that misses the ideas and actions of those marginalized members of the community.

Ballakrishnen and Silver, for example, chart both the oppressive feel of U.S. law schools' language cultures for international law students, and the ways that these students cope in these settings. In both their chapter and Lazarus-Black's research, we see that the growing population of international students is gaining ways of making its needs and problems more visible. Rendering visible the "taken for granted" or naturalized inequality in educational settings is one way that marginalized members of law school communities exert agency, often exercising choice in when, where, and how they push back. Herzfeld discusses the way that unrecognized or unseen processes can be resisted, despite their high levels of resilience:

> Here, then, is the larger structure of a form of colonial power that is visible but unseen. It is variously presented as common sense, obviousness, or, alternatively, as a matter of the merest detail. … In setting its face against … the contemptuous rejection of detail in favor of an overgeneralized and idealized "big picture," anthropology, with its respect for human versatility, can … call into question … the deliberately sustained invisibility of aspects of everyday life that make nonsense of the grand generalizations the public is asked to take for granted.
>
> (2015, 28)

Perhaps also it is no accident that it is at – and from – the margins that this taken-for-granted set of generalizations can be questioned, whether through the eyes of international students, "outsider" faculty and students, or others who stand at the edges of institutions. This is a place where the concept of inchoate power has much in common with the examples of imperialism described by Garth (2015), drawing on Bourdieu's conceptualization of the quiet workings of cultural capital and other features of backgrounded systems of assumed value. However, as we see throughout this volume, this is never a simple process: local contexts and historical developments give complex texture to this process in particular sites and times.

***

Thus we see that much can be learned from digging deeper in examining questions of what's taught, who gets in where, what it costs, and where students are going. Social and cultural factors are at work that lead to imbalanced – indeed, unfair – playing fields. The crucial role of law in democratic states means that this tilt at the beginning of legal careers can have far-ranging consequences for the operation of legal systems in capitalist states. This is further exacerbated by the hidden messages that law schools perpetuate, which make hierarchies that undermine equal access to justice seem natural – even morally preferable.

Conclusion

This volume outlines a multifaceted dilemma for would-be reformers of legal education. Hidden in apparently neutral curriculum, admissions and funding criteria, and faculty composition are deeply consequential fates for future lawyers – where they can and cannot go both in terms of their careers, and in terms of how they conceptualize the law. The hidden messages and subtle limitations of early legal training create barriers that impact the lack of lawyers for underserved communities as well as the availability of lawyers whose careers serve the interests of capital over citizens. Law is internationalizing and it is important to both understand and learn from how legal education is practiced around the world, with full attention to implicit messages and subtle structuring as well as to official goals and formal curriculum. This volume crosses boundaries in pursuit of that goal. In the process, it urges us toward a broader and more searching analysis of interactions between power and culture in legal education.

Acknowledgements

We acknowledge the crucial role of the National Science Foundation in providing funding for the conference from which this work developed: NSF 1650057, Legal Education in Crisis? Bringing Researchers and Resources Together to Generate New Scientific Insight. The American Bar Foundation in Chicago also provided vital support for that conference, offering logistical, financial, and intellectual resources. Following the conference, three of the participants founded an ongoing "Collaborative Research Network" under the aegis of the Law & Society Association: CRN #19, Organizers: Swethaa Ballakrishnen, John Bliss, and David Sandomierski. We also acknowledge with deep gratitude the crucial role of Dr. Frances Tung both in helping to organize and run the conference, and in shepherding this volume through a lengthy and complicated process involving reviews and revisions of the chapters.

References

Du Bois, W.E.B. 1903. *The Souls of Black Folk.* Chicago: A.C. McClurg & Co.

Garth, Bryant. 2015. Notes Toward an Understanding of the U.S. Market in Foreign LL.M. Students: From the British Empire and the Inns of Court to the U.S. LL.M. *Indiana Journal of Global Legal Studies* 22(1): 67–79.

Herzfeld, Michael. 2015. Anthropology and the Inchoate Intimacies of Power. *American Ethnologist* 42(1): 18–32.

Part I

Legal Pedagogies in Context(s)

1 Theory and Practice, Together at Last

A Heretical, Empirical Account of Canadian Legal Education

David Sandomierski[*]

Introduction

The tension between theory and practice in legal education has aptly been called both a "perennial" and "fierce" debate.[1] This narrative is not simply a Canadian one that happens to be "told by the winners" but rather exemplifies and perpetuates an older, transnational debate about the mission of legal education and the nature of law (Risk 2005, 313).[2] Is law amenable to the abstracting and theoretical treatment to which the university is best suited, or should its teaching remain grounded in everyday, actual practice?

In the common law world, the starting gun for this debate may have been Blackstone's installation as first Vinerian chair at Oxford in 1758. The Inns of Court had previously controlled all aspects of legal training through a clubby and closed practice of apprenticeship and meals. With Blackstone's inaugural lectures, the English universities not only began to claim ownership over law as a discipline, but established a foothold in legal education.[3] In the United States, the

* Assistant Professor, Faculty of Law, Western University. I gratefully acknowledge the financial assistance of the Social Sciences and Humanities Research Council of Canada, and the Faculty of Law, University of Toronto. For numerous suggestions for improvement, I would like to thank Angela Fernandez, Joel Bakan, and Blaine Baker; participants in the University of Toronto Faculty Workshop Series on April 3, 2017; the reviewers on the awards committee for the 2017 Roderick A Macdonald Graduate Student Essay Prize hosted by the Canadian Law and Society Association (for which this paper received an Honourable Mention); and the editors of this volume. The chapter incorporates research conducted under a Research Ethics Board Approval at the University of Toronto.

1 See Macdonald (1982, 585), Kyer and Bickenbach (1987).

2 For a series of significant episodes in the Canadian narrative, see Kyer and Bickenbach (1987) (the successful move by Caesar Wright and others to accredit the University of Toronto Faculty of Law over the resistance of the Law Society of Upper Canada in the 1950s); Arthurs (forthcoming 2019) (the hard-won control over curricular autonomy at Osgoode Hall Law School once it moved to York University in the 1960s); Willis (1979) (the successful move to inseminate the Dalhousie Law School with a mission of public citizenship in the 1910s); Common Law Degree Implementation Committee (2011) (the uproar caused by the Federation of Law Societies of Canada's attempt to mandate curricular competencies in the 2010s).

3 See Kyer and Bickenbach (1987).

establishment of "national" law schools in the nineteenth century, especially Harvard, were founded on the idea that an "American" law could be generalized and taught, and the prestige-seeking, imperializing project of American legal education began, with universities firmly asserting jurisdiction over the endeavour.[4]

Despite the incredible success of Oxford, Harvard, and hundreds of university law faculties across the common law world, the idea that universities provide an incomplete or unsatisfactory legal education has endured. To take a recent example, increasing calls on law schools to produce "practice-ready" lawyers have emphasized the perceived shortcomings of an overly theoretical approach to legal education.[5] While the recent financial downturn, combined with technological innovations disrupting the provision of legal services, provide a conspicuous explanation for the renewed pressure on law schools to become more "practical," recent events have not transformed, but rather amplified, an existing dynamic.

The dynamic is a deeply oppositional attitude between theory and practice. In caricatured terms, to the advocate of "practice," studying law in an academic environment can encourage navel-gazing, transcendental fantasies, and useless theorizing. To the advocate of "theory," a focus on "practice" is prosaic, overly instrumental, and insufficiently grounded in the ideals and principles of the justice system. While few serious commentators would subscribe to these views in their caricatured terms, an underlying spirit of opposition and othering animates the debate over legal education.[6]

The dominant discourse about legal education appears to be beset by two biases. First is the in-built predilection for viewing theory and practice in opposition. The perennial nature of the debate may have entrenched its terms to such a degree that its very grammar – the unacknowledged but agreed-upon rules of discourse – has become oppositional. In order to understand the mission of the law school freed from this "unsaid" oppositionality, a deliberate and laborious effort may be needed. In this regard, one can look to Anthony Kronman's (1993) *Lost Lawyer*, a major theoretical project to reconceive of the "lawyer as statesman," or the Carnegie Foundation's (Sullivan et al. 2007) extensive report arguing for the integration of the three "apprenticeships," as examples of sustained attempts to escape the oppositional paradigm in favour of a more integrative mode.[7] But these works are overwhelmingly the exception that proves the rule of oppositionality in the mainstream discourse.

The other hidden bias is the tendency to talk about legal education by focusing on the "macro" scale: curricula, institutions, the legal services market. Most of the discourse about legal education focuses on these programmatic, systemic, or top-down features of legal education. In part, this may be because within law schools, discussions about the mission or purpose of the institution arise only interstitially,

4 See Coquillette and Kimball (2015).

5 See, for example, Segal (2011); American Bar Association, Task Force on the Future of Legal Education (2013) [ABA Report]; Tamanaha (2012).

6 The debate about how much "theory" to teach in law schools is one clear example of this tendency. See, for example, Coleman (1995, 2579) ("my remarks are intended to defend the teaching of theory in the core of the law school curriculum").

7 See also Sandomierski (2014).

with curricular reform functioning as the "law school's primary heuristic device" (Macdonald 1982, 569). Whatever the reason, particularistic and empirical studies of legal education – that focus on actual practices, testimonials, habits, and attitudes – are historically in the minority, notwithstanding some recent bright lights.[8] Life does appear to be messier at a smaller scale, and it is at least possible that study at a more granular scale may help generate new ideas about the relationship between theory and practice.

This chapter reports on a study grounded in such an empirical, particularistic attitude, skeptical of the unsaid conventions about how we understand legal education. In the study, I have conducted semi-structured interviews with 67 Contracts professors from across Canada. These teachers taught first-year Contracts in the common law tradition at 17 different Canadian law faculties (including all the law schools in Canada outside Quebec, plus McGill, a bilingual law faculty in the primarily anglophone Montreal university). Forty-eight of the participants presented as male and 18 as female. They held diverse levels of teaching experience and varied positions, including tenure-stream (of all rank), sessional lecturers, adjunct professors, visiting scholars, fellows, and professors emeriti. Of these interviews, held between February 2013 and February 2017, I conducted 54 in person and 13 by phone and videoconference. I also obtained almost 300 syllabi, examinations and other course materials from my interview participants, and from eight others.[9]

Among my goals are to understand what Contracts professors intend to achieve in their course, to understand why they think these aims are important, and to compare their stated practices and aims with a limited amount of direct evidence of their teaching to determine whether there is a fit, or a gap, between their aspirations and their reality. The study has generated a rich series of data at different levels of generality: direct examples of teaching resources, accounts of teaching practices, explanations of the purpose and relevance of teaching choices, and more philosophical musings on the role of the law professor and law school. In this chapter, I examine this data for what can be learned about the relationship between theory and practice, when the starting point of analysis is classroom teaching and not curricular, institutional, or systemic design.

My analysis reveals two principal findings. (1) When professors speak about their teaching – their practices, strategies, goals, and rationales – they overwhelmingly emphasize the importance of practice. This is so despite the fact that professors articulate a wide range of goals, inspired by diverse theoretical ideas about law. What nearly unifies the participants in my study is the tendency to say

8 See especially Mertz (2007). See Noreau and Bonin (2017); Bliss (2017); Habermacher (in progress). See also Ballakrishnen and Silver, Biland and Israël, Deo, Lazarus-Black, Mertz, and Vanneuville, this volume.

9 I did not collect data on other markers of personal identity, such as race, First Nations status, sexual orientation, socioeconomic status, or disability. Instead, I chose to focus on correlations between professors' views and their markers of *professional* identity, such as work and academic background. For a full account of this study, including a more detailed description of its methodological approach and commitments, see Sandomierski (forthcoming 2019).

that a given theoretical or critical perspective is important because it produces "better lawyers." In describing their goals, methods, and rationales, the vast majority of professors aspire to treat theory and practice as mutually reinforcing. Theory flourishes, but in the service of "practical" training. And in a few cases, the reverse is also true: some professors articulate how a focus on "practice" can reinforce or deepen the theories to which they are committed.

(2) At the same time, when describing the mission of a law school or the role of a law professor *more generally*, this near consensus about the integration of theory and practice seems to break down. In these more general "mission" or "role" comments, professors are more likely to highlight the tension between theory and practice, or to advocate a view for one over the other. Only a minority resists the dichotomy, speaking of the need to integrate and balance theory and practice.

In the first section of this chapter, I discuss how, when talking about teaching, Canadian Contracts professors of different theoretical stripes justify critique or theory because it makes "better lawyers." This tendency paints a respectful and nuanced portrait of practice and leaves the impression that in conceiving their teaching, most Contracts professors aspire to treat theory and practice as mutually reinforcing. In Part II, I demonstrate how professors generally paint a more oppositional picture in speaking about their (or their institutions') role or mission. In Part III, I explore a few possible explanations that might account for the differential treatment of theory and practice between Parts I and II.

"Because It Makes Better Lawyers": The Practical Utility of Theory and Critical Perspectives

Commitments to "academic" values of theory and critique flourish among Contracts professors. While this prevalence might seem to vindicate the universities' so-called victory in the battle for control over legal education, the tendency to justify the importance of theory or critique in instrumental terms disturbs this narrative. When speaking about their own teaching, at least half of the participants in my study stated that teaching theory or critical perspectives was important because doing so makes "better lawyers." By contrast, only about four participants expressed some skepticism about the importance of practical utility. The sentiment that theory was important for its own sake was almost nonexistent.[10] This tendency suggests that professors have internalized "practice" as a core virtue of their teaching, and that they conceive "theory" as serving, and being integrated with, practice.

Reinforcing the depth of this integrative commitment is the sophistication and diversity of ways in which professors describe theory as informing practice. As I demonstrate below, Contracts professors' theories and commitments about law vary greatly, ranging from those with formalist commitments to the coherence of doctrinal rules, to realist preoccupations with policy, context, and politics; pluralist concerns with non-state normative systems; and those who seek to critique law from moral, economic, feministic, race, historical, and other perspectives. No one

10 The interviews were semi-structured so the issue may not have arisen in all interviews.

theory seems to be more, or less, amenable to the instrumental-practical justification that it makes "better lawyers."

Moreover, the formulation "because it makes better lawyers" serves to deepen and enrich what it means to practice – either by illustrating the specific skills and attributes of the better lawyer, or simply by associating the virtues of a particular theory with practice, and thereby imbuing "practice" with dignity and nuance. We see this respectful treatment of practice in comments by those professors who have, and have not, practiced law themselves.

Using Diverse Theories of Law to Produce "Better Lawyers" **Tout Court**

This Part's first section surveys the generic ways in which professors' various theoretical commitments make "better lawyers." Producing better lawyers is a commonplace justification for why it is important to expose students to theoretical or critical perspectives in first-year Contracts. Occasionally, professors will make the general case for the interrelation between theory and practice. As Professor 1 writes in the course syllabus:

> [Students should learn] to reason and work in the law of contracts at a high theoretical level. This is to say, move from a technical solution according to a certain system of positive law to a concept. And, returning from this concept, be able to understand the technical solutions that flow from it.[11]

In interview, Professor 1 says that "in the technical material there is an interplay between law and the totality of knowledge … Theory makes better practitioners."[12] Similarly, the very theoretically inclined[13] Professor 4 says:

> You do theory to help you with practice … I'm very theoretically inclined, but *theory for the purpose of theory is silly* … We want to know how to act in life and … that takes us to theory and philosophy.[14]

Professors of varying theoretical stripes connect their specific theories to the idea of making better lawyers. We see this among professors who exhibit a commitment to the formalist values of structure and coherence, as when Professor 8 strives to apply Peter Burke's idea of a taxonomy to private law as a whole, helping students "create a road map … to understand the situations they're dealing with."[15] Similarly, Professor 15, who "like[s]" the logic of contract law and who is

11 [001], Syllabus (2015–2016), p. 1 [Translation].
12 [001], Interview, 99–113, 284–292 [Translation]. Interview references are to line number(s).
13 Professor 4's main goal is to show that there is an "internal logic, a set of principles, that anchor contract law" (Interview, 7).
14 [004], Interview, 607–612 [emphasis added].
15 [008], Interview, 163–180; 152–157.

a "believer in rules," fitting "real life into these abstract … categories," "makes better lawyers."[16] Professor 27 speaks about how learning the "grammar" avoids one becoming "lost as a lawyer":

> There is a deepening narrative of what contract law … should be doing. But there's also a grammar and it does it in a particular way. If you don't understand the grammar, then you're lost as a lawyer. … There is [a] basic kind of conceptual bedrock which … law forces you to come to grips with. Otherwise you're just gassing around in the abstract.[17]

We also see the "better lawyers" justification from professors who exhibit realist commitments to the importance of "underlying" factors of policy, politics, and context. Thus, for Professor 67, "going beyond what's obvious" makes "a great lawyer."[18] Professor 56 argues that the "realist, policy-driven" question of "what is going on" should "always … stay[] with you as a lawyer."[19] For Professor 29, understanding how doctrine has "a solid foundation in public policy … makes you a better lawyer."[20] Professor 16 believes that "see[ing] law in context" and understanding that law "affects and is affected by other societal matters" "makes you a better lawyer."[21] And Professor 28 has seen that those students who "excel" at law firms are:

> ones that know that it's just not enough to look at the law on … paper or … doctrine … They search farther [and] try and figure out … where that particular rule came from, and what the context of that case was.[22]

Professors with other theoretical commitments also justify theory as a way of making "better lawyers." For example, Professor 3, who identifies with Marxism,[23] says:

> I try to encourage students to see what I believe is the truth of law, which is it's a battleground of ideology. …
>
> I tell them you're going to be much better lawyers if you understand that legal argument is about manipulating rhetorically and analytically, the grand arrogance of our collective culture. That's where you're going to be persuasive. That's where you're going to appeal.[24]

16 [015], Interview, 32, 283, 235, 323–325, 431.
17 [027], Interview, 403–412.
18 [067], Interview, handwritten notes of untranscripted interview, pp. 6, 8.
19 [056], Interview, 110–114.
20 [029], Interview, 217–222.
21 [016], Interview, 863, 862, 581–583, 866–867.
22 [028], Interview, 363–368.
23 [003], Interview, 108–109.
24 [003], Interview, 124–138, 234–238.

Specific Skills of the "Better Lawyer": Persuasion, Advocacy, Advising, Problem-Solving, Planning, Creative Lawyering

Law professors occasionally disaggregate what it takes to be a "better lawyer" into particular skills and attributes, which they also relate to their preferred theories of law. By far the most common instrumental reason for engaging with theory, or learning to "think critically," is that doing so will enable one to make persuasive arguments. Professors state this virtue both generally and as specifically related to making arguments in court.

The virtue of making better arguments transcends different theoretical approaches. We see it among the realists. Professor 31, for example, emphasizes that "judges know the result they want to reach and … fit it [into] … doctrine" in order to "signal the importance of … making persuasive arguments."[25] For Professor 50, highlighting factors that might "play a very persuasive role in the way a judge will jump" is important in order to "get to the heart of the judge."[26] For Professor 16, looking at the law "in a broader context … makes you a much more powerful advocate."[27] For Professor 11, it is important to understand how the "judge is also concerned with … policy implications" because "their job as lawyers is going to be to make arguments."[28] Professor 44 focuses on "disagreements in policy between the judges" in order to help students reflect on their "argument before the final court."[29]

But we also see the tendency among formalists. For Professor 4, the search for an inner logic serves a persuasive advocacy strategy:

> When they go into court, the judge wants to know, "Put these two cases together for me." … "Tell me why … I should follow this case as opposed to the other one?" … [Saying that cases are] contradictory [is] never the preferred answer … The judge will always prefer the answer that actually is able to reconcile the materials together.[30]

Aside from connecting specific theories to the skill of advocacy, many professors embrace the idea that exposure to a range of perspectives – the virtue of theory *generally* – trains persuasive argumentation. This aspiration can be considered consistent with the notion of equipping students with an "eclectic toolkit" (Kennedy and Fisher III 2006, 3) of different argument-types, and of training students to argue from both sides.[31]

Professors from across the theoretical spectrum express the aspiration to develop students' argumentative eclecticism. Both the strong formalist Professor 4 and the

25 [031], Interview, 201, 205–207, 230–232.
26 [050], Interview, 135–136, 166.
27 [016], Interview, 548–549.
28 [011], Interview, 421, 443–444.
29 [044], Interview, 684, 699–700.
30 [004], Interview, 279–292.
31 *Cf.* Kronman (1993, 98).

realist Professor 28 assert that their job is to "play devil's advocate"[32] and "won't share" personal political views.[33] Professor 50 doesn't "take a clear view on what is good or bad about particular cases" but wants students to "understand both sides" because "in practice [one needs to] fully and completely understand … the arguments [the other side is] going to make."[34] Professor 64, who ascribes to an "element of critical legal theory," tries to "minimize my opinion";[35] a "convincing" argument is one that "is going to be some combination of legal impact, policy effect, and values."[36] Professor 33 specifically cultivates the ability to make arguments by randomly assigning students positions based on themes of class, race, and power.[37] Professor 52 says, "Part of what makes a person a good lawyer is to be able to consider different perspectives."[38]

Professors also explain that the academic virtue of critical thinking – a term that receives a diversity of interpretations – helps to develop persuasive arguments. Professor 37 wants students to "hone their skills of imaginative insight and to think with an agile mind that's able to transcend boundaries" because one can "help your client better if you understand how to think in this much more creative and critical way."[39] For Professor 45, the ability to "offer some kind of critique" helps "persuade the court of a particular perspective, or to convince a court to move in a particular direction … The best lawyers, the great lawyers, are those who can construct the most persuasive legal arguments."[40]

While courtroom advocacy remains the more frequent type of practice that professors invoke for the relevance of theoretical perspectives and critical thinking, a series of other skills not directly related to advocacy surface. These too often flow directly from specific theoretical commitments.

Two professors specifically connect a pluralist focus on the "legal systems" of contracting parties to skills of planning, problem-solving, negotiation and drafting. Professor 42 says:

> I try to persuade students that contract is a dynamic and forward-looking mode of social ordering and that therefore it's a course about lawyers' involvement in the construction of little legal systems, each time they negotiate a contract. And although it's a planning exercise, a dynamic forward-looking exercise, there are all kinds of really good skills that are grounded in law, but are nonetheless skills. So, negotiation, figuring out how much to say when

32 [004], Interview, 427, 452.
33 [028], Interview, 236.
34 [050], Interview, 438–440, 486, 503–506.
35 [064], Interview, 743–750.
36 [064], Interview, 584–586.
37 [033], Interview, 480.
38 [052], Interview, 167–168.
39 [037], Interview, 274–277, 259–261, 318.
40 [045], Interview, 135–139, 112–113, 158–160. For various articulations on the virtues of critical thinking in legal education, see, for example, Nussbaum (2003); Elkins (1999).

> and where, determining how many of a client's instructions should be acted upon, *and* later on, maybe, having to convert a deliberately ambiguous or informal arrangement into codified form.[41]

Professor 36, for whom Stewart Macaulay and Ian Macneil were "formative," similarly states, "If one is concerned about training professionals who are effective problem-solvers in the world … the first and most important value should be the ability to navigate different normative systems."[42]

Problem-solving also flows from more traditional doctrinal approaches, as when Professor 48 states that "legal education trains you in relevance," a skill that can be taken to "any kind of problem solving,"[43] or when Professor 29 tries to get students "to see how what they are doing might be relevant to problem-solving in the real world."[44] And those who use more unorthodox methods of teaching also signal the virtue. For example, Professor 44's own office files serve as examples to show students "how we *use* the theory in everyday practice,"[45] and Professor 43, who has used a version of the flipped classroom to focus class time on problems for two decades, says that problem solving is "the *biggest skill* we give our lawyers."[46]

A number of professors also state that theoretical or critical perspectives help produce creative lawyers capable of effecting change. Professor 17 underlines the "arbitrariness and the contingency of [law to show that] it really is coming from … a particular place … I say to them: 'If you want to change it, if you want it to be different, you kind of have to know that.'"[47] Similarly, Professor 54 says that "all you need to do … as a lawyer" is to "identify what's uncertain, *why* it's uncertain, and what the potential arguments … to resolve the uncertainty *are*."[48] Professor 33 states that morality and public policy play a large role in the course because "that's where the most creative lawyering takes place."[49]

The Ethos *of "Better" Lawyers*

> *But what do you mean by better lawyers? … Are better lawyers … lawyers who are better people and more likely to be ethical? That's one way of being a better lawyer and*

41 [042], Interview, 79–95.
42 [036], Interview, 207–216, 247–259.
43 [048], Interview, 438–442, 700–715.
44 [029], Interview, 663–664.
45 [044], Interview, 226–235, 40–42.
46 [043], Interview, 1295–1300, 1146–1152. On problem-solving as an essential but often underachieved objective of legal education, see Rhode (2000, 36–38). See also Holloway and Friedland (2017, 421–423). The term "flipped classroom" is sometimes used to describe a method that replaces class time normally used for lecture with problem-based activities, with lectures pre-recorded for students to watch outside of class. See generally Abeysekera and Dawson (2015, 1).
47 [017], Interview, 332–343.
48 [054], Interview, 733–738.
49 [033], Interview, line 260. *Cf.* Klare (2011).

> *then the other way of being a better lawyer is they can manipulate the hell out of the law to win for their clients … And I think I'm doing both.* [50]

Up until now, we have treated "better" lawyers synonymously with being "more proficient" lawyers. But professors also express how theoretical and critical perspectives serve the goal of making "better" lawyers by addressing the ends lawyers serve. Professors include in this vision being "ethical," supporting marginalized communities, being aware of social effects, power imbalances, and diversity, and performing the "moral duty" to represent clients.[51]

Professor 3, whose quote opens this section, connects a focus on ideology with the lawyer's "moral role":

> A lot of people come into law school believing in justice. … I want to vindicate that belief rather than destroy it. … I'm going to show you that in the law, the struggle about what justice is is happening all the time … You cannot escape that moral role as a lawyer."[52]

Professor 63 emphasizes both a "realist" and "critical" perspective directly in order to "advocate for change … for members of marginalized communities or [those] less well-represented in the judiciary."[53] Similarly, Professor 33 exposes students to a "range of theoretical perspectives … because I don't want them to … *unknowingly* participat[e] in perpetuating something that is harmful to other people."[54]

Professor 35, who "takes a light *crit* approach … tying … the practical, everyday practice of law to theory," strives to expose students to "power relationships [and] the way socioeconomic resources are distributed" because lawyers should "be *conscious* and not stick their heads in the sand."[55] Professor 17 probes the context of a case in part to sensitize students to "diversity issues" and learn that they "have agency."[56] Professor 53 uses critical thinking to help students "challenge authority" because legal thinkers are:

> the ones that have to protect society from the government, from the police, from big business, from each other … They're the ones that have to say, "The emperor has no clothes."[57]

Practice as Important, Thick, and Mutually Constitutive with Theory

When law professors speak about their teaching goals, objectives, and practices, they predominantly describe their theoretical and critical perspectives as relevant

50 [003], Interview, 309–316.
51 *Cf.* Rhode (2000); Deo (2015).
52 [003], Interview, 269–286.
53 [063], Interview, 167–173, 153–154, 850–854.
54 [033], Interview, 374–377.
55 [035], Interview, 771–774, 303–313, 618–629.
56 [017], Interview, 202–234.
57 [053], Interview, 397, 434–440, 421–422, 398–403.

largely in the service of practice. They not only treat practice as a core objective, they endow it with a robust and principled content. There are also indications that for some of these professors, practice informs theory. As Professor 33 says:

> My experience practicing … was that you had to be extremely aware of the practical outcome of doctrines being interpreted in different ways. … If you [didn't address] the on the ground *consequences* … your legal argument was going to be rejected.[58]

Similarly, Professor 1 describes the mutuality of practice, "critical" thinking, and "professional aptitudes":

> A day at a law firm, in the legal department of a business, or in court will suffice to disabuse anyone of the idea that knowledge enables one to master the law *as it is*. …
>
> The jurist capable of critiquing his or her knowledge augments his or her professional aptitudes. … Critical work must accompany conceptual work in the learning of law.[59]

In such passages, where practice is specifically invoked to inform or complicate theoretical understandings, we see the inklings of a view that considers theory and practice as *mutually* reinforcing virtues, analogous to Anthony Kronman's *The Lost Lawyer*, in which the traits of deliberative wisdom and civic-mindedness simultaneously enable the "outstanding" lawyer to serve the interests of private clients and the public.[60]

Minority Report: The Attenuated Importance of Practice

Despite this near-consensus about the importance of practice, a minority of professors do express some reservations. This can take the form of distinguishing "thinking" from practicing law, as when Professor 58 writes, "[T]he focus is not on preparing you to write a professional Bar examination … or … legal opinions on complex contractual matters [but rather] … to do the legal thinking and research necessary to do so."[61] Occasionally, a professor is even more resistant:

> My objective is not to turn out legal *plumbers*. They're not doing contract law *plumbing* … I will gladly teach stuff that is practically *useless* [if I think it will help] … students to get some idea of the context of law.[62]

58 [033], Interview, 624–631.
59 [001], Syllabus, p. 2.
60 See Sandomierski (2014, 744–747). See also Holloway and Friedland (2017, 423–424).
61 [058], Syllabus (2007–2008), p. 2.
62 [047], Interview, 774–747.

Professor 22 altogether resists the notion of using theory for "practical implications":

> I tend to think the practical implications are not as important … The fundamental role is understanding, but that's not really going to change the world … philosophy is to understand the world, not to change it. And once you start changing it, you're not doing philosophy. Or you're not being academic.[63]

Earlier in the interview, Professor 22 speaks of the importance of applying understanding to real life fact situations.[64] It is when Professor 22 transitions from speaking about teaching to the role of "philosophy" or the "academy" that the skepticism about practicality surfaces. This transition nicely illustrates a broader tendency among law professors explored in the next Part.

Theory and Practice, Worlds Apart: Reproducing the Conventional Narrative

While it is relatively rare for law professors to assert the primacy of either practice or theory when discussing their teaching activities, the picture is somewhat different when discussions drift into the more abstract topic of what a law professor's role is, or what the mission of a law school (or faculty) should be. In these discussions, it is more frequent for professors to speak about the tension between theory and practice, or to assert that either academic or professional goals ought to be prioritized. There *are* professors who articulate the mission or role as being to integrate and balance theory and practice, but such comments are much less frequent than the attitude of integration in teaching outlined in Part I. Approximately 20 participants – including 11 who were also quoted in Part I – made comments that could plausibly be interpreted as reflecting, if not advocating, this oppositional construct. The conventional narrative about theory and practice surfaces in these comments.

The Perennial Debate

Professors disclose different responses to the debate, which almost all acknowledge as perennial or timeless. Some, like Professors 15 and 44, acknowledge the tension but treat it somewhat neutrally, suggesting that they have contended with it but ultimately figured a way to resolve it: they inhabit "both" sides of the divide:

> To what extent is the academic study of law … a preparation for practice and to what extent is it a *broader* intellectual discipline[?] … It's both …

63 [022], Interview, 198–240.

64 [022], Interview, 173–176 ("Why does classification matter? … What pre-conditions our … practical implications?").

> Acknowledging that people take this degree … to get qualified for the Bar … is relevant. And [it] is also what gives law schools their claim to be a distinct discipline.[65]
>
> One the finest articles on law teaching I've ever read … is … "The Law Teacher – A Man Divided Against Himself" … Are we academics, or are we people preparing students for practice? … I've been in that situation because … I've always done both![66]

Others describe the *impacts* of the tension. Professor 56, for example, intimates that tension is positive, in that it results in a less "boring" approach to teaching:

> If I didn't have to *worry* about training lawyers, I could … make it about the history or … theory. But … given that these people are not just being prepared for … PhDs in law, I think it wouldn't be right … [It] also would be more *boring* because law is about … sending people out into the real world and … *helping*, solving, resolving disputes. It's not just … creating articles that nobody reads![67]

By contrast, Professor 7 signals its harmful effects, arguing that the tension "drums" the enthusiasm out of students:

> The tension between learning what you need to be a lawyer … and the ambitions of law schools to teach law as a social phenomenon is not always easy for the students to navigate …The pressure from the *profession* … makes it hard for them to navigate those two objectives.[68]

Beyond acknowledging this debate as a fact, some go further, and engage in the terms of the debate – they take sides. Some professors fiercely assert the law faculty's separation from the profession. As Professor 40 says:

> There is a great deal of pressure upon the Faculty of Law to see itself as a kind of vocational training ground for the local bar … [I]t's not unknown for members of the Law Society … to come to [faculty] councils, and tell us … what we should be teaching … I won't do [what they ask] … There should be a divide of some sort. Not an absolute divide, but a divide nonetheless.[69]

Professor 40 doesn't practice law, but others who do express similar attitudes. Professor 2 has maintained a legal practice for 30 years and regularly receives

65 [015], Interview, 744–756.
66 [044], Interview, 27–37 (citing Bergin 1968).
67 [056], Interview, 567–586.
68 [007], Interview, 33–89.
69 [040], Interview, 865–905.

calls from former students asking for advice on active files. Yet, despite this affinity for practice – the course syllabus includes such highly practical goals as "negotiation, drafting, and interpretation" and "preparing and presenting claims"[70] – Professor 2 is among the most oppositional in describing the role of the law professor and law school:

> I do practice, it's important, but it is easily learned. What you must learn [in a law faculty] is the theoretical aspect of law, reflection and social critique. … The day where faculties of law stop playing this role, they will no longer belong in a university … I don't believe it is my role to [prepare students for practice]. My role is to enable them to be able to understand the law and once they have understood it, they will learn the rest.[71]

Professor 32 expresses a similar attitude in insisting on the term "jurist":

> You argue that you don't necessarily go to law school to be a lawyer … It's important that students consider themselves … to be *jurists* and not only proto-professionals who are learning the tools of the trade … It goes back I think to the old … trade school versus … academy *debate* … It's one of those … codes or symbols of keeping me grounded in the academic pursuit.[72]

The Law Faculty / Law School Distinction, like the academy / professional distinction, therefore functions as a guiding or structuring device for professors to prioritize an "academic" approach to studying law.[73] However, professors also invoke these debates to argue for the opposite, adopting a hostile tone toward the academy. Professor 12, for example, says that the *Arthurs Report* was "absolutely dreadful," because it "deprecated severely" Professor 12's "highly practical" work:

> [T]o the extent that the law schools repudiate the obligation to teach their students how to practice law, they're not doing what they should be doing. You would think it *monstrous* if the Faculty of Medicine said to its students, "We're not going to teach you how to cure people. We're going to teach you the *theory* of medicine." Medicine and law are professions, and the job of a profession is to *do things in the world.* [74]

Professor 60, hired many years before the *Arthurs Report*, stipulated as a condition of employment that Professor 60 "would not write." For this professor, who "never" wrote more than a case comment:

70 [002], Syllabus (2015–2016), pp. 2–3 [Translation].
71 [002], Interview, 225–242, 732–764 [Translation].
72 [032], Interview, 138–149. *Cf.* Pue (2005).
73 For further reflections on the relevance of the different terms "law school" and "law faculty," see, for example, Macdonald and McMorrow (2014, 717–720).
74 [012], Interview, 783–789, 409–418. See Consultative Group on Research and Education in Law (1983) [*Arthurs Report*].

> I always valued law school mainly as the way to prepare for a *profession* … as opposed to … an *academic discipline* in itself … And we're in a somewhat difficult position. [There's pressure] at a university [to] do what other professors do at the university. … But it's a *professional school.* [75]

Another senior professor argues that law schools *should* respond to the demands of the profession, and in particular the Federation of Law Societies of Canada's requirement that law schools train certain competencies.[76] This individual is the early adopter of technology who focuses on problem-based learning:

> We're talking about pushing articling into the law firm back into the law schools. There's a reason for it … In the good old days, [firms] could take articling students on … and charge them out to a company and they didn't mind. They can't do that anymore. … That's what the Federation of Law Societies['] … competencies piece is about …
>
> We're caught in a bind. … We're busy … going, "Oh! Come to us! … We're diverse! … We've got social access to justice! … We'll get you an internship here, and we'll give you that here" … We can't do that any longer because the firms, the big client, the buyer, has shown up at the door and said, "That's not what I want. … I want the kid who's ready to go now because I'm worried about my profitability …"
>
> And so we as law schools have to recognize that and gear up and transition.[77]

Each of the above three professors is an outlier in one sense or another: one has left the full-time academy, another never produced scholarship, and a third genuinely stands out in pedagogical approach. Their expressions are stronger than the norm. However, a number of other professors express similar views more mildly.

Professor 49, who compresses the doctrinal material into one semester, and focuses on reading real contracts for another semester, states simply, "I don't see why you *wouldn't* emphasize the practical side of contracts."[78] Professor 26 sees it as an "obligation to students" not to emphasize theory over a "practice-oriented approach … in emphasizing law as something that is usable as opposed to knowable."[79] Professor 54 tells students the practical benefits of course material "all the time," because "[legal reasoning is] really what they'll be doing as articling students and … that's what we're in large measure training them for."[80] Even Professor 57, who did graduate work bridging legal theory and philosophy, emphasizes that "[Reading case law is] an *enduring* skill that they need later as a lawyer. … Most of them are going to go on to be practitioners."[81] Professors

75 [060], Interview, 583–591, 284–291.
76 See Common Law Degree Implementation Committee (2011) [FLSC Report].
77 [043], Interview, 723–810.
78 [049], Interview, 216–217.
79 [026], Interview, 238–240, 523–527.
80 [054], Interview, 352, 366–368.
81 [057], Interview, 141–142, 235–236, 500–503.

occasionally refer to their own identity as practitioners. Comments such as "I'm sort of a practitioner; I'm not a theory person much myself,"[82] or "I'm trying to teach the course from a practical perspective … because I'm a practitioner myself"[83] relate pedagogical choices to a sense of personal role or identity.

This section has tried to emphasize how, notwithstanding the overwhelming tendency of teachers to treat theory and practice as mutually reinforcing virtues in their teaching, many professors do espouse an attitude that the academy and the profession, theory and practice, exist in opposition. But as with all stories, there are sub-plots, and the next section identifies the instances in which professors articulate – at the more abstract level – the notion that theory and practice can and should be integrated and balanced.

Balance and Integrate: A Secondary Narrative

There are signs that a secondary story is starting to be told about the nature and purpose of legal education. These professors capture the ethos of the attitudes about teaching illustrated in Part I in their general arguments that integrating theory and practice is both achievable and desirable.

Among the participants in my study, the most explicit champion of the integrative approach is Professor 62, who vigorously challenges the orthodox view:

> I find the distinction … between theory and practice or skills and theory, an *inane*, untenable distinction. …
> [P]art of the reason I think I was hired is because I'm kind of a hybrid academic/practitioner … [There is] an expectation that … we *explode* the distinction between theory and practice …
> I'm not just trying to help students become *lawyers*, … but rather … how to … lead a virtuous life as a lawyer … We're not trying to foreground and emphasize skills to the detriment of theory or … ideas. It's the opposite. It's trying to bring the two together. And it's trying to use skills and techniques as windows … into the ideas underneath them and underlying them, and to challenge them, to remake law and legal practice from the inside out.[84]

A number of factors combine to produce such an impassioned articulation: a prior intellectual commitment, the sense of an institutional mandate, a desire to resist the current "climate," and Professor 62's own ongoing experience practicing law.[85]

Such a confluence of factors is not common, but neither is it necessary to produce expressions of an integrative account. These can be more understated, as when Professor 51 (founder of a "contracts dance collective" with students), describes the "ideal" as being to "integrate and balance … doctrine, theory, and

82 [013], Interview, 630–631.
83 [065], Interview, 164–167.
84 [062], Interview, 455–513, 642–656.
85 *Ibid.*, 509, 524.

some practice."[86] Professor 16 similarly describes theory as a "container" or "framework" of law, and aspires to find the "right balance … connecting that theory to practical real-life examples."[87]

As expressive as these accounts are, they remain in the minority. The wider tendency is to describe the role or mission of a law school (or professors) within the conventional, oppositional framework. The disjuncture between that story and the near-consensus about integrating theory and practice *in teaching* is one of the mysteries revealed by this study. The next Part of this chapter tries to make some sense of this mystery.

Accounting for the Co-existence of Integrative and Oppositional Accounts of Theory and Practice

We might understand the meaning and purpose of legal education differently depending on the scale of what is studied. The conventional debate primarily views legal education from a macro perspective. This is true of scholarship that attempts to identify structural trends in legal education, of normative attempts to defend an academic mission, of reports emphasizing the role of market forces, and of curricular interventions, whether by the profession, academy, or third-party research institutes.[88] Theoretical or polemic interventions also tend to be pitched at a higher level of generality.[89] Such bird's-eye views produce an image of legal education akin to a territorial map, in which borders are clearly defined, factions coloured-in and homogenous. Just as in research about law, where "scale functions so that a specific perspective becomes embedded in forms of regulation and governance,"[90] the focus on macro scale in legal education research brings its own potential presuppositions. One of these presuppositions is the representation of theory and practice in oppositional terms.

Analyzing legal education from a different scale – that of the individual law professor – can produce substantively different insights. The insight that *in their teaching*, most professors do aspire to integrate theory with practice could simply not have been arrived at by a focus on curricula, institutions, or the market for legal services. By accessing accounts of legal education that are closer to professors' lived experience, we are able to generate new insights that are not as deeply entwined with conventional wisdom or as influenced by the hidden grammar of the discourse.

That said, while existing at a more granular scale, a focus on professors' accounts of their own teaching is also quite abstract. Professors' accounts make sense of an activity, law teaching, which itself is a marriage of two highly abstract

86 [051], Interview, 582–584.
87 [016], Interview, 467–480.
88 See, for example, Arthurs (1998); Tamanaha (2012); Arthurs (forthcoming 2019); American Bar Association (2013); Common Law Degree Implementation Committee (2011) [FLSC Report]; Sullivan et al. 2007 [*Carnegie Report*].
89 See, for example, Kronman (1993); Kennedy (1982).
90 Raso (2019) citing Valverde (2009); Valverde (2015); de Sousa Santos (1987).

endeavours, law and education. It is precisely because law professors are articulate and self-reflective enough to be able to discuss their objectives and goals so clearly that their words can converse directly with the mainstream discourse. Empiricism allows us to access the abstractions and representations not otherwise captured at the macro scale. The information discovered is not the discrete "data points" of "revealed preferences,"[91] but rather rich, thick, and layered testimonies. These directly inform the themes about legal education, but they are also subject to further meta-analysis, capable of broader generalizations. At very minimum, therefore, this study reveals the distinct value of a methodology grounded in an individual scale but focused on thematic and abstract, "stated preferences."[92]

More substantively, the interplay between Parts I and II of this chapter reveals how the terms of the conventional debate are woefully too superficial to explore the complexity of the relationship between theory and practice in legal education. It is certainly not enough to ask whether one should emphasize "practice" or "theory" in a law school. At a basic level, this study demonstrates that both elements play a key role in law teaching. To the extent that the co-existence of theory and practice emerges as an empirical "fact," the simplistic debate over *whether* theory or practice ought to be emphasized declines in significance. It is more productive to examine the dynamics between theory and practice.

One such dynamic is whether theory and practice are treated as oppositional forces or mutually constitutive virtues. If nothing else, asking this question illuminates the implicit bias toward an oppositional attitude. Raising consciousness may enable us to escape a default grammar and begin a more revelatory conversation. The observation that professors speak oppositionally sometimes, and integratively at others, shows how neither category is intuitively correct or unavoidable. Perhaps this work can serve to help legal educators think explicitly about how they *relate* different goals, objectives, features, and virtues of legal education (and not *just* theory and practice). When are we implicitly creating an either/or duality? Do we *believe* in virtues as mutually reinforcing? And if so, how thoroughgoing should we be in trying to implement that belief? This reflection can be useful for individual instructors, who might ask themselves what they believe in for their teaching, and how they would describe their role, and, if the answers to these questions differ, deciding whether they are comfortable with this difference.

91 *Cf.* Nelson et al. (2012–2013); Law Student Survey of Student Engagement, online: http://lssse.indiana.edu/.

92 Drawing on professors' subjective descriptions in this context shines a light on the potential advantages of foregrounding "stated" preferences in empirical research. As Edward Fischer writes, while revealed preferences are "highly sensitive to contextual and structural constraints, [and disclose] a necessary and pragmatic concern with what is possible," stated preferences are "less bounded by the practicalities of time horizons and collective action problems. They are able to consider 'what if' possibilities: what kind of person one would like to be, what sort of world one would like to live in" (Fischer 2014, 64).

A third type of insight derives from asking what might account for professors speaking in one way (integrative) about what they do, and another way (oppositional) about their role.

One account would downplay the apparent contradiction between Part I and Part II and argue that the profession and academy really are at war, and that the conventional narrative survives because it wrestles with the perennial, singular, animating tension of a law school as a professional school housed in a university. Professors *do* feel pressure from the profession to produce practice-ready lawyers and from the academy to produce scholarship. The tendency to speak of teaching in a way that "integrates" practice and theory is a response to structural conditions that are true and immutable – a response that can be broken down into separate steps.

The first step is for professors to bifurcate their roles as teacher and scholar in a way that mirrors the dichotomy between profession and academy. On this view, as a scholar, one pursues the academic virtues of theory, critique, and inquiry for their own sakes. As a teacher, one delivers the practicality demanded by the profession. There is no particular contradiction, because the law professor understands him- or herself as exercising two conceptually distinct tasks, inhabiting two distinct roles for different purposes. The oppositional descriptions of role or mission may reflect a high degree of self-awareness of the extent to which the law professor is a person "divided against [him- or her]self."[93] Law professors, like law schools, may lead a "double life" (Holloway and Friedland 2017).

The second step is that law professors strive to make "delivering" the practical education something they can live with. While the professional constraints are real, integrating one's theoretical and critical commitments directly into practical training transmutes the constraints into an exercise of autonomy. This interpretation would seem to align with the impression that the expressions of integration in teaching do not seem perfunctory but rather products of honest intellectual work. Integration signals professors becoming "creative non victims" vis-à-vis real, immutable pressures (Atwood 1972).

While attractive, this "split-role-creative-non-victim" explanation encounters difficulty in light of professors' reticence to acknowledge pressures from the profession as meaningful constraints. Professor 40 is virtually alone in describing teaching as a "pushback" against the local bar. Moreover, when I specifically asked professors about what constraints they do feel (and I did so, directly, 45 times, and more times indirectly), few alluded to pressure from the profession.[94] The most commonly cited constraints were time and competing demands, institutional

93 See note 66 and accompanying text.

94 Occasionally, student or faculty pressure to have common content across sections (motivated by a "core knowledge" expected in legal practice) arose ([013], [066]); [062] and [043] both spoke about the need to change pedagogy as a result of the changing nature of the market for legal services; and [007], quoted above, spoke specifically about how the tension between profession and academy "drums out" the enthusiasm of students and prevents navigating broad and technical understandings of law. A couple of professors mentioned the high cost of tuition and commensurate student demands to "give them what they are paying for" ([040]). All of these

culture (preference for research over teaching), administrative concerns (room layout and scheduling, limited administrative support for teaching initiatives, grading), attenuated student concentration because of laptop use, and displeasure with commercially available materials. *Fourteen* professors stated they felt "no" constraints whatsoever. Accordingly, while the "split-role" characterization may have a certain intuitive appeal (especially for the cynical), I do not believe it best characterizes the attitudes and commitments of the professors I spoke with.

An alternative account is that the difference between Parts I and II reflects a more systematic disjuncture between what law professors say and what they do.[95] Professors "say" oppositional things about role or mission, but "do" integrative things in their teaching. If there really is a gap, how should we deal with it? On the one hand, one could insist that this fact of disjuncture necessitates a remedial project. Some may feel that authenticity in legal education is derived from "meaning what we say"[96] and recommend an agenda to align one's beliefs about mission with one's pedagogy; a range of institutional modifications could follow.[97]

On the other hand, one could accept the fact of this gap and seek not to eradicate it but to better understand it. In the same way that it has become commonplace among the legal academy to assert that underlying factors provide a better account of legal decision-making than the words used by judges,[98] one could imagine a transformed framework for thinking about *any* issue on legal pedagogy or curricular reform along distinct two lines: how does this affect our understanding of role, and how does this affect teaching practices? If we were all "legal education realists," one could readily acknowledge that it is both the words we use *and* concrete actions that communicate meaning and intention. We could then cultivate an intellectual curiosity about both elements. Given the very common practice in Canada of simultaneously taking judges' words "seriously" and looking at "underlying factors" of policy, politics, and context, this type of duality would likely be natural to most professors.[99] Concretely, this would

indirectly make reference to pressure from the profession. Rarely does student resistance cause professors to actually change their approach.

95 *Cf.* Sandomierski (2017) (casebooks editors make strong claims to critical and realist perspectives, but convey ideas kindred to formalism in the sources they choose, how they structure the books, and the questions they pose).

96 See White (2004, 109).

97 Could the "teaching philosophy" section of teaching dossiers be supplemented with a reflection on mission? Could curricular reform begin to map out discrete skills progressions, in addition to substantive and thematic knowledge objectives?

98 On the ubiquity of this view, see Singer (1988, 465) (Review Essay of Laura Kalman, *Legal Realism at Yale: 1927–1960*, 1986). For an example of referring to judges' words as "rhetoric," see Posner (1977).

99 The examples used in this chapter may have given an erroneous impression that most Canadian Contracts professors are "pure" formalists or realists. In fact, by far the more common is the professor who takes doctrine seriously but seeks to supplement understanding with realist insights. I expand on this claim in *Aspiration and Reality In Legal Education* (Sandomierski forthcoming 2020). This tendency to take doctrine seriously is likely much more common in Canada than in the USA. See, for example, Marcovits

probably militate in favour of greater empirical studies into the practices of legal education within faculty as an offset to the more conventional and familiar practice of curricular debate.[100]

A third interpretation is that Contracts professors are genuinely committed to *both* oppositional and integrative views. The widespread goal of "making better lawyers" may not be so much a deft response to pressure, but a genuine commitment. This interpretation is interesting for at least two reasons. First, it accords with one interpretation of the co-existence of realist and formalist viewpoints observed in Canadian contract law casebooks; namely, that editors possess an "intellectual ambivalence."[101] To the extent that this ambivalence holds with respect to the "integrative" and "oppositional" attitudes, we move one step closer to considering ambivalence as a salient feature of Canadian legal thought.

Second, ambivalence makes categories such as "theory" or "practice," or "integrative" or "oppositional" less operative: if the prevailing norm is one of co-existence of different ideas, less hinges on characterizing a given attitude according to one category or another. Words such as "theory" or "practice" function less as contestants and more as ideal-types, or heuristics, for structuring reflection. When this happens, the centrality of these concepts to discourse is rendered contingent: they remain key only so long as they are useful for advancing understanding, and will (and should) be superseded when new concepts prove more useful.

Conclusion

Empirical research into the attitudes, goals, aspirations, and visions of relevance of legal educators is not only descriptive but generative. From the ground level, it mines the concepts that are of greatest relevance to the lived experience of legal education's protagonists: students and teachers. In the early to mid-2010s, Canadian Contracts professors do speak about theory and practice, vindicating the centrality of these concepts to the contemporary discourse. Professors' deeply held commitments, however, reveal that the "fierce debate" between the academy and profession, however favoured, only partially captures the dynamic between theory and practice. Professors passionately articulate the individual and creative ways in which their deeply held theoretical commitments assist them in making "better" lawyers – a "better" they believe in and seek to define. At the same time, when they speak about their role, many highlight a tension and oppositionality that is largely absent from their teaching.

What is most interesting about this dynamic is the apparent tension between these two tendencies. It suggests that the schism worth investigating is not the conventional one between theory and practice, played out on a macro level of curricula, institutions, or markets, but rather the professional self-conception of

(2012) (describing his approach of taking doctrine seriously as an outlier approach in the USA).

100 *Cf.* Macdonald (1982, 569) ("thoughtful curricular debate is a law school's primary heuristic device").

101 See Sandomierski (2017).

professors, played out at the individual level of pedagogical agency and role identity. That *internal* dynamic, that source of ambivalence, tension, and contradiction, may be a richer avenue to understand the practices, rationales, and downstream effects of legal education.

No amount of top-down interventions can elucidate the complexities of the mind. So long as we confine ourselves to the terms of the conventional debate, which seems increasingly epiphenomenal in light of the evidence of how professors understand their teaching, we may be doomed to "gas around in the abstract."[102] We may continue to incant old tropes whose operative significance has long since expired. It may be time to retire the time-honoured theory–practice debate in favour of a rigorous, empirical curiosity about legal educators' tendency and capacity to espouse multitudes.

References

Abeysekera, Lakmal, and Phillip Dawson. 2015. Motivation and Cognitive Load in the Flipped Classroom: Definition, Rationale and a Call for Research. *Higher Education Research & Development* 34: 1–14.

American Bar Association, Task Force on the Future of Legal Education. 2013. Working Paper, August 1. www.americanbar.org/content/dam/aba/administrative/professional_responsibility/taskforcecomments/aba_task_force_working_paper_august_2013.authcheckdam.pdf (accessed March 12, 2019).

Arthurs, Harry W. 1998. The Political Economy of Canadian Legal Education. *Journal of Law & Society* 25(1): 14–32.

Arthurs, Harry W. Forthcoming 2019. The Tree of Knowledge / The Axe of Power: Gerald Le Dain and the Transformation of Canadian Legal Education. In *Tracings of Gerald Le Dain's Life in the Law*, ed. G. Blaine Baker and Richard Janda. Montreal: McGill-Queen's University Press.

Atwood, Margaret. 1972. *Survival: A Thematic Guide to Canadian Literature.* Toronto: House of Anansi.

Bergin, Thomas F. 1968. The Law Teacher: A Man Divided Against Himself. *Virginia Law Review* 54(4): 637–657.

Bliss, John. 2017. Divided Selves: Professional Role Distancing Among Law Students and New Lawyers in a Period of Market Crisis. *Law and Social Inquiry* 42(3): 855–897.

Coleman, Jules L. 1995. Legal Theory and Practice. *Georgetown Law Journal* 83: 2579–2617.

Common Law Degree Implementation Committee. 2011 (August). *Final Report.* Federation of Law Societies of Canada, online [FLSC Report].

Consultative Group on Research and Education in Law. 1983. *Law and Learning.* Report to the Social Sciences and Humanities Research Council of Canada, Chairman Harry Arthurs. Ottawa: Social Sciences and Humanities Research Council of Canada.

Coquillette, Daniel R., and Bruce A. Kimball. 2015. *The Republic of Merit: Harvard Law School, the First Century (1817–1910).* Cambridge, MA: Harvard University Press.

Deo, Meera. 2015. Faculty Insights on Educational Diversity. *Fordham Law Review* 83: 3115–3153.

102 [027], Interview, 403–412.

de Sousa Santos, Boaventura. 1987. Law: A Map of Misreading. Toward a Post-modern Conception of Law. *Journal of Law and Society* 14(3): 279–302.

Elkins, James. 1999. Alternative Currents: One Teacher's Thinking about the Critical Thinking Movement. *Legal Studies Forum* 23(4): 379–389.

Fischer, Edward. 2014. *The Good Life: Aspiration, Dignity, and the Anthropology of Well-being*. Stanford, CA: Stanford University Press.

Habermacher, Adrien. In progress. *Institutional Culture and Legal Education at Select Canadian Law Faculties*. DCL thesis, Faculty of Law, McGill University.

Holloway, Ian, and Steven I. Friedland. 2017. The Double Life of Law Schools. *Case Western Reserve Law Review* 68: 397–427.

Kennedy, David, and William W. Fisher III. 2006. *The Canon of American Legal Thought*. Princeton, NJ: Princeton University Press.

Kennedy, Duncan. 1982. Legal Education and the Reproduction of Hierarchy. *Journal of Legal Education* 32(4): 591–615.

Klare, Karl. 2011. Teaching Local 1330 – Reflections on Critical Legal Pedagogy. *Unbound: Harvard Journal of the Legal Left* 7: 58–78.

Kronman, Anthony T. 1993. *The Lost Lawyer*. Cambridge, MA: Belknap Press.

Kyer, C. Ian, and Jerome Bickenbach. 1987. *The Fiercest Debate: Cecil A Wright, The Benchers and Legal Education in Ontario, 1923–1957*. Toronto: University of Toronto Press.

Law Student Survey of Student Engagement. http://lssse.indiana.edu/ (accessed March 12, 2019).

Macdonald, Roderick A. 1982. Curricular Development in the 1980s: A Perspective. *Journal of Legal Education* 32(4): 569–590.

Macdonald, Roderick A., and Thomas B. McMorrow. 2014. Decolonizing Law School. *Alberta Law Review* 51(4): 717–738.

Marcovits, Daniel. 2012. *Contract Law and Legal Methods*. New York: Foundation Press.

Mertz, Elizabeth. 2007. *The Language of Law School: Learning to "Think Like a Lawyer"*. New York: Oxford University Press.

Nelson, Robert, Ronit Dinovitzer, Gabriele Plickert, Joyce Sterling, and Bryant Garth. 2012–2013. *After the JD, Wave 3: A Longitudinal Study of Careers in Transition*. http://doi.org/10.3886/ICPSR35480.v1 (accessed March 12, 2019).

Noreau, Pierre, and Pierre-Olivier Bonin. 2017. Faire droit … devenir jurist. On file with author.

Nussbaum, Martha C. 2003. Cultivating Humanity in Legal Education. *University of Chicago Law Review* 70(1): 265–279.

Posner, Richard. 1977. *Economic Analysis of Law*, 2nd edition. Boston, MA: Little, Brown, & Co.

Pue, W. Wesley. 2005. Educating the Total Jurist. *Legal Ethics* 8(2): 208–221.

Raso, Jennifer. 2019. Unity in the Eye of the Beholder? Reasons for Decision in Theory and Practice in the Ontario Works Program. *University of Toronto Law Journal*. doi:10.3138/utlj.2018-0022

Rhode, Deborah L. 2000. Legal Education: Professional Interests and Public Values. *Indiana Law Review* 34(23): 23–45.

Risk, R.C.B. 2005. My Continuing Legal Education. *University of Toronto Law Journal* 55(3): 313–334.

Sandomierski, David. 2014. Training Lawyers, Cultivating Citizens, and Re-Enchanting the Legal Professional. *Alberta Law Review* 51(4): 739–760.

Sandomierski, David. 2017. Tension and Reconciliation in Canadian Contract Law Casebooks. *Osgoode Hall Law Journal* 54(4): 1181–1244.

Sandomierski, David. Forthcoming 2020. *Aspiration and Reality in Legal Education*. Toronto: University of Toronto Press.

Segal, David. 2011. What They Don't Teach Law Students: Lawyering. *New York Times*, November 19. www.nytimes.com/2011/11/20/business/after-law-school-associates-learn-to-be-lawyers.html (accessed March 12, 2019).

Singer, Joseph William. 1988. Legal Realism Now. *California Law Review* 76(2): 465–544.

Sullivan, William M., Anne Colby, Judith Welch Wegner, Lloyd Bond, and Lee S. Shulman. 2007. *Educating Lawyers: Preparation for the Profession of Law* [*Carnegie Report*]. San Francisco, CA: Jossey-Bass.

Tamanaha, Brian Z. 2012. *Failing Law Schools*. Chicago, IL: University of Chicago Press.

Valverde, Mariana. 2009. Jurisdiction and Scale: Legal "Technicalities" as Resources for Theory. *Social & Legal Studies* 18(2): 139–157.

Valverde, Mariana. 2015. *Chronotopes of Law: Jurisdiction, Scale and Governance*. Abingdon: Routledge.

White, James Boyd. 2004. Meaning What You Say. In *Law in the Liberal Arts*, ed. Austin Sarat, 109–139. Ithaca, NY: Cornell University Press.

Willis, John. 1979. *A History of the Dalhousie Law School*. Toronto: University of Toronto Press.

2 Teaching International Lawyers How to Think, Speak, and Act like U.S. Lawyers

Notes on Inchoate Power and the Imperial Process

Mindie Lazarus-Black

Introduction

This chapter draws upon ethnographic research and interviews with U.S. law faculty from two law schools about their experiences teaching attorneys from other countries who are enrolled in international LL.M. programs, the equivalent of a master's degree in law. Almost all the students trained originally in a civil law tradition, they have a wide range of academic and practical experience, and most of them are learning U.S. law in a second language. Professor #26, who teaches intellectual property in a Midwestern law school and sometimes in an intensive program in Thailand, explained the challenges she faces:

> So if I'm talking about a Cole Porter song to my Bangkok class, they've never heard of it. If I talk about Beatles songs … they don't know them well enough to know what I'm talking about … . The cultural differences are huge … I always take with me to Bangkok all kinds of stuff … like I bring a printout of a patent … and then they all come together while I'm sitting in the middle … and that seems to be a really good way to get them more comfortable … When I'm [in the U.S.], you'll never see me in a classroom in *anything* but a [business] suit … [but] in Bangkok I'm always informal. They tend to be more formal than I am a lot of times, because they've come from work.

The professor is in Bangkok to teach Thai lawyers how to think like a U.S. lawyer. That is usually accomplished by using the "signature pedagogy" of U.S. law schools, the Socratic Method (Carnegie Foundation 2007, 50).[1] Realizing, however, that her students are not only extremely formal, but they are also extremely reticent in English, she must change her style of instruction and sometimes the

1 The Carnegie Foundation Report defines "signature pedagogy" as a "key educational practice by which a given field creates a common frame through which it can induct new members" (2007, 50). The Socratic Method is "distinctive to North American legal education and quite sharply different from the method used in the United Kingdom, continental Europe, and, indeed, most of the world" (2007, 51).

language in which learning occurs. Instead of relying primarily on Socratic Method, she divides her students into groups. The students "talk like crazy" as they debate a matter in their own language. She explains: "And so I can get some of that dialogue started and I can get them thinking a little bit more about how to make the argument on each side." Yet she tells me that she is "tough" [meaning acts like a "real" law professor] when it comes to their exam: "And I tell them, don't vomit back the law to me; if you're not doing the analysis in the facts, you will get no points." Teaching in Thailand, the professor acknowledges, entails different attention to language, methods, customs, and appearances.

I examine for two reasons what occurs when U.S. law faculty teach non-U.S. attorneys how to think, speak, and act like U.S. lawyers. First, like Herzfeld (2015), I am interested in rendering visible mostly invisible patterns of interaction that deploy power in inchoate forms and that in this case have the consequence of making transnational classes sometimes paradoxical locales. I address as an anthropological question: "You teach? What is it that you do?" Are you "training"? If so, who, where, and to what extent? I investigate teaching as "work," as a labor process in which both faculty and students cross borders.[2] Like Barnes and Mertz, I seek to understand "what sort of real-world role model is provided to law students by the professors who are initiating them into their professional lives" (2018, 443). I also subject the work of legal education to questions of agency and structure that take place within the bureaucracies that constitute law schools in the U.S. and abroad. Such bureaucracies, as Graeber points out, are part of the "explosion of credentialism" that has occurred in so-called "advanced" economies like the U.S. (2015, 22) and in which "credentials function as *de facto* permission to speak" (Kendzior cited in Graeber 2015, 22). And yet as scholars who have studied the influence and consequences of race, gender, and socioeconomic status in U.S. JD classrooms have demonstrated, the process of educating lawyers and providing them with credentials—permission to speak—entails subtle and sometimes not-so-subtle forms of silencing.[3] Does the education of international lawyers entail similar processes?

2 My thanks to Carol Greenhouse who specifically referred to teaching as a labor process in her comments as discussant for the panel entitled "You Teach? What is it you Do? The Familiar/Strange in the Process of Instruction" at the American Anthropological Association, Denver, November 18–22, 2015.

3 Some classic and more recent studies addressing the silencing of white women, men and women of color, persons from socioeconomically disadvantaged backgrounds, and from other underrepresented groups in law school JD programs include: Banks (1988); Carnegie Foundation (2007); Costello (2005); Deo (2011–2012, 2015); Guinier et al. (1997); Granfield (1992); Grover and Womack (2017); Gutierrez y Muhs et al. (2012); Menkel-Meadow (1988); Mertz (2000, 2007a); Mertz with Njogu and Gooding (1998); Montoya (1999–2000); Moran (2000); Niemann (2012); Ogloff et al. (2000–2001); Schleef (2006); Sturm and Guinier (2007); Weiss and Melling (1987–1988); Williams (1991); and Working Group on Student Experiences, Study on Women's Experiences at Harvard Law School, Cambridge, MA (2004). An increasing number of studies examine how gender, sexuality, race, class, foreign national status, and other forms of diversity influence the experiences of law faculty (e.g. Barnes and Mertz 2012, 2018; Deo 2014; Gutierrez y Muhs et al. 2012; and Lopez and Johnson 2014). Florio and Hoffman's 2012–2013 study of JD students' experiences at

My second interest stems from my effort to understand better what Garth has called the "imperial process" (2015, 69) that governs the internationalization of legal education. The imperial process to which he refers had its origins in European imperialism. Today, Garth contends, the imperial process operates through educational markets that have led to the success of the U.S. in achieving its role in the "hierarchical global market in legal expertise" (2015, 73). He asks us to "explain sociologically what the patterns of import and export are and how they relate to larger questions of hierarchy and international political economy" (2015, 69–70). Examining the education of international lawyers reveals patterns of import and export with respect to the content of courses, styles of pedagogy, and the design of the programs. As I will demonstrate, it also reveals the circumstances under which law schools in other countries and non-U.S. lawyers contest the design of these programs, the content that is presented to them, the language of instruction, the styles in which they are taught, and how they are assessed in courses.

Examining how power and the imperial process are deployed in transnational legal education compels us to investigate how faculty contend with the vicissitudes of teaching lawyers from different academic and legal cultures. Broadly speaking, I use the term "academic culture" to refer to the norms and behaviors that govern teaching and learning in schools, as well as the actors who participate in varying ways in those processes. Academic culture includes such considerations as whether students are expected to voice their opinions in class, whether their attendance is recorded, and whether there exists a time that we, in the U.S., refer to as "office hours."[4] Academic culture in Thailand, for example, relies mainly on lectures, classes often include 150 or more students, students take notes and are not accustomed to speaking in class, they are expected to memorize a great deal of material, and they are usually tested in one final exam at the end of a course (Bliss et al. 2014, 223, 226).

"Legal culture" refers to the context in which law is made, implemented, and practiced, as well as where it is made and by whom. It includes the expectations and behaviors of its many representatives, whether scholars or practitioners. It comprises the assumptions and actions of those who teach law, how they teach and who they teach. Legal culture alerts us to the similarities and differences between solo practitioners and partners in legal firms. It attends to different relationships between law and the state in different nations. It also entails what lawyers do for clients and whether a particular problem is one that people believe the law should address. In Thai legal culture, for example, a law degree is an undergraduate degree and students do not think that learning to think like a lawyer means learning in class to argue both sides of a case. As lawyers, they will generally apply known statutes to their clients' cases. Moreover, matters such as the causation of injury and "justice" more generally are understood in other ways. The

University of Toronto is unusual in finding that gender was mostly not a significant variable in determining students' overall satisfaction with their legal education.

4 For critical discussions about the academic culture of U.S. law schools see, among other sources, Carnegie Foundation (2007); Granfield (1992); Guinier et al. (1997); Kennedy (2004); Mertz (2000, 2007a, 2007b); Philips (1988); Rapoport (2011–2012); Schleef (2006); and Sturm and Guinier (2007).

practice of tort law, for example, is profoundly influenced by Buddhism and ideas about karma, even if the codes are secular (Engel 2009; Engel and Engel 2010).[5]

My research shows that accommodation or resistance to differences in academic and legal cultures varies widely. For example, faculty members who have themselves studied abroad are aware of differences in academic cultures and respond to their own students accordingly.[6] Similarly, the topic of the law class matters; courses that rely heavily on statutory codes are less "foreign" to foreign attorneys trained in civil law. A more important finding is that differences in academic and legal cultures, and how those affect the politics of transnational legal education, are strongly influenced by the three different contexts in which faculty provide instruction. These contexts include: 1) classes that are part of the LL.M. program, but are taught in the students' countries of origin; 2) classes in the faculty members' home institutions specifically designed for international attorneys; and 3) classes for U.S. JD students. Relations of domination and subordination between institutions, faculty, and students are differently expressed and exercised in these three settings.

My discussion develops as follows. I describe first the programs in which this research unfolded, my research methods, and the participants in the study. In the three sections that follow, I portray what the faculty told me about teaching international students abroad, classes in which only international students are enrolled, and classes open to both international and U.S. JD students. For each context, I address how faculty manage the content of the courses they are teaching, what they "do" about the language of instruction, which pedagogical styles they choose, and how they test and grade their students. I argue that different bureaucratic and structural constraints operate in each of these contexts, challenging the professors to re-examine the labor process that constitutes their teaching while simultaneously reconstructing the agency of instructors and pupils. I explore how and when power is rendered and amended in each setting, as well as evidence for, and challenges to, the imperial process in transnational legal education.

Contextual Notes, Research Methods, and the Participants

The education of international law students has grown exponentially in the past few decades. The spread of the U.S. style of corporate law, neoliberal governance, and international trade, the movement of lawyers across borders, and a growing worldwide interest in human rights law, international commercial arbitration, and criminal

5 Other discussions of legal culture include: Engel and McCann (2009); Ewick and Silbey (1998); Friedman (1994); Galanter (1983–1984); Geertz (1983); Greenhouse et al. (1994); Konefsky and Sullivan (2014); Nelken (2004, 2009); and Rosen (2006). I am addressing legal culture specifically within the realm of educating lawyers and I illuminate the "faculty culture" (Task Force on the Future of Legal Education 2014, 15–16) in the two schools in which I worked.

6 Faculty #28 explained: "I've been an American law student, I've been a student in Europe, I know what it's like to sit in a classroom and only hear 20 percent, only hear 60 percent, only 40 percent … . I know it's not easy, I get that, and we can talk about this."

tribunals have encouraged a market for foreign attorneys trained in the U.S. and credentialed with an LL.M. degree.[7] In 2017 the ABA identified 178 schools that offered LL.M. programs, of which 59 listed programs specifically "for international lawyers."[8] With the exception of foundational work by Silver (e.g. 2006, 2011, 2012a, 2012b, 2013) and a few other studies, however, we have little information about the experiences of foreign LL.M. students, the faculty who teach them, and the administrators who admit and support them through their programs.[9]

My ethnographic research and interviews were conducted in 2008–2012 in two law schools, one in the Midwest and the second on the East Coast.[10] At each school, students were required to complete 24 credit hours of study, of which two classes were specifically designed for international students.[11] Some students in both programs earned credits towards the LL.M. degree in their country of origin or at another designated locale. They earned most other credits in classes with JD students. As part of my fieldwork, I spent considerable time in one admissions office, read hundreds of applications, and talked with program directors and staff. At one school, I was invited to attend classes for teaching legal research and writing to international attorneys taught by five instructors.[12] I also attended other events, such as orientation, Thanksgiving celebration, and graduation. I talked with students informally before and after classes, and conducted formal semi-

7 I draw this description from several sources, but especially from Garth's (2015, 72–73) summary of the important variables that led to the U.S. achieving its dominant role in global legal education. Other recent discussions of these trends include Aman (2015); Dezalay and Garth (2002, 2010); Garth (2013); Hupper (2015); Konefsky and Sullivan (2014); Liu (2008, 2013); Mattei and Nader (2008); Michelson (2015); Silver (2000, 2002, 2003, 2004–2005, 2009, 2011, 2012a, 2012b, 2013, 2015–2016); and Silver and Ballakrishnen (2018).

8 See www.americanbar.org/portals/non-us-lawyers.html (accessed June 28, 2017).

9 Silver finds, for example, that "reliable data on this population remains scarce" (2012a, 2389) and that even basic information, such as the number of international LL.M. students enrolled in U.S. law schools, their countries of origin, sources for funding their U.S. education, and their post-graduate activities, employment, and locations are unknown (Silver 2015–2016, 481–482). She explores the development of LL.M. programs designed to train foreign lawyers, the spread of U.S. law firms to international sites, and employment patterns of foreign lawyers. This project builds on her work, and includes interviews with faculty who teach LL.M. students, and participant observation in one admissions office and in legal writing and research classes. Trained in cultural anthropology, I ask different questions about how and with what consequences international students are "trained." See also Ballakrishnen (2012); Brand and Rist (2009); Lazarus-Black and Globokar (2015); Lazarus-Black (2017); and Spanbauer (2007).

10 Both schools are accredited by the ABA. In 2014, they ranked among the top 75 law schools in the country as measured by *U.S. News & World Report.* (See http://grad-schools.U.S.news.rankingsand reviews.com/best-graduate-schools/top-law-schools/law-rankings) (accessed October 28, 2014).

11 A few students at one school worked instead on independent projects.

12 I attended legal research and writing classes for international LL.M. students intermittently for five semesters, beginning in fall, 2009, and continuing through fall, 2011. In all, I attended 50 classes for a total of approximately 74 hours at different periods in each semester. I listened to instructors covering some of the same and some different cases and assignments.

structured interviews with 50 students from 22 countries across the two schools (Lazarus-Black and Globokar 2015; Lazarus-Black 2017).

To discover what it is like to teach in the three different contexts in which faculty work to credential international LL.M. students and export U.S. legal education, I turn primarily to interviews with 14 faculty members from the Midwestern law school and 18 faculty members from the East Coast school.[13] They taught classes such as introduction to the U.S. legal system, intellectual property, legal research and writing, securities, and constitutional law, as well as corporate law, public interest law, and civil rights. Thirty of the 32 interviewees had taught abroad. They taught primarily in China, other locales in Asia, and in Eastern and Western Europe.

The Midwestern law school faculty included seven men and seven women. When asked if he or she identified as a member of a racial, ethnic, or other minority group, seven responded "white" or "Caucasian," one as "African-American," three as "Jewish," two said they did not identify with any group, and one joked that he was a Democrat. Eight of the 14 had been educated at one of the top 20 law schools in the country. Their ages ranged from the mid-30s to the mid-70s. Four had taught for less than five years, seven between five and 15 years, and three for more than 15 years.

At the East Coast school I interviewed 13 men and five women. In answer to the question of whether they identified with a racial, ethnic, or other minority group, eight responded "white" or "Caucasian," one as African-American, six responded "no," one as "Jewish," one told me he was "uncomfortable with census categories," and another "preferred not to answer that question." Half of the interviewees at the East Coast school had attended one of the top 20 law schools in the country. They were older than their Midwest counterparts: five in their 50s, seven in their 60s, and two over 70. They also had more teaching experience: only one had taught for less than five years, six between five and 15 years, and nine for more than 15 years.[14] While there was variation in the demographic characteristics and teaching experiences of the faculty at the two schools, I found some striking similarities in their accounts of teaching foreign attorneys. I begin with teaching law overseas.

13 I used the "snowballing" method in the following way. I secured permission from the deans at each school to conduct my research and the deans provided me with the names of the administrators of the programs. The administrators then provided some names of faculty to contact. At the end of each faculty interview, I asked for names of other people to interview, noting that I wanted to talk to faculty with wide ranges of experiences working with foreign attorneys, including those who supported the international LL.M. programs and those who did not. I conducted 30 interviews with faculty in their offices or in a conference room, most of them of approximately one hour in duration. A few faculty members with extensive experience with the international attorneys invited me to return for a second interview. Two interviews, one from each school, were conducted by telephone.

14 I thank Brendan Tuttle for summarizing the sociological characteristics and educational, teaching, and work experiences of these interviewees. He calculated the law school rankings of the schools attended by the faculty based on *After the JD II* (Dinovitzer et al. 2009, 18). (Tuttle report to Lazarus-Black, December 12, 2013, on file with author)

Teaching U.S. Law Overseas

Of course, teaching U.S. law in Thailand is not like teaching U.S. law in Eastern Europe, nor is it like teaching U.S. law in China; there is always a politics of place in addition to a politics of pedagogy. Relationships between nations change over time, encouraging or discouraging international study, and as agreements between law schools wax and wane. Faculty who are preparing to teach abroad consult with their more experienced colleagues, but depending upon when and where they teach, faculty encounter differences in the backgrounds, experiences, and motivations of the students, encouraging (requiring?) them to re-think the training they provide. Nevertheless, certain patterns are clear. Professors find their work changes quite a lot when they teach overseas. For many, this labor entails interesting forms of accommodation for which they were not initially prepared. Faculty revealed four important patterns of import and export in the market for legal education.

First, when they go abroad faculty teach short intensive classes. The number of classroom hours, however, must conform to that of a semester taught at home. Professor #19 told me that whenever she teaches a class that introduces the American legal system to non-U.S. students it feels like "teaching BAR/BRI on steroids" as the course is especially "compressed" when it is taught abroad.[15] The upshot is that both teachers and students are together for an unwieldly number of hours at each class meeting—and sometimes—as in the Bangkok example—after the "students" have put in a full day of work as attorneys. Their instructors are aware of just how much material students can contend with in any class and they must adjust. Thus it is really difficult to teach a full semester of law when it is taught abroad. In mentioning this I am in no way condemning the editing process. Indeed, I would argue that sensible teaching requires it. My point is that classroom time is re-crafted in a way that is not familiar either to the pupil or to the teacher. It is, for them both, strange. Thus the content of a course is negotiated in part to fit classroom time. And Professor #14 told me that when he was teaching in Europe, he became accustomed to starting class ten minutes late. Academic culture there required that he do so.

Second, every faculty member I spoke with discussed the fact that the international attorneys have different levels of skill in speaking and writing English. (See also Silver 2013, 491.) Therefore, professors learn that they must speak in different ways and avoid what are for them familiar references. Faculty #19 explained one must be cognizant of how you speak, how much you speak, and what you speak about. In her words:

15 BAR/BRI is a short but intensive preparatory course for students who intend to take a state bar exam. It is operated by a private corporation and is expensive, but students experience pressure to take the course. Faculty #19's courses were taught for three hours per day for five days, followed by two days off, and then for another five days. Depending upon the agreement with law schools in other countries, the other school has offered three, four, six, and eight week sessions at one time or another. The same material would be taught at home over a fourteen-week semester.

> I mean I was never trained in ESL [English as a Second Language], but I think of it, as talking about complex subjects in accessible ways … Speaking slowly and clearly … which limits the amount of material you can go into. Limiting as much as possible extraneous cultural references to baseball and sports and sort of American, colloquial ways of describing things … Remembering that … if you make … ironic or sarcastic remarks … sometimes that's the only thing the student remembers.

Other faculty members change the readings they assign; Professor #7 told me she chose another textbook to teach contracts overseas because the authors' sense of humor was inexplicable to her students! Professor #32 learned: "There are some things you can't kid about. Relations between men and women are so different by culture that you have to stay away from that." In other words, irony, puns, jokes, music, movies, and sports are off the table. And so is American history. Faculty #12 told me that she had referred to "the Founding Fathers" in her classes for some time before she realized that the international attorneys had no idea about whom she was speaking. Moreover, she recognized: "Racism [in the U.S.] is impossible for them to—it takes a great deal of work for someone of another culture to work through what they have to work through in their own processing in order to analog U.S. racism … So, to the whole world, 1960s Civil Rights, is really incomprehensible basically."

Third, beyond adapting to time, language skills, and illustrative examples that might otherwise identify the professors as wise and witty, they must alter their teaching techniques and legal terminology. They learn that they can use some Socratic Method in their teaching style when they go abroad, but only some; academic cultures in other places have made the lecture format hegemonic. What do U.S. faculty do? Their work must change. They lecture more, write on the board, make students PowerPoint slides, summarize cases, provide handouts, create discussion groups, and engage the students in role playing. Professor #29 was cognizant of his need to pay attention to both academic and legal culture:

> [And] maybe I have to put more material up on a TV projector so they actually see the written word. And I wouldn't necessarily have to do that in front of a bunch of JDs. Maybe it's not just language though. Maybe it's a difference in fundamental meaning of a concept, like jurisdiction or notary. These are important legal terms that might have nuanced differences in other foreign legal cultures.

These sometimes fundamental or nuanced differences in legal concepts require shifts in power in which the *professor* must undergo new training. Professor #20 explained:

> Our problem is that we're talking about restitution and they're thinking Chinese restitution. I'm talking American restitution and neither of us realized for about an hour.

> And it's partly, it's about the market. We think in terms of contracts. They think in terms of justice. [In one case my students read] ... they auctioned off a safe, and the safe has a locked compartment. No key, right? This reduces the value of the safe. You buy this, there's no key. The buyer hires a locksmith and there's $30,000 in the locked compartment. Who gets the $30,000? In the United States, it's the person who bought the safe ... . It's absolutely opposite in China ... . The buyer gets to keep the safe but the $30,000 goes back to the estate!

In short, the script and the performance change when played abroad.

Fourth, references to the "imperial process" in the market for legal education emerged in several interviews, but to make different points. Professor #31 spoke explicitly about the export process in a way that Garth would predict—the U.S. is judged "the best" against the rest:

> it is the case now that intellectual property is one of the most significant exports of the United States; whether it's the entertainment industry or the pharmaceutical industry... [O]ur value, in terms of exports, is more embedded in intellectual property than it is in bananas.

In sharp contrast, Faculty #32 had astutely observed that U.S. LL.M. programs are successful only when the programs "fit" into the career paths of the attorneys and only when legal professionals accept English as the lingua franca of international law:

> We have had very bad luck in Japan [trying to set up programs] because it does not fit the Japanese pattern of progressive [career movement]. People who finish their law study in Japan tend to go right into a corporate structure ... [and] study in the United States does not fit that career pattern ... Not a great deal of luck with South America [either]. That's in part because we don't fit their career structure and there is more of a reluctance to be convinced that English is the international language of commerce anyway. Because, for example ... you don't get a Fulbright from South America unless you're fluent in Spanish.

Moreover, when U.S. professors teach foreign attorneys in the students' "home" they find that sometimes the students and the foreign law schools with which the U.S. programs have agreements rebuff "the imperial process." For example, Professor #32 explained:

> When we started our program in China ... the Chinese lawyers told us: "We can't spend nine months. We're too busy" ... So we said we'll split the difference. We will go to China and teach half the LL.M. program and then bring you here for one semester.

In other words, the program had to be re-imagined.[16]

Professors are challenged by students as well. Faculty #26 explained why international attorneys found U.S. intellectual property laws not "better" but strange and hypocritical:

> [T[here is a difference between developing and developed countries. And you have only to look at our history to see that. When the U.S. first started, it took three months to get a book across the Atlantic ... [and] there was no way people were not going to re-print those books here. And what's their justification? We can't afford not to; we have to have access to this information ... And a lot of the developing countries, if you listen to the argument that they're making, it's exactly the same argument. But now that we're developed, we don't want to hear those arguments.

Finally, sometimes faculty are challenged both by the students in their classes and by the administrators in the law schools in which they teach. Professor #31 confessed that when she taught in Eastern Europe she had a hard time keeping her students on track: they wanted to turn every issue into "just straight up policy debates," but they were not "the least bit engaged with the material [they were supposed to read for class]." She also encountered resistance from the law school when she submitted grades. Administration told her that her grades were too low and she had to re-grade all of the exams.

In short, teaching U.S. law to foreign attorneys in their countries of origin has a significant influence upon what and how much one teaches, the language of instruction, pedagogical practices and modes of examination, and the power that the faculty "normally" possesses over these matters. The faculty in this sample mostly molded their choices and performances to coincide with the very different academic and legal cultures in which they were working and to align as well with different structural and bureaucratic constraints. The process of "credentialism" changes in several ways when it operates abroad. Moreover, while there is evidence for the imperial process that Garth (2015) contends characterizes transnational legal education, that process is contested by faculty and administrators who design these programs and also by the students. As I demonstrate next, the work of teaching international attorneys changes in some ways, but not entirely, when faculty teach classes designed for those lawyers studying in the U.S.

16 My thanks to Nikky Greer who drew this point to my attention when she transcribed the interview. It is also the case that being able to complete the first half of a U.S. LL. M. program in one's country of origin dramatically reduces the costs of obtaining the degree, the amount of time one needs to be away from work, and relieves familial stress. It has enabled attorneys from a wider range of socioeconomic statuses to earn an LL.M. degree (Lazarus-Black and Globokar 2015; Lazarus-Black 2017). Law schools in other countries have begun to realize this and are developing their own programs to offer students legal education based on the U.S. model and without their having to travel abroad (Silver 2013–2014, 2901).

Teaching at Home in Classes Specifically Designed for Transnational Attorneys

At the time of my study, two types of classes designed for international LL.M. students were taught in the LL.M. programs in the U.S. schools I investigated. The first type included courses required for all international lawyers to complete the LL.M. programs. At one of the schools, these included a course introducing the U.S. legal system and another that provided "hands on" experience in legal research and writing. At the other campus, an introduction to the U.S. legal system took place during orientation and the two required classes were devoted to legal research and writing. I conducted participant observation in legal research and writing classes designed specifically for international students for two reasons. First, all the transnational lawyers shared that experience and so it was important to discuss it with them as part of my interviews about legal education. Second, I hypothesized that in those contexts I would learn a great deal about the presentation to global actors of U.S. law, legal processes, institutions, and legal practitioners. In this section, I draw upon my ethnographic observations of classes taught by five instructors and discussions with faculty members who taught them. What issues do teachers think are most important in their goal to train foreign attorneys to "think like a U.S. lawyer"? What kind of coaching do they provide to help them learn how to speak, write, and act like one? What messages do professors send to students about U.S. lawyers, their work, and their place in the global hierarchy? Do relations of domination and subordination shift when foreign attorneys study in the U.S., as opposed to studying in their countries of origin? Do we find evidence of the operation of an imperial process?

Teaching legal research and writing to international students in the U.S. shares some of the characteristics of law classes that are taught abroad. As I demonstrate in this section, professors teach more slowly, they are cognizant of the fact that their students have varying levels of spoken and written English, that they come from academic cultures with different styles of pedagogy, and that students may know little about American history or seemingly obvious references to sports, art, or music. When the faculty are instructing these students in the U.S., however, they have more time to achieve their teaching goals, they can provide sophisticated online research training, require more research and writing assignments, give more one-on-one attention to students' written work, and change the manner in which they grade.

Teaching over the course of a full semester gives the faculty additional time to unravel the process of "thinking like a U.S. lawyer." Professor #2 explained that thinking like a U.S lawyer differs from thinking like a lawyer trained in a civil law tradition in four critical ways: 1) common law relies upon precedent; 2) there is a U.S. cultural concept of "fairness" that influences lawyers, judges, and juries; 3) precedent is established through analogies; and 4) U.S. attorneys learn to critique both cases and statutes. To teach these principles, Professor #2 uses very concrete examples. Precedent and fairness, for example, can be illustrated first by the example of a teacher who awards good students with a cookie at the end of the day (good students come to expect a cookie), but who one day gives a good student a grapefruit instead. The class then discusses legal cases in which judges behave like consistent and fair—or inconsistent and unfair—teachers. The ways in which fruits and vegetables are similar to and different from each other introduces the concept of analogy. To illustrate the importance of thinking critically about cases and laws and being willing to challenge and change them, he introduces old cases and statutes that seem outrageous to contemporary attorneys. Lawyers who work in civil law traditions, he explained, are not trained to think creatively about framing cases nor are they accustomed to criticizing statutes. Thus Professor #2 consciously designs the work that civil law attorneys do when they learn to think like U.S. lawyers as a comparative and empowering process for them.

Teaching non-U.S. lawyers online legal research skills is another critical component of Professor #2's teaching goals. Students get access to online legal research services and are trained how to use them to find case law, statutes, law journals, and many other databases. The use of these research services is a novel experience for some students; these resources may not be available, or may not be readily available, to the attorneys in their home countries or in the specific work environments in which they are/were employed. I attended a training session and found the service quite remarkable; its astonishing complexity and capabilities sent a message about the resources and power of U.S. law and law schools, and also very clearly about the prominence of the U.S. in the international legal hierarchy.

I asked Professor #2 what he would do differently the next time he teaches this class. He mentioned two things. First, he would spend more time explaining and working with the students on legal citations because U.S. concepts about how one properly attributes sources is a component of its academic and legal cultures that differs greatly from that of other academic and legal traditions. Second, he would re-organize the class to enable even more one-on-one time with students to improve their oral and written skills in English. Apparently, he sensed his students had not yet met the requisite skills that would make them competitive in the imperial marketplace.

A colleague, Professor #1, had six years of experience teaching legal research and writing to international attorneys. In the first class of hers that I attended, she provided the students with an overview of the course and some guidelines.[17] "You will learn first how to read," she explained, "which might seem deceptively easy because you already know how to read. This form of reading, however, is different. It is to produce 'an authentic document,' by which I mean a document with original thought. It requires you to have critical reading skills." In this class, she continued, students would also encounter new forms of writing, including an "objective memo," such as one might write for a senior partner in a law firm, and a "persuasive memo, or we can call it a brief," that they would use later to argue a case before a panel of judges. One PowerPoint slide she presented that day included the following information:

17 I sat at the back of the law school classes I attended and typed notes; sometimes I can quote verbatim, but at other times the rapidity of the discussions meant I had to summarize the content of professors' and students' remarks. I use quotations only when I am certain I captured the speaker's precise wording.

> Tips for Reading Cases
> Read for a purpose
> While in law school you should read for two purposes:
> To learn the law.
> To learn to think like a lawyer.

Only later, as I began to analyze my fieldnotes, did I recognize that the slide was hegemonic; it presumed that the lawyers in the audience had not yet learned to think, read, or write like lawyers.

The class ended with a discussion of the first writing assignment. Students would read a case decided by the U.S. Supreme Court. They were to pay attention to the progression of the case from the lower courts, its facts, the questions the Court was asked to decide, and how the judges ruled. The brief they were to bring to class was to be brief: "Don't cut and paste most of the opinion … Quote only when there is such compelling language that you can't put in any other words. We call it 'the phrase that pays.'" Determining the "phrase that pays," of course, is quite a challenge if you were trained in English as a second language by memorizing vocabulary and rules of grammar.[18]

Over the course of five semesters, I intermittently attended classes in which the students worked on legal memos typical of those they might prepare if they were newly employed in a U.S. law firm. The professors taught the students how to write a memo using a formula they called "CREAC" (you can find it on google.com). What interests me as an anthropologist is not so much the formula, but rather the professors' accompanying remarks as they taught "CREAC." The following is an excerpt from one of the lectures I attended:

> "CREAC" … "C" … State your conclusion first … This [your memo] *is not a mystery novel* … "R" … State your primary rule that supports the conclusion … Think of this as a roadmap … You take the trip and then you have to give them [the senior partners] the map on how to get there … . "E" … Explain and prove the rule by analyzing the authority. You must educate your reader on the law … How did the court reach that conclusion? … [Provide] citations … . *Nothing is original.* Lawyers are obsessed with citations! … Without citations why should we believe you? … Citations are the bedrock of our legal system. *We don't care what you think.* We want to know what you are building on. Why can you predict the court will reason similarly? *This is lawyering—making a compelling case* … . "A"… Analysis … Apply the rule's elements to the facts. [Professor names two cases relevant to the assignment] … "C" … Conclusion. This is optional … Repeat if the memo is long.

18 Professor #2 explained that many of the LL.M. students, particularly those from Asia, learned English by the "translation method," a method that involves a lot of rote memorization. A student from China told me that he had had very little experience speaking English. When his English-language professors tested his skills, they generally used a multiple-choice format.

> [Summing up] ... Everyone wants the conclusion first... *The American reader is very lazy. He doesn't want to do any work at all.* You should not give any extra information. The reader should not have to look anywhere else. Here you have to put it in your [own] words. Do not give the boss the judge's wording [my emphasis].

The lecture provides several lessons about writing like a U.S. lawyer and also about what it would be like to work in a U.S. law firm. Legal writing is "objective," which means it is based on citations, it is not "art," and it is certainly not a mystery novel. A senior partner in a U.S. law firm is not interested in mystery novels and he or she (but the professor uses only the male pronoun on this occasion) expects a memo to be a roadmap to his client's success in court.[19] He has no interest in the junior lawyer's original thoughts and he is a lazy reader. This was one moment, among many I observed, in which the work of teaching U.S. law to non-U.S. attorneys included teaching, with a somewhat critical and cynical perspective, about the work that U.S. lawyers do. In another class that I observed, the non-U.S. attorneys learned about U.S. lawyers' obsession with time. Everything had to be done on time: "if an assignment is due at 3:00 it will not be accepted at 3:30. This is how American law operates." The students also learned that the profession was changing, that lawyers were moving into "boutique" work, and that "nowadays you are not going to come out of law school and cruise into a firm to make $250,000 a year."

I want to raise here an interesting point that came up in several of my interviews with the faculty and that has been observed by others who are studying the internationalization of legal education and the profession: namely, the fact that increasingly LL.M. students include attorneys who acquired a legal education abroad but who now, for a variety of reasons, are living in the U.S. and are likely to remain here. Some of them married U.S. citizens. Others had accompanied spouses whose employers had brought them to the U.S. A few already had a green card, sometimes won in the immigration diversity lottery, and a few were working on the process of obtaining one. In these situations, the LL.M. certificate became a prerequisite for taking a bar exam so that they could eventually practice law in the U.S.[20] Their presence changes the chemistry of the classroom. Professor #4 raised the point and phrased it this way:

> Some of the foreign students we have *are really Americans* [my emphasis]. In the sense that they come here to live here and they're not going back. Or they were born in a foreign country of an American working there. Therefore their basic language is English. So there's a great deal of variety.

19 In another semester, Professor #1's instructions included: "Your job is to inform the person higher up on the food chain in the form she expects."

20 At the time of this study, faculty members and administrators frequently mentioned New York and California as two states that allowed foreign lawyers with U.S. LL.M. certificates to sit for the bar. A one-year LL.M. program, of course, was much less expensive than a three-year JD program.

Teaching foreign attorneys *who are really Americans* alters class discussions because they have more knowledge about the content of U.S. law and how the legal system functions, as well as previous exposure (and perhaps for years) to U.S. history, news, and popular culture. They share with other students trained initially in civil law, however, a lack of experience with expository writing, knowledge about how U.S. lawyers use citations, how to argue both sides of a case, and how to creatively and persuasively present a case before a judge. My interviews confirm research by the Carnegie Foundation (2007), Michelson (2015), Silver (2013, 2015–2016), and Silver and Ballakrishnen (2018 and this volume) that points to the growing diversity of foreign attorneys studying in the U.S.[21] It is clearly no longer appropriate to sustain the imperialist notion that all international students be categorized and treated singularly as "foreign."

What specific pedagogical practices did instructors employ at home to teach international attorneys how to think, read, write, speak, and act like U.S. attorneys? All of them relied on mixed methods of instruction. They all sometimes used Socratic Method, but it was never the prevailing form of interaction.[22] Two professors I observed often posed a question to the class, rather than to an individual student, and waited for a volunteer. If no one responded, they explained how one should proceed. On occasion, the faculty had students work in small groups and several of them asked students to confer on a problem in class. During one class, the faculty member and her teaching assistant simulated an interview between a senior partner in a firm and a potential client. In another, students watched alumni argue cases before judges and listened to the judges' suggestions. There were classes devoted to the basics of legal writing, such as paraphrasing, quoting, footnoting, and editing. All the faculty read many drafts of various kinds of written work, and tutored students through assignments during conferences and office hours. Such individual attention is, of course, impossible when professors teach overseas in intensive classes of short duration. (I shall have more to say about office hours in the next section of the chapter.)

21 Silver and Ballakrishnen investigate the conflation of language and culture among students in JD programs who struggle with their identities as "American" or "international" because of their different backgrounds, language skills, and knowledge of U.S. culture (Paper presented at the Law & Society Association, New Orleans, June 2–5, 2016, and this volume).

22 Rakoff and Minow argue the Socratic Method has its place in the contemporary law school, but given the complexity of legal matters lawyers now face, there is a good argument to be made for incorporating other forms of pedagogy: "The fact is, Langdell's case method is good for some things, but not good for others … . Lawyers need to be able to consider solving problems not just through litigation, but also through alternative forms of dispute resolution, through legislation, and through regulatory or executive action" (2007, 600, 602). The literature urging revision of law school curricula and pedagogical practices is vast, but I want to draw readers' attention to work by Menkel-Meadow (2007), Mertz (2007b), and Rubin (2007) published in the same special symposium as the article by Rakoff and Minow cited here. More recently, we have witnessed important works by Aiken and Shalleck (2016), Southworth, Garth, and Fisk (2016), and Tejani (2016), incorporating the intellectual insights and practices of "the new legal realism" (Mertz, Macaulay, and Mitchell 2016).

The faculty struggled to persuade students to "speak up" in the manner of a U.S. attorney. That presentation of self, as I discussed earlier, is antithetical to academic cultures in which students are expected to play passive roles. Indeed, many international attorneys present themselves in class in a way that is antithetical to the ways U.S. lawyers are expected to perform. As Mertz has pointed out, U.S. law students learn to think of themselves as having not just a "different" way of thinking and speaking, but rather a "superior analytic ability" (2007a, 98) and that ability "turns out to depend in important ways on speaking (and reading, and writing) like a [U.S.] lawyer" (Mertz 2007b, 492, my insertion). They must speak fluently and quickly in English; they must be able to "take a stand."

Perhaps because "speaking up" in the manner of U.S. law students and lawyers is implicit to the U.S. meaning of legal professional, but was not part of these attorneys' former academic and legal cultures, role playing was particularly important in the legal research and writing classes I observed. For example, the professors assigned students to represent either the plaintiff or the defendant in a case involving a man who was chased and later apprehended by the police. The professors coached the students not only about how to construct their arguments, but also how to use the arcane language expected by U.S. judges. They gave instructions about how to behave like a lawyer that sometimes startled them (and me). A professor I observed but did not interview told students who were petitioning the court to begin with: "May it please the court. Make sure you begin with that sentence … . Next, introduce yourself. My name is — … I am here on behalf of [names plaintiff] … We respectfully request that the court grant the motion to suppress." She then reviewed with them the "bullet points" they were to cover. She explained: "You don't want to be reading. You want to be communicating." She also advised: "When referencing cases avoid saying things like 'I believe' or 'I think.' The court does not care about your personal mind set." Practicing before U.S. judges, they would need to present what Conley and O'Barr (1990, 67) call "powerful," as opposed to "powerless," speech. In the first class of one semester, Professor #1 explained that Americans were "litigious": "The word 'litigious' means to litigate. It means that American lawyers love to go to court, love to fight."

In addition to learning how to speak in court, the LL.M. students learned how to comport themselves and how to dress. Professor #7 told students that it was very important to make yourself look as tall as possible when speaking to a judge. He told a female student who was practicing her argument to: "Plant yourself. Don't lean. It invalidates or takes away from your argument." The students learned that body language is critical to perform successfully in court.[23] As she was preparing students for their presentation to the judges, Professor #1 moved her hands about a foot from her body and explained "this is about as much body language as you want to show. Be very self-contained." A few professors told their

23 Conley, O'Barr, and Lind refer to "presentational style" as "a comprehensive term including both verbal and nonverbal behavior. The latter includes what is commonly termed 'demeanor' or 'presence'" (1978, 1375, fn. 2). Their work examines how the presentational style of witnesses influences legal decision makers.

students not to wear jeans or Bermuda shorts. Slacks and a nice shirt or sweater were appropriate. It would not be a good idea for women to wear tight shirts. Baseball caps were also inappropriate.

My ethnographic experience in legal research and writing classes yielded two very different portraits of U.S. lawyers and the work they do. The foreign lawyers learned that practicing in a U.S. law firm is quite different from practicing law in court. The firm is firm: its senior partners care little for originality and they want to read memos composed with the fewest words possible. Less experienced attorneys work diligently, in a routinized manner, lining up citations. Professor #7 described it as an "apprenticeship." "Excellent work" is determined by the quality and brevity of your memo. And then the boss puts his name on it and takes all the credit. (In educational settings, we call this plagiarism.) This lawyer is not Atticus Finch, whose story, by the way, had convinced a good number of foreign lawyers to come to study U.S. law.[24] Atticus is a litigator. Litigators are warriors in pursuit of just causes. They use "bullets" when they present arguments, they "communicate" using "powerful speech" (with the exception of their deference to judges), and they engage in "original maneuvers." Litigators are tall, they constrain their body movements when they speak, and they dress respectfully. How would one know that despite the nation's obsession with baseball, it is not a good idea for a lawyer to wear a baseball cap to court?

In keeping with the objectives of the legal research and writing classes I observed, students were "examined" for their final grade according to their cumulative work on required assignments. Faculty assumed that final grades based on multiple projects ensured that students might do well in the course, even if they did poorly on one or two assignments. This method of assessment, however, was quite burdensome to the students, almost all of whom were accustomed to receiving a grade on the basis of an exam administered at the end of the school year. The LL.M. students I interviewed found unreasonable the degree of weekly homework they were assigned in the legal research and writing classes, and especially after they learned more about the academic culture of U.S. law schools.

An irony of these classes for foreign attorneys taught in the U.S. is that the students encounter a hierarchical bureaucratic ordering, what I will call a "homespun imperial process," about which they were not formerly aware. The curriculum is such that these required classes have "less value" than other law classes; students earn fewer credits than they earn in "real" subjects like constitutional or criminal law. Not surprisingly, then, students told me that they spent less time preparing for these classes. They learn, too, that the lack of prestige of the subject matter mirrors the lack of prestige accorded to faculty who teach these subjects.[25]Costello (2005) describes this same phenomenon in her study of students at University of California-Berkeley's Boalt School of Law, as do the authors of

24 *To Kill a Mockingbird* was cited often when applicants to the LL.M. programs explained their motivations for wanting to study in the U.S. (Lazarus-Black and Globokar 2015, 35).

25 On one occasion, Professor #1 acknowledged this hierarchy: "Legal Research and Writing is always the bastard stepchild, we know. Writing courses are considered less important. But you can't be a great lawyer if you can't write."

the Carnegie Report, who recognized that courses in which students learn "lawyering skills" "are most often taught by faculty other than those teaching the so-called substantive or doctrinal courses of the curriculum—a faculty that is not typically tenured and that has lower academic status" (2007, 87–88).[26] In other words, those who do the intensive, hands-on labor that is essential to building a global legal community in which lawyers can think, speak, write, and understand each other across borders are given secondary status in U.S. law schools.

To summarize, although I observed some evidence of the imperial process in legal research and writing classes taught in the U.S., these classes, like law classes taught abroad, are characterized by a great deal of faculty accommodation to differences in academic and legal cultures. In both contexts, too, international attorneys contest what and how much is expected of them. As the semester progressed, they spent less time preparing for legal research and writing classes than they did for more "substantive" subjects. Moreover, anecdotal evidence from my interviews suggests students register other protests in their end-of-term teacher evaluations and exit surveys that have ramifications for faculty hires and program design. In these rituals, students speak their minds and faculty and administrators listen. At both schools, they spoke to me regularly about offering new courses, revising the curricula, and re-structuring the programs. They reacted both to their own desire to improve the classroom experience and to suggestions from the students. Thus I found the consumers of legal research and writing classes taught in the U.S. exercise more clout in determining "patterns of import and export" (Garth 2015, 69) than is readily apparent. We encounter next different configurations of inchoate power, and different evidence of resistance and contestation to the imperial process, in classes for JD students.

Teaching International Attorneys in Classes Designed for U.S. JD Students

What happens when faculty members teach international attorneys in the U.S., but in classes specifically designed for U.S. JD students? Does the presence of international students alter the content of what they teach? Does it alter their linguistic and pedagogical styles? Given that "office hours" are not part of the academic culture of many countries, do international attorneys use them? What does the faculty say about that technique of power that Foucault (1979) identified as so crucial to the making of modern society—the examination? And, finally, does the presence of international LL.M. students in these classes reveal the dynamics of silencing in "credentialism" as part of an imperial process that shapes the market in legal education?[27]

26 This phenomenon has a long history. A 1970 survey of persons teaching "Legal Research and Writing" found these classes "were worth only one or two credit hours" (Ogloff et al. 2000–2001, 162). Rapoport (2011–2012, 1137, 1144–1145) makes clear the hierarchy continues.

27 At one school students in the LL.M. program for international students were not permitted to select certain classes whose primary content was tested by the Multistate Bar Exam (MBE) because seats had to be preserved for JD students. This is administrative silencing.

I found, almost without exception, that professors who regularly teach courses that devote significant attention to subjects tested in the Multistate Bar Exam (MBE) did not change in significant ways the content of their classes because of the presence of transnational students. Similar to findings by Israel and Vanneuville (2017) in their study of law classes in France, the materials professors cover in these classes are much affected by structural factors, including time constraints in delivering course materials and the need to teach to the test.[28] A great deal of the "work" of these law professors is to ensure that they are producing students who will be credentialed by passing the state bar exams. U.S. law professors are also pressed by administrators who are obsessed with law school rankings (Espeland and Sauder 2007, 2016).[29]

Nevertheless, a few faculty members who teach to the test told me that the presence of international students had some impact on the materials they covered in class and believed that JD students benefited from exposure to other legal cultures, as well as to concepts dear to the hearts of anthropologists—concepts like cultural relativism and ethnocentrism. Professor #14, who taught evidence and criminal and civil procedure, explained:

> Where it helps is that it causes me to teach my American students as the whole class including foreign students in a comparative way, which I didn't use to do. So now I can draw comparisons between systems and rules and the way things are done, which helps illustrate for everyone, including the Americans, why do we do things the way we do and [I] also let them know that *civilized people can do things differently* [my emphasis].

Thus Professor #14 found it important to debunk the notion that the U.S. system is necessarily better than the rest: "civilized people can do things differently." Professor #16, who had taught a variety of law classes over his extensive teaching career, including constitutional law and civil rights, told me students from China sometimes raised for class discussion the hypocrisy of the U.S. position on civil liberties; what was one to make of the situation in Guantanamo? Thus while their "mission" is to deliver the content tested by the state bar exam, Professors #14 and #16 voiced, and enabled students to voice, a critical perspective of U.S. law and policy. They were well aware of the ethnocentric attitudes and hegemonic assumptions about the superiority of the U.S. legal system that were held by the JD students they taught.

28 Israel and Vanneuville found that the heterogeneity of the student body, time constraints in delivering course content, the nature of civil as opposed to common law, and the need to prepare students for admission to the bar and magistracy entrance exams, constrain the content and pedagogical choices of faculty who are teaching law, even in one program designed to incorporate U.S. styles of pedagogy (2017, 164).

29 As many scholars have pointed out, some law schools develop LL.M. programs at least in part because they are revenue generating and those students do not count in terms of *U.S. News & World Report* rankings. See, for example, French (2015, 95–103) and Garth (2015, 73–74).

There was more leeway to change course content and to explore the experiences of international LL.M. students in subjects not tested in the state bar exams; professors teaching these courses labor under different structural constraints. Time devoted to comparative examples and advancing the theme of cultural relativism was more pronounced in these contexts. For example, Professor #15's course in international business attracted many transnational attorneys. He developed a pedagogical philosophy and strategy to encourage them to share examples of their legal cultures that presumed different ideas about what law "is," how it is made, and what lawyers "do." At the beginning of the semester, he asked the foreign students to stay for a few minutes after class because he needed their "help":

> I need their help because we'll be talking about things that are international that the U.S. students often, sometimes, think that the U.S. way is the only way to do things, or at least the best way. And I tell them I think it's really important that those views get challenged and that faculty can do that, but that sometimes it's much more powerful if it comes from one of their cohort, one of their colleagues. And so I strongly urge them to feel free to talk about their legal system and different ways they might be familiar with. I tell them it won't be perceived as a criticism of their host country. It won't be an insult to their colleagues in the classroom. I'm going to treat their comments as just another model. We're not going to talk about which model is better or worse, but about the strengths of this model and why you might do it one way and why you might do it the other way. And so I like to think that kind of conversation makes them feel comfortable and fully participating in the culture of the classroom in this country.

This exchange is important for course content in three respects. In asking for "help," Professor #15 reversed the usual status hierarchy that is presumed between faculty and students, but also in the imperial process in which it is assumed that U.S. law specifies "naturally" how things are or should be done. Simultaneously, he expressed an unusual awareness of cultural differences with regard to the meaning and appropriateness of "criticism" and "insult." He also encouraged his students to speak and to provide their peers with alternative possibilities. Professor #15's comments were especially astute, but he was not alone in his admiration of the knowledge and experiences that international attorneys brought to class.

In addition to the non-U.S. attorneys' ability to provide comparative examples based upon their experiences as practitioners in other countries, faculty teaching elective courses appreciated the "diversity" they brought to class, sometimes describing "diversity" in unexpected ways.[30] Professor #5, for example, told me he valued the *intellectual* diversity foreign lawyers conveyed in his class on international law:

30 In their responses to my question about the diversity of the students they were teaching, several interviewees offered information about the composition of the student body at the law school more generally. In that case, they typically mentioned gender, race, and ethnicity, and sometimes class, religion, and whether a student was the first generation in his or her family to attend college.

> I don't like the term ideology, a diversity of ideas, so I'm looking for people who approach law in different ways. I'm looking for people who ... come in with a, what we might call a natural rights approach, morality and law are not so separate, versus people who are more formalist in their visions about law. And for [students in my class] in international law in particular, I'm always interested in getting students who don't believe in international law because that enriches the environment where you actually have an ontological question of, is international law *law*?

Professor #13, who taught comparative constitutional law, mentioned the religious diversity these students brought to his classes, as well as the diversity of their political views. Voicing such alternative perspectives, he explained, was "enriching" to all of the students. And on occasion an alternative perspective might be shocking. Professor #11 told me that one student in his civil rights class reported: "Well, if somebody did that in my country, it wouldn't be a question of whether they could bring a lawsuit. It would be a question of whether or not they were shot."

What effect did the presence of non-U.S. students have upon faculty's linguistic and pedagogical styles? And how did those styles influence the experiences of the LL.M. students? Of the 32 faculty members I interviewed, 24 (75 percent) told me they always used a variety of pedagogical techniques. As has been found in earlier research, they lectured, encouraged class discussion, and sometimes employed Socratic Method.[31] The legal research and writing instructors also used a lot of role-playing, work groups, and multiple drafts of assignments. A few faculty members assigned collaborative projects, asked students to give presentations, and provided PowerPoint slides. Only four professors relied mainly on traditional Socratic Method, and one of these four only in a specific class in criminal law. Four told me their teaching style varied with the location in which they were teaching and according to the students' backgrounds.

Since most of the faculty I interviewed already used diverse teaching styles in their classes, it is not surprising that the presence of international students did not alter significantly their linguistic or pedagogical styles. They were well aware of the paradox faced by the international students; they were in the U.S. to experience learning law through Socratic Method—to learn to think like a U.S. lawyer—at the same time that their former academic and legal cultures, and sometimes their

31 My findings support those of Mertz with Njogu and Gooding (1998, 80) who report that Socratic Method can be used in a variety of ways, for different purposes, and with different consequences for students. Mertz found that at the time of her study of first-year contract classes at eight different laws schools the traditional Socratic Method was already "on the wane" (2007a, 142–144). She characterized the teaching styles of the faculty members in her study as: 1) "The Modified Socratic Teacher" (using extended Socratic dialogue but including some other forms of interaction); 2) "The Short-Exchange Teacher" (mixing shorter exchanges of Socratic dialogue with lecture and conversation); and 3) "Dialogic Lecturer" (relying mainly on lecture but including some student discussion) (Mertz 2007a, 144–169). The majority of faculty I interviewed, and the five I observed, employed a variety of teaching techniques with some modified Socratic Method.

oral and written skills in English, made this style of pedagogy extremely difficult.[32] The faculty also knew, however, that Socratic Method was difficult for U.S. JD students and their use of mixed teaching styles and modified forms of Socratic Method reflected that knowledge. For example, Professor #5 told me non-U.S. students regularly enrolled in his property class, but he did not alter his pedagogical style because he already used a "modified Socratic Method."[33] He put students into working panels composed of U.S. and international students and let the panels know in advance when they would be expected to report to the class. In his constitutional law course, Professor #11 called upon students in alphabetical order to ensure that "no one is shocked." On occasion, foreign students specifically asked him not to question them in class and he respected those requests. Professor #27 sent an email to his LL.M. students asking them if they were comfortable being called upon in class and he honored their responses.[34] Professor #7 told me she did not change her style when she taught contracts. Although she sometimes used Socratic Method, she did not like making *any* of her students, whether U.S. or international, uncomfortable.

The perspective that law school pedagogy should embrace diverse teaching techniques contrasts sharply, however, with the instructional style used by Professor #10, professor of criminal law and criminal procedure. He explained he relied heavily on Socratic Method because he viewed his role as "making an American lawyer." He assigned a great deal of reading for his classes and students were expected to articulate what they read. Over the years, he had found that the fast pace of his classes, the fact that many international attorneys were not fluent in English, and that they lacked knowledge about the legal system that he presumed his students already possessed, created a great deal of pressure on them. For these reasons, he discouraged students in the international LL.M. program from taking his classes and he had advised its administrators to that effect.

Professor #18 taught the first-year contracts course. He described his pedagogical style as "highly Socratic." He explained: "The direction of the course is

32 In my analysis of interviews with international lawyers I discovered two perspectives with respect to Socratic Method. On the one hand, some students identified this teaching style as one that encouraged individual thinking and promoted a freedom to debate that they found exciting. On the other hand, displays of bravado by some of the JD students were considered obnoxious and made them quite uncomfortable (Lazarus-Black 2017, 474–476).

33 Professors #15 and #16 also referred to their pedagogical styles as "modified Socratic Method." Professor #13 told me he uses "qualified Socratic." Professor #23 uses a "variation of that method, or a slow introduction of that method, when I teach these international classes to LL.M. students overseas." Professor #24 said: "I combine a sort of Socratic Method with sort of straight lecturing and with also giving examples and problems for the students to do, and they take extremely well to it."

34 He explained he did this for two reasons: "That's something I do because I don't want to embarrass them and I don't want to slow the class down for everyone else." He added that some students asked him not to call on them, some told him that they would volunteer when they were comfortable, and others replied that they would like to be called upon as long as he was "patient."

largely, but not exclusively, determined by student answers to questions." Professor #18 generally had only a handful of LL.M. students in his contracts classes; he was aware that the program's administrators steered students away from his classes. When he taught corporations, however, Professor #18 called upon LL.M. students to provide contrasting examples to the cases he had assigned "since American JDs tend to be both pretty insular and unaware of foreign legal traditions."

Professor #17 explained that she lectured for portions of her constitutional law class, but also relied heavily upon Socratic Method. She called on students and, even if they were initially uncomfortable, she didn't necessarily "let them off the hook." She moved on, however, if she felt a student was becoming embarrassed. In contrast to Professors #10 and #18, Professor #17 did not actively try to dissuade international students from enrolling in her class. Like them, she believed that Socratic Method was an essential component of law school pedagogy.

Professors #17, #25, #26, and #27 discussed with me the existence of a tipping point in terms of the number of international students enrolled in classes designed for JD students; it was educationally rewarding to have a few, but distracting and sometimes annoying to have too many.[35] In Professor #17's experience, the consequences of having international students in her classes depended on two matters: how many were enrolled and the students' personalities. A few quiet students had no consequence for the class. She had once had an international student, however, who was quite vocal and the other students in the class found him disruptive. Other faculty members complained that international students took up too much class time and caused the U.S. students to become dissatisfied with the pace of the course. It was rare for a faculty member who was discussing teaching classes for JD students to mention speaking more slowly or being careful not to use obscure historical, literary, or cultural references because of the presence of international students. Professor #18 identified another issue:

> They can generally be more demanding of my time—which per student unit they can take up more time because we have to fight through both language barriers and understanding barriers. While with the JDs it's usually just the understanding barriers. The law school general economic model is to have one professor for lots of students. That makes it quite difficult to spend—sometimes I have an hour or two per student per week [in office hours] for LL.Ms. [And] … I can't do that for all students.

35 Research on student diversity demonstrates that when there are only a few students of color in class they are reluctant to speak out "for fear that their comments will be taken as representing not their individual perspective, but instead the perspective of the group their peers believe they belong to" Deo (2015, 3150). See also Deo (2011–2012) and Moran (2000) on diversifying law schools. See Bell (1985–1986) for an important early review of the tipping point in hiring minority law faculty.

In other words, international students challenge the economy of professorial time both in class and during office hours. Professors who taught foreign students in this third context found the international students came often to office hours. Professor #14 was not unusual in commenting that they "ask a lot of questions after class rather than in class."[36] Faculty had two other interesting observations about the non-U.S. attorneys' use of office hours.

Their first perception had to do with the content of the conversations that take place; U.S. JD students do not ask their professors where they can find a Chinese market. A few professors were happy to provide this kind of information and one (Professor #21) took her foreign students to the "Chinatown" in her city. Others took international students to restaurants, two to visit their homes, and one sometimes invited students for a beer. This was particularly the case if the faculty member had taught abroad and had himself/herself been wined and dined—which is common in other academic cultures. A sense of reciprocity operates in these situations. Faculty #22 told me that legal research and writing instructors are often the "go to" people for the non-U.S. lawyers. Other professors, of course, did not imagine that that kind of attention is an appropriate use of their time.

Faculty and administrators noted a second difference. Periodically foreign students appeared at office hours or for administrative advising in small groups and then one or two students, who were most articulate in English, acted as the spokespersons for the others. They asked questions posed by classmates and translated the professor's responses. Professor #21 explained:

> [T]hey'll sort of send, kind of appoint two of them as delegates and have them come to see you to say, this is what we think was the point about, you know, the Smith case today. Did we understand this correctly? What did you mean when you said blah-blah-blah?

To my knowledge, this kind of cooperative learning activity is not characteristic of U.S. JD students' use of office hours. It is not possible, of course, when international students face two other critical components of U.S. academic culture in law school: namely, examinations and how students are ranked.

As noted earlier, the vast majority of the 50 international lawyers I interviewed had learned law in academic cultures that tested their competency in different legal subjects through examinations administered at the end of the school year. The LL.M programs, however, escalated the number, timing, and style of exams to which students were subject. A few professors had students do "practice" exams, but the results sometimes demoralized the foreign students; their grades shocked them because many had come from programs in which they had ranked at the top of their classes. Their responses to essay questions were typically too brief, a pattern verified by Professor #31, who told me: "I'm not use to getting an exam that's two paragraphs. I'd

36 Other faculty members who told me that the international students came often to office hours include Professors #5, #7, #11, #15, and #31.

give them a question for which I would have expected a couple of pages each at least. So, you know, a paragraph is standard." Not surprisingly, then, Faculty #20 observed: "They have no idea how to write the essay exam. None. Zero."

Because I did not specifically ask the question, none of the international attorneys I interviewed mentioned the existence of a pass/fail option in their country of origin.[37] Both of the schools in which I conducted research, however, had enacted pass/fail options for international students and faculty mostly appreciated that decision for a variety of reasons although, as we see next, a few expressed some reservations about that option.[38]

Professor #1 was strongly in favor of her law school's decision to allow international attorneys to decide whether to take their classes on a graded or pass/fail basis. She explained that most of the attorneys were returning to their countries of origin and that for them the LL.M. certificate—the credential rather than a transcript of grades—was what mattered. As an instructor of legal research and writing, she often advised students about which decision to make based on her experiences with them in the classroom and the written assignments they had already completed early in the semester. Some were relieved and others surprised when she counseled them to choose the pass/fail option. It was often the case that students arrived with unrealistic expectations about the difficulty of the program and/or their own English skills. Many had good test scores on the English-language admissions exam, but they could not manage without considerable stress rapidly delivered lectures, written assignments, or expository exams. The pass/fail option might not be a good choice, however, for non-U.S. students who might subsequently pursue a graduate program, a U. S. JD or S.J.D. degree, or who are "really Americans" and planned to practice law in the U.S. It is well established that employers use grades and rankings to screen applicants, reduce costs, and avoid hiring mistakes (Carnegie Foundation 2007, 33).

Professor #11 found the pass/fail option relieved student stress and made the chore of grading easier for him. He joked that he had always used his own curve to mark international students anyway, even prior to the establishment of the official pass/fail option. He worried that giving a student a grade of B or less might deprive that individual of a scholarship. Similarly, Professor #4 had learned that grades mattered in ways one could not always predict. A student of his applied to a very prestigious doctoral program, but "you can't get a grade lower than a B, and I gave him a B- or a C, so that knocked him out of that program."

Professor #5 also found the pass/fail option simplified his grading, but was concerned that it was a disincentive to learning:

> They can take their courses graded, just like the U.S. law students, or they can take pass/fail; it certainly eases their stress … . I think there's pluses or minuses

37 In the civil law traditions in which the majority of these interviewees had trained, law is an undergraduate degree. In one legal research and writing class I attended, the instructor asked the students how many of them had opted for the pass/fail option. There were ten in class and all but two had selected that option.

38 Within and across the two schools, there were different options for electing to take a class either for a grade or pass/fail.

> for that … I think it's better for them in some ways than having a transcript full of C's and B- and B+ they might otherwise get if they were seeking grades. On the other hand, I think it leads to some disincentives for them to participate in class. They just need to pass, how much do they really have to focus on each and every thing I'm doing? So that is something of a concern.

I did not systematically ask my interviewees how often they failed international students, but the interviews captured a few examples. Professor #11 was "pretty certain" that she had failed two students, Professor #18 had failed one student, and Professor #22 failed a "cavalier" student from India who just wouldn't do his work. However, Professor #26 explained:

> [W]e grade the LL.M. on a different scale. There is an assumption that LL.M. students do not fail, you know, so it's a little bit higher scale. And I have given B- to LL.M. students that I would give much lower grades to if it were a JD paper. And they are taken out of the JD curve if we have a curve, in those classes that have curves.

The attorneys I interviewed mostly reported very positive experiences interacting with their professors; I surmise, therefore, that they were not expecting to fail their classes. One must ask, however, if this separate grading system sends a message to all of the students about the hierarchical structural relationship between U.S. lawyers and their international colleagues; they are not evaluated in the same way and they are "not on the curve."

I turn, lastly, to the question of silencing in the matter of "credentialism." Silencing is the power to define or redefine a given situation exercised in sometimes blatant and sometimes subtle forms. As noted earlier, there is an extensive literature pertaining to the silencing of white women, men and women of color, persons from socioeconomically disadvantaged backgrounds, and members of other "historically underrepresented groups" (Niemann 2012, 449, 464). This research documents for these groups a reticence to participate in the highly competitive atmosphere of some classes, a lack of role models among the faculty, and feelings of dissonance, among other variables, as factors contributing to their less than full participation in law school.[39] My research finds that the silencing of non-

39 Costello found: "At the Law School, identity dissonance often presented itself through silence … . Silence was often a signal of alienation … . Silence could also be a sign of fear of failure," or "habitus failure," an identity dissonance between one's way of being in the world and expectations about student behavior and participation in law school (2005, 199). In her study, white heterosexual middle-class men experienced the least dissonance with the faculty and the law school environment. Students with multiple forms of personal identity, such as women of color, experienced higher rates of identity dissonance (2005, 204). Bliss (2017, 860) demonstrates that professional identity formation in law school is also influenced by the "job-path variable," and it seems reasonable to assume that the different past experiences of students in the LL.M. programs, as well as their future goals, would influence their attitudes, practices, and identities. These variables might also influence foreign attorneys' uses of silence.

U.S. attorneys shares some of these issues—they are also "differently situated" (Moran 2000, 2330) among their peers—but their status and consequent experiences are further complicated by matters of agency and structure that characterize learning law across borders. As we have seen, foreign attorneys must negotiate differences in academic cultures, legal cultures, and language skills. A few of the students I spoke with told me that they didn't volunteer in class because they had lost the thread of the professor's argument or because they could not speak up quickly enough. Others told me they did not want to speak in class because they were afraid their professors would not understand their heavily accented English—and that was potentially embarrassing. Still others self-selected silencing at the very beginning of the semester, as in the case of the attorneys who approached Professor #11 and specifically asked him not to call upon them. As Professor #15 recognized, some students thought challenging their professors might be insulting to them. The attorneys also use silence to protest their lack of interest in a subject or their boredom in class; I observed during my fieldwork that sometimes they chose not to engage with their instructors. (Like other students, they surf the web when they are bored.) Thus I watched these attorneys opt in and out of the education in which they are participants, even if they are "invested" in eventually winning the U.S. LL.M. In these ways, international students silence themselves. But that is not surprising. As Onwuachi-Willig reminds us: "Although silences can be self-negating, they also can empower" (2012, 143).[40]

Nevertheless, it was clear that transnational attorneys were also silenced as a consequence of the structural directives and system of accreditation of the ABA that credentials "real lawyers," and by administrators, faculty, and U.S. JD students. In sharp contrast to what happens when they teach abroad, professors who teach at home subjects tested by state bar exams make few changes to their course content or linguistic or instructional style because of the presence of international lawyers. The depth of the subject matter they must cover, not to mention the depth of oversight they experience from the ABA, law school administration, and *U.S. News & World Report*, weigh heavily upon them. A few students I interviewed complained to me that they were unable to take certain classes they had hoped to take. In their capacity as advisors, and with the best of intentions, administrators steered international students away from courses in which professors engaged heavily in traditional Socratic Method. Similarly, some faculty members dissuaded the international attorneys from taking their classes by suggesting that they could not master the content or rigorous requirements. For example, Professor #17 named an elective class on the federal courts as inappropriate for international LL.M. students. Unless a student intended to take the bar exam, she explained, there was no point in enrolling them in "tougher" classes that were "highly abstract" and presumed advanced knowledge of a subject.

40 See also Montoya's elegant and insightful work on the "interplay between the subordinating aspects of being silenced and the liberatory aspects of silence" (1999–2000, 266).

Professor #21 discouraged students from taking her employment law class because it dealt only with U.S. labor law and therefore it was "not useful" to them. Professor #22 dissuaded them from taking a class on immigration because it was "too difficult." Professors also engaged in silencing when non-native speakers were inarticulate or long-winded. A few were patient; others interrupted those students so that the pace of the class suited the expectations of the U.S. students. Finally, international students were silenced by their fellow classmates who dismissed them as peers in class and ignored them after class, phenomena that have been well documented by other researchers.[41] In their former training in law, they could miss classes and get notes from others, students shared outlines, and they formed study groups. They experienced no such camaraderie in the U.S. These practices implicate silencing as an inherent feature of the imperial process: the LL.M. students were overtly directed or "guided to" what and with whom they could study.

In short, the presence of international attorneys in classes designed specifically for JD students seemed to have relatively little influence on the content of classes, the faculty's attention to language, the styles of pedagogy they practiced, or to methods of examination if the subject matter was tested in the MBE, and more influence if the subject matter was elective. Agency and its structural constraints operated differently in the JD classes, but also in required as opposed to elective subjects. International attorneys were most likely to experience silencing when the stakes for faculty were highest. These findings underscore how state regulations sometimes make matters of international political economy superfluous; the local usurps the global in the race to ensure that students pass the bar exams.

41 Silver and others have found that a number of variables keep foreign and U.S. JD students apart. Among other factors, they may reside in different locales, experience discomfort in speaking in another language, participate in different classes and programs, lack opportunities to interact, and hold different future goals (Silver 2013, 474–475). An administrator from the Midwest (#9) pointed out that many of the LL.M. students are older, some have families they want to spend time with, others have no time to socialize because they are both studying and working on occasion for their employer via the internet, and often they "tap into communities from their country of origin that are already in the U.S." A 2011 report by the Law School Survey of Student Engagement (LSSSE), based on responses from 6,893 students from 21 law schools, also confirmed this lack of interaction between the two groups (Silver 2013, 478–486). In her study of law faculty, Deo reports that "structural diversity (i.e., diversity in numbers) does not lead automatically to interactional diversity (i.e., meaningful interaction among diverse students) or classroom diversity (i.e., meaningful diverse interaction in the classroom specifically); instead, these enhanced classroom experiences depend on adept facilitation by faculty and mutual respect among diverse students" (2015, 3115).

See also Dowd, Nunn, and Pendergast (2003) on students' experiences of diversity at University of Florida; Deo (2011–2012) on interactions among students of diverse backgrounds at the University of Michigan Law School; Grover and Womack (2017) on law students' stories of marginalization from across the country; and Silver and Ballakrishnen this volume.

Conclusions

In this chapter, I investigated what law professors *do* when they do the work of teaching international attorneys U.S. law and how to think, speak, and act like U.S. lawyers. In the two schools in which I conducted research, this work was accomplished in three contexts: in classes taught abroad, in classes taught in the U.S. specifically designed for international attorneys, and in others dominated by U.S. JD students. My discussion was designed to illuminate two theoretical issues. I asked how power in these programs and classes was deployed, by whom, in what ways, and with what consequences. What might interviews and ethnography reveal about otherwise inchoate forms of instruction? I also interrogated Garth's proposition that the U.S. dominates a hierarchical imperial process in the legal education market and sought to understand better its patterns of import and export.

I found that hierarchical relations of power, patterns of contestation, and an underlining imperial process, operate with some similarities across the three settings. In each context, the agency of the faculty and the students is deeply influenced by structural constraints imposed by the law schools in the U.S. and abroad, as well as by the complicated goals of school administrators in the U.S. who must generate revenues, and attend to the calculations of the ABA and the annual *U.S. News & World Report*. Within these constraints, too, faculty deploy power in their decisions about what, how, how much, and sometimes who they teach. In turn, students in all three contexts exercise power, negotiating their way in their own ways to obtain their "credential" and sometimes at a "price" other than that imagined by the law schools. Beyond these similarities, however, power and manifestations of an imperial process operate differently in each context.

U.S. legal education is mostly practiced quite differently when it is practiced abroad. Teaching U.S. law in other countries requires re-consideration of class time, course content, perceptive language sensibilities, an altered *modus operandi*, and recognition of and attention to similarities and differences in academic and legal cultures. What you *do* when you teach abroad changes—sometimes quite dramatically. Faculty recounted to me examples of changing texts, allowing students to talk to each other in their own language, and using various "props." Faculty must adjust their pedagogical styles to the hegemonic lecture format that prevails outside the U.S. And from what I can deduce, if pedagogy is not practiced differently abroad, it is mostly a very unfortunate experience for the instructor and the students. In addition, non-U.S. partners to these LL.M. programs impose considerable constraints, such as deciding how much time attorneys will spend abroad and how students are graded. I found that the U.S. exports legal education to a great many places, but not to every place, not without criticism, and not entirely in control of how such educational programs are designed or executed.

Teaching legal reading and research classes in the U.S. that are especially designed for transnational students requires that the faculty learn many of the skills and insights that professors learn when teaching abroad. They accommodate to many of the assumptions and rules of the academic cultures from which their students come. They are highly cognizant of the fact that their students are accustomed to lectures and of the students' different skills in oral and written English, and teach accordingly. Those I interviewed and observed used myriad teaching styles. They gave students a variety of assignments and spent extraordinary time seeing students individually and reviewing their written work. During these classes, they also taught the international attorneys about the work that U.S. lawyers do. Their portrayal of that work was sometimes laudatory and sometimes not—their comments sometimes critiqued directly the imperial process. Moreover, during their sojourn in the U.S. students became aware that their instructors' position within the bureaucracy of the law school was tenuous and that most were untenured. They encountered what I have called a homespun imperial process, one that differs from the global imperial process about which Garth writes. Modeling U.S. JD students, they adjusted their time accordingly.

When professors teach classes in the U.S. comprised mostly of JD students they are more likely to resist straying from the conventional academic norms of a U.S. legal education. This is especially true if they teach classes whose primary content is tested by state bar exams. These professors assign a great deal of reading and tend to use Socratic Method, although most with modifications. They lecture rapidly so as not to bore the U.S. students, they assume that what are for them familiar historical, social, political, legal, and cultural references are also familiar to the students they are teaching, and they draw upon these references "without thinking." Not surprisingly, it was common for these professors to comment about the international students' reticence in class. The professors in this sample who taught elective subjects, however, were more inclined to welcome transnational attorneys to their courses, to ask them about their experiences, and to draw comparisons about "how things can be done" in other places. They were cultural relativists who recognized that their U.S. JD students were not. Breaking through U.S. hegemony was critical to the knowledge they wanted to impart to their students. Whether teaching required or elective subjects, faculty commonly acknowledged that they graded the transnational attorneys with lower expectations and many were relieved to teach them "off the curve."

To conclude, the work of teaching transnational attorneys is challenging. Different relations of power and agency, different structural constraints, different forms of silencing, and different influences and effects of the imperial process characterize each of these classrooms. Within each site, however, international status is as critical a sociological variable in legal education as are the variables of race, gender, and class (see Silver and Ballakrishnen 2018 and this volume), but with some caveats. Rachel Moran once wrote: "Race is not merely an add-on to legal pedagogy, but rather one component in a larger debate about the meaning of law, legal education, and the legal profession" (2000, 2329). International LL. M. students are not minority students in the traditional sense in which Moran and other scholars have understood the meaning of that term. The diversity of these students stems from such variables as their exposure to different academic and legal cultures, their skills in English, their lack of knowledge of U.S. history and popular culture, and the diversity of their ideas about what law is and should do. And their status is complicated by the fact that international attorneys are representatives of nations caught up in imbalanced international political economies and legal systems that are unequally weighted. This chapter examined silencing, but the issue of voice—which ones matter and which don't—is constantly in play. The exercise, sources, and consequences of power and imperial practices are myriad, but these are contested—sometimes in the administrative design of these programs, sometimes by faculty, and sometimes by students.

Acknowledgements

I am grateful to the deans of the law schools for allowing me to conduct this research and to the administrators, faculty, and international students who participated both formally and informally to this conversation about teaching in different contexts. This chapter draws upon transcriptions of interviews and other research assistance by Marta Cuciurean-Zapan, Nikky Greer, Marie Schelle Solano, and Brendan Tuttle. Preliminary versions of sections of this chapter were presented at the American Anthropological Association, Denver, November 18–22, 2015, the Law & Society Association, New Orleans, June 2–5, 2016, and the NSF conference "Legal Education in Crisis? Bringing Researchers and Resources Together to Generate New Scientific Insights," Chicago, March 3–4, 2017. This work has been much enriched by Bill Black's perceptive questions and suggestions. I would also like to thank Carol Greenhouse for her insightful comments on an early draft of this chapter and Glenn Gottfried for a careful reading of a later manuscript that polished its style. Finally, I thank Meera Deo for her perceptive comments and questions about the experiences of U.S. law professors and Beth Mertz who, as always, gets right to the right points.

References

Aiken, Jane H., and Ann Shalleck. 2016. Putting the "Real World" into Traditional Classroom Teaching. In *The New Legal Realism, Volume 1: Translating Law-and-Society for Today's Legal Practice*, ed. Elizabeth Mertz, Stewart Macaulay, and Thomas W. Mitchell, 51–73. Cambridge: Cambridge University Press.

Aman Jr., Alfred C. 2015. Globalization: Legal Aspects. In *International Encyclopedia of the Social & Behavioral Sciences*, 2nd edition, Volume 10, ed. James D. Wright, 254–261. Oxford: Elsevier.

Ballakrishnen, Swethaa. 2012. Homeward Bound: What Does a Global Legal Education Offer the Indian Returnees? *Fordham Law Review* 80: 2441–2480.

Banks, Taunya Lovell. 1988. Gender Bias in the Classroom. *Journal of Legal Education* 38: 137–146.

Barnes, Katherine, and Elizabeth Mertz. 2012. Is It Fair? Law Professors' Perceptions of Tenure. *Journal of Legal Education* 61(4): 511–539.

Barnes, Katherine, and Elizabeth Mertz. 2018. Law School Climates: Job Satisfaction Among Tenured US Law Professors. *Law & Social Inquiry* 2: 441–467.

Bell Jr., Derrick A. 1985–1986. Application of the "Tipping Point" Principle to Law Faculty Hiring Policies. *Nova Law Journal* 10: 319–328.

Bliss, John. 2017. Divided Selves: Professional Role Distancing Among Law Students and New Lawyers in a Period of Market Crisis. *Law & Social Inquiry* 42(3): 855–897.

Bliss, Lisa Radtke, Sopit Cheevapanich, Damorn Kumtrai, and Panarairat Srichaiyarat. 2014. Moving into the Future: Legal Education in Thailand. In *Legal Education in Asia*, ed. Shuvro Prosun Sarker, 217–233. The Hague: Eleven International Publishing.

Brand, Ronald A., and D. Wes Rist, eds. 2009. *The Export of Legal Education: Its Promise and Impact in Transition Countries.* Burlington, VT: Ashgate.

Carnegie Foundation for the Advancement of Teaching. 2007. *Educating Lawyers: Preparation for the Profession of Law.* William M. Sullivan, Anne Colby, Judith Welch Wagner, Lloyd Bond, and Lee S. Shulman. San Francisco, CA: Jossey-Bass.

Conley, John M., and William M. O'Barr. 1990. *Rules Versus Relationships: The Ethnography of Legal Discourse.* Chicago, IL: University of Chicago Press.

Conley, John M., William M. O'Barr, and E. Allan Lind. 1978. The Power of Language: Presentational Style in the Courtroom. *Duke Law Journal* 1978: 1375–1399.

Costello, Carrie Yang. 2005. *Professional Identity Crisis: Race, Class, Gender and Success at Professional Schools.* Nashville, TN: Vanderbilt University.

Deo, Meera E. 2011–2012. The Promise of Grutter: Diverse Interactions at the University of Michigan Law School. *Michigan Journal of Race & Law* 17: 63–118.

Deo, Meera E. 2014. Looking Forward to Diversity in Legal Academia. *Berkeley Journal of Gender, Law & Justice* 29: 352–387.

Deo, Meera E. 2015. Faculty Insights on Educational Diversity. *Fordham Law Review* 83: 3115–3153.

Dezalay, Yves, and Bryant G. Garth. 2002. *The Internationalization of Palace Wars: Lawyers, Economists, and the Contest to Transform Latin American States.* Chicago, IL: University of Chicago Press.

Dezalay, Yves, and Bryant G. Garth. 2010. *Asian Legal Revivals: Lawyers in the Shadow of Empire.* Chicago, IL: University of Chicago Press.

Dinovitzer, Ronit, Robert L. Nelson, Gabriele Plickert, Rebecca Sandefur, and Joyce S. Sterling. 2009. *After the JD II: Second Results from a National Study of Legal Careers.* Joint Publication of the NALP Foundation and the American Bar Foundation.

Dowd, Nancy E., Kenneth B. Nunn, and Jane E. Pendergast. 2003. Diversity Matters: Race, Gender, and Ethnicity in Legal Education. *University of Florida Journal of Law & Public Policy* 15(1): 11–56.

Engel, David M. 2009. Discourses of Causation in Injury Cases: Exploring Thai and American Legal Cultures. In *Fault Lines: Tort Law as Cultural Practice*, ed. David M. Engle and Michael McCann, 251–268. Stanford, CA: Stanford University Press.

Engel, David M., and Jaruwan S. Engel. 2010. *Tort, Custom, and Karma: Globalization and Legal Consciousness in Thailand.* Stanford, CA: Stanford University Press.

Engel, David M., and Michael McCann, eds. 2009. *Fault Lines: Tort Law as Cultural Practice.* Stanford, CA: Stanford University Press.

Espeland, Wendy Nelson, and Michael Sauder. 2007. Rankings and Reactivity: How Public Measures Recreate Social Worlds. *American Journal of Sociology* 113(1): 1–40.

Espeland, Wendy Nelson, and Michael Sauder. 2016. *Engines of Anxiety: Academic Rankings, Reputation, and Accountability.* New York: Russell Sage Foundation.

Ewick, Patricia, and Susan S. Silbey. 1998. *The Common Place of Law: Stories from Everyday Life.* Chicago, IL: University of Chicago Press.

Florio, Cassandra M.S., and Steven J. Hoffman. 2012–2013. Student Perspectives on Legal Education: A Longitudinal Empirical Evaluation. *Journal of Legal Education* 62: 162–187.

Foucault, Michel. 1979. *Discipline and Punish: The Birth of the Prison.* New York: Vintage Books.

French, Jan Hoffman. 2015. At Play in the Field of Law: Symbolic Capital and Foreign Attorneys in LL.M. Programs. *Indiana Journal of Global Legal Studies* 22(1): 95–103.

Friedman, Lawrence. 1994. Is there a Modern Legal Culture? *Ratio Juris* 7(2): 117–131.

Galanter, Marc. 1983–1984. Reading the Landscape of Disputes: What We Know and Don't Know (And Think We Know) about Our Allegedly Contentious and Litigious Society. *UCLA Law Review* 31: 4–71.

Garth, Bryant G. 2013. Crises, Crisis Rhetoric, and Competition in Legal Education: A Sociological Perspective on the (Latest) Crisis of the Legal Profession and Legal Education. *Stanford Law & Policy Review* 24: 503–532.

Garth, Bryant G. 2015. Notes Toward an Understanding of the U.S. Market in Foreign LL.M. Students: From the British Empire and the Inns of Court to the U.S. LL.M. *Indiana Journal of Global Legal Studies* 22(1): 67–79.

Geertz, Clifford. 1983. *Local Knowledge: Further Essays in Interpretive Anthropology*. New York: Basic Books.

Graeber, David. 2015. *The Utopia of Rules: On Technology, Stupidity, and the Secret Joys of Bureaucracy*. Brooklyn, NY: Melville House.

Granfield, Robert. 1992. *Making Elite Lawyers: Visions of Law at Harvard and Beyond*. New York: Routledge.

Greenhouse, Carol J., Barbara Yngvesson, and David M. Engel. 1994. *Law and Community in Three American Towns*. Ithaca, NY: Cornell University.

Grover, Susan, and Nikeshia Womack. 2017. Stories at the Edge of Class—Marginalization in the Law School Experience. *Seattle Journal of Social Justice* 16: 41–70.

Guinier, Lani, Michelle Fine, and Jane Balin. 1997. *Becoming Gentlemen: Women, Law School, and Institutional Change*. Boston, MA: Beacon Press.

Gutierrez y Muhs, Yolanda Flores Niemann, Carmen G. Gonzalez, and Angela P. Harris, eds. 2012. *Presumed Incompetent: The Intersections of Race and Class for Women in Academia*. Boulder, CO: Utah State University Press.

Herzfeld, Michael. 2015. Anthropology and the Inchoate Intimacies of Power. *American Ethnologist* 42(1): 18–32.

Hupper, Gail J. 2015. Educational Ambivalence: The Rise of a Foreign-Student Doctorate in Law. *New England Law Review* 49: 319–447.

Israel, Liora, and Rachel Vanneuville. 2017. Legal Training and the Reshaping of French Elite: Lessons from an Ethnography of Law Classes in Two French Elite Higher Education Institutions. *Journal of Education and Work* 30(2): 156–167.

Kennedy, Duncan. 2004. *Legal Education and the Reproduction of Hierarchy: A Polemic Against the System*. New York: New York University Press.

Konefsky, Alfred A., and Barry Sullivan. 2014. In This, the Winter of Our Discontent: Legal Practice, Legal Education, and the Culture of Distrust. *Buffalo Law Review* 62: 659–745.

Lazarus-Black, Mindie. 2017. The Voice of the Stranger: Foreign LL.M. Students' Experiences of Culture, Law, and Pedagogy in U.S. Law Schools. In *Comparative Law and Anthropology*, ed. James A.R. Nafziger, 462–488. Cheltenham: Edward Elgar Publishing.

Lazarus-Black, Mindie, and Julie Globokar. 2015. Foreign Attorneys in U.S. LL.M. Programs: Who's In, Who's Out, and Who They Are. *Indiana Journal of Global Legal Studies* 22(1): 3–65.

Liu, Sida. 2008. Globalization as Boundary-Blurring: International and Local Law Firms in China's Corporate Law Market. *Law & Society Review* 42(4): 771–804.

Liu, Sida. 2013. The Legal Profession as a Social Process: A Theory on Lawyers and Globalization. *Law & Social Inquiry* 38(3): 670–693.

Lopez, Maria Pabon, and Kevin R. Johnson. 2014. Presumed Incompetent: Important Lessons for University Leaders on the Professional Lives of Women Faculty of Color. *Berkeley Journal of Gender, Law & Justice* 29: 388–405.

Mattei, Ugo, and Laura Nader. 2008. *Plunder: When the Rule of Law is Illegal.* Malden, MA: Blackwell Publishing.

Menkel-Meadow, Carrie. 1988. Feminist Legal Theory, Critical Legal Studies, and Legal Education or "The Fem-Crits Go to Law School". *Journal of Legal Education* 38: 61–85.

Menkel-Meadow, Carrie. 2007. Taking Law and _____ Really Seriously: Before, During and after "The Law". *Vanderbilt Law Review* 60: 555–595.

Mertz, Elizabeth. 2000. Teaching Lawyers the Language of Law: Legal and Anthropological Translations. *John Marshall Law Review* 34(4): 91–117.

Mertz, Elizabeth. 2007a. *The Language of Law School: Learning to "Think Like a Lawyer".* Oxford: Oxford University Press.

Mertz, Elizabeth. 2007b. Inside the Law School Classroom: Toward a New Legal Realist Pedagogy. *Vanderbilt Law Review* 60: 483–513.

Mertz, Elizabeth, Stewart Macaulay, and Thomas W. Mitchell, eds. 2016. *The New Legal Realism, Volume 1. Translating Law-and-Society for Today's Legal Practice.* Cambridge: Cambridge University Press.

Mertz, Elizabeth, with Wamucii Njogu and Susan Gooding. 1998. What Difference Does Difference Make? The Challenge for Legal Education. *Journal of Legal Education* 48(1): 1–87.

Michelson, Ethan. 2015. Immigrant Lawyers and the Changing Face of the U.S. Legal Profession. *Indiana Journal of Global Legal Studies* 22(1): 105–111.

Montoya, Margaret E. 1999–2000. Silence and Silencing: Their Centripetal and Centrifugal Forces in Legal Communication, Pedagogy and Discourse. *University of Michigan Journal of Law Reform* 33: 263–327.

Moran, Rachel F. 2000. Diversity and Its Discontents: The End of Affirmative Action at Boalt Hall. *California Law Review* 88: 2241–2352.

Nelken, David. 2004. Using the Concept of Legal Culture. *Australian Journal of Legal Philosophy* 29: 1–26.

Nelken, David. 2009. Law, Liability, and Culture. In *Fault Lines: Tort Law as Cultural Practice*, ed. David M. Engel and Michael McCann, 21–38. Stanford, CA: Stanford University Press.

Niemann, Yolanda Flores. 2012. Lessons from the Experiences of Women of Color Working in Academia. In *Presumed Incompetent: The Intersections of Race and Class for Women in Academia*, ed. Gutierrez y Muhs et al., 446–499. Boulder, CO: Utah State University Press.

Ogloff, James R.P., David R. Lyon, Kevin S. Douglas, and V. Gordon Rose. 2000–2001. More Than "Learning to Think Like a Lawyer": The Empirical Research on Legal Education. *Creighton Law Review* 34: 73–244.

Onwuachi-Willig, Angela. 2012. Silence of the Lambs. In *Presumed Incompetent: The Intersections of Race and Class for Women in Academia*, ed. Gutierrez y Muhs et al., 142–151. Boulder, CO: Utah State University Press.

Philips, Susan Urmston. 1988. The Language Socialization of Lawyers: Acquiring the "Cant". In*Doing the Ethnography of Schooling: Educational Anthropology in Action*, ed. George Spindler, 176–209. Prospect Heights, IL: Waveland.

Rakoff, Todd D., and Martha Minow. 2007. A Case for Another Case Method. *Vanderbilt Law Review* 60: 597–607.

Rapoport, Nancy B. 2011–2012. Changing the Modal Law School: Rethinking U.S. Legal Education in (Most) Schools. *Pennsylvania State Law Review* 116: 1119–1154.

Rosen, Lawrence. 2006. *Law as Culture: An Invitation.* Princeton, NJ: Princeton University Press.

Rubin, Edward. 2007. What's Wrong with Langdell's Method, and What to Do about It. *Vanderbilt Law Review* 60(2): 609–666.

Schleef, Debra J. 2006. *Managing Elites: Professional Socialization in Law and Business School.* Lanham, MD: Rowman & Littlefield.

Silver, Carole. 2000. Globalization and the US Market in Legal Services—Shifting Identities. *Law and Policy in International Business* 31: 1093–1150.

Silver, Carole. 2002. The Case of the Foreign Lawyer: Internationalizing the US Legal Profession. *Fordham International Legal Journal* 25: 1039–1084.

Silver, Carole. 2003. Regulatory Mismatch in the International Market for Legal Services. Northwestern University School of Law Public Law and Legal Theory Paper. http://law.bepress.com/nwwps/plltp/art29.

Silver, Carole. 2004–2005. Winners and Losers in the Globalization of Legal Services: Situating the Market for Foreign Lawyers. *Virginia Journal of International Law* 45: 897–934.

Silver, Carole. 2006. Internationalizing US Legal Education: A Report on the Education of Transnational Lawyers. *Cardozo Journal of International and Comparative Law* 14(1): 143–175.

Silver, Carole. 2009. *Agents of Globalization in Law: Phase I.* Law School Admission Council Research Report Series. Grants Report 1–9. March, 2009.

Silver, Carole. 2011. The Variable Value of US Legal Education in the Global Legal Services Market. *Georgetown Journal of Legal Ethics* 24: 1–57.

Silver, Carole. 2012a. States Side Story: Career Paths of International LL.M. Students, or "I Like To Be In America". *Fordham Law Review* 80: 2383–2440.

Silver, Carole. 2012b. Coping with the Consequences of "Too Many Lawyers": Securing the Place of International Graduate Law Students. *International Journal of the Legal Profession* 19(2–3): 227–245.

Silver, Carole. 2013. Getting Real about Globalization and Legal Education: Potential and Perspectives for the US. *Stanford Law & Policy Review* 24: 457–501.

Silver, Carole. 2013–2014. Globalization and the Monopoly of ABA-Approved Law Schools: Missed Opportunities or Dodged Bullets? *Fordham Law Review* 82: 2869–2902.

Silver, Carole. 2015–2016. What We Know and Need to Know about Global Lawyer Regulations. *South Carolina Law Review* 67: 461–483.

Silver, Carole, and Swethaa S. Ballakrishnen. 2016. Mind Your Language. Presentation to the Law & Society Association, New Orleans, June 2–5, 2016.

Silver, Carole, and Swethaa S. Ballakrishnen. 2018. Sticky Floors, Springboards, Stairways & Slow Escalators. *University of California Irvine Journal of International, Transnational, and Comparative Law* 3: 39–70.

Southworth, Ann, Bryant Garth, and Catherine Fisk. 2016. Some Realism about Realism in Teaching about the Legal Profession. In *The New Legal Realism, Volume 1. Translating Law-and-Society for Today's Legal Practice*, ed. Elizabeth Mertz, Stewart Macaulay, and Thomas W. Mitchell, 74–94. Cambridge: Cambridge University Press.

Spanbauer, Julie M. 2007. Lost in Translation in the Law School Classroom: Assessing Required Coursework in LL.M. Programs for International Students. *International Journal of Legal Information* 35: 397–446.

Sturm, Susan, and Lani Guinier. 2007. The Law School Matrix: Reforming Legal Education in a Culture of Competition and Conformity. *Vanderbilt Law Review* 60: 515–553.

Task Force on the Future of Legal Education: Report and Recommendations, American Bar Association. 2014. www.americanbar.org/content/dam/aba/administrative/ professional_reponsibility/report_and_recommendations_of_aba_task_force.authcheckdam.pdf (accessed October 27, 2017).

Tejani, Riaz. 2016. "Fielding" Legal Realism: Law Students as Participant-Observers? In *The New Legal Realism, Volume 1. Translating Law-and-Society for Today's Legal Practice*, ed. Elizabeth Mertz, Stewart Macaulay, and Thomas W. Mitchell, 95–118. Cambridge: Cambridge University Press.

Weiss, Catherine, and Louise Melling. 1987–1988. The Legal Education of Twenty Women. *Stanford Law Review* 40: 1299–1369.

Williams, Patricia. 1991. *The Alchemy of Race and Rights: Diary of a Law Professor*. Cambridge, MA: Harvard University Press.

Working Group on Student Experiences, Study on Women's Experiences at Harvard Law School, Cambridge, MA. 2004. www.law.harvard.edu/students/experiences/ExecutiveSummary.pdf.

3 In the Law School Classroom

Hidden Messages in French Elite Training

Émilie Biland and Liora Israël[*]

Introduction

To understand French elites and their educations, it is crucial to grasp an important fact specific to France's national structure: the duality of the higher education system, which is split into universities and *grandes écoles*. While universities are open to all and espouse an egalitarian view of higher education, access to many *grandes écoles* (literally, the "great schools") may be limited by highly competitive entrance examinations requiring two years in a *classe préparatoire*, a program preparing would-be applicants to take the exam. As Pierre Bourdieu demonstrated in *The State Nobility* (1998 [1989]), the majority of French elites have taken the *classes préparatoires* and *grandes écoles* path that selects and legitimizes the upper classes in fields as diverse as the sciences and humanities (in the *Ecoles Normales Supérieures*, ENS), business (in business schools such as HEC), and engineering, each field with its own specialized schools. A second series of competitive exams, supported by the *Instituts de Sciences Politiques* (IEP; Institutes of Political Science) of Paris and elsewhere in France and, more marginally, universities, determines access to the *grandes écoles* for civil service, such as the *Ecole Nationale d'Administration* (ENA; National School of Administration) and the *Ecole Nationale de la Magistrature* (ENM; National School for the Magistrate).

Despite all that, the legal and medical disciplines traditionally stood apart: centered in the universities, they had not been in competition with the *grandes écoles*. Setting aside the private organizations that prepared applicants for entrance exams, in fact, university training in law and medicine seemed to successfully hold on to its monopoly and prestige. This assessment, based in the accustomed dualistic divide between universities and *grandes écoles*, is problematic for at least two reasons, however. Firstly, it tends to assume that law is only studied in universities, when early in our research we observed that it is found in many other curricula. Most notable among them are the notorious *grandes écoles*, which have long included courses in law, whether they are intended to train students for positions directly handling legal matters or not. Understanding how elites are trained in law thus means delving into the entirely neglected question of legal teachings outside the university. Comprehending the content and development of this education should make it possible to grasp the

* Translation by Ian Douglass and Juliette Rogers.

conceptions of law that are passed on by instructors, describing the legal corpuses thought to be useful in preparing students for their future roles and the forms of socialization in law experienced by these elites-in-the-making, as they simultaneously enter into relation with the State and politics (Commaille and Duran 2009).

A second point also justified our study. While we were writing our research proposal in 2008, the French legal world was shaken by a controversy arising from a decree enacted a year earlier that broke the monopoly of university-based law schools over access to the bar, their prerogative since the Middle Ages. Indeed, the decree created the possibility for graduates of two masters degree programs in law of the IEP of Paris (commonly and hereafter called Sciences Po) to present themselves for the bar exam without a university law degree. This change and the ensuing mobilization of law professors are indeed indicators of a second strategic front, relating to the formation of a legal elite comprised of business lawyers. This is the new "market" that interested Sciences Po when it requested that the monopoly be broken – a break that had in fact already been made, although much more discretely, by the *grandes écoles* of business, which had been offering an increasing number of programs for lawyers which targeted the business world. Looking at law outside of Faculties of Law was thus essential to understanding the competitive development of a now-international market for the training of elites (both in and outside of law). Indeed, the *grande écoles'* investment in legal training took place in a general context in which institutions of higher learning had started to compete internationally. This shift changed the inter-institutional space of conflict, tending to put the norms of excellence in France into perspective and leading to the emergence of new skills (Wagner 2007, 65).

Faced with an especially incomplete literature largely composed of jurists' observations or vague monographs on the *grandes écoles*, we decided to address the question taking three approaches: 1) at the socio-historical level, intended to broadly reconstruct the teaching of law in these institutions since 1958; 2) through a more classic sociological analysis based on interviews and documentation of law's place in various curricula today; and 3) through a specific methodological approach – observation – making it possible to follow legal instruction as it is actually dispensed in these institutions. While rooted in the first two, our chapter is primarily focused on the third approach, based on observations of law classes at the *Ecole des Hautes Etudes Commerciales* (HEC; School for Advanced Study of Business)[1] and Sciences Po in 2009 and 2010. From an epistemological perspective, direct observation of these law classes without limiting ourselves to analyzing teaching materials (plans, handouts) meant situating ourselves unambiguously in an approach to law "in action" rather than a purely text-based understanding of law. Indeed, observation allows us to grasp what is in play in the concrete teaching of legal subjects, above and beyond the announced program and orientations declared by institutions and their representatives (what the sociology of education calls a "formal curriculum"), in order to get through to the hidden, or at very least implicit, curriculum (Musgrove 1968). What conception of law is actually promoted in classes? Which models of lawyer are students led to identify with? What

1 HEC is the most prestigious business school in France.

relationships are built between instructors and students? These concrete questions are the essential lines of thought guiding our inquiry. Elizabeth Mertz has demonstrated that law courses convey far more than mere content; after all, she says, their objective is to inculcate a specific way of thinking that is seemingly depoliticized, abstract, distinct from morality, and ultimately well adapted to capitalist ideology (Mertz 2007). Would the law classes we observed at HEC and Sciences Po lead us to the same conclusions? And more broadly, what are the implicit norms (on the nature of law, the "good" lawyer, the legal system) that are passed on to future economic elites through this teaching?

Taking an approach favoring empirical research on law and justice (Israël 2008) and ethnography in institutions (Béliard and Biland 2008), from the outset we were convinced of the value of conducting research over a relatively long period in the chosen institutions (several months in each field site) in order to respond to these questions. More specifically, we decided to focus our research protocol on groups of people who knew each other,[2] composed of teachers and students involved in legal programs. Putting this approach into practice nonetheless ran into two kinds of obstacles. For one thing, we were lacking French references in the sociology of education, which has only recently started using classroom observation as a significant research technique. The classroom has indeed been the "black box" of the sub-discipline (Derouet et al. 1987). Recent work has indeed made observation central to analysis of educational transmission (Deauvieau 2007), or even of the transformations of scholastic reproduction.[3] Scholars have gradually integrated British Marxist sociology (introduced in France by Jean-Claude Forquin (1983)) into French approaches focused on the symbolic violence of academic institutions (Bourdieu and Passeron 1970) and moved beyond American interactionism, which is quick to consider that student socialization is stronger outside of the classroom than inside (Becker et al. 1961). Regardless, research on the *grandes écoles* in civil service is based on written sources and interviews more than on direct observation of courses,[4] and ethnographic work on law largely favors courthouses over lecture halls, making Mertz's book a welcome exception. Consequently, we also built our position as observers by adopting methodological skills and theoretical frameworks forged from other topics.

There was a second obstacle between us and fieldwork: although we are specialists in the political sociology of law, we were not trained in Faculties of Law. We were (and still are) not lawyers. Although the usual research sites of political sociology can create some skills in public law, we were complete novices in the subjects of the courses we were going to observe (ranging from contract law to merger and acquisition law). Because we intended to study not only the context of interactions but the transmission of legal knowledge as well, this ignorance proved to be embarrassing. However, since apprenticeship happens by taking courses (also true for researchers),

2 In other words, the "*groups d'interconnaissance*" of Beaud and Weber (2003).

3 See the special issue on the subject entitled "Les classes populaires dans l'enseignement supérieur. Politiques, stratégies, inégalités" of *Actes de la recherche en sciences sociales* 183(3), edited by Beaud and Convert (2010).

4 Eymeri (2001); Gervais (2007); Oger (2008).

this initial situation was not detrimental. In a classic ethnological strategy, we situated ourselves as apprentices with the law professors we interviewed, so as to encourage them to explain the knowledge that they intended to hand on in the classroom. We also tried to analyze the cognitive content conveyed in classrooms in relation to classroom physical and interactional materials. While not denying the specificity of legal matters, we used tools and concepts from the sociology of institutions and socialization that are partially transferable to other disciplines.

Our chapter follows this progression, as attentive to the discursive and cognitive patterns of legal education as it is to the institutional frameworks making them possible and giving them substance.[5] It focuses on the legal training of future public and private sector leaders in order to analyze the place of knowledge in contemporary modes of regulation and domination (Ihl, Kaluszynski, and Pollet 2003). We will first analyze the changing place of training in law and professors' pedagogical methods in both schools so that we can discuss the relative specificity of the legal education dispensed in these institutions, which, in addition to being more elitist than universities, were also more rapid to take a vocational approach.[6] We will then study the definitions of law and kinds of lawyers that were promoted in the courses by crossing analysis of course content with examination of the practical conditions of their expression. This analysis shows that by presenting the law as practical knowledge, these courses teach students to play with the economic and political rules of financial capitalism and to put themselves in the service of its dominant actors.

Grandes Écoles of Law?

To analyze HEC and Sciences Po's positions on the legal terrain, we consider three major dimensions: the institutional dimension, to take account of their position relative to faculties of law; the curricular dimension, making it possible to identify the kind of law that is taught there; and the pedagogical dimension, to demonstrate how it is passed on in acts, in relation to French and North American university models.

From General Law to Law for Lawyers

As mentioned earlier, Sciences Po and HEC have recently begun to train lawyers, especially for the upper echelons of the bar working in very large firms (the vast majority of which are Anglo-American) whose clients are mostly businesses. This

5 This chapter is part of a broader research project entitled "Élidroit. La place du droit dans la formation des élites du privé et du public depuis 1958. Quels savoirs juridiques pour quel mode de gouvernement" (The legal training of elites of the private and public sectors since 1958: Which legal knowledge for which mode of government?). This project was funded by the French National Research Agency (ANR) (ANR grant ANR-O8-GOUV-65) for 2008–2012.

6 It should be mentioned that the injunction to "professionalize" programs is now quite present in universities, although it manifests itself more at the masters' level (in occupationally oriented masters' degrees combining internships and coursework) than at the undergraduate level, where teaching is still mainly theoretical and based in large lectures.

development is transforming the legal teachings offered in these schools, which were long associated with the general culture common to high-level civil servants for the former, and to businessmen in the latter.

Since HEC's founding in 1881, "legislation" was already one of the dozen subjects in its program (Merleau 1981, 16): "For the entire first part of the twentieth century, the established teaching system was thus quite marked by the concern of acquiring the titles of academic nobility (…) Law becomes the core discipline of the program" (Abraham 2007, 42). Moreover, until World War II, the only instructors with university credentials were the professors of law (Merleau 1981, 85). Even during the first two decades after the war, prestigious professors from Paris' only university-based law school taught at HEC, and spoke frequently at Sciences Po for that matter (Biland 2013, 52). In other words, while it was still a "'school for catching up' for a bourgeois youth kept at a distance from higher education," (Abraham 2007, 43) the business school modeled itself on the university and the primary contact between them was through legal instruction.

This relationship was significantly impacted when HEC moved from Paris to a new campus in the southern suburb of Jouy-en-Josas in 1964. This move coincided with other important changes. Starting in the mid-1960s, the school administration promoted teaching "through case studies" inspired by the Harvard Business School, setting itself apart from the traditional French university lecture. Disciplines associated with management grew in importance, while "more academic subjects [lost] importance" (Abraham 2007, 43). Moreover, after a decade of growth, HEC began to form a body of permanent professors, only few of whom met the requirements for French university faculty (possessing an accredited doctorate or the *agrégation*).[7] Professors from La Sorbonne only rarely took the trip to Jouy-en-Josas. In the early 1970s, the new Department of Law recruited several of its members from the bureaucracy of the national tax administration and charged them with developing courses in taxation. These tax specialists were imbued with a culture of civil service that was lacking in the other programs offered at HEC (management, then marketing and finance), and they gradually made law into a specialization. Law's contribution to the "general business culture" that graduates should possess has obviously not disappeared, as attested by the mandatory law course for first-year students. Moreover, starting in the 1980s and coming into full force in the 1990s, the notion of criminal liability of the legal person (introduced into the Penal Code[8] in 1994) and media coverage of legal cases involving CEOs provided a new argument for giving legal training to all future management: sensitized to "penal risk" and knowing enough to surround themselves with legal counselors capable of warning them, they would be able to innovate and develop businesses while "securing" decisions.[9] In a book devoted to

7 The *agrégation* is a selective examination qualifying instructors to teach at the university level. In law it is a prerequisite for reaching full professorship.

8 *Nouveau Code pénal français*, article 121–2.

9 HEC professors are in line with a wider trend to promote legal security: Vanneuville (2008).

HEC, an article collectively written by its law faculty touted the result of law and taxation instruction, which had shifted away from accounting and toward management: "Law no longer being only a technique, it becomes a major strategic element" (Lenglart et al. 1994, 184).

In so doing, legal education also paves the way for another objective. Counting on the growth of legal careers in the executive management of major corporations, modeled on General Counsels in the United States, HEC law professors aim to train business lawyers, whose ranks have become more numerous, highly trained, and recognized. They are also interested in the development of the legal and fiscal consulting market. So since its creation in 1985, a major entitled "Fiscal strategy and international law"[10] has been offered (as part of the third-year curriculum) to prepare for both of these career paths. The professors behind this program explained in interviews that this positioning with auditing and financial consulting firms and internal legal positions was a way of not "being rude to" universities or the bar. HEC has not openly announced their intention to train future lawyers, and has not contested the university monopoly of conferring degrees. By taking this conciliatory approach, HEC has been able to renew its ties with Faculties of Law – first with a university in the southern suburbs of Paris (Paris 11), and then the two prestigious faculties of the Latin Quarter (Paris 1 and 2). For 25 years, the "Law" major has accepted an annual entering class of about 50 students,[11] half from the *grande école* and half from partner universities, although the outcome is inegalitarian: students from HEC are awarded the equivalent of a masters' degree and thus may apply to the bar, but students from the university do not receive a degree from HEC.

For the first graduates of the major (whom we interviewed), the school being a path to the bar was not a major factor in their choice: the major financial consulting firms (mainly Arthur Andersen at the time) came directly on campus to seek their future employees. On the other hand, the fusion of the occupation of legal counselor and the profession of lawyer, which took effect on January 1, 1992, soon allowed these consultants to become lawyers without an examination. In the years that followed, HEC students aiming for legal and judicial careers increasingly pursued legal classes at the university – encouraged by teachers who wanted to ensure that students applying to the bar would be able to meet the academic requirements. Marking another change, a growing proportion of these students abandon taxation for business law (especially mergers and acquisitions) and practice in large law firms (mainly corporate departments). The instructors that founded the major have gotten these firms involved through philanthropy (funding the HEC foundation), advising on policy (on the Orientation Committee, which is consulted on the program and internships), and teaching (several courses are given by lawyers). At the same time,

10 This is the only major explicitly intended for future jurists; law is nonetheless taught in other, more recent programs with lower enrollments, notably the "Arts and creation management" major headed by a law professor and the "Alternative management" major co-founded by a law professor.

11 In 2007–2008, this was the fourth most popular major, trailing well behind finance and marketing (with about 80 students each), but close to the "entrepreneur" track and ahead of economics (Lambert 2010, 120).

the HEC legal department has struggled to reach the standards of "excellence" vaunted by the school administration for the past 15 years.[12] Thus far, few professors have reached the given objective of publishing in prominent international journals, a kind of evaluation that many decry for its incompatibility with the discipline of law, which is nationally based and less mathematical. The major manages to keep its position at the *grande école* nonetheless, thanks to the recognition its degrees enjoy on the "Paris market."

In other words, compared to Sciences Po's current strategy (which we explain below), HEC's law professors, who are relatively isolated in the institution and have less prestigious job titles than their university colleagues, have been discreet in their arrangements with the bar and university alliances, rather than seeking publicity and competition. One of the professors behind the major, now retired, sums up his aim with expression "Small is beautiful."[13] HEC is not – and probably never will be – a *grande école* for law, and it is not trying to create an entire law program through the doctorate or recruit the most prominent lawyers. But it is holding on to a niche position that meets the aspirations and financial expectations of some students. While the founding of the law school at Sciences Po contributed fully to the institution's rather aggressive transformation under the leadership of media-savvy director Richard Descoings, law is still peripheral at HEC as a research discipline, and in the minority in terms of teaching. The fact remains that HEC is more invested in law than any other French *grande école* for business[14] and enjoys a high reputation in the upper echelons of the bar.

Sciences Po's 2007 arrival on the legal education scene threatened this advantage. Law had also been taught there for a very long time, but mainly as public law: the so-called "Public service" program, which is traditionally the most legitimate and prestigious of the French public service programs, included a non-negligible legal component. From its base on the rue Saint-Guillaume in Paris's 7th *arrondisement*, the school competed with university law schools for access to the highest level of the civil service during the latter half of the twentieth century. Its multidisciplinary curriculum and the presence of high-ranking civil servants on the faculty proved to be advantageous for preparing the entrance examination for ENA, the gateway to top government positions. However, at the time a number of students from the Parisian bourgeoisie did "their law" at the same time as "rue Saint-Guillaume."[15] This tendency to accumulate degrees from multiple institutions (law/Sciences Po, law/

12 At the head of the HEC group since 1996, Bernard Ramanantso championed this change by recruiting a more internationally diverse faculty, seeking international recognition in the form of rankings, and developing research according to North American standards.

13 Interview March 11, 2010.

14 The other two business *grandes écoles* in Paris, École supérieure de commerce de Paris (ESCP) and École supérieure des sciences économiques et commerciales (ESSEC), also teach legal matters, even offering law programs. But law is most prominent among HEC's required courses, and there are more law professors there than in the others.

15 A great many French politicians have taken this double program, often capped by a degree at ENA.

business school, Sciences Po/ENS) has risen distinctly since the 1980s. Competition between institutions of higher learning (especially to become a business lawyer) is also seen in how the most privileged students seek to pair up the schools the most favorable to the accumulation of cultural, symbolic, and social capitals.

The most decisive turn came after the 2007 decree,[16] with the founding of a law school at Sciences Po offering two masters' degrees ("Economic law" and "Legal and judicial careers") and a doctoral program in law. Its creation was consistent with the institution's dual positioning, tending to stick to the business school model (Garrigou 2001) while developing an ambitious scientific policy (based on the possibility of hiring a great number of teachers relative to other institutions). As two members of our Élidroit research team have shown (Vanneuville 2013; Myriam 2013), university academics experienced the 2007 decree and founding of the law school as genuine provocations and, worse yet, an exercise in "unfair competition" from an institution that, unlike universities, had significant means at its disposal and the ability to select its students. Furthermore, university-based academics challenged the quality and the very seriousness of the education provided at Sciences Po in the ensuing controversy, through a petition and contentious appeal. Indeed the decree made it possible to admit novice law students into its masters' degree programs, making them eligible to take the bar exam after only two years. Two years of study instead of four or five? Little surprise that many university academics of all political stripes described the program as "third-rate." In this domain, the most influential law firms, while hoping to avoid upsetting their usual purveyors of young employees, made it understood that they looked favorably on the creation of a law school that would contrast with the university, perpetually accused of being too disconnected from actual practice.[17]

The reactions came quickly, especially from the director of the law school. In a particularly incisive text published in a thematic journal issue devoted to the teaching of law in the early twenty-first century (Jamin 2010), he responded to various objections raised by the university legal community by dismissing Paris 1 and Paris 2's concerns as being about their "shares of the market in the competition" for hiring in major Parisian firms, which lay hidden behind their proclaimed defense of general interest. He refuted the selectivity and means argument, pointing to universities' ability to be selective after the undergraduate level, and the relatively high level of resources available to them, as he had experienced it as a

16 Arrêté du 21 mars 2007 modifiant l'arrêté du 25 novembre 1998 fixant la liste des titres ou diplômes reconnus comme équivalents à la maîtrise en droit pour l'exercice de la profession d'avocat, J.O. 8 avr. 2007, p. 6609.

17 The founding of the National Council of Law, on April 29, 2008, was part of this context of change and renewal. It is formally "charged with a mission of reflection and proposition on the teaching of law, on relationships between establishments that offer this teaching and concerned institutions and professors, on the education and employment of jurists and on the orientations and on the modalities of research in law" (Décret no 2008–420 du 29 avril 2008 portant création du Conseil national du droit, J.O. 2 mai 2008, texte 19, art. 2; Conseil national du droit, viewed March 8 2011, from www.conseilnationaldudroit.fr).

professor in Lille for 12 years. He countered the supposed inadequacy of the legal instruction dispensed at Sciences Po by citing the dispensations that already existed for certain students of *grandes écoles* in France as well as examples from the United States, Great Britain, Japan, and even McGill University in Quebec (where he started out as a teacher), where the programs are shorter. Finally, he challenged the model holding that "legal culture" had to be passed along so gradually and include mastery of dogmatics.

This last remark leads to the heart of the debate relevant to our chapter. Beyond Science Po's relatively triumphant posture on the law market, it arrived on the scene claiming a new way to learn and practice law. Several quotes were particularly eloquent in conveying this point of view. In this first quotation, the director of Sciences Po's law school describes the old-fashioned perspective associated with the universities' approach to teaching law:

> I think that most French jurists are convinced that (…) the right legal apprenticeship – which they endlessly tell us is the prerogative of doctrine – would require knowledge of as many elements of the system as possible, without which the students could never manage to make it function, understand its internal workings, use the right analogies, or even critique and reform it.
>
> (Jamin 2010, 132)

He counters this conception of law and its teaching, described as being terribly dated, with the conception of legal realism, from René Démogue in France to Duncan Kennedy in the United States,[18] which he describes as a shift from knowledge of what law is toward a knowledge of what lawyers do. He maintains that courses at the Sciences Po law school take this perspective, and are judged to be in line with both the highest international university standards and business law firms' need for flexibility and creativity. The director then enumerated seven orientations characterizing the choices made at Sciences Po:

1 Connect the teaching of law to prior knowledge of the humanities;
2 Emphasize the fundamentals (by distinguishing between the legal essentials and the non-essentials);
3 Stop thinking of legal instruction as isolated from other fields;
4 Privilege multidisciplinarity;
5 Develop experience through internships in professional settings;
6 Do not limit it to dogmatics[19] (think of practice as the real legal theory);
7 Use interactive teaching methods with the students.

18 This kinship is up for discussion, especially since the Law and Society Association is the more likely heir to American realism than critical legal studies, which is much more resistant to empirical approaches, but this is beyond the scope of this text.

19 By "dogmatics," he means a focus on abstract legal doctrines and theory without attention to how law works in practice and in society.

It is easy to identify the example of American law schools behind the promoted model. They begin after undergraduate studies and reconcile professional training (as attested by the bar's recognition of their degrees) and multi- and inter-disciplinary coursework (law and economics, law and society, and critical legal studies, to give some examples) – and also use what is called the Socratic teaching method, which since Charles Langdell has relied on close interaction between the teacher and students to arrive at a maieutic of legal thought.[20]

As we have seen, HEC's and Sciences Po's positions on the legal education market contrast with each other. Admittedly, the same firms invest in both schools and court their best students. But Sciences Po has a larger mass of students, with two masters' programs instead of one – and more importantly it has placed itself in direct competition with the Faculties of Law by obtaining the right to confer degrees and tempting professors away from university law programs. Ever since, inter-institutional confrontation has expanded from being between universities and *grandes écoles* to occurring amongst *grandes écoles* as well. The position of the Department of Law within HEC does not permit it to be a direct rival to the Sciences Po Law School.[21] Instead, HEC has deepened its partnerships with universities – creating its first undergraduate program with the *Université de Versailles Saint-Quentin-en-Yvelines* in 2007, and a joint masters' degree with Paris 1 in 2010[22] – thus reaffirming its position on the legal education market. In other words, it would be an oversimplification to think of relations between the two institutional types only in terms of duality and competition. Both types have become porous, notably through the circulation of students (for HEC) and professors (for Sciences Po).

Moreover, comparison of the two *grandes écoles* shows that the internal logics of each weigh on their positioning relative to other institutions and structure two opposing poles of *grande école*/university relations: alliance for HEC, conquest by Sciences Po. While encroaching on university territory, in a way Sciences Po is more "university" than HEC. Its Law School is directed by a professor of private law who is a former lawyer and secretary of the *Conférence du Stage*[23] and a recognized specialist in contract law and legal history. He is making a strong mark on the school, as seen in his public engagement in the defense and promotion of the institution; he is developing thinking on legal pedagogy and even on the very definition of legal matters. This distinctive strength for law within the school itself is not found at HEC, which actually delegates the academic dimension of legal

20 For more about this model, its hegemony, and its current crisis, see Johnson (2010).

21 The number of faculty members remains especially limited: it has recently gone from seven to nine permanent professors (out of approximately 100 for the entire school).

22 This allows (public) university students to get an HEC degree. We should point out that at the same time, the Sorbonne law school at Paris 1 and the Paris 2 law college are transforming the organization of legal studies, changing the rules for selection, strengthening certain programs, and creating new labels intended to improve their renown among thousands of students and employers. Some Faculties of Law outside of Paris are following suit.

23 The "conference du stage" (trainee conference) is a rhetorical competition that has traditionally distinguished the elite of novice lawyers; this is how most presidents of the bar association earned early recognition.

training to the university while providing multidisciplinary perspectives and contributions from non-academic professionals on its end. By calling on professors of law that are recognized both in the academic world and among practicing lawyers, Sciences Po manages to have it both ways. The 15 professors of the Law School all have classic meritocratic careers, although the number of instructors trained outside of France is growing. They are almost entirely men (14 of 15),[24] 10 have passed the *agrégation* examination leading to the grade of full Professor of Law at the university; four of them are also lawyers. Although two researchers from the *Centre National de la Recherche Scientifique* (CNRS; National Scientific Research Center) with more multi-disciplinary profiles are further from this university-career type, they teach very little in the masters' program.

The Centrality of Contract Law in Both Programs

One commonality is shared by both schools: both on the rue Saint-Guillaume and in Jouy-en-Josas, contract law has a privileged position in legal instruction. At HEC the required first-year course is officially "Introduction to law," but as the person responsible for it explained,[25] faculty members have decided to make it into a course on contract law. The aims of law and its conceptual and geographical sources are addressed, but only in the "prolegomena" (introduction), the main bulk of the course being devoted to various steps of "contractual life" (working up a contract, effects, execution). At Sciences Po, the contract law course is part of the common curriculum for the first semester of the "Economic law" and "Legal and judicial careers" masters' programs. Significantly, it is taught by the Law School director himself, which makes this course an example of the specificities Sciences Po promotes where law is concerned. This specificity is furthermore noted by students: their informal interactions after class highlight its atypical character, in contrast to other courses that they consider less innovative. The professor actively embodies in person what is supposed to be taught in this class; he promotes the new curriculum, selects the department team, and repeatedly drops reminders of his central position in the program. For their part, students see this personalization as typical of the original approach to the field of law that is under construction in the new institution.

These initial courses, and contract law courses more generally, thus emerged as strategic sites for observation. For one thing, contract law is a fundamental aspect of private law, at the top of the academic hierarchy of legal specializations as a valued skill for the economic elite of lawyers, whom these schools intend to train. For another thing, the teaching of contract law has a particular methodological and epistemological appeal for our study. In fact, the

24 The given numbers date to the time of the study.

25 This conversation took place after class on November 18, 2009. Since the course concerns the entire class cohort, it is divided into three sections that are usually taught by different instructors. The head teacher teaches one of the sections and prepared the 200-page course reader.

previously cited book by Mertz (2007) is based on an ethnographic study specifically of first-year contract law courses in eight American law schools (varying according to several academic and social criteria). While we have no intention of adding another comparative example or two, which would make little sense given the differing national contexts, choosing to concentrate on contract law courses does allow us to extend some of Mertz's methods to our study and compare some of the results more easily (see box). Among the particularly interesting orientations that Mertz has uncovered, we single out a type of questioning that is relevant to our field sites, and one kind of result that could be contrasted with our own conclusions.

What does it mean to learn to read the law – case reading and reading legal texts more generally being central to these forms of learning? What kind of pedagogical relationship is established by the instructor, and to what effect on students' understanding of the law? Lastly, what worldviews do these teachings lead to? Using an ethnographic method relying heavily on techniques from linguistic anthropology (full transcription, coding), Mertz and her team highlight how pedagogical practices (the Socratic method in this case) are relatively homogeneous among the observed courses and combine to pass on a way of reading cases that is above all a manner of legal thinking. From this, the teaching of law seems less like teaching content than apprenticeship in a way of thinking, with strong ideological connotations despite its claims to technicality and neutrality.

Box 3.1 Field Sites: The Content and Methods of Observation in the Two Schools

At HEC, Émilie Biland focused on the program for the final year (Master 2), called "Fiscal strategy and international law" from November 2009 through June 2010. For her observations, she chose two courses described as "emblematic" by the faculty and former students she met during research preparations: one course of 12 3-hour sessions entitled "Corporate Group Strategies" taught by two senior lawyers in Anglo-American firms (observation of the last two classes in the course), and another called "The Business Game" (a case study that in 2010 focused on France Télécom, the largest telecommunications company in France), held in seven "tutorial" sessions with a group of five students and two or three lawyers and concluding in a day of defenses (five sessions were observed). To be able to compare with the instruction offered by permanent HEC faculty, Biland attended one session of the mandatory first-year course ("Introduction to law") and a second-year elective course ("Intellectual property law"), both taught by the same permanent female faculty member. Biland conducted semi-structured interviews with eight lawyers participating in course instruction, seven permanent HEC professors (one of whom was retired), and three university professors in Paris (one retired).

Liora Israël applied a distinctly different observation protocol for Sciences Po, due to her schedule availability and because she had read Mertz's book (based on observations of first-year contract-law courses in eight law schools) in the interim. She chose to conduct extensive observations of the contract law course offered in the first semester of masters' degrees in law at Sciences Po. Altogether, nine of the 10 2-hour sessions were observed, between September 9 and December 16, 2010. Although practical instruction given directly by lawyers was not observed at Sciences Po, it seems to have traits quite comparable to instruction at HEC in the "Fiscal strategy and international law" major, especially because firms of comparable characteristics (and in some cases, the same firms) are involved in teaching at both institutions.

Like all ethnographic studies, limited in time and space by necessity, observations of this course cannot be used to make immediate generalizations. Nonetheless, the fact that this course is part of the core curriculum for both of the Law School's masters' programs and taught by its charismatic director, combined with the subject's prominence in the program's focus on "professionalization," all justify our choice of focus. If it cannot be taken as representative, it is a core example of the approach that justifies the Law School's claim to be unique. The attention our analysis pays to the importance of exchanges with teachers, as well as to relating course characteristics with those of participants, justifies the decision to invest in this site rather than scattering the research across the variety of courses offered at the Sciences Po Law School. Ethnographic analysis of a closely followed course is also the method that Stacey Burns used to study a first-semester civil procedure course (Burns 1997), related to the same concern for making fine-tuned connections between pedagogical methods, the circulation of exchanges, and the kinds of legal skills that are held in esteem.

Ultimately, although the observation strategies differed between schools, they are more complementary than divergent: the HEC study makes it possible to compare several kinds of teaching and teachers, while the Sciences Po study provides an in-depth account of a key course in the curriculum. Combining the two reduces the risk of metonymy, consisting of taking a part (of a given course) for the whole (the entire masters' program) while avoiding the pitfall of observations that are too periodic to be methodical. Moreover, since the formal progressions and program schedules and content of the studied schools are different from those of relatively comparable institutions such as universities, it was impossible to conduct a term-by-term comparison between them.

Despite the differences between the observed classes, data was collected using a similar method: classes were transcribed in real-time, as exhaustively as possible, including student contributions, classroom behavior, and the like. Before and after each class, attention was paid to student conversations about the course supplemented with private interviews with students at other times. Additionally, at the end of each class a discussion was held with its professor, including his or her remarks on the class, the receptivity of the students, the latest news on the program, or how our research was progressing. Delphine Thivet made complementary observations at the Legal Careers Forum (*Forum des Métiers du Droit*) at Sciences Po, where law firms in partnership with the school presented their conceptions of the profession and their interest in its degrees. Lastly, in both field sites, observations were supplemented by the reading of course materials made for students and various documents related to the program (website, articles, interviews conducted as part of our larger project by Rachel Vanneuville at Sciences Po).

An Anti-University Pedagogy of Law?

In order to probe the ways of thinking that are relayed in law courses, as Mertz did, one has to begin with analyzing how this transmission works. Specifically, we will begin our ethnography of law courses by examining teachers' pedagogical practices paired with the models of transmission to which they refer. Sciences Po and HEC are positioned in two distinct ways from the outset, at least as far as discourse is concerned: distinguishing themselves from the French university model characterized by lectures combined with discussion sections and training in dogmatics (di Rosa 2010) and succumbing to the seductions of the American legal teaching model, associated with a double imperative to efficiency and globalization. Although it is not boasted of, there are references to the Socratic method at Sciences Po in verbal exchanges between students and faculty. At HEC, the university model serves as a negative example. North American methods do show through, at least implicitly, in classes taught by lawyers immersed in an Anglo-American working world. Beyond their impact, what kind of pedagogy can actually be observed in these classes?

The Challenge of Breaking Away from the Lecture

In the contract law class at Sciences Po, the fundamental tension created by time limits seriously impacts the course. Indeed, to cover the foundations of contract law in 24 classroom hours (ultimately reduced to 20 hours due to the cancellation of two sessions), the course is unavoidably taught at breakneck speed. As the instructor made clear in the first session, it relies on sustained preparation work (4–6 hours a week, based on reading the textbook[26] and at least two recommended manuals), and is delivered at an especially intense pace. Although it is not technically a lecture course, since the students should have worked beforehand to have a basic understanding of the issues relevant to the session, neither is it a dialog-based course where a protracted and genuine conversation can develop between teacher and student, as the Socratic method recommends.

There are several factors allowing us to understand why the course as it is given is far from the Socratic method. First of all, although it is for beginning masters' students, some of those students have already studied law while others came from a general studies program, often at Sciences Po. It should be pointed out that students can also be divided into those who pursued their prior education in France and those who came from abroad (which, in the case of law, is an especially

26 The textbook is comprised of three volumes of 200 or so pages each for this course alone.

significant criterion).[27] This student heterogeneity is one of the most perceptible limitations in instituting an interactive relationship with the class. In the very first session, while the instructor was presenting how he works and the recommended texts for the course, a student launched into a long technical question. Slightly irritated, the instructor responded: "I think there's 80% [of the class] that doesn't understand." Time constraints and student heterogeneity – and thus a highly variable ability to get involved in long comparable exchanges with each student – contribute to making a hybrid pedagogical model in which the professor does not dictate knowledge but rather relies on texts and student participation, which is often limited to isolated interjections (a single answer to a question from the teacher, an occasional question to clear up a point). In only one session was there a sustained exchange with a student that lasted several minutes, on how it may or may not be possible to describe the interpretation made in the decision of a real-estate litigation involving a farmer and his wife as "paternalistic."[28]

As for HEC, in the required first-year course, barely any students had prior exposure to the law,[29] and the time allotted to the course left twice as long as Sciences Po (40 hours) to cover a similar plan. Regardless, the pedagogical relationship the professor established resembled that of the course at Sciences Po. It seems that the persistence of the lecture model, despite the proclaimed distancing from some of its traits, could be credited to the teacher's academic socialization, as she had done her graduate studies at Paris 2 and had no foreign experience. The professor in particular objects to the two-part outline associated with university teaching: "I don't do my course with a I and a II. We aren't at the law school. That's part of the reason that I came to HEC. We don't make an *agreg*[*ation*] outline. I laugh more," she explains to students at the beginning of the session – but still without getting rid of outlines

27 According to masters' program administrative staff, at least 30 of the 62 students enrolled in the observed course came from the Sciences Po university undergraduate program, meaning that their prior education was not exclusively in law, and only seven students entered through the masters' program admission process, which normally only deals with students who have an undergraduate degree in law in France. Moreover, two students were admitted through the CEP (*Convention éducation prioritaire*; Priority Education Agreement) procedure, which is a kind of affirmative action established by Richard Descoings for disadvantaged neighborhoods. The rest of the student body came through foreign recruitment or exchange programs, either at the undergraduate or masters' level, but 12 of them are nonetheless French citizens (exclusively, or in some cases with a double nationality), which puts the still rather striking international dimension into perspective.

28 It may not be trivial to add that this long exchange, which in some ways can be compared to those described in American studies, took place during the session following a long conversation between the researcher and instructor about Mertz's book. As in quantum physics, ethnographic observation sometimes modifies the observed results: the course would probably not have been the same if a sociologist had not been in the room with the instructor's authorization.

29 In 2010, only 11 applicants having chosen the "legal sciences" option were admitted (of a total of 381 admitted students) (HEC Paris, "Admission sur classes préparatoires," at www.hec.fr/Grande-Ecole/Admissions/Admission-sur-classespreparatoires).

for the essays that some students have to prepare at home. However, clearly neither the Socratic method nor the "active pedagogies" developed in the mid-twentieth century for primary and secondary schools experiencing the influx of a more socially diverse student body[30] serve as secondary references. HEC is an elitist institution: teachers accept questions from the students because they are seen as "gifted" and "interesting." And when the intense student social life on campus makes them less attentive to their classes than they should be, the professors question them to stimulate their interest in the class. During the two sessions that were observed, there was on average one exchange every 10–15 minutes – quite far from Mertz's counts. Like at Sciences Po, teachers are still in a position of "knowing" rather than assuming a posture of midwife.[31]

Courses that are taught by lawyers in the major at HEC present another situation. For one thing, there are fewer students (15–20 in "Corporate Group Strategies" compared to 40–50 in the classes described above). Additionally, professors and students are not separated by the incline of the lecture hall and instead are seated in identical comfortable chairs around a table in the meeting room of a law firm in a fashionable neighborhood. Sessions are organized very differently, since at least half of the session is devoted to a presentation of a fictional case (involving leveraged buy-outs[32] or mergers and acquisitions in the three observed sessions) by a group of four students standing in front of their classmates and teachers while commenting on their PowerPoints. This interactional setting is no longer defined in scholastic terms, but according to professional norms. There are considerably more exchanges, the students interrupting the lawyer almost as often as he interrupts them. And yet the asymmetry of roles remains: during their presentations students should be able to maintain the flow of their arguments without being destabilized by frequent, sometimes provocative, interruptions (a lawyer to a female student: "You're starting out like you're going to lose across the board! Are you sure you aren't lawyer for [the opponent]?"). Here knowledge is evaluated on the same level as endurance, self-control, and the ability to respond well. This kind of course is an implicit reference to the presentations that junior associates make for the senior partners for whom they work. Observations of sessions of "The Business Game" confirm this hypothesis: the group that we followed was led by a partner of about 40 with visibility on the Paris market and two junior associates in their 30s, for

30 The process taking place at this historical moment in French education is referred to as "massification" Bonnéry (2007).

31 To conclude our comparison between the American and French models at the *grande école* level, analysis should be made of the variable personalization of the relationship to students, which we could not develop in our already-long chapter. It seems that there is more educationally related exchange at HEC and Sciences Po than at universities. At Sciences Po this occurs through regular e-mail exchanges between professors and students; at HEC the professor prefers the telephone. But in neither instance are students addressed by name, unlike in the United States where the practice helps to establish the "dialogue" held in such esteem.

32 A leveraged buyout (LBO) is buying a company with bank loans, facilitating the acquisition and tax deductions.

whom the stakes were not only passing knowledge along to students but also living up to the senior partner's expectations. For that matter, he asked the junior associates more questions than the students, who were consequently spectators of enacted hierarchical relations in the firm.

Are the prime models national (or even international) universities, or the profession? The space of pedagogical models observed in these classes is strongly conditioned by instructors' socialization and social milieu. Accordingly, the "American-style" role-playing sessions at Sciences Po are run by an instructor from Great Britain who is familiar with the American model. The practical limitations (group size, number of course hours) also count, but they are dependent variables as much as they are explanatory ones. By limiting the number of classroom hours and requiring considerable work from duly selected students, Sciences Po can claim to give them as much as a law school, in less time. By taking courses off campus, reducing group sizes, and bringing practicing lawyers into the curriculum, HEC can describe its last year as "professionalizing." The high variability of these pedagogical practices is an indicator of the tensions pulling these *grandes écoles* between pedagogical models transformed by the internationalization of the institutions and between the worlds of school and work, the intersection being where they situate themselves. In the first instance, "dialogue" is reduced to the strict minimum; in the second it takes place under the interactional order of major law firms. Those of *grandes écoles* professors indeed do still espouse the classic French lecture, historically situated itself,[33] as the model for university courses. However, alongside that, North American maieutics implemented in the law schools seems to be a positive model that at least in theory values classroom exchanges. To define the specificities of *grande école* legal instruction, the legal resources used in the name of these pedagogical methods merit a closer look.

French Legal Resources

In order to more deeply analyze these programs' similarity to the American model, the type of law being taught must be taken into consideration, because the programs follow the continental tradition, not the Anglo-American common law tradition. As Mertz demonstrates, the Socratic method's master–student model for dialogue is especially well suited to showing the antagonistic structure of legal relationships in an adversarial system. In addition to this dualism, precedent is important in common law: law is learned by discussing the precedents set by case law through a series of examinations of cases. In contrast, the law courses we observed at Sciences Po and HEC teach French contract law: they are based on a layering process connecting legislative foundations with knowledge of legal precedent. At Sciences Po, students are instructed to bring their copies of the Civil Code, and the instructor often asks

33 Since the 1902 *lycée* (high school) reform, lectures have taken the place of teaching through written exercises (Héry 2007).

them short questions to ensure that they know the main articles (or sections of the Code). The students receive a handout that presents changes to contract legislation, up through plans for reform under discussion at the Ministry of Justice. Lastly, they should know precedent: "Perhaps some of you have never read an order of the Final Court of Appeal [*Cour de Cassation*], so we're going to read it together. I warn you that an order from the Final Court of Appeal is very challenging," said the instructor, as he initiated the students into handling legal doctrine. Student assignments are typically commentaries and essays, to prepare students for the "final stretch." After this exercise, which the instructor considered something of a failure, he said he was surprised that the students "don't question anything" and do not know how to present their outlines, while going on to state a second later, "I could care less about outlines, there's one that didn't give an outline and I gave him a passing grade, no problem." The students also encountered difficulties writing commentaries on texts: "They all start like an essay" in the instructor's opinion. Despite his criticism of university formalism, all of his remarks were still directed at correcting classic elements of French academic rhetoric (a structured text, presentation of the outline, introduction to a commentary, the formal difference between an essay and commentary).

Knowledge of legal resources is not as valued at HEC. References to the codes (Civil Code in the introductory course, Intellectual Property Code for the course on the subject, Business Code for the corporate strategies course) are often limited to mentioning the number of the article in question. Few articles are read completely through, and it is rarely required that they be memorized. Speaking of the rule of evidence in employment contracts, for example, the teacher said, "It's article L113–1 of the CPI. Rest assured, I'll give you the article, but that's not the important part. It's really the reasoning that matters." It is likewise rare for them to read orders, the instructor preferring that students reformulate them in their own words, favoring fundamental comprehension over the form, and above all aiming for definitions of concepts. To define the notion of "fault of a third party" in the introductory course she explained it thusly:

> I'll give you a typical example, really well-known precedent: A trucker parks his rig and leaves the key on the dashboard. The rig is stolen: removal of an earthbound motor vehicle. There is no exemption of liability, because the vehicle was not locked.

There was a bibliography in the handout, but in the interview the professor seemed to have forgotten it, indicating that the course alone was enough. Lastly, a few pages were set aside for doctrine, but verbal references to it are rare. Another indicator of the distancing from the academic approach to law is in the nature of assignments. The legal essay is a rarity, reserved for students who are absent the day of the in-class multiple-choice examination. In addition, the exercise of writing a commentary on an order, a rite of passage in the first year of a university program, is absent here: students are evaluated at the end of the session by a fictional case-study often consisting of preparing a contract. Lastly, unlike American programs where trial simulations are commonplace, court activities are rarely mentioned.[34] To the contrary, as the Law faculty puts it, the course is primarily interested in "diagnostic, prescriptive law, from above," which serves to prevent conflict or at least avoid trial (Lenglart 1994, 182). As we will see later in this chapter, the professional outcomes of teaching weigh heavily on how law is taught and how legal resources are used.

How to explain these differences between Sciences Po and HEC? Why are legal resources studied in much greater detail at Sciences Po, despite the fact that it presents the same distinctly French stratification of legal resources as HEC? This contrast can be understood through the different position each school assumes on the market for legal training, presented earlier. It is evident that Sciences Po aims to replace the university in preparing students for the bar and ENM examinations.[35] The pressure of these exams (whose content is beyond Science Po's control) is probably the most powerful impediment to a genuine distancing from the form, and even more the content, of law as it is taught in the university. At HEC, however, the legal fate of students is still uncertain. Although it is required, the first-year class is mainly addressed to students not intending to become lawyers. Even within the major, passing the bar exam is far from students' concerns. The internship from January through March is the opportunity for them to try out their "vocation" as a jurist. Several decide to work in the legal division of a major bank to keep this other professional possibility open. In addition, the mandatory 18-month internship after passage of the bar examination discourages some students, who are interested in rapid access to well-paying careers that do not require them to be a member of the bar, such as working in the legal services division of a company. Lastly, the most purely legal classes are delegated to partner universities, which take responsibility for preparing students for the examination. In short, HEC is less tied to the constraints of examinations and can prepare its students more directly for their probable professional futures in the business world.

34 Another law professor at HEC said, in an interview on February 3, 2010, "When I comment on a decision from the Final Appeals Court, I don't explain why there was an appeal and what the Final Appeals Court is. I simply say, in the Barbelivien/Montagné case, there was a song that was used by Flunch [a restaurant chain] without the agreement of the authors and composers. We thought that their moral rights had been violated, period! The fact that there was opposition between the Appellate Court and Final Appeals Court, I don't address that." This professor is referring to the "arrêt du 2 avril 2009 de la 1re Chambre civile de la Cour de cassation," which imposed the primacy of the moral rights of the author (Civ. 1re, 2 avr. 2009, Bull. civ. I, no 416).

35 This limitation was particularly noticeable in the beginning of the second-to-last session, in which the instructor commented on the success rate of the preceding class cohort in these examinations.

Law, Knowledge for Economic Practice

Although HEC's program features more situations of projected legal practice than Sciences Po, where this dimension culminates in the second year of the masters' program,[36] it is still central to the curriculum. Studying how future professional roles are presented – thus considering instructors as agents of students' future-oriented socialization – will allow us to arrive at the sociopolitical conceptions of law that are thus passed along, building on Mertz's thinking.

Enacting and Learning Roles

Facing instructors who physically and verbally incarnate several ways of being jurists, students are led to project themselves into professional positions that are presented as desirable. Our classroom observations, combined with our previous observations (characteristics of the professor, the course's place in the program, etc.) made it possible for us to identify the range of professorial postures and anticipated professional types.

Being a Jurist: Instructors Incarnating the Law

The director of the Sciences Po law school presents himself as a multi-positioned actor in the legal world (Boltanski 1973). If his class is like a lecture, it is mostly because of how he plays the professorial role. Very tall, with a beard and bow tie, he is both particularly invested in teaching and rather enthusiastic about the subject he teaches. As a good French law professor, he typically positions himself as a producer of doctrinal analysis. However, beyond mentioning his doctorate or one of his case comments, sometimes printed in the handout or e-mailed to the class between sessions, he depicts himself more as someone engaged. This engagement takes many forms, be it legislative (when he lets it be understood that he is involved in the discussion of contract law reform at the Ministry of Justice), academic (by saying of a text in passing, "I assign it for comments in the *agrégation*"),[37] and in the practice of law. To lend clout to his interpretations of precedent, he emphasizes his relationships with influential magistrates like his "friend" Guy Canivet, former president of the Final Court of Appeal and member of the Constitutional Council. However it is mainly his past experience as a lawyer and current experience as arbitrator that is revealed in his references to specific cases: "I've found myself pleading the absolute nullity of a contract ten years after

36 This progression is ensured by a shift in faculty, especially between the first year of the masters' program and the second, which is more specialized. The website of the "Economic law" masters' program specifies that "the first courses are taught by **academics** and courses later in the program more by **practitioners**" (bold in the original) (SciencesPo Ecole de Droit, Master Droit économique, viewed July 21, 2017, from www.sciencespo.fr/ecole-de-droit/fr/content/master-droit-economique).

37 This lets it be understood that the director is a member of the selection committee that chooses who will have access to university law professor positions.

it's ended"; "Don't do like I did the first time I plead"; "My 2009 ruling isn't exactly satisfactory for responding to the client who consulted me."[38]

This positioning may be interpreted in two ways. The teacher first of all gives a peek into his trajectory of social success through law by mentioning his non-Parisian and relatively working-class origins, far from the Parisian legal world.[39] In contrast he allows glimpses of regular frequentation of economic elites, mentioning lunch with second in command of the LVMH group (Louis Vuiton Moët Hennessy, a major French luxury company) to speak with him about the law school, that he regularly spends time with lawyers that drive Ferraris, and his dinners with Parisian notaries. In addition to what students probably find to be a rather impressive life, his personal multipositionality is analogous to the law school's own position, formed without a prior tradition (at least in private law), claiming academic and legal excellence and recognition in the business world.

HEC instructors' presentations are made very differently, partly because none of its faculty members have accumulated the same level of social and symbolic attributes as several of Science Po's law school instructors, and partly because, as we have seen, the institution positions itself as a complement to other actors in legal training, namely universities and lawyers. Having observed courses taught by a female professor with both little research recognition and little involvement with law firms (not the case for all HEC faculty) and courses taught by lawyers, we were struck by the differences. The former stresses her availability to students (including outside of course time), repeating the definitions of concepts multiple times, confirming that everyone has noted certain things. In this sense she demonstrates a pedagogical sense that is closer to secondary teaching than it is to the university level. She moreover plays on complicity with the students with funny remarks ("I'll use the Asterix method: I'll stop breathing until you find the answer"), in contrast with the image of the serious and distant professor alone on his dais. She makes law into a learned discipline, using numerous Latin expressions ("Should we evaluate it *in concreto* or *in abstracto*?," "We apply the law of *res perit domino*") and constantly insists that concepts should be mastered. This positioning is particularly strong in her intellectual property rights course, where she announces in the first session that it is her "favorite subject." When she relates Beaumarchais's wrangles with the Comédie Française or the conflict between Alexandre Dumas and Auguste Maquet, the pleasure she takes in connecting history, law, and artistic life is evident.

This simultaneously enthusiastic and intellectual posture tells us about law's position at HEC. First, law here is never mono-disciplinary or strictly specialized, but always in resonance with other fields of knowledge – history and literature in this case, finance elsewhere (see below). Next, situating law as an intellectual and literary discipline relates to practices of distinction as compared with more practical disciplines

38 This concerns the distinction between a sales contract and a service contract.

39 In one session the director told the class that when he began his studies in law, someone told him that he'd "have to speak Latin and that you need the memory of a horse or elephant."

(like accounting or marketing) and with those based on mathematical reasoning (finance, economics). In so doing, law occupies a segment of knowledge that is barely found at HEC, and might attract students who were admitted after literary *pré-paratoire* studies. Lastly, fostering an interest in the law corresponds to the generalist purpose of the coursework in the first two years. Although most of the students will not become jurists, they should have had a taste of it to be able to call on legal counsel in their future professional lives. In an institution where the playful aspect of knowledge is valued (seen especially in competitions and prizes to be won), enjoyment of learning is seen as a guarantee of their later mobilization.

At the moment that career paths take shape, in the third year, courses show another incarnation of law and a somewhat different vision of the material. Law is as allied with other disciplinary fields as ever, as we will see, but the literary and intellectual dimension has yielded to the technical and problem-solving. It is no longer about convincing students of the conceptual richness of the material but training them in its most relevant practical applications. The lawyers teaching at this level embody a professionalism directly out of their working environment: mandatory and commonplace use of PowerPoint (which the previously discussed teacher promised to adopt … next year), suit and tie, speech peppered with expressions in English, reasoning more in diagrams than in texts. The lawyer-instructor we observed in "Corporate Group Strategies" does little to adapt his posture for teaching: since this class takes place at his law firm, he is directly connected to his intranet; he is able to call on his usual assistant and he arrives for class at start time while leaving as soon as it ends. He moreover refers to several aspects of his "daily life" at work, such as recounting a closing procedure: "We take half a day to put the documents in order. The table isn't long enough to contain them all. It's an ordeal. That comes from the Anglo-Saxons: they ask for documents that have no purpose." His colleague from Sciences Po says nothing to discredit this: "When you are faced with the real world, you'll find yourself buried in paper." These prosaic accounts give glimpses of the job, alongside the advantages that students will experience directly in the classes taught in firms with beverages, snacks, office supplies, and newspapers free for the taking. And even in the intellectual property course, the instructor explicitly mentioned the (high) salary prospects, telling students, "You can make a good living off your passion."

Becoming a Jurist: The Course as a Space of Future-Oriented Socialization

Beyond these anecdotes, these students are indeed projecting themselves into the market polity (Boltanski and Thévenot 2006 [1991]). Encouraged to position themselves in a competitive space (competing law firms, between lawyers and bankers, between companies) and to assert their own financial ambitions,[40] they also learn that their role is to serve their clients' financial interests.

40 In an interview on January 13, 2010, a lawyer told us, "They are people who want to make a good living, no question. I think that they come to HEC in that state of mind […]. The starting salaries of junior partners generally start at around 65,000–70,000

At Sciences Po and HEC alike, students are invited to imagine a future as a business lawyer (or, less often, an in-house counsel). Although the professor from Sciences Po sometimes refers to judges,[41] it is usually by presenting them as interlocutors or even adversaries:

> There, you're going to plea, and you say: "With the precedent there's still an inconsistency, Your Honor, I'm not making it up …" And there, you upset the magistrate because he hasn't kept entirely up to date with the precedents and you're waving it in his face.

The lawyer-instructor is presented as a practitioner, a jurist that takes action. All his actions have to be thought out in relation to the consequences they are supposed to produce: "You've got to pay attention to what you write when you're a lawyer, because it will be read by a judge who, having imbalanced information, will take everything you write at face value, even e-mails." At HEC the students also have to know precedent and be able to use it, but the trial setting is only rarely brought up because legal counsel serves precisely to avoid such procedures, which are as costly for the company's image as they are for its finances. Students are led to project themselves into contract negotiations or pre-litigation and other procedural alternatives to going to trial (such as arbitration).

In addition to baseline professional relations and activities, there is an implicit generational division of labor in firms. To the junior associates falls the bookwork of documentation, and to experienced partners client relations, as the previously mentioned lawyer teaching at HEC verified in interview: "I'm really interested to read the outcome of the research done by the intern. It entertains me a lot. But I'm not going to join in, go looking for legal information myself." Hearing jurists rather humorously defined as "theologians" and even "textually obsessed," Sciences Po students are also given to understand that a jurist's place is reading, classification, and commentary, at least in the first years of practice. However, the instructor includes the strategic role of jurists, as well, by highlighting his relations with business leaders on several occasions. The teaching presence of these lawyers, still practicing or converted to academia, gives a sense of different segments of this professional world and the diversity of roles in firms. The lawyers who teach at HEC, the great majority of them HEC alumni themselves, embody models of professional success, unquestionably exemplary (some are reputed to be "bigwigs of the Paris market"),[42] but accessible because they are from the same inner circle. When students attend classes in law firms, they trade in their post-adolescent jeans and t-shirts, common in first- and second-year classrooms, for business attire

euros a year. We all have token fees. That's in English firms. In American firms it's between 90,000 and 100,000 euros, so that's considerable money for people who are just leaving school."

41 For example, in a session in October the director said, "Tomorrow you're in practice, you're a judge, don't do like I did!"

42 This expression was used by an HEC professor during a discussion on October 21, 2009.

(slacks, jacket, shirt, sometimes even cufflinks for many men; skirt or pantsuits for many women). In these "situational" classes, they are presenting themselves to instructors who intend to identify the best of them for pre-hire internships, and so they try to demonstrate a professional conformity right down to their attire. This is obviously not the only setting for such anticipatory socialization through contact, as it also reaches into the educational sphere, with individuals from the professional milieu of reference. Such socialization has been widely discussed concerning ENA and Sciences Po's preparatory program for the ENA entrance examination (Bellier 1993). That the same mechanism also works for business lawyers demonstrates that this professional space, little institutionalized until the 1980s (Boigeol and Dezalay 1997), is now invested in its own reproduction.

The supposedly distinctive properties of business lawyers are presented in class, especially when client relations are raised. Described as non-lawyers, or at least "less-lawyers," clients have concerns other than law alone, and those concerns may even be in contradiction with legality. At Sciences Po, the professor stresses the tensions between what the client wants and the normative evaluation of success or failure of a legal procedure: "I'm speaking in very, very real terms here. Your client will say: 'I don't give a damn about enforcement, what I want is as much money as possible'." The connection with the client inherent to the classic practice of the profession raises a contradiction between the legal definition of the situation, which is established normatively, and how it is evaluated in practice, according to the decision's actual economic effectiveness. Clients demand that their legal counsel show creativity or even genius that allows them to maximize profit without running afoul of the tax administration or the court. The previously quoted lawyer-instructor thus explains to HEC students that rapid mergers (between two holding companies after a leveraged buyout) for purely fiscal ends are not permitted: "You have to find an additional explanation to justify the merger. It's up to us to use our imaginations."

Legal Knowledge and Power[43]

The commercial evaluation of legal activity takes shape around a broader conception of law, as an instrument in the service of clients' power in firms. Consequently, business law courses convey an instrumental vision of law[44] that is nonetheless political. This conception makes sense from the multidisciplinary perspective that is developed throughout the course: far from being knowledge

43 To conceptualize the relationship between knowledge and power we refer readers to the work of Michel Foucault, who asserted "that there is no power relation without the correlative constitution of a field of knowledge, nor any knowledge that does not presuppose and constitute at the same time power relations" (1995 [1975]). We thus wonder which simultaneously academic and professional power(s) are constituted by legal knowledge (and more precisely, contract law).

44 "Law isn't an end unto itself. [...] When you train managers you have to show them that law is a tool for an economic issue," a previously cited HEC professor told us in interview.

serving its own needs, law should meet extralegal demands, both strategic and financial. In short, the legal method put in the service of economics contributes to legitimating financial capitalism, whose outcomes are only rarely discussed.

An Instrumental Conception of Law

At Sciences Po, the frequently used metaphor of the "toolbox" illustrates this pragmatic resource for economic action. Doctrine is presented as highly political and controversial, as is the role of judges (potentially activists for the left).[45] Lawyers' practices are mainly presented as outcome-oriented, inseparably economic and political, rather than concerned with formal and procedural correction: "It's a game, I love that, getting clauses cut from contracts," the instructor said. In its very brevity this formulation is telling of the essential dimension of this conception, common to both schools: its playful imagery reveals a relationship to law that is marked by its partial legitimacy and the pursuit of the clients' interests. In other words, rather than thinking of legality as prescriptive and authoritarian, instructors teach students to use it strategically, in a context of negotiation rather than coercion. It is a matter of doing things "with the law," not being subjected to it (Ewick and Silbey 1998). Lewis Kornhauser[46] is cited to remind students that it is possible to negotiate "in the shadow of the law" and that most contracts do not end up in court. The lawyer teaching at HEC points to a contradiction between the rationality of the law (backed by the Final Court of Appeal, which invalidated the system sanctioning managers leaving merger procedures that were still underway) and the rationality of the firm (trying to have an efficient system of incentives and sanctions) to highlight how difficult it can be to make these two spheres fit with each other. These legal games are aimed at satisfying clients at various levels of the entrepreneurial structure and optimizing businesses' financial situations. Indeed, said the professor at Sciences Po, "a client is obsessed by recovering his funds, and the lawyer's work isn't done when he gets a ruling on the principle." In other words, a lawyer's practical intelligence aims to satisfy the client above and beyond respecting the law. It should even sometimes be able to work around certain challenges and in so doing place economic activities in "zones of less legal resistance" (Boltanski and Chiapello 2005 [1999], 400) in which capitalist logics are subjected to fewer constraints.

The political and economic outcomes of these uses of law are particularly manifest in the Corporate Group Strategies course at HEC: the contracts that students draft based on fictional cases concern firms' internal power structures. These

45 Speaking of consumer law relative to deceptive claims from mail order companies leading their customers to believe that they had won a fortune, the professor said, "So the judges say to themselves, 'We're fed up – certain political outcome – but we're judges, we can't pronounce political decisions, so we'll look for some trick in the toolbox'."

46 Lewis Kornhauser is a professor at New York University School of Law and a recognized specialist in economic analysis of law; he was an invited professor at Sciences Po the year of this course.

contracts regularly address the political rights of stockholders, meaning the right to vote on the board relative to their share of capital. Of central importance to corporate law, the notion of "group" is the focus of case studies (incorporated company, limited liability company, joint stock company, holding, subsidiary), each with its own limitations and specific resources that could be subject to arbitration. A version of law that serves to defend the majority stockholder, promote those in the minority, or to develop incentive strategies for managers, as it is taught at HEC, indeed depicts law as a science of government – of businesses. In the service of stockholders, law is never entirely isolated: the "legal considerations" in students' PowerPoint presentations are always followed by "accounting considerations."[47] It is a matter of determining the fairness of the exchange, the difference between real and book values, or calculating the number of stocks to release and the merger bonus as well as the post-merger balance sheet. And within these legal considerations, students are encouraged to combine different subjects, such as internal and international taxation or business law and taxation. The ways in which they present their knowledge is in line with this multidisciplinary approach, the figures tending to set the tone for the law in the name of the financial outcome of activities and decisions: figures (in thousands of Euros or as a percentage) are ubiquitous in student presentations, as are diagrams charting their flows.

To hirers' way of thinking, HEC graduates have the advantage of multidisciplinarity, able to handle a variety of business-related subjects and thus have informed discussions with a variety of relevant actors (bankers, legal, fiscal, and financial directors). Central to the school's position in the legal training market, multidisciplinarity is all the more promising since number-oriented fields (accounting expertise and auditing) and law (legal counsel and litigation) have grown closer to each other since the 1990s, under the "multinationals of law" that hire its graduates (Dezalay 1992). Firms seek the same commitment to multidisciplinarity at Sciences Po, even to the detriment of legal knowledge. A lawyer from the Clifford Chance firm explained this bluntly at the Legal Careers Forum held by the Sciences Po Law School and Sciences Po Avenir.[48] While presenting a case study, he declared, "we actually do very little law." Instead, he said, business lawyers are more investigators than jurists, and must gradually acquire an overall understanding of all the relevant elements for a case.[49] Later the same day, another lawyer from the same firm stressed the "accompanying the client" aspect of the profession, which presupposes "not sticking to law." Quite clearly these lawyers intended to make graduates of the Sciences Po Law School understand that their potential absence of initial training in law is more of an advantage than a handicap as far as they are concerned. Such a description also reveals professional

47 "It's not explicit [in the instructions], but students know it: it's HEC's specialty. We removed the taxation part, it was too heavy," a lawyer told us when we were questioning him on this presentation structure.

48 The Sciences Po career center.

49 This observation was made by Delphine Thivet on Thursday, April 8, 2010.

practices that are far indeed from the court and trial. They are not trained in the art of pleading, and the great criminal lawyer is no longer the major figure of reference. After all, it is about drafting a consultation or preparing a contract, not writing submissions or preparing pleas. And instead of training to address the bench and before a quickly moved public, students should train to communicate with the relevant "authorities," and more importantly to accompany their client (banker, legal director, or a major company) to the confidential negotiating table at a prestigious head office. Mandatory use of PowerPoint software moreover recalls the practices of strategic advisors, presentations for the board of directors, and general meetings.

A Capitalist Law?

Is it possible to get past analogies with the main figures of contemporary capitalism (bankers and financial consultants/auditors) and consider that the conception of law promoted in these schools has an affinity with the spirit of capitalism, as Mertz deems the case for American law schools, or in other words, with the ideology that justifies engagement in this type of economic system?[50] The pragmatic aim of law, whose uses are over-determined by economic imperatives, seem to confirm this hypothesis. An even closer study would probably show that the vision of capitalism – market, industrial, project-based – is ambiguous, varying from course to course. Previous observations have indicated that when labor disputes are taught at HEC, students are encouraged to take the director or management's side rather than that of unionists or strikers (Abraham 2007). Stock-market capitalism is taught in the Corporate Group Strategies course and closely connected with financial knowledge acquired at another point in the program. Lastly, in the Sciences Po course, the confidential relationship between lawyer and client, central to the imagined network and set of projects forming the new world into which these students will move (Boltanski and Chiapello 2005, 107 onward), holds a prominent position. Although these visions are theoretically distinguishable from each other and correspond to different segments (including generational) of capitalist elites, our analysis leads us to consider them as convergent. Indeed, what is important in each is putting legal knowledge to work for economic interests (of the boss, the stockholder, or the client). The theoretical conception that puts the law in the service of the economic finds concrete expression in student socialization through the gradual clarification of the aspired-to social and economic position as well as the construction of a half theoretical, half practical taste for legal tactics. At a time when the ethic of a calling (Weber 2001 [1930]) seems weakened – in interviews, several lawyers mentioned the job's temporal demands as providing little incentive for the youngest – the possibility of reconciling intellectual satisfaction and social success through a specialization in law seems like a non-negligible advantage.[51]

50 What Boltanski and Chiapello (2005 [1999], 8) describe as the new "projective city."

51 Focused on the classroom and instructors, our research does not allow us to systematically describe the social and academic characteristics of the students who choose this

At least in the HEC legal program,[52] the intellectual legitimation of practice still does not mean encouragement of reflexivity or critique. It is true that the female professor of "Introduction to law" acknowledges that some "tyrannical bosses" provoke strikes. In "Corporate Group Strategies," the lawyer-instructor even thinks that "everyone is shocked" by leveraged buy-outs in which the managers divvy up hundreds of billions of euros or by investment funds created with insufficient equity capital. In the introductory session of "The Business Game," the entire class was shown a documentary highlighting the possibility that France Télécom's upper management might bear responsibility for the suicides of several of its employees. But such an issue never showed up again during the other sessions. More than that, the institutional setting and the social properties of the actors contribute to reducing the impact of these observations. No-one comes back to the employee suicides in the ensuing discussion of the film. How could they, with the company's fiscal director himself in the room? The professional lens of the educational program justifies the participation of practitioners – who would find criticizing their institution from within difficult – and strongly promotes technical learning, especially of the law. In the process, it contributes to overshadowing the political issues intrinsic to the instruments by focusing on mastering their operation and the constitution of a social capital in the milieu of reference. Significantly, as the lawyer-instructor of the Corporate Group Strategies class put it, it is by adopting technical measures (such as limiting the authorized level of debt for financing an operation) that the observed problems are resolved. In short, far from criticizing the core of capitalism, these examples are focused on a few of its excesses, either individual (hoodlum bosses) or technical (prudential rules). In describing HEC as a school "without ethics but that imposes none," one professor[53] reflects our perceptions based on observing classes: law does not justify the high-finance economy, it is merely presented as a technique that is useful to it. It is this lack of an alternative ethic that makes this knowledge so adaptable to the dominant ideology.

The situation at Sciences Po is more ambiguous, because the professor considers critique to be an integral part of his teaching,[54] whether in reference to legal realism or critical legal studies. In his discourse, the pragmatism of handling the law in the service of economic interests coincides with its objectification in critiques from the social sciences and humanities. Indeed, in both cases, law appears to be both the object and the stake of endlessly renegotiated power relationships. This association between the promotion of the dogmatic approach to law and theoretical critique

program. Interviews with graduates who became lawyers indicate that they are heirs (children of jurists or members of other professions) and children of the cultivated middle classes (or, more rarely, of the working-class strata) who are particularly drawn by the "intellectual" image of law (relative to other specializations at HEC).

52 Although they are clearly in the minority, other HEC professors do engage in critical analyses of capitalism.

53 This conversation took place October 21, 2009.

54 This dimension is not entirely absent at HEC since the creation of the "Alternative management" program.

allows the instructor to reconcile economic utilitarianism and academic reflexivity. Critique of the dogmatic approach is thus made in the name of two kinds of realism, one utilitarian and practice-based and another intellectual, in relation to this current of legal analysis in North America.[55] To analyze this posture we must return to the differentiated place of critique in France, where it is made more at the margins of the university, and in the United States (which Sciences Po claims as its model), where it reached the hallways of the most prestigious universities in the 1980s (Unger 1986), as Duncan Kennedy (1982) attests.[56] We will content ourselves here with wondering if it is really possible for Sciences Po students to appropriate their instructor's heterodox vision in the 20 densely packed course hours allotted to its teaching. This vision seems to more closely match that of the Doctoral program, which pursues purely academic objectives.

Conclusion

Through the knowledge passed along and interactions with the faculty, law courses are instances of secondary socialization in the sense that they are host to "the internalization of institutional 'sub-worlds'" through which students are said to acquire "knowledge [related to their future role] in the division of labor" (Martuccelli 2003, 189). As Mertz emphasizes, this socialization includes a process of normative acculturation, in this case to capitalist ideology, through the intermediary of economic law and the figure of the business lawyer. Ethnographic observation is an especially useful method for grasping these various dimensions of legal training.

In our research on the education of elites in law, this method was the indispensable supplement to the formal comparison between institutions of higher learning. Limiting oneself to classroom observations, necessarily reduced relative to all the courses offered by a given institution, would run the risk of excessive generalization. However, when put in connection with the other resources of our research (primarily interviews and documentary research), instructors' practices make sense in relation to broader institutional positions, student recruitment practices, and representations of career opportunities. Opening the black box of the classroom to study what instructors are teaching, both with and alongside legal knowledge, allows us to identify similarities between programs, resemblances that are sometimes obscured by the strategies of distinction between institutions. This method particularly highlights the challenges in reconciling pedagogical innovation with being embedded in a national framework for professional training that greatly limits the leeway available to instructors. Additionally, more so than in the formal curricula, the purely ideological dimension of the conveyed knowledge is perceptible in anecdotes of experiences, minor ordinary occurrences, and other tales of client relations. These elements are

55 The history of legal realism has clearly shown how Holmes (the founder of legal realism) was directly exposed to pragmatic philosophy at Harvard University through regular contact with Pierce, Dewey, and (especially) James.

56 In the intervening years, to be sure, Critical Legal Studies has receded under pressure from other movements in U.S. academic law.

scattered throughout the courses and they reveal how much the law in action can, and sometimes must, distance itself from law in books.

In the specific case of business law, the tacit image conveyed is that of law in the service of a company that takes shape over the course of instruction. This occurs in classes that are otherwise differently situated and whose students have different occupational trajectories. Across these differences, students learn that law is a medium for business strategy, one become mundane because it is reduced to the rank of one technique among many – but one that nonetheless is quietly indispensable to juridicalized capitalism.

References

Abraham, Yves-Marie. 2007. Du souci scolaire au sérieux managérial, ou comment devenir un "HEC". *Revue Française de Sociologie* 48(1): 42–66.

Beaud, Stéphane, and Bernard Convert, eds. 2010. Les classes populaires dans l'enseignement supérieur. Politiques, stratégies, inégalités . *Actes de la recherche en sciences sociales* 183(3).

Beaud, Stéphane, and Florence Weber. 2003. *Guide de l'enquête de terrain*, 3rd ed. Paris: La Découverte.

Becker, Howard S., Blanche Geer, Everett C. Hughes, and Anselme L. Strauss. 1961. *Boys in White: Student Culture in Medical School.* Chicago: University of Chicago Press.

Béliard, Aude, and Émilie Biland. 2008. Enquêter à partir de dossiers personnels. Une ethnographie des relations entre institutions et individus. *Genèses, Sciences sociales et histoire* 70(1): 106–119.

Bellier, Irène. 1993. *L'ENA comme si vous y étiez.* Paris: Seuil.

Biland, Émilie. 2013. Quand les managers mettent la robe. La participation prudente des écoles de commerce à la formation des avocats d'affaires. *Droit et société* 83: 49–65.

Boigeol, Anne, and Yves Dezalay. 1997. De l'agent d'affaires au Barreau: les conseils juridiques et la construction d'un espace professionnel. *Genèses. Sciences sociales et histoire* 27: 49–68.

Boltanski, Luc. 1973. L'espace positionnel. Multiplicité des positions institutionnelles et habitus de classe. *Revue française de sociologie* 14(1): 3–26.

Boltanski, Luc, and Ève Chiapello. 2005 [1999]. *The New Spirit of Capitalism*, translated by Gregory Elliott. New York: Verso.

Boltanski, Luc, and Laurent Thévenot. 2006 [1991]. *On Justification: Economies of Worth*, translated by Catherine Porter. Princeton, NJ: Princeton University Press.

Bonnéry, Stéphane. 2007. *Comprendre l'échec scolaire. Élèves en difficultés et dispositifs pédagogiques.* Paris: La Dispute.

Bourdieu, Pierre. 1998 [1989]. *The State Nobility: Elite Schools in the Field of Power*, translated by L. Clough. Stanford, CA: Stanford University Press.

Bourdieu, Pierre, and Jean-Claude Passeron. 1970. *La reproduction. Éléments pour une théorie du système d'enseignement.* Paris: Éditions de Minuit.

Burns, Stacey. 1997. Practicing Law: A Study of Pedagogic Interchange in a Law School Classroom. In *Law In Action: Ethnomethodological and Conversation Analytic Approaches to Law*, ed. Max Travers and John F. Manzo, 265–287. Aldershot: Ashgate/Dartmouth.

Commaille, Jacques, and Patrice Duran. 2009. Pour une sociologie politique du droit: Présentation. *L'Année sociologique* 59(1): 11–28.

Deauvieau, Jérôme. 2007. Observer et comprendre les pratiques enseignantes. *Sociologie du travail* 49(1): 100–118.

Décret no 2008–420 du 29 avril 2008 portant création du Conseil national du droit, J.O. 2 mai 2008, texte 19, art. 2; Conseil national du droit. www.conseilnationaldudroit.fr (accessed March 8, 2011).

Derouet, Jean-Louis, Agnès Henriot-Van Zanten, and Régine Sirota. 1987. Approches ethnographiques en sociologie de l'éducation: l'école et la communauté, l'établissement scolaire, la classe. *Revue française de pédagogie* 80: 73–108.

Dezalay, Yves. 1992. *Marchands de droit. La restructuration de l'ordre juridique international par les multinationales du droit.* Paris: Fayard.

di Rosa, Antonio. 2010. L'enseignement du droit. Un modèle en équilibre (précaire) entre théorie et pratique. *Jurisprudence. Revue critique* 1(1): 241–259.

Ewick, Patricia, and Susan S. Silbey. 1998. *The Common Place of Law: Stories from Everyday Life.* Chicago, IL: University of Chicago Press.

Eymeri, Jean-Michel. 2001. *La fabrique des énarques.* Paris: Economica.

Forquin, Jean-Claude. 1983. La "nouvelle sociologie de l'éducation" en Grande-Bretagne: orientations, apports théoriques, évolution (1970–1980). *Revue française de pédagogie* 63: 61–79.

Foucault, Michel. 1995 [1975]. *Discipline and Punish: The Birth of the Prison*, translated by Alan Sheridan. New York: Vintage Books.

Garrigou, Alain. 2001. *Les élites contre la République. Sciences Po et l'ENA.* Paris: La Découverte.

Gervais, Julie. 2007. *La réforme des cadres de l'action publique ou la fabrique d'un 'nouveau' corps des Ponts et Chaussées. Impératifs managériaux, logiques administratives et stratégies corporatistes (fin du 20e siècle).* Doctoral dissertation, Institut d'études politiques de Lyon, Université Lumière Lyon 2.

HEC Paris. Admission sur classes préparatoires. www.hec.fr/Grande-Ecole/Admissions/Admission-sur-classespreparatoires (accessed February 18, 2011).

Héry, Évelyne. 2007. *Les pratiques pédagogiques dans l'enseignement secondaire au 20e siècle.* Paris: L'Harmattan.

Ihl, Olivier, Martine Kaluszynski, and Gilles Pollet. 2003. *Les sciences de gouvernement.* Paris: Economica.

Israël, Liora. 2008. Question(s) de méthodes. Se saisir du droit en sociologue. *Droit et Société* 2008(69–70): 381–395.

Jamin, Christophe. 2010. L'enseignement du droit à Sciences Po: autour de la polémique suscitée par l'arrêté du 21 mars 2007. *Jurisprudence. Revue Critique* 1(1): 125–136.

Johnson, Eric E. 2010. A Populist Manifesto for Learning the Law. *Journal of Legal Education* 60(1): 41–64.

Kennedy, Duncan. 1982. Legal Education and the Reproduction of Hierarchy. *Journal of Legal Education* 32: 591–615.

Lambert, Anne. 2010. Le comblement inachevé des écarts sociaux. Trajectoire scolaire et devenir professionnel des élèves boursiers d'HEC et de l'ESSEC. *Actes de la recherche en sciences sociales* 183(3): 106–124.

Lenglart, François et al. 1994. Droit et fiscalité, une discipline de management. In *L'École des managers de demain, Les professeurs du groupe HEC*, 179–186. Paris: Economica.

Martuccelli, Danilo. 2003. Introduction. In *La construction sociale de la réalité*, ed. Peter L. Berger and Thomas Luckmann, 5–40. Paris: Armand Colin.

Merleau, Marc. 1981. *Histoire d'une grande école. HEC 1881–1981.* Paris: Dunod.

Mertz, Elizabeth. 2007. *The Language of Law School: Learning to "Think like a Lawyer".* New York: Oxford University Press.

Musgrove, F.W. 1968. The Contribution of Sociology to the Study of Curriculum. In *Changing the Curriculum*, ed. J.F. Kerr, 96–106. London: University of London Press.

Myriam, Aït-Aoudia. 2013. Le droit dans la concurrence. Mobilisations universitaires contre la création de diplômes de droit à Sciences Po Paris. *Droit et société* 1(83): 99–116.

Oger, Claire. 2008. *Le façonnage des élites de la République. Culture générale et haute fonction publique.* Paris: Presses de Sciences Po.

SciencesPo Ecole de Droit. Master Droit économique. www.sciencespo.fr/ecole-de-droit/fr/content/master-droit-economique (accessed July 21, 2017).

Unger, Roberto Mangabeira. 1986. *The Critical Legal Studies Movement.* Cambridge, MA: Harvard University Press.

Vanneuville, Rachel. 2008. Sécuriser le droit pour mieux gouverner les conduites: les enjeux sociopolitiques de la promotion contemporaine de la sécurité juridique. *Revue Gouvernance* 5(2). doi:10.7202/1039101ar

Vanneuville, Rachel. 2013. La formation contemporaine des avocats: aiguillon d'une recomposition de l'enseignement du droit en France? *Droit et société* 1(83): 67–82.

Wagner, Anne-Catherine. 2007. *Les classes sociales dans la mondialisation.* Paris: La Découverte.

Weber, Max. 2001 [1930]. *The Protestant Ethic and the Spirit of Capitalism*, translated by Talcott Parsons. London: Routledge.

Part II

Class and Market in Legal Education

4 Legal Training as Socialization to State Power

An Ethnography of Law Classes for French Senior Civil Servants

Rachel Vanneuville

What legal training do French senior civil servants receive and how does this socialize them into exercising state power? This specific subject, linking law and state, is part of French history, marked by the importance of the place occupied by law in the construction and legitimization of a highly centralized state (Genet 1990). This central role has resulted in the affirmation of law as both a tool and a form of knowledge for government, notably with the development of a law guaranteeing and justifying the specific status of the state (administrative law, distinct from private law). Correlatively, this centrality of law has also made law faculties important in the training of civil servants. The historical primacy of these faculties in training for the highest administrative posts was, however, superseded at the end of the nineteenth century (Gatti-Montain 1987), and especially after the Second World War with the establishment of the *École Nationale d'Administration* (*ENA*, National School of Administration) in 1945. The creation of the school aimed to standardize and democratize senior civil service training, and to give "the sense of the state" to the students thus trained (Gaillard 1995) (Box 4.1). This conception of the training was based on a desire to create distance between the teaching of civil servants and training done by law faculties, which were judged too narrow and too theoretical. Since its creation, the *ENA* has thus proposed a series of classes designed to train "generalist" civil servants (law, economics, international relations, etc.), classes associated with periods of internships in administration and in companies, representing around half the course (now lasting two years). The teaching is provided by practitioners, most often senior civil servants themselves.

Box 4.1 The ENA: Training Students to State Power

The *ENA* is a selective post-graduate program, open to graduates and, to a smaller extent, to middle-ranked civil servants. It welcomes roughly 100 students each year. Despite its founders' wish to democratize administrative recruitment, the portion of students belonging to upper-middle and upper classes has always been high (about 70% between 2005 and 2014) (Rouban 2014). Most of them studied in Parisian universities (especially Sciences Po Paris, renowned as a gateway to the power elite) before entering the *ENA*.

Énarques – aka *ENA* alumni – staff key public institutions: they dominate in the *grands corps* (prestigious administrative bodies like the *Conseil d'État, Cour des Comptes, Inspection des Finances*: Council of State, Court of Auditors, General Inspectorate of Finance) and they often lead ministers' offices as well as administrative departments. More and more alumni work in business affairs as senior managers.

The *ENA* thus contributes to the reproduction of the "state nobility" (Bourdieu 1996).

Congruous with the legal-rational conception of the state, law classes dominated the *ENA*'s curriculum when it was created, contributing to making legal capital the bureaucratic capital *par excellence* (Bourdieu 1996). However, from the 1960s onwards, the primacy of law was reconsidered, notably to the benefit of economic knowledge (Biland and Kolopp 2013). This transformation was linked to the process of managerial reform of the French state and the concomitant promotion of economic knowledge as state knowledge (Dulong 1997). This sheds light on the specific place of the *ENA* in the landscape of French higher education: a breeding ground for the "state nobility" (Bourdieu 1996), the *ENA* contributes to defining legitimate skills to access positions of power, by accrediting and diffusing the knowledge and tools judged useful to governance. It is consequently the target of state reform groups and involved in conflicts relating to the knowledge with which the state elites must be equipped. In this capacity, the *ENA* constitutes a privileged observatory to investigate the place of law as government knowledge. As many studies have demonstrated (Dezalay and Garth 2002; Georgakakis and de Lassalle 2008), challenges to law and lawyers in the field of state power are common in numerous countries. However, law is still taught at the *ENA* and remains valued knowledge in the training of senior civil servants. But what type of knowledge is it? Or more precisely: what comprises the law classes delivered to current students? From which visions of law and its uses are they formed? How does this inform us about the role of law and lawyers in the regulation of the contemporary state? This chapter proposes to respond to these questions.

This inquiry into the *ENA* is part of joint research focusing on the legal training delivered to French elites since 1958.[1] It highlights the nature of this training and its changes over the last 50 years in order to question the transformations of the place and the role of law as a tool and core form of knowledge of government. Previous research had left an odd void. On the one hand, despite the importance of law in the construction and legitimization of the French state and, more broadly, in the regulation of French society, few academic studies exist on the legal training of the power elites, whether they operate in the economic or state sectors.[2] In terms of the *ENA*, although the training of civil servants in law has been the subject of several publications (Conseil d'État 1988; Revue administrative 1996), these accounts are derived from actors who are themselves engaged

1 Entitled: "Legal training of elites from the public and private sectors since 1958" the research project was funded by the *Agence Nationale de la Recherche* from 2009 to 2012.

2 More broadly, legal training in France has not been the subject of many studies.

in legal training (senior civil servants, lawyers, etc.). On the other hand, although there is a large selection of studies on what in France are called "elite schools" (selective schools that bring together students from the most privileged social categories and that train for economic, administrative and cultural positions of power), they show little interest in the actual content of the training. As to the *ENA*, previous studies inform us about the genesis of the school (Gaillard 1995), the sociology of its students and teachers (Eymeri 2001), and the nature and modalities of the socialization that occurs there (Eymeri 2001; Oger 2008). Yet, not including some recent exceptions (Biland and Kolopp 2013; Kolopp 2013), they remain reserved about the content of the training (as, for example, the way in which it prepares civil servants to practice their profession). In other words, there is a lack of knowledge of the "cognitive equipment" (Biland and Kolopp 2013) of the elites, whichever type they may be. The joint research project of which this chapter is a part thus sought to shed light on this unexplored area by investigating the legal training in several elite schools, including the *ENA*.

Conducted with Émilie Biland, this inquiry into the *ENA* included archival work; interviews with heads of the training, professors and students; and in-class observations. This chapter is primarily based on the material from the latter source, drawing centrally on approaches from two research fields. On the one hand, it borrows from work on the sociology of curriculum (Margolis et al. 2001) demonstrating that, beyond the formally prescribed knowledge and its content, classrooms are places of – implicit or explicit – transmission of know-how and values. This chapter more specifically considers classrooms as places of "anticipatory socialization" where one acquires "values and orientations found in statuses and groups in which one is not yet engaged but which one is likely to enter" (Merton 1968, 438). On the other hand, in line with works on sociology of law, it also considers the political dimension of law by conceiving it as a vehicle for particular visions of the world (Bourdieu 1987; Mertz 2007). Given the importance, in the French tradition, of the construction of law as the language of the state, the legal teaching at the *ENA* can thus be envisaged as a form of "socialization" to the state. Law, especially public law, conveys a set of representations of the relationships between state and civil society, state and market, all while defining the modes and boundaries of legitimate public action (Chevallier 1979). By observing law classes at the *ENA*, then, our objective was to bring to light the frameworks of perception and action in which the future senior civil servants are trained.

In the first section, I will specify the nature of the legal training delivered at the *ENA* and the political stakes linked to it, and detail the material on which the chapter is based. The second section will demonstrate how contemporary law classes contribute both to socializing students into their civil service role, and to establishing a Weberian conception of the state. But, as will be explained in the third section, the classes also encourage students to "play" with law and to adopt an instrumental relationship with it, feeding a managerial vision of the state. Although the double orientation of this education reflects battles over the role of law and lawyers in the state, it is also part of the transformations of legal teaching in France, which tend to bring about a vision of law distancing itself from the positivist conception[3] that has been dominant up until now.

The Political Stakes of Legal Teaching

The historical work that we conducted on the *ENA* enabled us to reconstitute the transformations of legal training from its beginning and to highlight the conflicts about it. Without returning in detail to this history (see Biland and Vanneuville 2012), it is important to point out its salient features as they illustrate the stakes of today's legal training.

Law at the ENA*: A Historical Glance*

When the *ENA* was founded, learning about law was considered self-evident and permeated the entire curriculum, rather than having its own separate space. Law teaching was monopolized by the members of the Council of State, who also occupied positions of responsibility within the school (chairmanship of the board of directors, management of the school). The Council of State is the highest French administrative court: born in 1799, it is considered to be the creator and guardian of administrative law. It is also one of the *grand corps*, in other words, one of the most prestigious organs of the administration (Box 4.2).

Box 4.2 The Council of State as a Core Institution of the French State

The council has two major prerogatives: as a judge, it controls the legality of administrative acts. As such it sets up and organizes public law. Through its counseling function, it also advises the executive branch on the preparation of bills, ordinances and many decrees, thus participating in, and controlling, their drafting, and helping to ensure the legality of administrative action.

In addition to these official functions, the council is also a breeding ground for high administrative positions. Through a variety of legal procedures, members of the council head administrative departments, act as directors of legal services or join ministers' personal staff. This has fed the continuous presence of Councillors of State in key positions in government.

From the middle of the 1960s, however, this supremacy of law and lawyers at the *ENA* was brought into question. The contestation was supported within the

3 According to Garcia-Villegas (2006, 351): "The main characteristics of [the French conception of law] are the reduction of the notion of law to written official law; the belief in law as a complete and coherent system of positive norms that in most cases must not be interpreted; confidence on deductive reasoning as the best – if not the only – method for the application of law; and the conviction in the neutrality of [law]."

school by those upholding the primacy of economic knowledge – and who, at the same time, worked to promote the managerial reforms of the state. This "managerial nebula" (Bezes 2009, 194) was very critical regarding law and the Council of State, accusing them of inhibiting the development of the "modernization" of the state. For these critics, law was a factor of rigidity in addition to rendering, through its complexity, the administration opaque. At the *ENA*, the curriculum then opened itself up to economic and managerial subjects, to the detriment of legal subjects. The members of the Council of State also lost the management of the school at the end of the 1970s. To respond to the critics, internal and external to the school, the Council of State initiated a "strategy of relegitimization" (Lochak 1993, 14). At the *ENA*, this translated into the setting up of a new class in 1977, designed to teach the drafting of legal texts.[4] Attention must be paid to this class as it became emblematic of legal training at the *ENA*. To what extent could the creation of a legal drafting class respond to the criticisms leveled at law?

The idea presiding over the creation of this class was twofold. On one hand, learning to draft the law requires knowledge of the central legal principles: it is thus a means to ensure that students would have at least a minimum level of legal knowledge. Indeed, it was, according to the assessments conducted by the Council of State during the 1970s (Conseil d'État, 1976–77), partially because civil servants lacked legal knowledge that law was of poor quality. In fact, at the *ENA*, while up until the 1960s most students were law graduates (around 60% of the cohorts), this then greatly diminished (around 30% in the 1970s, less than 20% from the early 2000s). On the other hand, and more importantly, legal drafting in a clear and legally sound manner was thought to be the way to make law into a factor of administrative "efficiency" and "rapidity," according to the terms employed by a Councilor of State (Revue *f*rançaise d'*a*dministration *p*ublique 1989, 29). "When legal texts, and principles are clear," explained the same councilor, "the application is easy" (*ibid.*). As expressions of administrative language and style, legal texts then became a medium for the rehabilitation of the role of law in the state *via* the attention paid to the teaching of their "good" drafting at the *ENA*. By improving the formal quality of texts, the members of the Council of State could demonstrate that law was able to participate in the "modernization" of the state. In doing this, they were also striving to conserve the power of their own institution within the state. From the 1980s onwards, the Council of State effectively renewed its role by highlighting its function of legal advisor to the government, especially with regards to legal texts, the drafting of which it is its duty to control. From the 1970s onwards, the council members initiated a series of actions designed to valorize the importance of the good drafting of texts in the administration and also to establish their control (production of circulars on the rules of drafting texts from the middle of the 1970s; publication of manuals in the 1990s and early 2000s; creation in different ministries of services dedicated to the quality of regulation in the early 2000s). In this sense, the roll-out of legal drafting classes at the *ENA* constituted one of the supports to the extension of

4 In France, we can indeed take seriously that it is civil servants that write the law (Chevallier 2011).

the advisory function of the Council of State: this class institutionalized the importance of legal drafting in the school training for state power.

With that much at stake – maintaining the importance of law and lawyers at the heart of the state – the legal drafting class, renamed "legistics" in the very early 2000s, is today presented as the heart of legal teaching at the *ENA*, as explained in an interview with the Councilor of State responsible for legal training:

> It is something that the ENA is the only one to do, being as it is a teaching centered on legal drafting, legistics as they call it … and that, it is taught nowhere else but in the ENA […] It fits perfectly with the school, both because you can't learn it elsewhere and because it is essential learning: whatever position you will further occupy, one day or another, any ENA student will be confronted to the drafting of a text.

For these reasons, this chapter first and foremost centers on legistics classes.

Observing Law Classes at the ENA *Today*

During our fieldwork, the teaching of legistics was divided into (1) framework lectures on public law which set out the major principles by which law is ranked and organized (the hierarchy of norms, the different categories of legal norms and their specificities); (2) legal drafting methodology lectures; and (3) lectures correcting legistics exercises. There were also other law classes: for example, general lectures on European Union law, followed by a drafting exercise transposing European directives into French national law; and classes on the law of territorial authorities (founded on two case studies, these classes combined a framework lecture on each case study, illustrating the main legal principles involved in the case; and simulation exercises in the form of role-plays, in which the students had to propose a legal solution to an administrative problem). Added to these classes was an "in-depth law elective" that consisted of drafting an administrative report on a given topic ("administration and freedoms" at the time of our study), which occurred in small groups of four students. Almost all teaching positions were filled by members of the Council of State (14 out of 16 in 2009–2010), mostly men (three women only).

The material on which this chapter is based is composed of observations that we made from March to December 2010: three (of four) legistics methodology lectures, three (of seven) framework lectures on public law and three lectures correcting legistics exercises. Added to these are the observations from a framework lecture on public procurement and from two "role-play" lectures linked to this same theme, together with the launch day of the "in-depth law elective." We were not able to attend classes on European law, which had already been delivered before our arrival in the field. In total, we observed 27 hours of classes. The courses were transcribed as extensively as possible, by including the participation of students, their behaviors and those of their professor, the interactions between students and professors. Before and after the classes, we also paid attention to students' discussions regarding the class and, when possible, conducted informal interviews with the students and professors. To the 18 informal interviews with the professors were added formal interviews with the heads of studies, the Councilor of State in charge of coordinating legal teaching, as well as a former legistics professor.

Our method and the brevity of the observation period did not allow us to investigate the effective socialization of the students, that is, the way in which the classes influenced them. They did enable us, though, to gain access to the visions of the state, of the role of civil servants, of the exercise of power, which are transmitted through the legal discourse of the professors.

The Drafting of Law as a Discipline

"We are going to have four sessions together this year on legistics, which consist in teaching you a craft," announced the professor during the introduction to the first class of methodology. "It is not only at the Council of State [...] that we draft legal texts, it is all the time," he continued. In saying this, the professor reminded the students that legal drafting is a constituent of the activities of all civil servants and that this is so because law is the language *par excellence* of the state. That which is transmitted in these classes can be analyzed on two levels: the necessary steps to learn this language, in which the expected qualities of a "good" civil servant are visible; and the rules of legal drafting, which are a vehicle for representations of what a "good" administration should be.

Disciplining Spirits

The language of law is foreign to many students, as can be seen in their frequent amazement when confronted with legal formulations:

PROFESSOR: (lecture correcting legistics exercises): Page 10, Article 2 ... (*Interrupts the exercise to address a student*) ... you seem stunned by this article!

STUDENT: Honestly, when reading things like: "program composed of an ordered sequence of shows comprising images and sounds" [to describe a televised program], it is rather grandiose! (*Laughs*)

PROFESSOR: [...] Communication law is written like that. It is written in a somewhat counter-intuitive, a somewhat absurd manner, and it is important to try and understand what is being said behind all that. The difficulty of the dossier, is to translate into French (*emphasized by the professor*) what is written here in law (*emphasized by the professor*). Unfortunately (*smiling while saying it*), whatever your future profession, you will have to put up with these texts, because they are written like that! The idea is to become familiar with them, to try and understand them. We are going to make an effort.The phrase "to make an effort" straightaway indicates that, in the methodology classes, learning this form of drafting is presented as tedious: "You should see it as a game, really, you have to see it as a game, well, not literally, it is not really fun," said the professor. The legistics classes seem to derive from a formal school model. This model implies that "the learning has to be somewhat 'laborious', that it does not occur spontaneously but at the price of dedication and effort" (Maulini and Perrenoud 2005, 151). Through the rigor and precision that it demands, this learning is indeed laborious: the professors teach the terminology and standard conjunctions, how to count the paragraphs of a text, reminding students of the necessity of correctly placing commas and words, indicating turns of phrase to be avoided:

PROFESSOR: (lecture correcting legistics exercises): We use passive formulas to say what is happening: "is inserted," "is integrated." There were at least two examples where students used the infinitive: "must insert." (*A series of "what?" ironically bursts out in the classroom.*) It's not catastrophic, it is a language like any other, there are rules, you just have to learn them.The writing of law resembles a "discipline" (Foucault 1977), insomuch as it is composed of a series of methods, rules and definitions, of techniques which mean that one is not in the "truth" unless obeying a "discursive police" (Foucault 1977, 37):

A text that does not come easily is a text that is legally problematic. So you will quickly know if you are in hot water when you are drafting it. If what you are drafting does not stick, that means that there is a problem,

declared the methodology professor. It is only by acquiring automatic thinking that the students will succeed in drafting within the rules: as is repeated in the methodology classes, it is necessary to "learn by heart" the formulas, to acquire the "mechanisms" of reading and drafting, and the "reflexes" of reasoning. The questions to ask before drafting are always "like the 'who, what, when, where' when you were young," again said the professor. Furthermore, the latter incarnated these interiorized rules when, several times, he evoked that, to justify a drafting proposition, he did it according to "feeling," "to instinct." In an interview, he explained that the power to "sense things" is necessary for the senior civil servants who often work under pressure. While the *ENA* "was not conceived as a place of transmission of the knowledge, [...] deemed acquired" (Eymeri 2001, 122), the legistics classes were, however, developed according to a classical model of knowledge transmission. The academic character of the teaching is also reflected both in the exercises given to the students, such as the fill-in-the-blanks texts that they must complete, as well as in the very form in which the classes are given: the methodology classes, like most of the exercise-correction sessions, take place in lecture halls welcoming more than 150 people, with poor acoustics, making interactions between students and professors difficult (the smaller classrooms, with a capacity of around 30 students, are also used as lecture halls). This arrangement encourages lecture-style (*cours magistral*) teaching, where the professor imparts his/her knowledge according to an academic and formal model (Macherey 2011). While the methodology professor made an effort to liven up his discourse (by being humorous), all the other professors adopted more of a monotonous tone, which made their quite technical classes even more dry. Exchanges with the students serve mostly as an opportunity for professors to ask questions of comprehension or guidance in reading the documents distributed ("What are you looking for in the dossier?"; "What can you take from this definition?"). The students are thus required to be attentive and studious, which also applies to the posture that they must adopt while drafting a legal text. Evoking the "intellectual approach" that presides over drafting texts, the methodology professor recalled the first question to ask: "What is expected of me?" Indeed, it is always to "respond to a command," which requires the civil servant to share the concerns of the commander and to assume the "identity" of the ministry or service in which he/she presides.[5] The students, however, have a rather distanced relationship with this pedagogical form: they do not hesitate to leave and return to class, they take few notes, those with laptop computers surf the internet, organize their files … . Although this description of the students might lead to the hypothesis that the discipline linked to the drafting of texts is differently assimilated, it must be noted, however, that most of them at least "comply" just by attending the class (while absenteeism is frequent, as one of the heads of studies indicated to us) and by completing the required exercises. Legistics indeed counts for the final ranking,[6] evaluation being part of the formal school model of these classes (Maulini and Perrenoud 2005).

Although the mastery of legal language attests to the possession of specific knowledge contributing to establishing the legitimacy of civil servants (Weber 1995, 292–293), it also reflects the possession of a specific ethos. Learning to draft laws requires a set of qualities: it demands precision, rigor, technique, and is based on the respect of specific language forms. All of these qualities draw the portrait of a conscientious, formalistic, conformist bureaucrat. The professors themselves, with reserved manners, dressed in dark suits and ties, or strict outfits for the women, personify the respect of good manners, the rigorous and lackluster posture required of the future civil servants (Eymeri 2001).

The Rules of Drafting: The Good Forms of the State

By learning to draft law, the students also learn what the state is and the specific position that they occupy within it. The classes of legistics consist of learning how to conform drafting to the rules and procedures defined by law. Among these rules, respect for the hierarchy is the predominant principle. The hierarchy of norms is the subject of the framework lecture delivered before the methodological sessions: understanding it is defined as fundamental, as it is necessary to know where to position the text to be drafted or modified, and how to draft it. A series of drafting prescriptions incessantly recall the strong interconnection between legal drafting and the bureaucratic pyramid. This is the case for the

5 The classes of legistics form part of the "memorandum model" repeated by the students, of which Jean-Michel Eymeri demonstrated the socializing force (Eymeri 2001, 138): "Always 'context-setting'–'You are the director of the cabinet of the prefect of …', 'Technical Advisor, the minister asks you to …' – accompanied by a dossier of 50 to 80 pages composed of diverse documents of which one must 'make a summary' in the form of a several-page memorandum 'for the attention of the' hierarchic supervisor, supposed to propose a solution." This exercise contributes to the production of "conformist, docile, policed" individuals (Eymeri 2001, 147).

6 At the end of their studies, the students are ranked according to their grades, and choose their posting depending on their place in the ranking.

drafting of text titles, to be adjusted depending on their normative stature – "The higher the text in the hierarchy of norms, the more the title will have a general and formal scope. The lower you descend, the more technical you are"; the numbering of legal articles – Roman numerals must be used for the first subdivisions of articles to indicate that there is a "conceptual unit"; and even the terminology to adopt when describing the same situation, different according to the stature of the texts – "In a decree by the Prime Minister, the people 'are tasked' with the execution. They are 'responsible' if it is a decree by the President," explained the methodology professor. To a student who asked if the difference in formulation would have repercussions for the people in question, the professor responded in the negative, but he added that "it is not very chic to put, for a decree by the Prime Minister: 'they are responsible' and for a decree by the President: 'they are tasked'."

Legal drafting is thus learning the hierarchical order of the administration and the differential value of the diverse positions within the state, the grandeur being reserved to the highest of them. It is also the learning of an "organic" vision of the state, to refer to Émile Durkheim's work (1996). The students' attention is drawn to the fact that their main contribution to legality will consist of drafting parts of texts, as recalled by the methodology professor:

> You have to be conscious, in the test, that your text will not be an entire draft bill: it will be a series of articles destined to be inserted into a greater draft bill. In real life, it is the same: each administration works on a part and then you have an overall text.

They will also have to redraft existing texts, as the same professor summarized: "We rarely ask you to shake the columns of the temple, we settle for changing the roofing or repainting the facade." The fact of belonging to a collective of legal "do-ers" is thus made clear in the classes, a collective in which each person has a role to play, at the same time emphasizing the historical continuity of the administration that is created through these incessantly reworked texts. This historical depth, and the necessity to preserve it, is also shown in the instructions for manipulating legal language: "For pity's sake, use the intemporal present!"[7] recalled the methodology professor, also specifying that the modifications carried out on a text are not autonomous from the initial text: "We always work in relation to the source text. So pay attention to it." It is also important to consider what has been established and to take care of it: "You are not in the position of a dreamer starting with a clean slate. You know (*emphasized by the professor*) to consider the context." Like law, the administration is a fabric forever being mended (Latour 2009), of which the civil servants are the tireless little hands.

The last salient point of the representation of the state disseminated in the law classes consists of a reminder of the limits of the civil servants' powers. In addition

7 Cf. Bourdieu: "the use of indefinites and of the intemporal present (or the 'juridical future') [is] designed to express the generality or omnitemporality of the rule of law" (1987, 820).

to reoccurring references to Articles 34 and 37 of the Constitution (that define the domains of intervention of the legislative and executive powers), which it is necessary to "know by heart," the future civil servants are also reminded that they must respect the prerogatives of the political actors – "The parliament is sovereign, it can modify your project," stressed the methodology professor – and adopt a posture of political neutrality – "When you modify a text, you are not to prioritize the order of the articles depending on your political priorities," recalled the same professor. Similarly, while correcting an exercise, another professor specified: "I advise you to avoid adverbs and value judgements. Try to remain as neutral, as concise and as precise as possible. Even if you propose a solution, you are not there to judge it." The work of the future civil servants is also restricted by the monitoring to which it will be constantly subjected. The students are thus repeatedly reminded that their texts will be inspected by the Council of State. More generally, the administrative and constitutional judges are omnipresent in the classes through the exposure of their jurisprudence, the professors thus demonstrating the centrality of jurisdictions in the good working order of the state.

All these classes thus contribute to outlining a hierarchical administrative apparatus collectively produced by qualified, methodical civil servants who are neutral and respect the forms. Correct use of legal form ensures its coherence, permanence and legitimacy. "The importance of the rule of law, is something that remains in mind because it is hammered home in the classes," said a student between classes; a rule of law essentially taking the form of the state as protector of rights and individual freedoms, in accordance with the liberal conception that imposed itself from the 1980s onwards (Chevallier 1999). "Alongside the repressive purpose," stressed the methodology professor with regards to sanctions, "it is imperative to think of guarantees and processes. That is what makes the difference between rule of law and authoritarian state." The *ENA* professors produce a vision of the administrative state close to Weber's "legal" type of domination (Weber 1995). As such, the training constitutes one of the resources contributing to adoption of "the common-sense belief in the existence of a clear distinction 'of nature' between the so-called 'political' domain and the so-called 'administrative' domain" (Eymeri 2003, 76).

By drafting the law, the future civil servants are thus tasked with being the guardians of the temple of the state. But their power within the state, and their means of exercising it, are also framed within the learning of law.

Law as a Resource of Power

At the *ENA*, legal teaching is "a somewhat mechanical, technical education," explained the legal training coordinator during an interview. This was echoed by the methodology professor when he compared the rules of drafting to "cooking recipes," or the drafting formulas to a mechanic's "set of wrenches." This "technification" is not unique to legal training: it is part of the instrumentalization of knowledge that developed at the *ENA* from the 1970s onwards, contributing to making the figure of the civil servant "operational": "the knowledge is thought of as an instrument in the service of action and decision-making" (Biland and Kolopp

2013, 243). The instrumental conception of knowledge is also linked to pedagogical innovations put in place in the early 2000s, including the role-plays, which aim to put the students in simulations to resolve a problem. They require, as a professor explained in an interview, not the learning of abstract law but knowledge of how to use legal tools. In other words, ways of manipulating law are also transmitted in the classes. Here the students are invited to "play" with law. They also learn that this game has to fit with efficiency requirements.

Playing with Law: The Power of Knowing How to Translate

Although, as previously demonstrated, the legistics classes teach that the drafting of a text must conform to a series of rules within the legal system, they also invite the students to think about these rules not merely in terms of constraints: respecting the discursive police of legal language, although it restricts the range of possible discourses, also enables one to "formulate, and to indefinitely formulate, new propositions" (Foucault 1977, 32). The rules are thus presented to them rather as a drafting "framework," just as they are constantly reminded during each correction exercise: there is not only one possible solution. In other words, the students are urged to play with the potential offered by these drafting rules. The professors thus show them the room to maneuver that they may have at their disposal, by explaining how, for example, despite the principle of codification on the basis of established law, it is possible to propose a codification amending existing law, and how it is possible to step outside the principle of "congruent forms" (the principle requiring that a text made in a certain form may only be repealed, annulled or amended by respecting the same forms). Although the texts that they must draft are always in response to a request from their hierarchy, the professors show them the possibilities opened by legal drafting, also informing them of the power at their disposal to direct political choices, sometimes expressing this explicitly:

PROFESSOR: (in-depth law elective): Because you are lawyers, practitioners, you are directed towards the action, you are at the interior of the legal system, you are the advisors of a minister who may sometimes modify the texts. Thus, you have the position of the writer of the text, of the legislator. It is the same thing for a judge, who can make law evolve, who is at the interior of the system.Like the judge who writes law in a permanent back-and-forth between cases and texts ("A civil servant must think like a judge," a professor told us at the end of a class), the *énarque*'s power resides in his/her position as a "simultaneous translator" (Eymeri 2003, 56): "Am I able to translate *that* into pertinent, adequate, legal terms that comply with the hierarchy of norms? Here lies the skill, eh!" explained the methodology professor, the "that" referring as much to the political demand to be satisfied as to the social reality concerned. The way in which the political actors are presented, as hardly interested in questions that are "too technical," tends to reassure the students in the feeling of power imparted by their legistics knowledge. "Like the devil is in the detail, it is the texts that make the difference," explained the methodology professor.

The legistics classes thus aim to make the students aware of the fact that their role of legal "scribe" is close to an "effective delegation of power" (Eymeri 2003, 55), linked to this capacity to put into legal form the social world that is at the heart of the symbolic force of law and the power of the state. However, this power conferred by the capacity to manipulate law is also subjected to strong constraints external to law, which tend to "desacralize" it to a certain extent.

A Law that Must Prove Its Worth

Creating the legistics classes at the *ENA* at the end of the 1970s reaffirmed the place of legal language and norms in the administrative sector by demonstrating that law could participate in the managerial reforms of the state. Although attention to the formal dimension of legistics, privileging the correction and legal clarity of the texts, is particularly accentuated in the classes, it is nevertheless combined with attention to the "material" dimension of legistics, highlighting the content and the application of texts (Flückiger 2007a, 14). Behind these two definitions of legistics (formal and material) reside different visions of legitimate modes of action of the state, the first associated with the principle of legality, the second with the principle of efficacy (Flückiger 2007b, 83). A preoccupation with the efficacy of texts has been an integral part of the classes at the *ENA* from the beginning. It stems from a shift in the conception of the effectiveness of law, starting from the principle that legal validity alone cannot ensure obedience (Chevallier 1993). In the 1980s, the preoccupation with efficacy was centered on the conditions for the application of texts and on the sanctions they imposed, two issues that are still stressed in today's classes. On the one hand, the students are taught that, to be effective, the rule must be adapted to social behaviors, which requires that attention be paid to the delays of the application of texts – "It is here that you show that you are pragmatic and you demonstrate your common sense with regards to an economic and concrete reality," explained the methodology professor in relation to the delays to be expected before a text comes into application. On the other hand, the rule must be obeyed, hence the attention paid to the nature of the sanctions accompanying a new legal obligation – "How to put in place a regime of sanctions? It is very important, open your ears," warned the methodology class professor before listing all the questions that must be posed to choose adequate sanctions. Thus defined, the preoccupation with efficacy requires extra-juridical considerations to be included in the making of the texts, but it does not bring into question the intrinsic value of law as a tool of action. Observing contemporary classes tends, however, to indicate that attention to efficacy combines with efficiency requirements, shifting legal drafting into an economic and financial logic.

The students thus learn that the first question that any text drafter "must" ask himself/herself is of the very utility of the text. Such a question implicitly suggests that law can constitute an obstacle to administrative action. Indeed, respecting legal formalism is sometimes described by professors as a burden: knowing the tricks to circumvent burdensome legal requirements demonstrates "that you are sufficiently pragmatic not to set in motion an infernal machine each time," said one professor;

"codifying rights in a new constitutional text would present the disadvantage of rigidity," warned another. In the class on public procurement, the professor explained that "formalism, justified by the preoccupation of moralizing public spending, may to some extent be a source of a certain economic inefficiency by increasing the transaction costs. This formalism may also play out to the expense of competition."

"You are not only required to produce good legal constructions!" said a professor during a correction exercise, after having explained the necessity of considering the political relevance of proposed solutions and not "weighing down" the already existing legal corpus. Although this comment refers to the lawyer's posture of translator previously evoked, the students are nevertheless urged to somewhat think beyond law, to adjust their propositions depending not only on the objectives but also on "cost." The detail that the professor in charge of the public law framework lectures dedicates to impact analysis is indicative of the rise in power of these efficiency requirements assigned to law. Made compulsory by a bill in 2009 for a series of legal texts, the impact analysis measures, *ex ante*, the effects of the new regulation across a range of domains (administrative, social, environmental, economic and financial effects) and their objective is "to balance the costs and benefits in normative production" through the realization of a cost-benefit analysis (Rose-Ackerman and Perroud 2014, 106). Noting that this 2009 bill resulted from the assessment that there were too many laws and that it was necessary to stabilize the rules governing their production, the professor continued by explaining that "the fundamental idea of the impact analysis is eventually to not (*emphasized by the professor*) draft a bill if the impact assessment comes to the conclusion that it is unnecessary or that the analysis is unbalanced." He distributed to the students a memorandum co-authored by the Council of State that had been sent to administrative departments in order to push for the implementation of this procedure. He then insisted on its importance: "The preoccupations of the impact analysis, they are your (*emphasized by the professor*) preoccupations. … The approach of the impact analysis is essentially the approach of good legistics." As two sociologists of law commented, regarding new efficacy requirements for law: "The evaluation of the profitability of the legal system is conducted in a negative way, in other words, by referring to its inability to manage the social reality" (Lascoumes and Serverin 1986, 146). Today, to serve state action, law must not only prove its utility but also its compatibility with contemporary policies seeking to diminish the costs of public action (Bezes 2005).

This orientation in the ways of thinking about law converges with the development of New Public Management principles in the French administration since the early 2000s, which especially encourages the development of methods for calculating the costs of regulation and envisaging the rules in terms of performance (Lasserre 2004). Significantly, the legistics classes are integrated into the "Public Management" module, one of the three modules put in place during the reform of the *ENA* in 2006, and presented as making it into "A school of state reform."[8] Furthermore, although legistics is at the heart of the legal curriculum, the latter also includes

8 "*Présentation générale de la scolarité*" ("General Course Introduction"), brochure given to new students, 2009.

role-play classes where the "purely instrumental" character of law (Lascoumes and Serverin 1986, 146) is promoted. The students are encouraged to choose the legal device necessary for the resolution of a given administrative question (at the time of our observations: the construction of a carpark in a prefecture), each student having a specific administrative role to play (regulation office agent, financial services agent, secretary-general of a prefecture, etc.). It is through conducting a cost-benefit analysis depending on a set of criteria (ease of realization, economic cost, aesthetic quality, litigation risk, etc.) that the students can succeed in identifying the best legal solution. Law then appears subordinate to other interests at play, of which the prioritization will model the adopted legal solution. In this instance, as summarized by one of the professors at the end of the class: "Finance commands law." It is also expected that those assuming the role of lawyer will protect the administration against "litigation risks," an omnipresent expression in role-play classes, and also often mentioned in legistics ones. The use of law is thus tied to accounting concerns: it must prevent the administration from losing money and time by protecting it from litigation. But it is also presented as a tool "like any other" of public decision-making, the value of which is indexed to its performance.

Evoking the transformations of legal rationality under the managerialization of the state, one author thus noted: "A legitimacy founded on the *regularity* of procedures ... is substituted by a legitimacy founded on the *efficiency* of the actions undertaken ... . Law is no more than an *instrument*, that has no value *in itself*, but only depending on the *results* that it obtains; *the efficiency becomes the condition and the guarantee of its legitimacy*" (Chevallier 1993, 128). The law classes at the *ENA* are thus part of, and participants in, this transformation in ways of understanding law, which is closer to an American realist conception under which "law is conceived as a tool dedicated to solve problems and not as an abstract and autonomous system of rules like in the French vision" (Garcia-Villegas 2006, 361). This utilitarian vision of law is even more likely to be assumed by the students, as their academic profile has particularly changed over the last few years. As Rouban (2014) showed, they still mainly graduate from Sciences Po Paris (more than 50% in the last cohorts), but the latter has changed by opening its curriculum to public and private management. Moreover, an increasing proportion of *ENA* students graduate from business schools (21.8% of the class of 2000). This basic training facilitates receptiveness to managerial concerns.

Conclusion: Tensions Surrounding Law

The legal training at the *ENA* is ambivalent. On one hand, law classes are closely linked to a positivist vision of law, which is derived from a belief in its intrinsic force: "We start from the idea that law must be respected and that, even without criminal penalties, people respect law," affirmed a professor. On the other hand, they contribute to "desacralizing" law, by teaching students that law's legitimacy is subject to the demonstration of its social efficiency. This double orientation is part of the reaffirmation of the value of law as a form of state knowledge, by presenting law both as the framework of a state affirming its "rule of law," and as an efficient instrument of the state's own action.

Nevertheless, this ambivalence also reveals tensions surrounding the representation of law, and reflects the battles taking place outside the *ENA*. On one hand, the position of the Council of State as the quality controller of law is at stake. As a specialist of legistics remarked: "Whereas formal legistic is mainly an affair for lawyers, material legistic is by no means an exclusivity of persons with legal training or a field of activity for which lawyers are better prepared than persons having another professional background" (Mader 2001, 121). In fact, the issue of the quality control of law is the subject of battles for appropriation within the French state, as members of economic and financial corps claim to have the monopoly over this control (Hainque and Montin 2011). In this context, valuing the formal dimension of legal drafting is also a means for the members of the Council of State to promote the specificity of their expertise. On the other hand, the defense of French law in the contemporary global competition among legal systems is also reflected in this attachment to the formal characteristics of law. As written by the Councilor of State Catherine Bergeal, legistics professor at the *ENA* at the beginning of the 1990s, France:

> should know how to use the strength of its long experience in legislative drafting – abstraction, brevity, and clarity – in the face of the growing influence of the common law, both in Europe and in states in transition to democracy. Political influence also depends on the language of law and on the way we think about it.
> (Bergeal 2008, 3)

Whatever the outcome of these battles regarding the law, their very existence evidences the common acceptance of the necessity to evaluate the *quality* of law: law as a value in itself is not taken for granted anymore. The watchword of quality has been promoted by both the OECD and the European Union since the 1990s through a set of programs dedicated to improving the quality of regulation (Groulier 2015; Radaelli and Meuwese 2009). As Pollitt and Bouckaert (1995, 3) note in their book on the managerial transformation of European public administration: "'Quality' has become a central term in our contemporary rhetoric. It is scarcely conceivable that anyone would wish to argue against it: like virtue, it seems unopposable," and all the more so that it is an "elusive concept" (*ibid.*, 11). As such, this watchword could be seen as a form of "inchoate power" through which neoliberal policies have been increasing their hold over governments (Herzfeld 2015). Legal training seems to be one of its vehicles.

The transmission of an instrumental vision of law is not specific to the *ENA*: it also characterizes transformations of legal training in other elite schools (Derouet and Thivet 2015; Biland and Israël, this book) and, more broadly, contemporary reforms to legal teaching across France (Israël and Vanneuville 2014). A series of new legal training programs destined for the elites of the private sector have indeed been established since the early 2000s, endeavoring to link law with economics, as a precondition to producing lawyers "of excellence" adapted to an increasingly competitive market for legal services. The promotion of a utilitarian vision of law to students destined to work for the public and private sectors would feed the process of rapprochement between the French administrative and economic elites described by recent scholarship (Denord, Lagneau-Ymonet and Thine 2011). More generally, French transformations of legal training echo the reforms that are occurring in numerous foreign countries (Flood 2011), and confirm that legal teaching is a key issue in the legitimization of the status of law and of lawyers in the regulation of contemporary societies.

References

Bergeal, Catherine. 2008. Avant-propos. *Courrier juridique des finances et de l'industrie, special issue: La légistique. Ou l'art de rédiger le droit.* June: 3–6.

Bezes, Philippe. 2005. Le renouveau du contrôle des bureaucraties. *Informations sociales* 126: 26–37.

Bezes, Philippe. 2009. *Réinventer l'État. Les réformes de l'administration française (1962–2008).* Paris: PUF.

Biland, Émilie, and Sarah Kolopp. 2013. La fabrique de la pensée d'Etat. Luttes d'institutions et arrangements cognitifs à l'ENA (1945–1982). *Gouvernement et action publique* 2(2): 221–248.

Biland, Émilie, and Rachel Vanneuville. 2012. Government Lawyers and the Training of Senior Civil Servants: Maintaining Law at the Heart of the French State. *International Journal of the Legal Profession* 19(1): 29–54.

Bourdieu, Pierre. 1987. The Force of Law: Toward a Sociology of the Juridical Field. *TheHastings Law Journal* 38(5): 805–838.

Bourdieu, Pierre. 1996. *The State Nobility: Elite Schools in the Field of Power.* Stanford, CA: Stanford University Press.

Chevallier, Jacques. 1979. Les fondements idéologiques du droit administratif français. In *Variations autour de l'idéologie de l'intérêt général*, ed. Jacques Chevallier, 3–57. Paris: PUF.

Chevallier, Jacques. 1993. La juridicisation des préceptes managériaux. *Politiques et Management Public* 11(4): 111–134.

Chevallier, Jacques. 1999. *L'Etat de droit.* Paris: Montchrestien.

Chevallier, Jacques. 2011. La place de l'administration dans la production des normes. *Droit et société* 79: 623–636.

Conseil d'Etat. 1976–77. *Modern Management and Public Service* (unpublished).

Conseil d'Etat. 1988. *Rapport sur la formation juridique des fonctionnaires* (unpublished).

Denord, François, Paul Lagneau-Ymonet and Sylvain Thine. 2011. Le champ du pouvoir en France. *Actes de la recherche en sciences sociales* 5(190): 24–57.

Derouet, Antoine, and Delphine Thivet. 2015. L'enseignement juridique comme socialisation à une élite économique: le cas de l'École Centrale. *Cahiers de la Recherche sur l'Education et les Savoirs* 14: 47–67.

Dezalay, Yves, and Bryant Garth, eds. 2002. *Global Prescriptions: The Production, Exportation and Importation of a New Legal Orthodoxy.* Ann Arbor: University of Michigan Press.

Dulong, Delphine. 1997. *Moderniser la politique: Aux origines de la Vème République.* Paris: L'Harmattan.

Durkheim, Emile. 1996 [1893]. *De la division du travail social.* Paris: PUF.

Eymeri, Jean-Michel. 2001. *La fabrique des énarques.* Paris: Economica.

Eymeri, Jean-Michel. 2003. Frontières ou marches? De la contribution de la haute administration à la production du politique. In *La politisation*, ed. Jacques Lagroye, 47–77. Paris: Belin.

Flood, John. 2011. *Legal Education in the Global Context. Challenges from Globalization, Technology and Changes in Government Regulation. University of Westminster School of Law Research Paper* no. 11–16. Legal Services Board. www.legalservicesboard.org.uk/news_publications/latest_news/pdf/lsb_legal_education_report_flood.pdf (accessed May 22, 2019).

Flückiger, Alexandre. 2007a. *Les racines historiques de la légistique en Suisse.* Séminaire Commission Européenne, Université de Genève, October 19. http://ec.europa.eu/dgs/legal_service/seminars/ch_fluckiger.pdf (accessed May 22, 2019).

Flückiger, Alexandre. 2007b. L'évaluation législative ou comment mesurer l'efficacité des Lois. *Revue européenne des sciences sociales* 45(138): 83–101.

Foucault, Michel. 1977. *L'ordre du discours.* Paris: Gallimard.

Gaillard, Jean-Michel. 1995. *L'ENA, miroir de l'État de 1945 à nos jours.* Paris: Complexe.

Garcia-Villegas, Mauricio. 2006. Comparative Sociology of Law: Legal Fields, Legal Scholarships, and Social Sciences in Europe and in the United States. *Law & Social Inquiry* 31(2): 343–382.

Gatti-Montain, Jacqueline. 1987. *Le système d'enseignement du droit en France.* Lyon: Presses Universitaires de Lyon.

Genet, Jean-Pierre, ed. 1990. *L'Etat moderne. Genèse. Bilans et perspectives.* Paris: CNRS.

Georgakakis, Didier, and Marine de Lassalle. 2008. *Where Have All the Lawyers Gone? Structure and Transformations of the Top European Commission Officials' Legal Training, n°38.* EUI-RSCAS Working Papers, European University Institute (EUI), Robert Schuman Centre of Advanced Studies (RSCAS).

Groulier, Cédric. 2015. La "gouvernance réglementaire" de l'OCDE: vers une "globalisation légistique"? *Revue du droit public* 3: 763.

Hainque, Michel, and Jean-Charles Montin. 2011 (May). *Better Regulation in France.* http://regulatoryreform.com/wp-content/uploads/2015/02/Hainque-and-Montin-BETTER-REGULATION-IN-FRANCE-2011.pdf (accessed May 22, 2019).

Herzfeld, Michael. 2015. Anthropology and the Inchoate Intimacies of Power. *American Ethnologist* 42(1): 18–32.

Israël, Liora, and Rachel Vanneuville. 2014. Enquêter sur la formation au droit en France. L'exemple des formations extra-universitaires. *Revue Interdisciplinaire d'Etudes Juridiques* 72(1): 141–162.

Kolopp, Sarah. 2013. De la modernisation à la raison économique. La formation en économie à l'Ena et les déplacements des lieux communs de l'action publique (1945–1984). *Genèses* 4(93): 53–75.

Lascoumes, Pierre, and Evelyne Serverin. 1986. Théories et pratiques de l'effectivité du droit. *Droit et Société* 2: 127–150.

Lasserre, Bruno. 2004. *Pour une meilleure qualité de la réglementation.* Paris: La Documentation française.

Latour, Bruno. 2009. *The Making of Law: An Ethnography of the Conseil d'Etat.* Cambridge: Polity Press.

Lochak, Danièle. 1993. Quelle légitimité pour le juge administratif? In *Le droit administratif en mutation*, Publications du CURAPP, 141–151. Paris: PUF.

Macherey, Pierre. 2011. Le cours magistral (1). http://philolarge.hypotheses.org/1013 (accessed May 22, 2019).

Mader, Lucius. 2001. Evaluating the Effects: A Contribution to the Quality of Legislation. *Statute Law Review* 22(2): 119–131.

Margolis, Eric, Michaël Soldatenko, Sandra Acker and Marina Gair. 2001. Hiding and Outing the Curriculum. In *The Hidden Curriculum in Higher Education*, ed. Eric Margolis, 2–15. New York: Routledge.

Maulini, Olivier, and Philippe Perrenoud. 2005. La forme scolaire et l'éducation de base: tensions internes et évolutions. In *Les formes de l'éducation: variété et variations*, eds. Olivier Maulini and Cléopâtre Montandon, 147–167. Brussels: De Boeck Supérieur.

Merton, Robert. 1968. *Social Theory and Social Structure*. New York: The Free Press.

Mertz, Elizabeth. 2007. *The Language of Law Schools: Learning to "Think Like a Lawyer"*. New York: Oxford University Press.

Oger, Claire. 2008. *Le façonnage des élites de la République. Culture générale et haute fonction publique*. Paris: Les Presses de Sciences Po.

Pollitt, Christopher, and Geert Bouckaert, eds. 1995. *Quality Improvement in European Public Services*. London: Sage.

Radaelli, Claudio M., and Anne Meuwese. 2009. Better Regulation in Europe: Between Public Management and Regulatory Reform. *Public Administration* 87(3): 639–654.

Revue administrative. 1996. *La formation et le recrutement des hauts fonctionnaires en France. Revue administrative*, special issue.

Revue *f*rançaise d'*a*dministration *p*ublique. 1989. *Quelle formation pour les fonctionnaires? Revue française d'administration publique*, special issue, 51.

Rose-Ackerman, Susan, and Thomas Perroud. 2014. Les études d'impact et l'analyse "coûts-avantages": modèles américains et traditions juridiques françaises. *Revue française d'administration publique* 149: 105–122.

Rouban, Luc. 2014. La norme et l'institution: les mutations professionnelles des énarques de 1970 à 2010. *Revue française d'administration publique* 3(151–152): 719–740.

Weber, Max. 1995 [1921-1922]. *Économie et société. 1 Les catégories de la sociologie*. Paris: Pocket.

5 The Perennial (and Stubborn) Challenges of Affordability, Cost, and Access in Legal Education

Stephen Daniels[*]

Introduction

> "caught between a rock and a hard place"
> "there is no answer, no magic bullet, no easy solution"
> "we will continue to muddle through"

These phrases (Kramer 1993, 65) aptly describe the current situation with regard to the challenge of financing legal education. The rock is the tuition students must pay and the debt they must incur to do so. The hard place is the bleak job market into which they graduate, along with the diminishing number of people willing to invest in such an expensive and uncertain opportunity. The problem admits to no clear remedy and perhaps all legal education can hope for is to somehow get by with incremental adjustments – as it has before.

Written a generation ago by John R. Kramer, then dean of Tulane Law School, the phrases remind us that financing legal education is a perennial and stubborn challenge. Kramer was a trenchant and prescient commentator on legal education's financial challenges. The basic issue in his view was the business model underlying the way in which the enterprise operated and how that model became so deeply entrenched. It is the basic issue today as well. Simply, are students willing to borrow higher amounts to pay increasing levels of tuition in light of the jobs and salaries they can expect upon graduation? The model's logic, best described as a value proposition, depends on the answer being yes.

Kramer wasn't so sure of that answer and of the business model's sustainability. He worried about the economist's idea of elasticity – that the demand for law school seats is highly sensitive to the expected value.[1] Writing in a time when law

* Research funded by the American Bar Foundation and by a grant from AccessLex Institute. The American Bar Endowment provides an annual, unrestricted grant to support American Bar Foundation research. The author was the consultant/reporter for the American Bar Association Task Force on the Financing of Legal Education (hereafter ABA Task Force) and would like to acknowledge the Task Force's Chair Dennis Archer and its members. The views expressed are the author's alone.

1 In the late 1980s economist Ronald Ehrenberg argued, "The market for law students 'behaves' in a manner that economists would consider quite rational from the

school enrollments were leveling-off after a long and dramatic increase, he saw a problematic future. What happens when the value – the well-paying lawyer jobs – is no longer there? He, and a few others, thought the jobs may not be there, leaving the value proposition resting only on overly optimistic student perceptions of job opportunities (White 1989, 729). He said, "Research to date has yielded no firm answer to the question of how elastic the demand for legal education is" (Kramer 1987, 240). He thought a reckoning was sure to come and come soon, with the business model itself imploding – but it didn't.

One could argue that legal education has muddled through, with the business model working passably for many years. That is, until enrollments plummeted after 2010 in the wake of the Great Recession.[2] The question today is whether that reckoning has now finally arrived. One member of the recent American Bar Association Task Force on the Financing of Legal Education (ABA Task Force 2015), himself a dean struggling with the same concerns as Kramer, thinks the answer is yes.

Taking a lesson from Kramer, this chapter focuses on that business model. It is divided into three substantive parts. The first two provide an historical context without which today's challenges cannot be fully understood. One looks at financing in post-World War II legal education to understand the business model itself – its development, logic, and how it became so entrenched. The next adds a longitudinal exploration of seldom-analyzed data on key patterns and changes in post-World War II legal education. Specifically, it looks at the number of schools, enrollments, and tuition. These patterns and changes are a key part of the story and today they seem not so well understood or even known. The 1970s into the early 1980s are especially important as the number of schools and enrollments increased dramatically and then leveled off – a dynamic behind Kramer's concerns about the business model's sustainability.

The final part treats the changes in enrollment and job prospects in the wake of the Great Recession as a kind of rough natural experiment for Kramer's concern about the business model and demand elasticity. He saw dire times for legal education, but students continued to come and continued to borrow increasingly to do so – at least until 2010. Post-2010 data on enrollment and employment paint a sobering picture for most of legal education. Only the top schools, where job prospects remained relatively robust, are an exception.

The Value Proposition Business Model: Affordability and Access

Some Context for the Business Model

Financing legal education has always had two sides that can be characterized as a "chicken and egg" relationship (Swords and Walwer 1978, 1881).[3] First and

perspective of the participants." The investment students made was sensible given the job opportunities and salaries (Ehrenberg 1989, 629).

2 For a more optimistic view *see* Simkovic and McIntyre (2014), arguing there is a long-term income benefit for a law degree compared to just an undergraduate degree, even if one graduates into a down job market.

3 *Also see* Swords and Walwer (1974, 265–271, 276–280).

foremost is the need of law schools to fund their operations. The funds can come from a variety of sources. They may come directly from a governmental source or from private sources such as contributions to the school. The funds may come from the tuition and fees a school charges to attendees, especially for private schools.

Regardless, the entire enterprise depends on the student's ability to pay the tuition. As an important, early 1950s ABA special committee noted ominously, the lack of tuition-paying students means a lack of revenue, which threatens the very survival of legal education.[4] This is the second side and the student must be able to pay tuition as well the other costs involved. Writing about the mid-1950s Peter Swords and Frank Walwer found that available funds for both scholarships and loans were limited. Aside from any financial aid, a student's resources consisted of "those provided by the student himself or herself, those provided by the spouse, and those provided by parents" (Swords and Walwer 1974, 282–283).

While legal education as we currently know it is largely a post-World War II phenomenon,[5] two trends that started before the war are particularly important. Each made affordability and access decidedly more problematic. Each helped shape the context for the emergence of the value proposition business model as a way of dealing with the chicken and egg issue.

The first is insidious – the long-term erosion of support for public higher education, including public law schools. Publicly supported higher education providing inexpensive access was far truer in the past than today. For some public law schools, like University of California-Berkeley Boalt Hall and University of California-Hastings Law School in the 1930s, tuition itself was free, although some fees may have been charged (Barnes 1978, 232). In 1933, those fees in nominal dollars were $102 for Berkeley and $100 for Hastings – less than $2,000 in 2018 dollars.[6] The days of low-cost or tuition-free law school, of course, are long gone.[7] For the 2018–19 academic year *in-state* tuition and fees for those two California schools was just north of $49,000.[8]

The second trend involves the long-term efforts of the American Bar Association (ABA) to shape the nature and structure of legal education, especially with regard to part-time legal education and schools not accredited by the ABA (the ABA began formally accrediting law schools in 1923).[9] Part-time legal education was far more available in the deeper past than now and offered a way for students to address the

4 *See* American Bar Association Special Committee of the Conference on Personal Finance Law (1952–53).

5 *See* Stevens (1983, 205–231).

6 Unless otherwise noted, all data on the number of schools, enrollment, tuition, and employment used come from one of two sources: Spinelli's Law Library Reference Shelf (n.d.) or ABA Section of Legal Education and Admissions to the Bar (n.d.).

7 Swords and Walwer (1978, 276–280), for example, reported a 129% increase (in constant dollars) in *in-state* public school tuition between 1955 and 1970; long-term trends in tuition are discussed in Part III.

8 The lowest stated figure for *in-state* tuition and fees in 1933 was the University of Oklahoma at $16 in nominal dollars or $314 in 2018 dollars; the figure for *in-state* tuition and fees for 2018–19 was $20,903.

9 *See* Stevens (1983); *also see* Abel (1989, 40–73).

financing of their legal educations by working and taking late afternoon and/or evening classes. Depending on the point in time, some of these schools with part-time programs were ABA-accredited schools, but not many. Of 85 ABA-approved law schools in 1933, 11 had part-time programs and 89 non-approved schools had such programs.

Over time, the availability of this kind of opportunity declined. In writing about the ABA's efforts in the first half of the 20th century to control the structure and size of the legal education market and the legal profession, Richard Abel noted that part-time programs were prime targets. Typically found in stand-alone schools often serving immigrant and lower/working class aspirants, these programs helped fuel a rapid growth in the number of law schools and, concomitantly, in the number of lawyers (Abel 1989, 57–58). The ABA expended substantial effort to drive as many of these schools as possible out of business by withholding accreditation using ABA-created standards few of these schools could meet.

In Abel's words, "The virtual demise of unapproved schools [in the first half of the 20th century] has also meant the decline of part-time law study … The ABA campaign against unapproved law schools disproportionately affected part-time study" (Abel 1989, 57). Among the major consequences was the affordability of and access to legal training. Abel said, "the decline of part-time schools has rendered legal education financially less accessible to students from poorer backgrounds. Evening instruction makes it far easier for students to support themselves by working" (Abel 1989, 58). In 2018, three-quarters of ABA-approved or provisionally approved schools showed at least some part-time enrollment, but this should not be taken as a return to greater part-time opportunities for students. Of those with part-time students, approximately one-half had less than 75.

Even if slowly, access to legal education became increasingly problematic for those of limited means – and was always problematic for women and minorities. The profession in the first half of the 20th century and the schools that trained lawyers were largely white, male, from northern European backgrounds, and more well off than not. Few seemed concerned, except to ensure this did not change.[10]

Perhaps the major pre-World War II exception, at least with regard to class and ethnicity, was Alfred Reed. Writing in 1921, he argued:

> Humanitarian and political considerations unite in leading us to approve of efforts to widen the circle of those who are able to study law … It is particularly important that the opportunity to exercise an essentially governmental function (the practice of law) should be open to the mass of our citizens.
>
> (Reed 1921, 398)

10 *See* Auerbach (1976, 40, 108–129) on the early 20th century efforts to maintain the profession's social structure and characteristics.

One favorable commentator noted that he "championed the cause of evening law schools" because of their role in broadening access (Brown 1938, 43–45). Reed's ideas on access, however, were widely and strongly condemned by the organized bar.[11]

The concern over access gained some traction after World War II as the legal profession and legal academy explored the challenge of financing legal education in the future. It is seen in the early 1950s with the ABA special committee that looked beyond self-funding by students/families, and the meager scholarship monies then available. The committee warned:

> The people of this country would not countenance any standard that would result in all lawyers coming from the well-to-do or socially-elect classes. This result would be fatal in a modern democracy such as ours because those classes have no corner on ability and the lawyer is not only an officer of the court but also a public servant.
>
> (ABA Special Committee 1952–53, 314)

Still, diversity and access, it seems, didn't go beyond being "available to the barber's son on no more onerous terms than the broker's" (Dean 1964, 419), or perhaps more radically, the "son of a Sicilian immigrant shoemaker " (Barnes 1978, 229). Women constituted a mere 3% of law students at ABA-accredited schools in 1950, and publicly available data on minority enrollment did not even appear for accredited schools until the early 1970s. Minority students were 8% of all students at accredited schools in 1975, women were 23%.

World War II and the GI Bill

World War II had a profound effect on law schools, as it did on all of higher education. Enrollments "dropped dramatically during World War II" (Abel 1989, 74), as the pool of potential law students went into military service. By 1943 total law school enrollment dropped below 4,300. The war reduced Northwestern Law School's "enrollment to a very small level" (Rahl and Schwerin 1960, 52–53), and even law professors switched to roles supporting the war effort in the military and elsewhere. At Iowa, "student enrollment dropped dramatically during WWII … to a low of 23 in 1943. Law students and most faculty left to serve in the war" (University of Iowa 2008/2012). Baylor's law school "ceased operations from 1943 to 1946 during World War II" (Baylor University n.d.). All told, eight schools, including Baylor, closed for some amount of time during the war and reopened afterward.

The government's plans for the immediate post-war period brought the original GI Bill, which provided broad access to education and training generally through its financial support of students in broad array of settings.[12] It saw higher education and training as public goods and it was the first major

11 *See* Auerbach (1976, 110–116).

12 The Servicemen's Readjustment Act of 1944.

foray into higher education funding by the federal government. Its impact on legal education was immediate and dramatic. Baylor's law school "reopened in 1946 … (and) experienced a rapid increase in enrollment from about 100 in the fall of 1946 to 402 in the fall of 1949" (Baylor University n.d.). From its low of 23 students in 1943, after the war Iowa's "law enrollments swelled to record levels. Nearly 500 students were enrolled in 1947 and the school adopted special acceleration programs to move the bulge through as quickly as possible. By 1950, enrollments had stabilized at around 400." Enrollments swelled, "thanks largely to the GI Bill" (University of Iowa 2008/2012).

There does not yet appear to be a study that explicitly and systematically explores the impact of the original or subsequent versions of the GI Bill on legal education. Writing in 2004, about the Boston College Law School, Brandon Bigelow (himself a 1990s-era Navy veteran and Boston College Law School graduate) presents a rare case study on the impact of the GI Bill. He notes that the war "presented challenging times for Boston College – and indeed, nearly destroyed the law school" (Bigelow 2004, 3). There were only six graduates in June of 1945 and the law school's finances were "dire" (Bigelow 2004, 14). The immediate post-war period was one of opportunity because of the GI Bill. "Returning veterans, flush with money provided by the federal government through the Servicemen's Readjustment Act of 1944 … financed an ambitious transformation of Boston College Law School from a well-respected regional school to one of national stature" (Bigelow 2004, 3–4).

Given the generous educational benefits and allowance for living and other expenses, the original 1944 GI Bill most certainly had a substantial impact on legal education. At least with regard to affordability it provided a breadth of access not seen before or since. Bigelow points out that it paid tuition directly to the school with a relatively high limit – high enough, for instance, that Boston College Law School could raise tuition into the 1950s and still stay comfortably within the limit ($500). The living allowance was paid directly to the veteran. Only nine of 110 ABA-approved schools with a full-time program had a full-time tuition exceeding the limit in 1949. In short, said Bigelow, "economically, veterans returning to law school found themselves in pretty good shape … With tuition and most living expenses paid, veterans left the (Boston College) law school unencumbered by debt" (Bigelow 2004, 20–21).

Of course, the GI Bill was also an enormous financial boon for law schools – and a badly needed one. Bigelow's Boston College provides an example.

> Perhaps the most dramatic and concrete effect of the massive influx of veterans was economic. In 1941–42, the law school held a reserve of approximately $32,000; by 1945 … that amount had shrunk to a mere $1,693. Increasing tuition from $300 to $350 for the day session in 1947, and to $400 in 1948, the law school was able to rebuild its capital position. By 1948, the law school held more than $162,000 in reserve.
>
> (Bigelow 2004, 18–19)

One might not be going too far in saying the 1944 GI Bill rescued legal education financially by making it quite affordable for large numbers of veterans to attend law school with the federal government covering the tuition. It remedied, at least temporarily, the lack of tuition-paying students and revenue, which was threatening the survival of legal education.

The Korean War GI Bill and subsequent benefit programs for veterans were less generous, but not meaningless. What they meant for legal education is unknown. Because of their lower level of support, the lower numbers of veterans leaving the service at the same time, and the different environment for law schools, the impact is likely to have been less dramatic than the 1944 version. As the initial surge of veterans passed through law schools enrollments dropped in the middle 1950s.

Even with its relatively short-term impact the original GI Bill provided one effective model for financing legal education and higher education generally. Most importantly, it solved the chicken-and-egg issue by fully addressing both schools' revenue needs and students' ability to pay the level of tuition driven by those needs. Its short life highlighted the need for a business model moving forward.

Financing Legal Education Beyond the 1944 GI Bill

The Starting Point: Two Key Assumptions

Despite its success and generous public benefits, the original 1944 GI Bill was not destined to be the model going forward. There was little political support for a similar, broad-based program of direct governmental funding. Most, but not all, approached the challenge of financing legal education in terms of a model radically different than the GI Bill – some variant of a value proposition not unlike the one still at the heart of the law school business model today. Two linked assumptions were key. One was empirical and the raison d'etre – responding to a shortage of lawyers reaching well into the future. There needed to be a robust legal education system to do so. The other was more ideological and framed the approach for underwriting that system – that legal education is a private good and government should stay out.

The Shortage of Lawyers

For the earliest post-war commentators discussing the financing of legal education, the pervasive assumption was a substantial lawyer shortage – not just an immediate shortage, but an expanding need into the indefinite future. This assumption was at the foundation of the ABA special committee's report addressing the financing of legal education in the post-GI Bill years. Among the reasons given for the need of a new, sustainable business model for legal education was "too few properly trained lawyers in the United States" (ABA Special Committee 1952–53, 316). Even the initial influx of post-war students supported by the GI Bill would not be enough for the future as the population increased and the economy grew.

An ongoing lawyer shortage – and a conspicuous optimism about an expanding need for lawyers – animated an interesting 1957 article by Professor Charles Joiner. He looked into the future and saw a robust market for new lawyers. Examining indicators of population and economic growth he predicted a substantial need for more lawyers by the early 1970s saying, "it would not be unrealistic to predict that there will need for … forty percent more lawyers in 1970 than in 1955" (Joiner 1957, 469).

Examining projections for increases in college enrollment Joiner also saw an increasing pool of potential law students through the early 1970s. To meet the growing need for lawyers "graduating classes must increase by more than fifty percent in fifteen years" (Joiner 1957, 472). His prediction, however, turned out to be a bit off. Enrollment in ABA-approved law schools increased by just over 130% between 1955 and 1970 – a robust market indeed (see Part III below). Regardless of the veracity of Joiner's analyses, the article clearly suggested to his readers that the necessary jobs part of the value proposition was a certainty.

Joiner was by no means alone in his view of a lawyer shortage. Writing in 1968, Martin Katzman – who then was the Assistant Director, Economic Analysis, Office of the Vice President-Planning and Analysis, University of California-Berkeley – reported on an economic analysis done for the University of California to determine whether or not the university needed to expand legal education. Based on the analysis, Katzman argued that there was indeed a shortage of lawyers based on available economic indicators. The exact extent of the shortage, however, could not be determined. He concluded by saying, "our analysis suggests the *direction* but not the *distance* we ought to go in choosing the number of lawyers to educate" (Katzman 1968, 176). Even though he could not judge that distance, the value proposition's logic was built into Katzman's economic analysis. Apparently assuming that potential law students are reasonably rational economic actors, his argument was that they would apply to law school if there was a long-term return on the investment in legal education.

Contrary to the great optimism, law school enrollments declined in the middle 1980s, leading commentators like Kramer to begin raising concerns about the value proposition and its built-in assumption about the need for lawyers.[13] The decline, however, was short-lived (see Part III below) and others argued that the value proposition remained quite viable. Writing in 1989, as part of a symposium on student debt, economist Ronald Ehrenberg reported on his economic analysis that modeled the market for potential law students and concluded, "while tuition increases have outpaced starting salaries law school attendance, on average, still appears to be a worthwhile investment" (Ehrenberg 1989, 629).[14] Still, Ehrenberg warned, the investment may not be worthwhile for some because of the varying job prospects among different types of school (public and private, "higher" or "lower" quality).

13 *See* Vernon and Zimmer (1985).
14 *Also see* Yarbrough (1989).

The Value Proposition and Legal Education as a Private Good

At its heart, the value proposition sees legal education as a private rather than a public good. It is, after all, based on the individual student's gain from his/her long-term investment. Any broader or public good, it seems, would be a side-benefit – society having the diverse lawyers it needs. What that might mean in practice – sufficient in terms of what and whose legal needs – was always somewhat hazy, as if things would just get sorted as lawyers capitalized on that investment.

The value proposition's logic always has had a flaw in terms of that side-benefit. Even Ehrenberg saw it despite his otherwise positive assessment. He admitted, "High debt tuition and subsequent debt levels may discourage students from low-income families from entering law school. High debt levels may also discourage law students from entering low paying fields of practice (e.g., public interest law)" (Ehrenberg 1989, 629).[15] Kramer was more acerbic, worrying that the model itself may attract a particular kind of student, saying law school "seats may be filled with many more students who, as they become lawyers, do so with the single-minded objective of milking the profession for all it is worth in order to be able to pay retrospectively for their legal education" (Kramer 1987, 240–241).[16]

The idea of legal education as a private good in conjunction with the assumption of a substantial lawyer shortage were the central ideas in the ABA special committee report. The report deserves attention because its purpose was to present "a recommended plan for use by [ABA] approved law schools for conducting a student loan program" (ABA Special Committee 1952–53, 312). If not *the* first it was among the very first places in which the value proposition was laid out explicitly, authoritatively, and in detail. It is especially important in light of the GI Bill's success and the ABA's perspective then on the federal government's role in financing legal education – which should be none.

A series of interconnected reasons drove the report and its argument for a non-governmental loan program. Three were broader in character and took the lead. The first was the lawyer shortage – "there are too few properly trained lawyers in the United States" (ABA Special Committee 1952–53). The second was the challenge of making legal education available because "the cost of education of all kinds has risen greatly and is still rising," and to make it available to more people "without regard to financial status or social standing" (ABA Special Committee 1952–53, 312). This did not, however, mean any kind of full commitment to diversity. It was to make it "available to poor boys of the requisite character, ambition, and ability"

15 *Also see* Yarbrough (1989).

16 The concern with the impact of law school debt and affordability on access to justice has received renewed attention in the aftermath of the Great Recession. For example, a 2013 report of an Illinois State Bar Association commission said, "Contrary to popular belief, there are not too many lawyers in America; instead, there are too many lawyers with student debt preventing them from providing affordable legal services to the middle class" (Illinois State Bar Association 2013, 21).

(ABA Special Committee 1952–53, 315). It would be another generation before women and minorities were even noticeable in law schools.

The third recognized that most schools at the time did "not have sufficient funds to furnish the necessary financial assistance to qualified and deserving students" (ABA Special Committee 1952–53, 312). Based on a survey of ABA-accredited law schools, the report noted some progress in building up scholarship funds. Regardless, while scholarships may help the top students, they will do little for the bulk of the students. The report tried to assess the then current state of loan programs by individual law schools. Few of the schools responding to the survey had any program; and for those that did the funds available were inadequate to fill the gap left by the meager scholarship funds (ABA Special Committee 1952–53, 316).

Three other reasons were decidedly different, and perhaps more important. The first was the overriding need for operating funds. A loan program would provide schools with the funds needed to meet "their present financial difficulties which are pressing upon them more and more by reason of inflation, increased costs, and expenses, and particularly the necessity of increases in teachers' salaries" (ABA Special Committee 1952–53, 313). In other words, schools need and/or want to charge higher tuitions and a loan program would help students pay the increased fare. The second would enhance public support for legal education and the legal profession by making financial help available to those "poor boys." The third, and related, "a loan program would be a distinct asset in the public relations program of the American Bar Association" (ABA Special Committee 1952–53, 313).

The report also devoted detailed attention to a loan program's design and operation – including amounts to be borrowed, interest rates that might be charged, and varying repayment possibilities. The bottom line was that loans should be repaid over a period of time with interest rates that would not place the new lawyer in any financial or moral peril. In words that would resonate for many today, the report stated that "If the debt is too great, it can scar the soul ...it will invite a tendency to avoid repayment and to moral decay. It may become so burdensome that it leads to hopelessness, despair, and even bankruptcy" (ABA Special Committee 1952–53, 318).

A loan program can work, the report said, because "education is a long-range capital investment capable of returning high yields. The difference between the cost of a legal education and its value in terms of lifetime earnings is proportionately much greater than the return ordinarily experienced on invested capital. The average annual earnings of lawyers exceed that of skilled industrial workers by almost $5,000 per year. This greater annual return makes legal education a sound investment" (ABA Special Committee 1952–53, 314). This value proposition works because the report assumed there were too few lawyers.

The GI Bill, of course, presented a fundamentally different approach to making law school affordable. It saw education as more of a public good. What makes the ABA report especially interesting, in light of the original GI Bill's success, is its strong rejection of *any* government involvement in a loan program or any other program for helping students pay for law school. While grudgingly accepting the government's help "for those who made such sacrifices in the armed forces, we feel that under normal conditions it is socialistic in concept, would suppress initiative in the individual student, destroy self-reliance, and undermine individual integrity" (ABA Special Committee 1952–53, 315).

Indeed, the report presented loans (privately funded with no governmental involvement) and its version of the value proposition not just as a sustainable business model, but also as a bulwark against an existential threat. If a privately funded and privately run loan program is not developed, the report said, "the alternative may well be for the government to intervene and grant such aid, which will inevitably lead to the socialization of the legal profession or at least legal education, and tend towards a totalitarian state" (ABA Special Committee 1952–53). Governmental intervention "will destroy our present educational system with its freedom of thought, expression, and spirit, as it exists today" (ABA Special Committee 1952–53, 316).

While the value proposition and seeing legal education as a private good has won out over the long term, at least one radically different approach was proposed. Writing in 1964, Cornell law professor William Tucker Dean argued for a program – a business model – that would see legal education as a public good. Pointing to Alfred Reed's arguments about the legal profession, one of Dean's starting points was that "Everyone will agree that the lawyer is a member of a public profession with responsibilities in a democratic society" (Dean 1964, 417). As such a public good, "it is important that this 'special professional order' be drawn from the widest possible sources in our society" (Dean 1964, 418).

Dean agreed with the ABA report on the need for a sustainable source of revenue and for making legal education available to a broader range of students (Dean 1964, 419). He rejected the idea of long-term student borrowing because the pool of possible law students was already tilted toward the affluent, saying, "college graduates are primarily the sons and daughters of upper-income citizens" (Dean 1964, 418). "If this method [long-term borrowing] were applicable to higher education generally, its effect on legal education might not be too serious" because that pool would be much broader. Instead of borrowing for law school, Dean said society generally should pay as it does for public grammar and high school – at least for a substantial proportion of law students (half or more).

Dean asks, where will the money come from? His answer is direct and clear: "That it can only come from the Federal Government is apparent at the purely practical level" (Dean 1964, 426). One finds no talk of creeping socialism or threat of totalitarianism in Dean's discussion, but instead the idea that the federal government has been involved in financially supporting students. Among the more recent programs noted was the post-World War II GI Bill and National Science Foundation fellowships, which "re-emphasized the inevitable role of the Federal Government in higher education" (Dean 1964, 427). Other areas of higher education were receiving substantial federal support, while legal education was not, an observation to which others pointed as well.[17] Legal education, as a special, public profession should also receive federal aid: "A well-trained

17 *See* Manning (1969).

profession, open financially to able citizens of every income group, is a vital element in the preservation of the Republic" (Dean 1964, 427).

Dean's plan, however, was not dependent on the assumption of a large and increasing number of well-paying jobs (Dean 1964, 429).[18] His plan would create National Legal Scholarships and a National Legal Scholarship Commission. While not everyone would need such a scholarship or choose to apply, he assumed that most applicants would apply. Those applying would be required to take the LSAT (at the time, not all schools required it). Unlike the GI Bill, Dean's plan was purely meritocratic. Scholarships would be awarded based on performance on the LSAT, with the commission determining the cut-off point for receiving aid based on "periodic evaluations of the future demand for legally-trained professionals" (Dean 1964, 429).

A scholarship recipient would choose a school and the commission would disburse money directly to that school for the full amount of tuition along with funds to cover books and room and board. Apparently, there would be no partial scholarships. Those not applying for a scholarship or those not receiving one would need to find other ways to finance their legal educations – school scholarships, loans from the school or other sources, or work to help finance their educations.

Dean readily admits that the impact of his meritocratic plan on legal education would be "complex," with "different schools ... affected in different ways" (Dean 1964, 430). It would be a boon for top schools, but it could pose real problems for some schools of what he called marginal quality – schools that would find it difficult to attract full-tuition paying students. He did not envision a parallel, large-scale loan program for those not receiving federal scholarships. We can't know what he might say about his meritocratic plan today (Dean retired in 1988 and passed away in 1999) in light of more recent evidence surrounding bias and the LSAT or bias and other standardized tests, suggesting the impact may be complex in ways he could not foresee or expect.[19]

The Value Proposition, the Federal Government, and Education as a Private Good

Of course, Dean's plan did not prevail. An approach built on the value proposition idea did. Still, one key argument of Dean's did prevail – the necessary involvement of the federal government. In fact, law schools eventually had the decision on the institutionalization of the value proposition made for them by the federal government with the passage of the Higher Education Act (HEA) of 1965 and subsequent amendments and reauthorizations.[20] While not the first federal foray into higher education, one commentator described the HEA as the first "significant,

18 It is not clear that Dean accepted the oft-stated idea of a substantial shortage of lawyers.

19 *E.g.*, Kidder (2001); Kidder and Rosner (2002).

20 *See* Hegji (2014)

coordinated approach to higher education at the federal level that would actively foster broad access" (Brown 2016).[21]

Among other things, the HEA and later amendments created Pell Grants, a number of targeted scholarships and grants, Parent Loans for Undergraduate Students (PLUS loans), Guaranteed Student Loans, Direct Loans (subsidized and unsubsidized), Stafford Loans (subsidized and unsubsidized), and Work-Study Programs.[22] Finally, with regard to access, one part of the 1972 amendments to HEA not dealing directly with financial aid to students or institutions must be noted – Title IX, which "is a comprehensive federal law that prohibits discrimination on the basis of sex in any federally funded educational program or activity."[23]

One other key program especially important for legal education was not a part of HEA – the Middle-Income Student Assistance Act. "Passed in 1978 MISAA made guaranteed subsidized loans available to students apart from income or need" (Brown 2016, 4). In a 1987 article on the affordability of law school, Kramer highlighted this measure's importance for law student borrowing, saying:

> Law students did not begin to use Guaranteed Student Loans to a significant extent until after 1978, when the Middle Income Student Support Act removed some income eligibility limitations applicable to Guaranteed Student Loans. By 1980–81, law students had $210 million in Guaranteed Student Loans … [that covered] 66% of private school and 78% of public school tuition in that year.
>
> (Kramer 1987, 252)[24]

By the end of the 1980s the value proposition was firmly institutionalized. Writing in 1989, the Consultant on Legal Education to the American Bar Association, James White, noted "a significant number of law schools are financed almost totally by student tuition and fees" (White 1989, 731). And what provides the funds for tuition? Said White, "The single most important factor in financing legal education has been … student loans. Students have been able to pay for the increasing costs of law school study only through development of a national loan system" (White 1989, 729). Somewhat ominously, he added, "Students have been willing to borrow in large part because their perception of job opportunities after graduation has been optimistic" (White 1989, 729).

21 Brown's title is taken from President Lyndon Johnson's remarks as Johnson signed the Higher Education Act of 1965 (Brown 2016, 203).

22 *See* Brown (2016) for a detailed description.

23 "Overview of Title IX of the Education Amendments of 1972," United States Department Of Justice, www.justice.gov/crt/overview-title-ix-education-amendments-1972-20-usc-1681-et-seq.

24 Kramer's article provides a detailed explanation of the programs in existence in the middle 1980s (federal as well other loans programs) and the impact of changes made during those years that made borrowing more advantageous to students as tuitions were increasing. He also reviews some potential programs suggested by those within the legal academy for addressing the increasing levels of debt, such as income-based repayment plans and public service loan forgiveness programs. *Also see* Vernon (1989).

Without these federally backed loans, said Kramer, "legal education as we know it today would not exist" (Kramer 1987, 252).[25] The loan system was propping up a highly problematic business model. He opened his 1987 article on affordability noting, "law schools for the last twenty years have been testing the elasticity of demand for their product" (Kramer 1987, 240). The evidence at the time, he said, seemed to suggest a surprisingly inelastic demand law schools did not fully understand. At some point the demand would inevitably diminish as the value proposition stopped working. The prospects beyond the turn of 21st century of an increasingly "debt-driven regime" worried him greatly (Kramer 1987, 241). Kramer did not live to see the reckoning he feared. He passed away in 2006, as law school enrollments were increasing again.

The Great Expansion and Rising Tuition

Schools

What motivated observers like Kramer was something that might have been seen as a good thing by earlier commentators – the great expansion of legal education combined with tuition levels that kept most schools in decent financial shape. That expansion included not just more law students to fill the seats in existing schools but more schools. The demand seemed – at times – almost inexhaustible.[26]

As World War II started there were 109 fully or provisionally accredited schools – 49 public and 60 private. For the 2018–19 academic year 201 schools were accredited (83 public and 118 private). Three periods of increase stand out: the immediate post-World War II years (1948–1950) with 12 new schools, half private; the substantial increase in the 1970s with 24 schools, 20 private; and the less substantial, but still important increase in the early 2000s with 18 schools, 15 private.[27]

A single explanation for the patterns of increase, especially for new private schools, is hard to discover. One might hazard an explanation for the periods of greatest increase as a clear response to an identifiable need based on a systematic assessment akin to Dean's plan. No such assessments, however, were made. Instead, individual entities – schools, state governing boards, and so on – made their own decisions for their own reasons. If they sought ABA accreditation, the process required a localized feasibility study to explore "the demand for legal education and the need for lawyers in the area."[28] In light of the ABA's standards for accreditation, that feasibility study

25 He noted a 1986 amendment to the HEA, which no longer required that students applying for loans in the federal program from being treated as dependents. This meant there was no longer an expectation that parents would be contributing to the student's support, meaning students could qualify for larger loans.

26 *See* Ruud (1972).

27 The figures in this paragraph exclude the three law schools in Puerto Rico. The 2018–19 figure is net of law school closures, mergers, splits, and consolidations that occurred since 1948. The most recent count of non-accredited schools is 32, *see* Law School Admission Council (n.d.).

28 *Approval of Law Schools: ABA Standards and Rules of Procedure* (as amended, 1979), 39.

seemed to be largely geared toward showing a potential market for students whose tuition dollars would cover a school's operating costs.

Enrollments

While the precise connection between the number of schools and demand for law school seats might be hazy, there clearly has been a substantial increase in enrollment since World War II. Figure 5.1 shows the increase in total JD enrollment in accredited public and private schools since 1943, as well as enrollment overall. The extremely low level of enrollment in 1943 shows dramatically the impact of the war on law schools – the figures are so low they don't even show as points on the graph. By 1947 with the war's end and the GI Bill, total enrollment increased from 4,248 in 1943 to 42,411 in 1947, an increase of 898% over the 1943 figure.

Even though the number of schools increased in the immediate post-war years, enrollment dipped in the early to mid-1950s as the World War II and Korean War veterans moved through legal education. It regained ground in the 1960s – enrollment in 1970 represented an increase of 104% over the 1960 figure. The reasons for this decade's increase are unclear. Some may be related to the federal government's involvement via the HEA of 1965, but as noted above it had limits on financial aid. Some may simply have been a result of the early "baby boomers" moving through the education system.

The 1970s brought 24 new schools (mostly private) and more increase in enrollment. The greater capacity provided by the new schools was important. Those 24 new schools accounted for 34% the increase in enrollment between 1970 and 1980. There was clearly a demand for law school seats, more than could

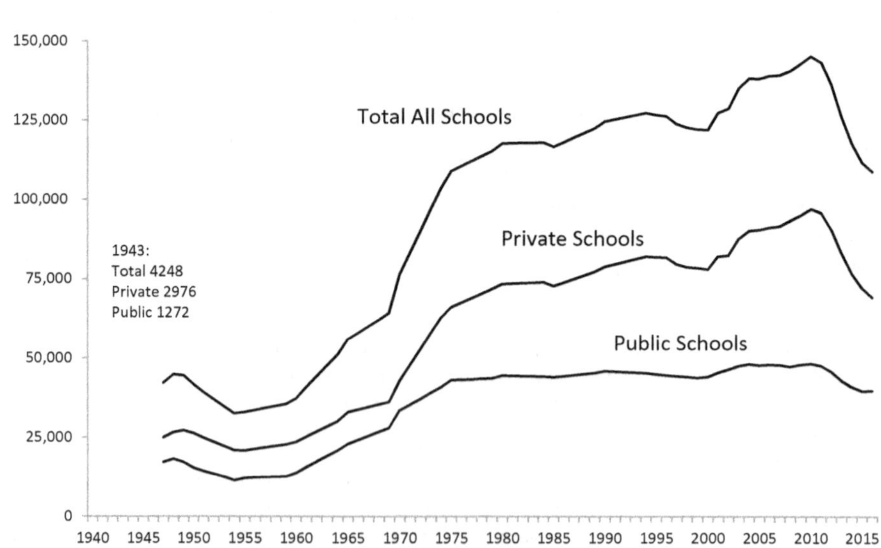

Figure 5.1 Total JD Enrollment: 1943–2016

be handled by the older schools alone, especially the older public schools. It was this substantial increase in the 1970s that so worried Kramer, who was not sure of a concomitant increase in employment opportunities.

The possible reasons for the increase in the 1970s are perhaps a little clearer than those in the 1960s. Loans were more broadly available, something important given that 62% of students were enrolled in higher-tuition private schools (new and already existing schools). Loans were doubly important given, as Figure 5.1 shows, the overall enrollment trend from the mid-1970s onwards was driven by private school enrollment.

Perhaps more important, as Figure 5.2 shows, was the rapid and unexpected increase in female students in the 1970s. Figure 5.2 sets the changes in the number of enrollees – total, female, and minority – from to 1950 to 1960 to zero and then subtracts the respective figures from the changes in enrollment numbers in each subsequent decade to show the increase or decrease compared to 1950–60. There is one exception to the pattern – for 2010–15 the figures for change between 1950 and 1955 are used. Because figures for minority enrollment are not available for years earlier than 1973, rough estimates are used for 1950, 1960, and 1970, based on the percentage of female enrollment for each year (women were 3% of enrollment for 1950 and 1960, and 8% in 1970; minorities were 8% of enrollment in 1973). For each decade the left-hand column represents the change in the total number of enrollees from the beginning to the end of the decade. The middle column represents the change in the number of female enrollees and the right-hand column represents the change in the number of minority enrollees.

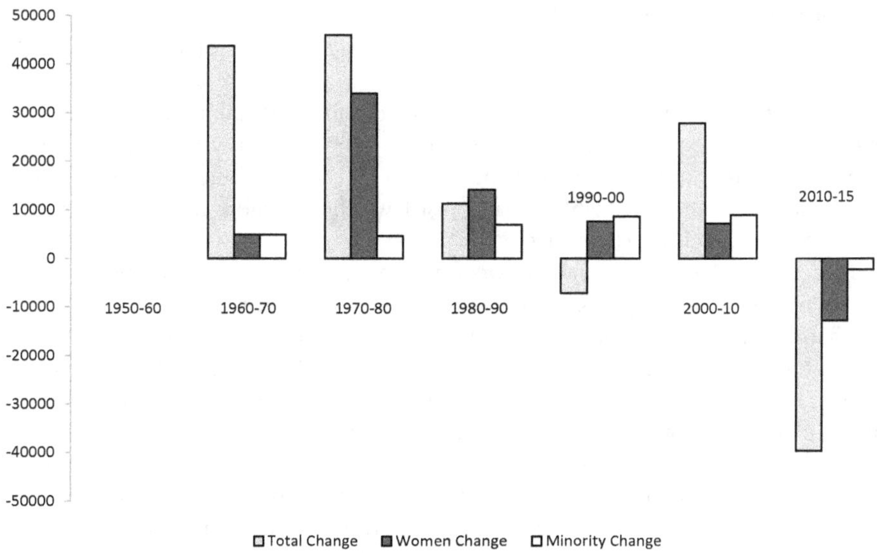

Figure 5.2 Change in Enrollment by Decade Compared to 1950 to 1960

Note: Change from 1950 to 1960 set to zero, and that figure subtracted from change in later decades to show increase or decrease compared to 1950–60.

Between 1960 and 1970, women accounted for only 12% of the increase in enrollment. Between 1970 and 1980, women accounted for 80% of the increase. While female enrollment continued to increase after 1980, the increases were much smaller. The reasons for this influx of women are unclear. One might simply point to the passage on Title IX in 1972 as the explanation and it undoubtedly played a role by opening the doors for women with its prohibition of gender discrimination. But opening the doors isn't enough and neither is just referring to the women's movement.

The picture is more complex. For instance, a national survey of 1971 college seniors (done by Educational Testing Service) about their plans upon graduation showed that few respondents were interested in any further education, only 38% – and most of them were men, 69% of the 38%. Very few of those interested in more education were interested in law school, only 12% of that 38%. And of those interested in law school only 11% were women. (Of women with post-graduation plans, only 4% were interested in law school (Baird 1973, 18).) A similar survey done in 1961 did not even include women, "since more than 90% of all students selecting law are men" (Warkov and Zelan 1965, 1).

That 1971 survey showed that perceptions of discrimination may have played a role. Both male and female respondents thought it:

> more difficult for women to gain admission to professional schools of business, medicine, and law, and this impression of discrimination is particularly prevalent among women in relation to medicine and law … it is not unreasonable that it discouraged or deterred more women than men for applying for further study in these fields.
>
> (Baird 1973, 102)

The lack of money also played an important role for both men and women with regard to further educational plans generally, but more so for women (Baird 1973, 126–127). Interestingly, respondents across all racial/ethnic groups thought "admission procedures [overall and not just law schools] more likely to be tainted by sexism than racism" (Baird 1973, 85).

Title IX may have opened the doors for women, but evidence like this begs the question of why *so* many women decided to go to law school. Obviously, there is much we still do not know about the influx of women, their changing views of legal education, or the views of their job prospects. The influx of women, nonetheless, exacerbates Kramer's concerns given the lack of any apparent evidence of substantial job opportunities for women at the time.

In the next decade, 1980–90, the long upward trend in enrollment seen in Figure 5.1 flattened out. Figure 5.2 shows that women, now along with minorities, were the driver of what was a modest increase in total enrollment. By 2000, women accounted for approximately one-half of enrollment and minorities accounted for 21% (57% of all minority enrollees were women; and minority women accounted for 24% of all women). Regardless, it appeared that the force behind the earlier big increases in total enrollment was exhausted. There would not be substantial increases in the number of women wanting to go to law school; and while minority enrollment continued to increase, it would never bring the kind of increases seen earlier.

In the new century the pattern changed once more and it would seem any Kramer-esque pessimism was misplaced. Eighteen new schools opened and overall enrollment rebounded between 2000 and 2010, though not to the magnitude of earlier increases. Women, however, were not pushing this new increase. It was men, especially non-minority men, who accounted for 48% of the increase.

After 2010, the enrollment bottom fell out endangering the viability of numerous schools. Female enrollment declined – and sharply – for the first time, and especially for non-minority women (female minority enrollment declined only marginally). Male enrollment, especially for non-minority males, declined too. Non-minority female enrollment accounted for 36% of the 2010 to 2015 decline and non-minority male enrollment accounted for 57%.[29]

In the wake of those declines Kramer-esque pessimism reigned and the idea of a value proposition itself was strenuously attacked in ways not seen before. The days, to use a term from another arena, of "irrational exuberance" regarding job prospects were over. Where students during the great influx of the 1970s may have faced little information dampening any overly optimistic perceptions of their job prospects, not so in the post-recession years – especially for women. The challenges faced by women in tightening job markets were regularly highlighted.[30]

The image of debt-ridden, unemployed graduates was pervasive in the media as was criticism (if not outright condemnation) of legal education and its cost. Legal education's "failings" were widely and intensely discussed (and continue to be) at a level unlike anything in the past, especially via social media and numerous specialized websites. There was nothing in the past to compare what some call the "scamblog movement" and to a series of consumer fraud complaints filed against individual law schools for allegedly defrauding students with regard to employment opportunities.[31] From Kramer's perspective the post-2010 enrollment declines – and maybe even the fraud complaints – should not be surprising if

29 The remaining 7% of the decline came from minority students. One commentator, using empirical materials, has argued that some schools targeted lower LSAT minority students as a way to prop-up their dangerously declining enrollments and tuition dollars. *See* Taylor (2015).

30 *See* Bell (2017); American Bar Association Commission on Women in the Profession, www.americanbar.org/groups/diversity/women/.

31 *See* Outside the Law School Scam (2013, 2017). "We haven't won yet. Not until the cost of law school tuition approaches rationality and we don't have large numbers of law grads roaming the streets unable to work in the field they trained in. For me, this wasn't about sticking it to the law schools (OK, maybe a little bit). My personal goal was more focused on curbing the avarice of the law schools at the expense of their students." *Also see* Segal (2011) on whether the value proposition really works; Shaer (2012) on consumer fraud complaints against law schools; Barnhizer (2012). *See* Espeland and Sauder (2016) for the role ranking systems may have played in the reporting of employment data by schools.

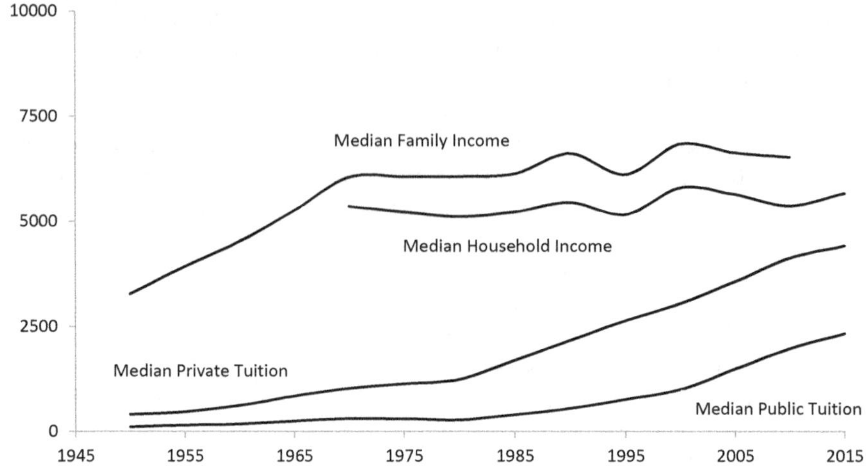

Figure 5.3 Family Income, Household Income, and Law School Tuition (1949$)

potential law students began questioning the value of a substantial investment in legal training. His day of reckoning appeared, finally, to be at hand.

Tuition and Debt

For the value proposition to work, students must go into debt to cover the cost of their investment. Tuition, of course, is *the* major cost component and as Figure 5.3 shows – in constant dollars – it has increased substantially over time, especially since the 1980s. Tuition has increased for both private and public schools, with private schools (where most students matriculate) naturally being more. As a reference point for affordability, Figure 5.3 also includes median family and household income (again in constant dollars). Importantly, after 1970, the former levels off and the latter stays within in a narrow range after its introduction in the graph in 1975.[32] Tuition simply kept increasing. In 2015, 10 schools had tuition that exceeded the median household income.

Increasing tuition was a part of Kramer's concern about the value proposition's sustainability because it meant increasing borrowing by students, thereby making the availability of good paying jobs all the more important. Writing in 1989, he lamented:

> Tuition is still running ahead of the cost of living … How does one pay the piper? … We deplore dependence on them [loans], but, at the same time, we heap them even higher upon the bent backs of our students, human subjects of our experiment on manageability.
>
> (Kramer 1989, 656)

32 See Kramer (1989) for a more contemporaneous discussion of rising tuition along with law school budgets and expenditures.

To aggravate the problem, he also pointed out that "the true range of debt burdens our graduates confront remains uncertain. We have no good evidence because few have the time or the money, or indeed the incentive to collect the data" (Kramer 1989, 672). Today there is some useful evidence, and highlighting Kramer's concern it gives one pause about debt and the elasticity of demand for law school seats.

The ABA Task Force found that the vast majority of contemporary law students borrowed to pay for their legal education– almost 90%. "The amount borrowed by students has increased substantially in recent years even after adjusting for inflation" (ABA Task Force 2015, 8). The reason – "full tuition prices have increased at a greater rate than discounts."[33] The spring 2016 (AY 2015–16) LSSSE survey showed for respondents graduating that year with law school debt the typical amount (in 2016 dollars) to be between $80,000 and $100,000 for public school graduates and between $120,000 and $140,000 for private school graduates (for 25% of private school graduates the debt exceeded $160,000, and the comparable percentage for public school graduates was 7%).[34]

A Kramer-esque Experiment on the Value Proposition

Has Kramer's day of reckoning finally come? Has the test of the value proposition and the elasticity of demand for what law schools offer finally played out in the real world? The post-recession environment can be seen as rough, natural experiment for Kramer's concern about the sustainability of the value proposition business model. Like Ehrenberg, Kramer believed the "market for law students 'behaves' in a manner that economists would consider quite rational from the perspective of the participants" (Ehrenberg 1989, 627). True to the value proposition's logic, students stopped coming after 2010 amid the questions about employment and legal education's investment value.[35]

Kramer typically talked in big picture terms, implying that the value proposition is problematic for all schools and for all students. Perhaps more telling is what lies beneath the big picture and the differences among schools. Not all schools will necessarily suffer the same fate in terms of enrollment, meaning the business model may not be so problematic. Assuming there are any schools with substantially better employment outcomes, they may still offer a good investment. Other schools may offer decidedly bad investments and the value proposition may not be a sustainable business model at current tuitions.

33 The ABA Task Force also found that "tuition discounting through grants and scholarships occurs, is widespread, and is generally increasing" (ABA Task Force 2015, 7).

34 LSSSE is the acronym for the Law School Survey of Student Engagement, an annual survey of students at participating law schools conducted by the Indiana University Center for Postsecondary Research, http://lssse.indiana.edu/who-we-are/. The statistics shown are from the author's analysis of the spring 2016 raw data (n=16,616 respondents) provided by LSSSE.

35 Even Ehrenberg – writing in 2013 – thought the business model was "breaking down because of the collapse of the job market for new lawyers" (Ehrenberg 2013, 98).

The crucial question is what is happening in the broad middle where most law schools operate and where most lawyers are trained. Any business model or system of financing legal education has to work for this broad middle. Too often, attention is given to schools seen as the "bad" ones – the ones with supposedly the worst outcomes who fuel the idea of legal education as a scam.[36] They are the easy target as if they are the problem and once they are dealt with all will be well. In other words, a symbolic effort with no real attention to the fundamental challenge of financing legal education.

Figures 5.4 (private schools) and 5.5 (public schools) offer some simple visual evidence of what is happening beneath the big picture. The figures are organized around five pairs of bars, each pair represents a group of schools based on the average of a school's yearly median LSAT over time – median LSAT score for full-time students for each academic year between AY2006–07 and AY2016–17.[37] The groups are designated simply as G1 through G5, with G1 schools having the lowest LSAT scores and G5 schools the highest. This scheme is used as an alternative to the *US News* rankings schools.[38]

The bars themselves present two sets of substantive data. The first set (the gray bars in each figure) is comprised of school-level employment data taken from the ABA's Law School Employment Database and aggregated for each group of schools (all the schools in a group together). Specifically, for each group, it is a percentage calculated by dividing the total number of reported graduates from 2011 to 2016 who obtained full-time, long-term, bar pass-required positions (FTLBP) by the total number seeking employment.[39] Aggregating in this way over a number of years puts the focus on the underlying dynamic rather than year-to-year variations.

The FTLBP category generally constitutes the largest percentage of employment outcomes for each school in the database and these are the hoped-for jobs for most students. The category also has the virtue of being an unambiguous one unlike, for example, JD-preferred – which each school can define in a variety of unique ways. The starting year used is 2011 because it is the first year for which such detailed data were collected. It is also a good starting point because it comes just as the post-2010 enrollment decline was about to start.

The second set (the white bars in each figure) is comprised of data from the annual ABA 509 disclosures and aggregated for each group of schools. Specifically,

36 *See* Sloan (2018); Crittenden (2018); Kreighbaum (2017); *also see* sources in note 32.

37 Averaging over a period of time provides a measure not affected by year-to-year variations before and after the post-2010 enrollment declines.

38 It is the approach used by the ABA Task Force (2015), and a very similar approach was used in Taylor (2015).

39 The figures do not include all schools for the time period covered, only those who had a graduating class in 2011 and not those whose first graduating class came later. Because two schools switched from private to public during the time covered – what are now New Hampshire and Texas A & M – the private/public in the two figures are based on the status of these schools at the start of the time covered, meaning they are counted as private schools.

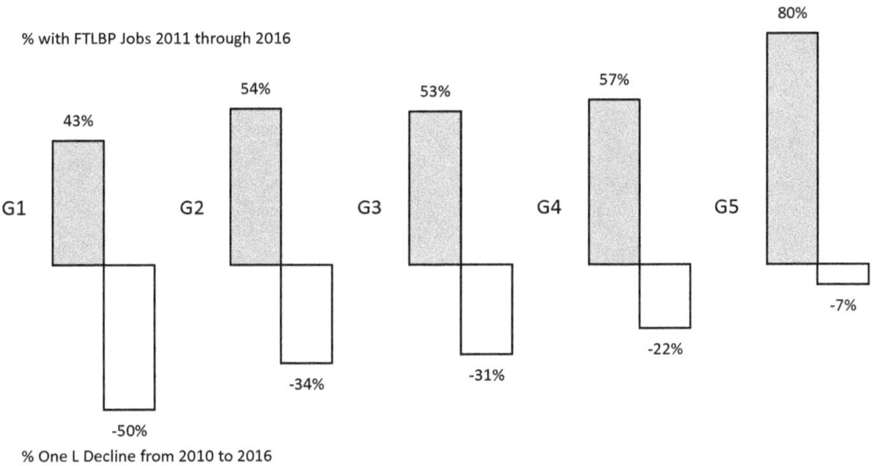

Figure 5.4 Private Schools by LSAT Group: % Graduates with FTLBP Jobs and % One L Enrollment Decline

for each group, it is the percentage difference in One L enrollment for each group of schools between fall 2010 (the peak enrollment year) and fall 2015 – how much new, first-time enrollment went up or down in 2015 compared to 2010. One L enrollment is used rather than total enrollment because it is a more immediate indicator of the schools' attractiveness.

The pattern in Figure 5.4 for private schools (these schools account for two-thirds of all job seekers) is clear. As the percentage of graduates obtaining FTLPB positions increases, the decline in One L enrollment gets smaller. The G5 private schools would appear to still offer a good investment for students and so the schools are attractive even if students borrow a substantial amount. One suspects this has always been the case. These schools, however, train only a minority of law students – just 26% of private school job seekers between 2011 and 2016, and only 17% of all job seekers.

Private G1 schools account for almost one-quarter (23%) of the private school job seekers and 15% of all job seekers. They are the ones garnering most of the attention recently and they offer a decidedly bad investment in light of the employment outcomes. Their graduates face a daunting challenge in getting an FTLPB position (one suspects this has always been the case), and the schools have endured the most dramatic declines in One L enrollment. For some of them the value proposition's reckoning may be close at hand, if it hasn't already arrived. As of this writing, three of the private G1 schools are closing.[40]

That broad middle of private schools (G2–G4) accounts for one-half of the private school job seekers (one-third of all job seekers). Their graduates fare better than the private G1 graduates, but nowhere near as well as the G5 graduates. Collectively, just over one-half (55%) of their students obtain a FTLPB position.

40 For Charlotte and Whittier law schools, *see* Olson (2017a, 2017b); for Valparaiso, *see* Whitford (2018).

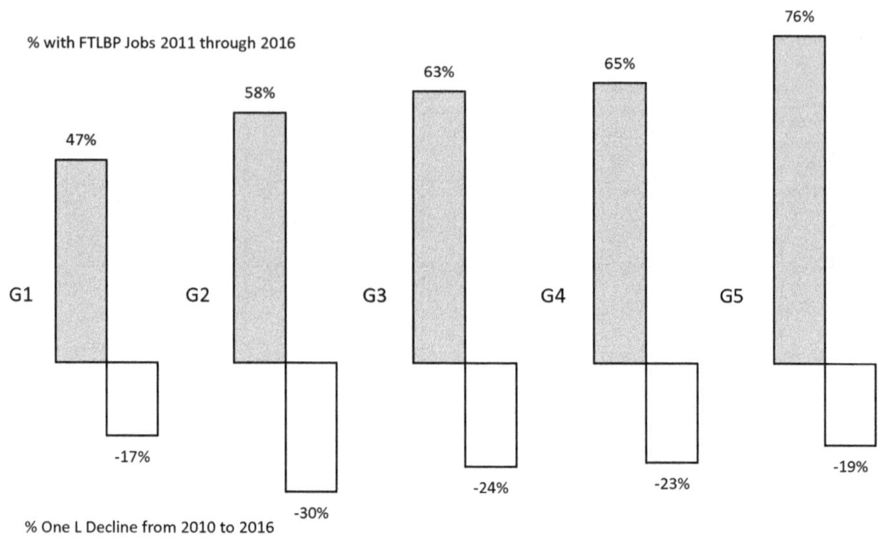

Figure 5.5 Public Schools by LSAT Group: % Graduates with FTLBP Jobs and One L Enrollment Decline

For them, and their students, the value proposition's value is not all that great, especially in light of the higher private school tuition. Together their enrollment declined by 29%.

It is questionable whether this is a sustainable business model for the G2–G4 private schools unless they see substantial enrollment increases, or unless they drastically reduce the cost to students, or unless employment prospects at sufficient pay somehow appear. The first is unlikely, the second is unrealistic for most, and the last is beyond their control. Perhaps all these schools can do is muddle through with incremental adjustments that better prepare their students for the available jobs while finding ways to somewhat reduce costs to students (or minimize increases). This doesn't address the underlying problem of the business model itself, but it is at least a recognition of the challenge. For all but those G5 schools, it would seem that it is live by the value proposition, die by the value proposition for private schools.[41]

Figure 5.5 presents the same material for public schools (which account for one-third of all job seekers) and the pattern is different in one key respect. Public G1 schools had the lowest percentage employed in FTLPB positions *and* the smallest One L decline. They will be examined below. Without them the pattern is similar to that in Figure 5.4 for private schools. While not as negative, the pattern is not especially positive.[42]

41 The correlation between a private school's percentage One L decline from 2010 to 2016 and its percentage of the total number of graduates between 2011 and 2016 with FTLPB position is a robust .60 (sig=.000).

42 The correlation between a public school's percentage One L decline from 2010 to 2016 and its percentage of the total number of graduates between 2011 and 2016 with

The value proposition seems to make sense for only a minority of public schools and their graduates. Like their private school counterparts, public G5 schools have the best record for FTLPB positions, although at a slightly lower level. They accounted for just over one-quarter (26%) of the job seekers and only 9% of all job seekers. The largest percentage of public school job seekers were from the G2–G4 schools – the broad middle. Two-thirds of public school job seekers were from G2–G4 schools (23% of all job seekers) and they fared better than their higher-tuition, private school counterparts. Sixty-three percent found FTLPB jobs compared to 55% – suggesting that the value proposition may work somewhat better for these public schools (with their lower tuitions) and their students.

Public G1 schools are eccentrics. They don't fit fully fit the value proposition pattern. They account for a very low percentage of the graduates in the market – 8% of public school graduates and 3% of all graduates. They are like their private counterparts in having the lowest percentage of graduates landing a FTLPB position; but rather than having the greatest decline in One L enrollment, they have the lowest for public schools. Only G5 private schools had better enrollment figures.

Other factors are apparently at work with the G1 schools. Four are a part of an historically black college or university, and a fifth is a newer school with a substantial minority enrollment. Two of the reaming four public G1 schools are very low enrollment schools and the only law schools in their sparsely populated states (the Dakotas). And the final two are local, lower cost law schools in Illinois (Northern and Southern). Although beyond the scope of this chapter, they require further investigation.

These findings are by no means definitive with regard to the future viability of the value proposition-based business model. Nonetheless, in light of Kramer's concerns they are sobering as evidence of a problematic business model for legal education. The value proposition makes sense only for a minority of schools and a minority of students. Perhaps, as Kramer said, legal education may be able to muddle through for a while, but sustainability is problematic.

Conclusion

John Kramer worried deeply about the perennial and stubborn challenge of financing legal education. He also worried about the ability of law schools to prepare for his day of reckoning or to even see it coming. Given legal education today he would be very worried indeed. As he wrote a generation ago there is still "no magic bullet, no easy solution. As always we will continue to muddle through together" (Kramer 1993, 65). Some current critics of legal education might not even grant the muddling through.[43]

Without a fundamental change – like the original GI Bill or something akin to Professor Dean's fully federally funded National Legal Scholarship program or

FTLPB position is .28 (sig=.006). If G1 schools are excluded the correlation rises to .42 (sig.=.000). While not as robust as the correlation for private schools, it is still an important indicator of the value proposition at work.

43 *See* Tamanaha (2012)

some better alternative for training people to provide needed legal services – muddling through may be as good as it gets. This may be so if – in line with some literature on organizational change – we see muddling through as incremental change within a set of institutional constraints an organization cannot alter. Barring fundamental structural change in institutional constraints (controlled primarily by the ABA), most change will be gradual with some contingency and randomness. Not all adaptions will be successful and not all organizations will even try to adapt, but some may try and succeed.[44]

One of the important observations of the ABA Task Force was that at least some schools are trying different ways of delivering the services they provide, with innovations being planned and/or instituted to meet their challenges (ABA Task Force 2015, 11–14).[45] Some schools, to reduce costs and enhance access, are trying hybrid programs allowing students to take more classes online. One school has an honors program based around a two-year practicum that is designed to give students intensive, hands-on training and better entry onto the local job market. Others are revising their third-year curricula to better prepare their students to compete in a changing employment market. Another now requires its JD students to complete full-time, course-connected residencies-in-practice as part of a highly experiential curriculum that is two-and-one-half years long. And there are others.

In effect, as the ABA Task Force observed, the adaptations schools are trying are natural experiments. It is muddling through as experimentation.[46] They are the incubators of new directions *and* an exacting market proving ground. Moving forward these experiments may well be the source of practical solutions and models, allowing others to see what can be done, how, and with what success. They can also show what may not work, and this is equally important. Of course, nothing guarantees that individual schools – or even most schools – will follow any particular set of adaptations or that any will make much difference with regard to the value proposition's viability.

There is another possibility, another experiment that looks beyond law schools and sees their challenges as an opportunity – the development of an alternative professional role, a non-lawyer professional akin to mid-level professionals in the health care arena. This would be a licensed professional trained outside of a traditional law school at a lower cost, a professional to serve particular legal needs at an affordable price. In 2012, Washington State created such a mid-level professional called a limited licensed legal technician or LLLT. This is a formally trained (at minimum a two-year program plus substantial clinical requirements), licensed and regulated professional, authorized to provide a narrowly prescribed set of legal services without the supervision of a licensed attorney in a well-defined practice area. Again, live by the value proposition, die by the value proposition.

44 *See* Hannan and Freeman (1977), Hannan and Freeman (1984)

45 *Also see* Daniels, Katz, and Sullivan (2014).

46 A recent book on the history of American higher education sees experimentation as the key to its success; *see* Labaree (2017).

References

Abel, Richard. 1989. *American Lawyers*. New York: Oxford University Press.

ABA Section of Legal Education and Admissions to the Bar. n.d. www.abarequireddisclosures.org (accessed March 11, 2019).

ABA Special Committee of the Conference on Personal Finance Law. 1952–53. Loans for Law School Students. *Journal of Legal Education* 5(3): 312–323.

ABA Task Force on the Financing of Legal Education. 2015. Appendix D, Separate Statement by Luke Bierman, Dean, Elon University School of Law. www.americanbar.org/content/dam/aba/administrative/legal_education_and_admissions_to_the_bar/reports/2015_june_report_of_the_aba_task_force_on_the_financing_of_legal_education.authcheckdam.pdf (accessed March 11, 2019).

Auerbach, Jerold. 1976. *Unequal Justice: Lawyers and Social Change in Modern America*. New York: Oxford University Press.

Baird, Leonard. 1973. *The Graduates: A Report on the Characteristics and Plans of College Seniors*. Princeton, NJ: Educational Testing Service.

Barnes, Thomas Garden. 1978. *Hastings College of the Law: The First Century*. San Francisco, CA: Hastings College of the Law Press.

Barnhizer, Daniel D. 2012. Cultural Narratives of the Legal Profession: Law School, Scamblogs, Hopelessness, and the Rule of Law. *Michigan State Law Review* 2012: 663–689.

Baylor University. n.d. Baylor Law History. www.baylor.edu/law/index.php?id=930137 (accessed March 11, 2019).

Bell, Jacqueline. 2017. Women See Another Year of Slow Gains at Law Firms. *Law360*. www.law360.com/articles/946586/women-see-another-year-of-slow-gains-at-law-firms (accessed March 11, 2019).

Bigelow, Brandon. 2004. The Impact of the GI Bill on Legal Education: A Case Study of Boston College Law School, 1949–1959 . *Law School Publications*, Paper 51. http://lawdigitalcommons.bc.edu/law_school_publications/51 (accessed March 11, 2019).

Brown, David. 2016. "We Have Opened the Road": A Brief History of the Higher Education Act. *Higher Education Review* 12: 1–7.

Brown, Esther Lucile. 1938. *Lawyers and the Promotion of Justice*. New York: Russell Sage Foundation.

Crittenden, Jack. 2018. Arizona Summit Second of Three InfiLaw Schools to Lose Accreditation. *The National Jurist*, June 19. www.nationaljurist.com/national-jurist-magazine/arizona-summit-second-three-infilaw-schools-lose-accreditation (accessed March 11, 2019).

Daniels, Stephen, Martin Katz, and William Sullivan. 2014. Analyzing Carnegie's Reach: The Contingent Nature of Innovation. *Journal of Legal Education* 63(4): 585–611.

Dean, William Tucker. 1964. Who Pays the Bills? The Cost of Legal Education and How to Meet It. *Journal of Legal Education* 16: 416–432.

Ehrenberg, Ronald. 1989. An Economic Analysis of the Market for Law Students. *Journal of Legal Education* 39(5): 627–654.

Ehrenberg, Ronald. 2013. American Law Schools in a Time of Transition. *Journal of Legal Education* 63: 98–112.

Espeland, Wendy, and Michael Sauder. 2016. *Engines of Anxiety: Academic Rankings, Reputation, and Accountability*. New York: Russell Sage Foundation.

Hannan, Michael, and John Freeman. 1977. The Population Ecology of Organizations. *American Journal of Sociology* 82(5): 929–964.

Hannan, Michael, and John Freeman. 1984. Structural Inertia and Organizational Change. *American Sociological Review* 49(2): 149–164.

Hegji, Alexandra. 2014. *The Higher Education Act (HEA): A Primer*. Congressional Research Service. www.hsdl.org/?view&did=749333 (accessed March 11, 2019).

Illinois State Bar Association. 2013. *Final Report, Findings and Recommendations on the Impact of Law School Debt on the Delivery of Legal Services.*

Joiner, Charles. 1957. The Coming Deluge: How Goes Our Ark? *Journal of Legal Education* 9(4): 466–472.

Katzman, Martin. 1968. There is a Shortage of Lawyers. *Journal of Legal Education* 21(2): 169–176.

Kidder, William. 2001. Does the LSAT Mirror or Magnify Racial and Ethnic Differences in Educational Attainment? A Study of Equally Achieving "Elite" College Students. *California Law Review* 89(4): 1055–1124.

Kidder, William, and Jay Rosner. 2002. How the SAT Creates "Built-In Headwinds": An Educational and Legal Analysis of Disparate Impact. *Santa Clara Law Review* 43(1): 131–212.

Kramer, John. 1987. Will Legal Education Remain Affordable, By Whom, and How? *Duke Law Journal* 1987: 240–275.

Kramer, John. 1989. Who Will Pay the Piper or Leave the Check on the Table for the Other Guy? *Journal of Legal Education* 39(5): 655–695.

Kramer, John R. 1993. Deans and Presidents: Sharing in Bankruptcy or Maybe the Cash Cow Won't be Able to Moo. *The Law School and the University: The Present and the Future*, in American Bar Association Section of Legal Education and Admissions to the Bar, Occasional Papers 6, 55.

Kreighbaum, Andrew. 2017. Calls for Tougher Oversight of For-Profit Law Schools. *Inside Higher Ed*, November 15. www.insidehighered.com/news/2017/11/15/accreditors-scrutiny-florida-law-school-renews-concerns-over-oversight (accessed March 11, 2019).

Labaree, David. 2017. *A Perfect Mess: The Unlikely Ascendancy of American Higher Education*. Chicago, IL: The University of Chicago Press.

Law School Admission Council. n.d. Non-ABA-Approved Law Schools (US). www.lsac.org/choosing-law-school/find-law-school/non-aba-approved-law-schools (accessed August 5, 2019).

University of Iowa. 2008/2011. Law School History and Milestones. First prepared for presentation to the US District Court, Northern District of Iowa Historical Society, April 11, 2008, updated Fall 2012, by N. William Hines. https://law.uiowa.edu/law-school-history-and-milestones (accessed March 11, 2019).

Manning, Bayless. 1969. Financial Anemia in Legal Education: Everybody's Business. *American Bar Association Journal* 55(12): 1123–1128.

Olson, Elizabeth. 2017a. For-Profit Charlotte School of Law Closes. *New York Times*, August 15, B3.

Olson, Elizabeth. 2017b. Whittier Law School Says It Will Shut Down. *New York Times*, April 20, B4.

Outside the Law School Scam (blog). 2013. A Brief History of So-Called Scamblogging: Where We Are and Where It's Going. *Outside the Law School Scam*, May 5. http://outsidethelawschoolscam.blogspot.com/2013/05/a-brief-history-of-so-called.html (accessed March 11, 2019).

Outside the Law School Scam (blog). 2017. What's Next for the Scamblog Movement? *Outside the Law School Scam*, February 20. http://outsidethelawschoolscam.blogspot.com/2017/02/whats-next-for-scamblog-movement.html (accessed March 11, 2019).

Rahl, James, and Kurt Schwerin. 1960. *Northwestern University School of Law: A Short History.* Chicago, IL: Northwestern University Law School.

Reed, Alfred Z. 1921. *Training for the Public Profession of the Law: Historical Development and Principal Contemporary Problems of Legal Education in the United States with Some Account of Conditions in England and Canada.* New York: Carnegie Foundation for the Advancement of Teaching Bulletin No. 15.

Ruud, Millard H. 1972. That Burgeoning Law School Enrollment. *American Bar Association Journal* 58(2): 146–148.

Segal, David. 2011. Is Law School a Losing Game? *New York Times*, January 8. www.nytimes.com/2011/01/09/business/09law.html (accessed March 11, 2019).

Shaer, Matthew. 2012. The Case(s) Against Law School. *New York*, March 4. http://nymag.com/news/features/law-schools-2012–3/ (accessed March 11, 2019).

Simkovic, Michael, and Frank McIntyre. 2014. The Economic Value of a Law Degree. *Journal of Legal Studies* 43: 249–289.

Sloan, Karen. 2018. ABA Seeks to Stay InfiLaw Accreditation Suits. *Law.com*, August 9. www.law.com/2018/08/09/aba-seeks-to-stay-infilaw-accreditation-suits/?slreturn=20190009165610 (accessed March 11, 2019).

Spinelli's Law Library Reference Shelf. n.d. *Official Guide to ABA Approved Law Schools (1926–2012).* https://home.heinonline.org/titles/Spinellis-Law-Library-Reference-Shelf/Official-Guide-to-ABA-Approved-Law-Schools/ (accessed March 11, 2019).

Stevens, Robert. 1983. *Law School: Legal Education in America from the 1850s to the 1980s.* Chapel Hill: University of North Carolina Press.

Swords, Peter, and Frank Walwer. 1974. *The Costs and Resources of Legal Education: A Study of the Management of Educational Resources.* New York: Council on Legal Education for Professional Responsibility.

Swords, Peter, and Frank Walwer. 1978. Financing Legal Education. *American Bar Association Journal* 64(12): 1880–1885.

Tamanaha, Brian. 2012. *Failing Law Schools.* Chicago, IL: The University of Chicago Press.

Taylor, Aaron. 2015. Diversity as a Law School Survival Strategy. *St. Louis University Law Journal* 59: 321–383.

Vernon, David. 1989. Educational Debt Burden: Law School Assistance Programs – A Review of Existing Programs and a Proposed New Approach. *Journal of Legal Education* 39: 743–771.

Vernon, David, and Bruce Zimmer. 1985. The Demand for Legal Education: 1984 and the Future. *Journal of Legal Education* 39(2): 261–298.

Warkov, Seymour, and Joseph Zelan. 1965. *Lawyers in the Making.* Chicago, IL: Aldine Publishing Company.

White, James. 1989. The Impact of Law Student Debt Upon the Legal Profession. *Journal of Legal Education* 39: 725–734.

Whitford, Emma. 2018. Another Law School Will Close. *Inside Higher Ed*, October 31. www.insidehighered.com/news/2018/10/31/valparaiso-law-school-will-close-following-unsuccessful-attempt-transfer-middle (accessed March 11, 2019).

Yarbrough, Marilyn V. 1989. Minority Students and Debt: Limiting Limited Career Options. *Journal of Legal Education* 35(5): 697–707.

6 Market Creep

"Product" Talk in Legal Education

*Riaz Tejani**

Introduction

How we talk about a problem structures how we try to solve it. The language we use has the dual effect of narrowing the field of possibility while foreclosing, often irreversibly, pathways to alternatives. Legal education in the U.S. today—study toward the primary professional law degree—is rife with problems. These include, among other things, outsized tuition, unreasonable graduate debt, falling job outcomes, unstable bar passage rates, variable information transparency, questionable professional preparation, contribution to a graduate oversupply, underemphasis on teaching quality, heavy emphasis on reputational rankings, and, as in the rest of higher education, administrative bloat.[1] Considerable ink has been spilled describing and normatively addressing these problems in what is now a cottage industry of legal education crisis and reform writing. This industry has been professionally inclusive; while law professors have generated a large volume of the key commentary, so too have social researchers, law and business journalists, non-governmental organizations and activists, students and alumni, and certain regulatory actors. Meanwhile, the content of their discussions has been less ideologically diverse. Over approximately ten years of observations of legal education, first as a non-traditional student, then as a faculty member, then as an empirical researcher, I have come to observe the growth of the "market" as metaphor to describe the underlying nature of U.S. law school operations and training. In this chapter I argue that this apparent capture of legal education commentary by "market" ideology is a recent extension of wider developments labeled as ***neoliberalism***, and I suggest that this capture limits the solutions available while posing heightened danger to broader social justice as it becomes embedded in the training of legal advocates and lawmakers.

The first reaction may be that ***market*** is not merely a metaphor. Our law and economics friends might complain that legal education does not just behave "like" a market: it *is* one. I want to provisionally concede that point even while harboring doubts about it for reasons discussed near the end of this piece. For now, this

* The author thanks Elizabeth Mertz and Eugene McCarthy for valuable input, as well as Ryan Griffiths for extensive research assistance on this piece.

1 For more on these dilemmas see e.g. Tejani (2017).

chapter does not attack the market-*ness* of U.S. legal education at the ontological level—that is to say at the level of underlying reality.[2] It rather addresses the dominance of market language such that coexisting realities "during the J.D." may become crowded out or elided.

Metaphor is a common feature of language that allows it to describe new or changing objects, events, substances, or circumstances with categories we already possess and understand. Metaphors work particularly hard in the worlds of law and legal culture, where new cases constantly bring unfamiliar facts to a preexisting matrix of rules and standards. Metaphors in this regard are more than just linguistic tricks or tropes; they are the tools by which we make sense of and sort out complicated facts. As Lawrence Rosen says:

> To speak of one's body as a "temple," home as a "castle," intellectual life as "a marketplace of ideas," or equality as "a level playing field" is far more than mere wordplay: Such metaphors connect what we think we know with what we are trying to grasp, and thus unite, under each potent symbol, those diverse domains that must seem to cohere if life is to be rendered comprehensible.
>
> (Rosen 2006, 9)

In life as in law, the ability to analogize and distinguish new cases and old ones structures how we choose to resolve them.[3] The choice of metaphor, therefore, is "more than mere wordplay" because it can have an immediate impact on actions we take or the solutions we devise to grapple with lived reality.

In order to become the dominant reality for participants, the image of a "market" must be embedded in the minds of a network of actors. Anthropologists have been studying this in important ways. Writing about Wall Street trading culture in the years prior to the Great Recession of the late 2000s, Karen Ho describes how traders and bankers themselves "ma[d]e markets" rather than simply entering into any pre-existing ones (Ho 2009, 4).[4] To operate smoothly,

2 Some in the interpretive social sciences such as my own field of anthropology might add that there really is no "underlying" reality beneath experience, and that our perception and interpretations are the only stable reality to speak of. I will not go that far. Rather than assert the impossibility of the underlying reality in contrast to the perceptual one, I acknowledge the coexistence of the two indicated at the very least by the structure of language. See e.g. Lakoff and Johnson (2003).

3 Roscoe Pound and others described the principle of "common carriers" in similar terms. "[C]onsider how starting from a principle as to the duty of a common carrier the precepts worked out for the carter were extended in one line to the stage coach, to the railroad, to the trolley line, to the autotruck, to the airplane, without calling for new rules as one type of carrier succeeded another. Consider how in another line they were extended to telegraph, telephone, radio, gas, electric light, and power. Then note how lawyers worked out a broader principle as to duties involved in a public service, which has enabled our law to deal with one after another of these rapidly developing agencies of public service by affording a starting point for reasoning" (Pound 1946, 46–47).

4 This has also been referred to as the "performativity" of markets; see e.g. Callon (2007). See also, Tham (2017).

the "reality" of the stock market had to be accepted by its participants, but to be accepted by participants the concept of the "market" had to appeal on a linguistic level to a critical mass of them.

Applied to education, "market" has been a controversial heuristic. Comparing it to its commercial counterparts, higher education in many ways confounds the metaphor. The object of its so-called market is more diffuse, complicated, and processual. Educations are not fungible goods or delivered services; they possess some overlap with these, but they must in large part include the input skill, effort, determination, and sometimes luck of the students they seek to benefit. Traditional educations impart more than mere "knowledge" or "capacities" or "human capital." They convey communal values, ideal behaviors, civic solidarity, and senses of belonging. In more recent decades, some institutional actors in higher education have determined it expedient to omit these latter roles to focus instead on the informational or capacity-building roles. Doing so allows them to emphasize a putative augmentation in human capital—an increased ability among graduates to complete economically valuable tasks.

Applied to legal education, the situation gets still more complicated. Though law graduates are and should rightly be expected to accomplish several key tasks such as issue spotting, research and citation, and memo and brief writing, this is far from the balance of their responsibilities. Today more than ever, credentialed jurists should also be able to weigh and resolve ethical dilemmas; understand the differences between law, justice, and morality; and envision themselves in the larger tapestry of civic institutions and engagement that enable their profession in the first place. If legal education is a "market," then which of these things is the good, product, or commodity being traded? Technically, when licensed advocates bill clients, it is for time spent on the key tasks listed above.[5] But the legal academy, the professional bar associations, the bench, and the informed public would object to the omission of the philosophical entanglements of legal education simply because they don't generate use- or exchange-value. Does the "market" commodity then describe the *entirety* of a legal education—the skills *plus* the values—or the symbolization of this education in the J.D. diploma students receive upon completion? Or is the commodity instead the "opportunity" to pursue that credential which comes with the very real risk that a student "consumer" may be among a percentage of aspirants unable to finish for any number of reasons? This second definition at least takes into account the reciprocity problem mentioned above: an education is the interaction of teaching services and materials *and* the student's own effort and determination to learn successfully.

With this in mind, the remainder of this chapter argues that the legal education reform debates have been discursively "captured" by a kind of market fundamentalism—what social researchers have come to call neoliberalism. Part one establishes the importance of this argument, building on theories in the fields of economic and legal anthropology, as well as political economy. Part two describes

5 Recent changes in legal service delivery and billing have made "task based" billing more common, though still not the norm.

the method by which the chapter will portray and evaluate the prevalence of market language in legal education drawing on antecedents in linguistics, anthropology, and law school reform debates. Part three lays out empirical evidence of the occurrence of market language across key sectors of the legal education crisis and reform dialogue including law school marketers, journalists, activists, and law scholars. Part four then offers an analysis of this evidence including, integrally, a subsection that considers the most viable counterclaims to the argument it supports here. Finally, part five offers concluding remarks to underscore the implications of these points for broader legal education, social justice, and social theoretical discussions.

Conceptual Framework

Serious efforts to confront product talk in legal education must be inherently interdisciplinary. To begin, the concept of "market" has traditionally been considered an economic one. Some trace its modern origins to the writings of Adam Smith who envisaged the market as a singular web of social relations mediated by money and operating as the most efficient form of exchange predicated on individual pursuit of self-interest (Hann and Hart 2011, 25). More broadly, this form of exchange came to require strong institutions to issue and certify the value of money, as well as robust infrastructure to allow its extension over larger and larger populations and geographic space.[6] Today the market is understood to mean *both* the underlying principle of actor-to-actor exchange *and* the system of institutions and infrastructures that allows this.

Smith also suggested that the aggregate pursuit of self-interest in market activity is regulated by an "invisible hand." Though not used directly to describe any market in Smith's own writing, the metaphor of the invisible hand has been widely applied in this fashion in the centuries since.[7] Under a commonly adopted application, the "invisible hand" metaphor posits a hidden mechanism by which resources are best used and least wasted when individuals maximize their own needs or "enjoyment," and it argues that no intermediary is better suited to determining "enjoyment" than the individual herself. Thus for partisans of the superiority of market systems, few or no internal norms are required to ensure that the system operates appropriately. On the other hand, many have argued that the market needs regulatory discipline to continue operating stably over time. This opposition between market-based normativity and positive or regulatory normativity would set the stage for the global battle between capitalism and social protectionism documented later in the writings of many critics.[8] This chapter builds on those writings by examining the dramatic substitution of market

6 See e.g. Duina (2011).

7 Some point to the analogy and potential uptake of "invisible hand" in Darwin's "natural selection" theory. See Callinicos (1999). Others have argued that Darwin's theory was so economic in nature that the thinker will soon supplant Adam Smith as the father of modern economics. See Frank (2009).

8 See e.g. Polanyi (1968 [1944]); Horkheimer and Adorno (2001 [1944]); Fraser (2013).

fundamentalism for traditional positive normative thinking that is occurring at the heart and soul of U.S. legal academic training.

This being the case, are there even alternatives to the market metaphor? There seems to be some difficulty answering this question in recent years both in higher education generally and in legal education specifically. Many have protested the incursion of marketization into colleges and universities, but traditional ways of thinking have limited those critics' capacity to suggest alternatives. I will argue that sociocultural anthropology offers an important theoretical resource for posing such alternatives. The study of exchange in anthropology has yielded important lessons that continue to be influential. In 1922 Bronislaw Malinowski described the "Kula ring," a form of ceremonial exchange where an apparently low value (to Western eyes) ornament was circulated among tribes across vast oceanic distances in the Trobriand Islands (Malinowski 2002 [1922]). In addition to the methodological revolution this work set off, it argued convincingly that "primitive" gift exchange served a larger and more complex political purpose than previously thought. The exchange value of the object, therefore, was something that far exceeded the apparent use-value of the object—so much so that it justified risky sea voyages among tribes. This distinction did not preclude a simultaneous market economy however. Marcel Mauss would later argue that gift economy and market economy coexisted around the "Kula ring" system. The Kula itself was a solemn exchange imbued with deep significance while a separate barter system for basic necessities remained to support the other (Mauss 1970 [1954], 22–23). If the Kula was characterized by amity and cooperation, the latter allowed for tough bargaining and personal economic gain (Mauss 1970 [1954], 22–23). This single example illustrates the value cross-disciplinary readings bring to the legal education reformist capacity to envision alternatives. From it we see the possibility and wisdom of maintaining *both* market and non-market forms of exchange—perhaps with one embedded in the other. In other words, the Kula ring, as depicted by Malinowski and Mauss, is but one prominent example of the unique contribution anthropology might bring to discussions of economy going beyond market exchange. This example might not have emerged without the groundbreaking advent of extended fieldwork by Malinowski.

This early research into "primitive" exchange inspired an entire subfield of economic anthropology. There, ethnographic researchers have since turned to the study of exchange (Weiner 1992), money (Maurer 2005), finance (Ho 2009), debt (Hart 2016), value (Graeber 2001), and property (Riles 2004). Arguably, the greatest achievement indexed by these works has been a growth in long term, deeply engaged, qualitative behavioral studies of economy by scholars rigorously trained in ethnographic methods.[9] Though this has coincided with the growing influence of "behavioral economics"[10]—the subfield of economics dedicated to

9 Significant because of the confusion with journalism.

10 See e.g. Sunstein and Thaler (2008).

the practices and meanings of economy to real people—it has curiously remained separate and apart from the formative canon in that field.[11]

Economic anthropology may not yet have revolutionized economics, but it has influenced broader social theory. In *The Great Transformation*, the Hungarian-American economic anthropologist Karl Polanyi argued, at the time cogently, that the developing story of Western capitalism would likely be structured as a bipolarity between "free marketeers" on the one hand and "social protectionists" on the other (Polanyi 1968 [1944], 201–205). These poles were evident in Polanyi's era respectively as the titans of industry advocating against labor and natural resource regulations in the name of national growth, and the trade union and civil rights advocates organizing for legal protections against unrestrained market behavior. Much like Marx's historical dialectic, Polanyi's "double movement" would, he felt, ultimately produce a synthesis or resolution in the form of embedded or socially conscious markets that combined profitability and social sustenance. Like Malinowski, Polanyi can conceive of economic structures beyond the market.

And yet, even Polanyi's model has encountered some criticism. The political philosopher Nancy Fraser offers an update to the double movement that better accounts for civil rights era "emancipatory" social movements as a third gravitational force on the evolution of capital (Fraser 2013, 129–130). The sociologist Fred Block sought to update Polanyi with a more modern understanding of what "society" is after deindustrialization and globalization (Block 2008). And the name Polanyi arises at least ten times in *A Brief History of Neoliberalism* by the influential British geographer David Harvey. Common across these varied revisitations of the "double movement" is a dissatisfaction among contemporary theorists with the way "society" was, for Polanyi, simply a romantic *other* to economy (Harvey 2005). In other words—and this may be a truism today—society and economy do not sit neatly as separate spheres. Empirical ethnographic studies of neoliberalism have become especially useful in demonstrating the complexity of intertwining social and economic spheres, with economic modalities envisioned as encompassing more than just markets.

But these studies offer a second key benefit as well: recouping the study of society without romanticizing it as *other* to economy. Ethnographies of neoliberalism study society in its everyday, point-to-point materiality, and this has become paradoxically more valuable as "the social" faded beneath increasingly economistic approaches in politics and law. Noting this, Carol Greenhouse has said that, "It was politics that abandoned *society* as social—the basis of social security—and failed the people with whom anthropologists most readily identified, that is minority communities at the social margins" (Greenhouse 2011, 34 [emphasis in original]).

11 Behavioral economics has so far assimilated psychology and sociology over anthropology, perhaps because of the far more positivist approaches of these neighboring disciplines.

Others have studied the role individual meaning-making plays in fashioning larger economic structures like "the market" (Ho 2009, 4). Applied to the higher and legal education contexts, some have shown how this meaning-making role is itself the product of learning to mobilize and master specialized discourse (Urciouli 2010). Still others explain in grounded ethnographic detail how modern day financial markets could not function but for their deep installation in the imagination of everyday traders (Ho 2009, 4). By highlighting the "discourse" of markets as constructive of their social reality, these studies also illustrate anthropology's disciplinary lineage. Broadly influential across the social sciences, Emile Durkheim early on introduced the "social fact" as a key object for social research in the 1890s (Durkheim 1982 [1895], 50).[12] Economic ethnographies drawing upon this lineage denaturalize the market concept, revealing it to be a matter of tacit agreement among participants (i.e., socially constructed) rather than of an independently produced (i.e., precognitive) reality.[13] Building on that scaffolding, this chapter unpacks different uses of the market metaphor across several legal education "stakeholders" in another effort to denaturalize its role through emphasis on underlying language.

This approach owes much to the work of Elizabeth Mertz on linguistic ideology in the law school classroom. Mertz has shown how traditional U.S. legal epistemology makes law school study a process of acquiring new linguistic patterns and structures for ultimate application to messy real-world problems (Mertz 2000, 2007).

> These ideologies structure and reflect the social uses of language and text in legal contexts, and thus, I argue, provide a key foundation for "thinking like a lawyer." In this sense, one thinks like a lawyer because one speaks, writes, and reads like a lawyer. Some would associate thinking like a lawyer with superior analytic skills in a neutral sense; I would instead characterize the acquisition of lawyerly "thinking" as an initiation into a particular linguistic and textual tradition found in our society.
>
> (Mertz 2007, 3–4)

This claim has much in common with observations by Sarat and Felstiner that the *practice* of law may also entail deployment of specific discursive moves that distance legal problems from moral or emotional ones in client consultations (Sarat and Felstiner 1995). Drawing upon this line of studies, I suggest here that

12 From Durkheim we inherit the notion that a social fact is a fixed truth only once it is agreed upon by a critical mass of the group, community, or society. A common example is "race." Race is a social fact both as a distinguishing feature of humanness, as well as in the qualities that characterize any particular racial group. Racial identifiers are "factual" because we say they are. Supporting this is the observation that so-called racial boundaries change over time. See e.g. Haney-Lopez (1994).

13 By "naturalize" I refer to the process by which concepts and ideas are made to feel fixed or eternal. The concept of "race" described in the preceding note has come to be viewed as a function of human nature. "Denaturalize" then refers to the opposite process.

the prevalence of "product" talk in law school reform dialogues is indicative of a new development: the incursion of market ideology into longstanding legal epistemology. I further suggest that this may indicate the legal academy is becoming increasingly "captured" by this way of thinking, and therefore foreclosing alternative imaginings of its problems and solutions. Product talk, in other words, may illustrate one way in which "thinking like a law professor" increasingly means "speaking like an economist."

Approach

This chapter observes marketization at the level of discourse, or language in action, an approach already adopted by others in the legal education context. Bryant Garth addressed the contemporary law school "crisis" as a rhetorical move on the part of certain commentators seeking to advance their own careers as critics (Garth 2013). Talk of crisis, Garth says, is a recurring feature of the U.S legal profession and tends to coincide with periods of broader economic scarcity or socio-cultural integration. With the relatively recent accreditation of a number of new fourth tier law schools, among which several are for-profit, today's crisis rhetoric, says Garth, is reminiscent of statements circulating around the advent of new law programs in the 1930s that welcomed Catholic and Jewish aspirants into the profession (Garth 2013). These tend to reinforce professional hierarchy and often imply that professional saturation and ethical dilemmas are only a problem for the "bottom" (Garth 2013).

Here I look not for textual instances and interpretations of crisis, but for occurrences of statements about reform that naturalize the law school economy as a "market." I look, in short, not for "crisis talk" but for "product talk." As I define it, this category of law school reform speech will include not only literal occurrences of words like "product" and "market," but also non-literal occurrences where these words may not appear but where legal education is understood as a commodity to be exchanged and consumed within a network of individual, "rational" buyers and sellers. As discussed here, the occurrence of these terms and referents does not point to a naturally existing object or process. It rather produces those objects and processes as "natural" in the first place.[14]

In this usage the unit of analysis becomes the bounded utterance or "speech event" of law school commentators. Borrowed from the anthropological linguist Dell Hymes, "speech event" refers to a statement by one actor directed to at least one other.[15] In this case, the sample gathered is from online available sources so

14 This approach to look at speech as constitutive of ideology and power has been called "critical discourse analysis." See Fairclough (1995).

15 See Hymes (2013, 52). "The term speech event will be restricted to activities, or aspects of activities, that are directly governed by rules or norms for the use of speech. An event may consist of a single speech act, but will often comprise several … . It is of speech events and speech acts that one writes formal rules for their occurrence and characteristics."

that primarily Internet archived speech events are presented.[16] These texts are here represented according to the category of "speaker": law school institutions; legal education journalists; prospective, current, and former law students and activists; and academic lawyers.

To gather their statements, I ran Internet and Westlaw searches for different combinations of the terms "law school," "legal education," "JD," "law program," "economy," "market," and "product" "within" ten and fifteen words of each other. The search was limited to the past fourteen years. For each "hit," the relevant sentence was excerpted along with at least one sentence before and after. The resulting events were then entered into a spreadsheet tagged with their author or speaker and URL source. This method resulted in approximately fifty significant speech events. These were then organized by spreadsheet according to the category of speaker, and closer analysis was then applied to verify the usage of the terms produced the meaning targeted by our small survey. This led to the exclusion of several occurrences where "market" referred, for example, not to legal education *as* a market but rather to "job market" for legal graduates—a related but distinct usage of the term. This also led to exclusion of occurrences of "product" such as, for example, "work product" or simply "outcome of this law school"—again conveying related but distinct or non-specialized meanings. In gathering the commentaries by legal academic experts, our search of Westlaw excluded occurrences of "product talk" by judges within published case law, or by regulators in formal policy documents. With a growing body of opinions and court documents from lawsuits against law schools themselves for misrepresentation, breach of contract, and so forth, a robust study of this type of speech is better left to a separate, dedicated study. This work limits its look at "expert" commentary to academics published in law and policy journals with one exception where content from an unpublished interview with one high profile academic was included as indicated below.

The resulting matrix represented here, then, consists of thirty speech events gathered from across the legal education reform sector in late 2016 and early 2017.[17] It is not intended to be a scientifically generalizable sample; it does not permit the conclusion that everyone or most are speaking in these ways. It does, however, lead to a conclusion about the way a significant group of speakers in this area frames the content of discourse surrounding legal education—which is observably described here across a variety of key speech arenas as a product or commodity traded on a market.

Evidence of Product Talk

"Product talk" refers to a category of speech that treats its object as a commodity to be exchanged on a market. It tends to naturalize both the commodity quality of the

16 I hesitate to narrow the title of the piece to "Online Product Talk," however, because many of these utterances first appeared in distributed print form. Web archiving here acts as a sort of "filter" on selection of such examples, so that a print-only search might result in more "hits."

17 Several "hits" appearing in a single text will be treated as parts of a single speech event.

object, and the market quality of its exchange network. At least four general types of product talk in legal education can be identified based simply upon the speaker involved. The first is that issued (or reissued) by law school marketers. This can be further subdivided into marketing to student consumers (future, current, and former), and marketing to employer consumers—those looking to hire new lawyers. The second type includes utterances from professional journalists; this category is slippery in that several "activists" are published in national news outlets, and Internet blogs now span the border between activism and journalism both in content and in form. This problem has been addressed here by treating the primary affiliation of the speaker as the basis for categorization. The third is that issued by activists and advocates for legal education reform. And finally, the fourth category of product talk comes from law scholars—full or part-time law faculty and administrators with institutional appointments. Although related in some senses to institutional product talk, this category accounts for the independence afforded law scholars from their affiliate schools under the protections of academic freedom and security of position.

Law School Marketers

This first category of "product talk" includes speech acts made in pursuit of law school marketing. Whereas some of these examples might be produced by business offices and specific marketing personnel, others come from administrators speaking in support of the school's public image in the community. Two subtypes of this kind can be specified; the first includes utterances directed at student consumers, and the second includes speech acts directed at employer consumers.

I sought to gather examples of product talk from among the full spectrum of law school rankings according to *U.S. News and World Report.* Interestingly, none of the *U.S. News* "Top 20" schools appeared to formally use product talk as we have defined it in their online literature. Any references to "products" and "markets" at those institutions' websites tended to be about Products Liability courses or scholarship, or about research into financial markets. Turning next to law schools ranked 20 to 100 and then 100 onward according to *U.S. News*, I began finding responsive hits. Several of these include content generated not by the law school itself, but rather by a journalist about the school or its niche (sometimes quoting a member of the school). However, because this content has been affirmatively republished by the institution, with implicit endorsement, I treat it here as institutional speech. The remainder of this subsection presents these utterances in the two distinct groups described above: (1) legal education as a product to be consumed by *students*, and (2) the output of law schools as a product to be, apparently, consumed by *employers.*

Directed at Student Consumers

Representations of law school education as a product for student consumption were relatively abundant. At the College of William and Mary Law School, for example, a 2010 "news" piece about interdisciplinary team teaching in a Law and Economics course quoted one of the professors about the suitability of this approach at the university given its history. "'William and Mary—America's first university—is a true university, and we can integrate the strengths of law school and the arts & sciences,' said [Alan] Meese. 'Such integration can produce a better *product* for our students'" (Zagursky 2010).[18] Spoken by a law and economics expert, this first occurrence may already hint at the source for reasoning that has popularized market discourse in law.:

At Wake Forest, meanwhile, a "news" page reproduced the language of a *Wall Street Journal* article quoting several legal education experts around the country including several law deans:

> "Adding new degree programs is like a company diversifying its *product* lines. If demand for one sags, you've still got alternative sources of revenue coming in," said Paul McGreal, dean of the University of Dayton School of Law, which now offers master's degrees for nonlawyers and practicing attorneys alike.
>
> (Wake Forest University School of Law n.d.)

Spoken initially by a dean, quoted by journalists, and then reproduced by a law school touting its own creation of a non-professional master's program—a strategy adopted widely in part to survive declining applications and enrollments—this utterance makes an overt analogy to private manufacturing—underscoring the commercial, as well as the fungible nature of the degree options available to students.

Resulting from the merger of two struggling law programs in 2015 (Wahlberg 2015), Mitchell Hamline School of Law has been forced to place financial solvency at the center of its operational choices. To some, therefore, the occurrence of product talk within its own literature would seem expected. In September 2016, the school reposted an article from the State Bar magazine touting the new program's career focus as a differentiated educational commodity. The article quoted directly and indirectly the school's dean:

> Unlike many schools, Mitchell Hamline is seeing higher enrollment in the new academic year, with the new class bigger than previous Mitchell and Hamline classes combined. The school has been recruiting aggressively but also has a great *product* to offer and is attracting students from all over the country, Gordon said. It is the largest law school in the region, defined as Minnesota and its border states.
>
> (Mitchell Hamline School of Law 2016)

The overt mention here of "product" is complemented by the more implicit reference to its market. Pointing to the growing size of the incoming class, the distances from which new students hail, and the student population relative to

18 All emphasis on the words "product," "market," "consumers," etc. in excerpts in this section has been added.

neighboring schools, the statement suggests the school's great "product" is reaching a larger "market" of student consumers.

Directed at Employer Consumers

In addition to the treatment of students as consumers in language produced or referenced by law school institutions, a related subtype of product talk inverts the heuristic to view educated students as the "product" and legal employers as their consumer market. Fordham University School of Law, for instance, includes in its web pages a description of its efforts to train students in law practice at a level sufficient to obtain small firm attorney positions. As legal profession writers point out, the traditional approach for smaller firms was to allow the well-resourced large firms to "train" new graduates in practice skills like memo, motion, and contract drafting, and then absorb these trained professionals once they left "BigLaw" due to burnout or forced attrition. "Fordham Law's Apprenticeship Program," meanwhile, "is designed to provide a win-win experience for recent J.D. graduates and employers who do not traditionally hire straight out of law school" (Fordham University School of Law n.d.). To accomplish this:

> The Apprenticeship Program enables employers to hire, full-time for one year, a recent J.D. graduate. The employer benefits from the *product* of a Fordham Law education—a professional ready, willing, and able to hit the ground running and make immediate contributions, whether in a small to midsize law firm or in-house setting.
>
> (Fordham University School of Law n.d.)

Other schools describe their graduates as "products" for employer consumption in literature about clerking for local judges, meaning in a sense the local bench is the consuming market. One website quotes just such a consumer as saying:

> Two of my last four law clerks have been Campbell Law graduates, and these two particular students are first-class. They can hold their own with anybody from any law school in the country in terms of the thoroughness of their research and ability to write. I know that the *product* that Campbell Law is turning out right now is world-class.
>
> (Campbell University School of Law n.d.)

Finally, it is important, before moving on, to acknowledge the rare instances I found of *negative* use of product talk in law school institutional materials. Here, as if in response to the wider circulating language of fungibility and consumption, some schools may cite primary utterances on the part of faculty or students that distance that institution from the wider economism. Such uses appear to emphasize humanism, and suggest the experience in *this* particular program is superior for its ability to match the humanism of the student with the humanism of the education offered. One such instance appears on the web page for the University of Nebraska-Lincoln College of Law—notably, the institution where Roscoe Pound initially taught and became Dean (University of Nebraska-Lincoln n.d.).[19] In an excerpted testimonial, the College proudly quoted a member of the Class of 2016 as saying, "Life as a non-traditional student with four children presents a unique set of challenges. Yet I've thrived because Nebraska Law has always treated me as a person and not as a *product* of legal education."[20]

And finally, at least one law school's web page uses "product" even more explicitly in the same sense, but leaves the identity of the consumer more open-ended. According to Chapman University School of Law:

> There is a crisis in legal education right now; there is a crisis in the practice of law right now. Law practice has changed as a result of technology, globalization, and economic pressures. The *market* for legal education's *product*, law graduates, has diminished. And now, for the first time in decades, the *market* for legal education has diminished. Law schools cannot remain the same in this environment.
>
> (Moliterno 2013, 73)

Here, the consumer could be read as any type of legal employer, but it could also be the clients of legal services themselves. Meanwhile, deployment of product talk in these last four examples above is more complicated than may appear on its face. While statements that describe law graduates as the "product" and employers as the "consumer" appear interpretively bounded, a wider perspective that captures their contextual use offers a different picture. Even when law schools appear to use the "employer as consumer" meaning in promotional materials, these quotes can still also intend to sell their unique legal education experience to students. In other words, posts on law school websites that tout how prepared students are for employment will be read by potential students as well as employers; and students will likely care a great deal that they are represented as desirable to potential employers.

To conclude this initial section on marketing, let me offer some interim takeaways. First, most use of market metaphor is positive, negative is rare. Second, these positive uses are usually linked with reassuring students about job possibilities. Third, "market readiness," both for students and employers, is framed as the solution to an otherwise confounding job shortage in the legal profession. Fourth, this "market" frame is not generally problematized, but used to paint a positive picture. Finally, and perhaps most obviously, the "product" can be training offered by a school, or the students offered to employers.

19 This is interesting because Pound was associated with the Legal Realists, some of whom saw the future of American legal education heading towards the understanding of law as a behavioral "social science." See e.g. Tejani (2016).

20 http://law.unl.edu/john-duggar/ (1/18/17).

Journalists

When they write sympathetically of law school governance or business practices, journalists are sometimes—as above—cited and mobilized by institutions in marketing and web literature. More and more often, however, they have written critically about legal education, hewing to the larger criticism that law school attendance is increasingly an economic "losing game" (Segal 2011a). Like many of their counterparts in the legal academy (*infra*), journalists seem to feel the problem is *insufficient* rather than *too much* marketization. The *New York Times* writer David Segal has been perhaps the most vociferous in this regard. "With apologies to show business," he writes:

> there's no business like the business of law school. The basic rules of a *market* economy—even golden oldies, like a link between supply and demand—just don't apply. Legal diplomas have such allure that law schools have been able to jack up tuition four times faster than the soaring cost of college. And many law schools have added students to their incoming classes—a step that, for them, means almost pure profits—even during the worst recession in the legal profession's history.
>
> (Segal 2011b)

Segal's line of attack here has become familiar. Market insulation has created the bubble; market discipline must be its solution. Although one might not expect theoretical nuances of the "market" concept to appear in journalistic statements, one could reasonably hope that if the concept is applied, the justifications for it might also be. Instead, statements such as this take the terminology for granted and question why full-time academics have not themselves better launched this critique. (As alluded to in the previous section, one reason may be that those already intimately familiar know that law schools do not, strictly speaking, just generate "products" for a market.)

In her article entitled, "Law School Is Buyers' Market, With Top Students in Demand," the *New York Times* business writer Elizabeth Olson describes intense competition for elite students with ranking-boosting indicators as a kind of market. On the one hand, this appears to be yet another usage, in which law schools appear as consumers while "top" students appear to be the commodity (Olson 2014). Olson is not alone in textualizing this conception, and, given her area of expertise, her doing so makes sense. On the other hand, if it is a "buyer's market," giving students greater bargaining power, then students themselves are the consumers with legal education as the product. Regardless of its exact meaning, as more and more credible writers describe contemporary legal education in terms of a market, the "reality" of this heuristic further crystalizes. Moreover, as they apply the market trope to the law school economy in different and divergent ways (e.g. the market for students, the market for educational products, the market for graduates), one begins to suspect that it is less a coherent system of meaning than a metaphor reproducing itself virally through ongoing imitation.

Reporting on a high-profile misrepresentation case against Thomas Jefferson School of Law, *Bloomberg* contributor (and law professor) Noah Feldman explains that:

> [I]t's significant that a California court is allowing her case to go to trial. It places the spotlight on an important question about how law schools in particular and universities generally recruit students. How accurate must they be in describing their merits and the accomplishments of their graduates? Is a school's promotional material like advertising for any other *product*? Or should institutions of higher learning be held to a higher standard?
>
> (Feldman 2016)

Here, product talk in journalism may be fed by product talk in litigation, in effect further illustrating the concrete effects of metaphor.[21] The student in question sued for misrepresentation in law school promotional materials requiring the judge to evaluate whether such material could be compared to similar materials for other goods and services.

Elsewhere, a *Bloomberg* writer deployed similar language without the words *product* or *market*, while instead focusing on the concepts of price, sale, and supply.

> Tuition generally accounts for about half of a law school's budget, according to a 2011 report by Hanover Research, which also noted that it would be cuckoo to raise the *price* of a degree when people already have doubts about what these schools are *selling*. The best a dean can do is try to keep a healthy headcount, which means it's a good time to make yourself a part of an increasingly scarce *supply* of heads.
>
> (Kitroeff 2015)

Here, the overt reference to law school education as the "sale" of something is striking; it allows us to compare conceptions of legal education against higher education more generally. Do we tend to speak of a liberal arts education in even very "practical" subject matter like chemistry, economics, or public policy as the "sale" of the learning content, teaching service, or the degree itself? Is law school reducible to "sale" because it brings more palpable economic benefit on completion? If so, should we rethink this as the predicate benefit becomes more and more ephemeral?

Meanwhile, among new media journalists, application of similar language is also prevalent. Whereas one might expect the overt ideology among marquee print capitalist outlets, one might expect subversion of this among new or web-only publications. This seems not to be the case with *Above the Law* (*ATL*), a highly critical and well funded online publication tracking developments in law, legal profession, and legal education. *ATL*'s staff writer Joe Patrice hinted at the primary basis for the site's ongoing criticism. "We give law schools a lot of grief around here for being too expensive and not recognizing the true value of their *product*" (Patrice 2013). Applying it unapologetically in the new media format—

21 These effects are described in Lakoff and Johnson (2003).

one that carries the "real-time" validity of a high-level blog—*ATL* uses some form of product talk in most of its legal education criticism.

As above, some journalists have recently used product talk in a negative sense worth highlighting. One legal academic writer publishing online under the blog heading *Excess of Democracy* wrote in early 2017 that:

> [S]chools have been developing degree programs specifically for non-lawyers. If we use crude terms and call law school a "*product*," then the legal education "industry" has "innovated," responded to the "*market*," and developed a new "*product*."
>
> (Muller 2013)

Using product talk in scare quotes the writer calls these "crude terms," demonstrating a self-awareness about their usage not commonly found in new or old media publications on the topic.

To summarize, journalists writing critically of law schools tend to urge more attention to the "market" and this framing seems to go unproblematized. Journalists use "product" and "market" in multiple ways, but the wider impact of the metaphor can be seen in its expansion through terms like "price," "selling," and "supply"—and in how it might impact applications of analogies in case law in a way resembling that described by Lakoff and Johnson. And even new social media writers, who might be expected to be more self-conscious about metaphors, mostly accept the "market" metaphor uncritically.

Online Activists and Students

While many online activists in the movement for reforming legal education began to speak out while they were in law school, classifying them as "students" is complicated. If they were students at the time of their writing, they most likely were no longer upon our analysis of it. Even if we treat them here as "activists" in the sense of working to draw more attention to critical issues of legal education reform, they may not view themselves solely as activists as they engage in research, fundraising, teaching, law practice and so forth. For this reason, the activists/students category is something of a residual category to capture speakers who have gone through some form of law school training themselves, who advocate changes in law school regulatory oversight, but who lack affiliations as either a member of an educational institution, a journalist, or a faculty member.

One high-profile individual is the researcher-activist Kyle McEntee, founder of the organization Law School Transparency (LST). McEntee is an attorney and technologist who became a leading activist figure in efforts to reform legal education starting around 2009. His work gathering and aggregating outcome data has forced law schools to report more honestly, and students to choose schools more carefully. He is a passionate and caring policy advocate, with an inclusive and rigorous intellectual approach. His approach is also market-based. The premise of LST is that greater information works in the service of more rational market behavior. This way of framing the issue treats the robust information LST provides as illuminating the quality of legal education as a "product." Writing on the changes to come after the admissions "bubble" began to deflate, McEntee said:

> Overall, elite schools won't look much different than today's law school—a professional and graduate school hybrid that tries to simultaneously serve both the legal profession and the pursuit of knowledge. Nevertheless, they will feel different because the educational *product* will be more skills-oriented.
>
> (McEntee 2013)

As we will see, talk of the educational "product" is relatively common among institutional and faculty commentators alike. What is striking here is the adoption of similar discourse from those who are outside and critical of the institutional context but part of the powerful mainstream press, and those who are outsiders to the mainstream business and trade press as well. Product talk used in this way, across quite different domains, has been intended as a kind of revolutionary tool intended to overturn the longstanding professorial talk about legal education as a form of liberal education, philosophy of public policy, or engaged citizenship.

It might be interesting to examine whether the emergence and predominance of those characterizations may have in part been a reaction against the "critical legal studies" movement of the late-1960s through 1980s which had absorbed many of the structural critiques about law launched during the free speech, civil rights, anti-war, and Watergate eras. Senior faculty trained in those years may have been steeped in an idea of legal education as, precisely, a form of high-level liberal arts and rhetorical training, and would have resisted the kinds of market-based economism inspired by neoliberalism in the post-1980s era. Significantly, then, product talk—before becoming amplified as a solution to the law school tuition and enrollment bubble—may have emerged as a kind of pragmatic, generational rebellion against the critical idealism of the CLS era and its intellectual offspring.

How earnest or cynical this use of product talk might be in particular instances is another question. Do students and activists adopt product talk because they believe in it normatively or do they do so because they feel somehow compelled to use this description under the weight of economic hegemony in their world?[22] Speaking not of legal education specifically but rather the openness of law schools to recruit from all undergraduate majors, one student on a college admissions board justified free choice of major on the basis that everything is business, and that therefore law schools are interested in everything:

> Because if you think about it, all organizations are ruled by laws and contracts of some sort. Also, they need to bring in money and they use money; they create *product* and they *market* themselves, etc. As the others have said, get thee to the Career Office and line up internships in your fields of interest.
>
> (DustyFeathers 2017)

22 See *infra*.

While this is not direct talk of law school as a market, it does effectively essentialize law school as "in the service" of market behavior—a classic law and economics position trickled down to the pre-undergraduate student discussion boards.

Returning to the more conventional use, another student commented on the use of misleading information in recruitment at one ABA law school.

> [S]he thinks they're fudging some data in the sense that only the top people are reporting their salaries to Cal Western and of course every school uses "propaganda" I mean they are selling a *product*—legal education and its not cheap. They have to make it seem respected etc.
>
> (Wtracing 2008)

This student, posting anonymously in the pre-law admissions board *Law School Discussion,* appears resigned to the use of misleading information—"propaganda"—because law schools are in roughly the same enterprise as all other commercial entities: "selling a product." Once again, this resignation suggests a kind of cynicism that accepts rather than hails the market behavior of legal education institutions.

And finally, one additional example comes from another anonymous student, posting at the online site College Confidential and writing about the "no questions asked" federal student loan support for attendance at any ABA law school:

> Congress is looking at messing with highly-endowed schools' rights to use their endowments as they wish, with a goal of shifting more funds towards student expenses/tuition. Congress should back off. The private sector could solve this problem if government would stop messing with the situation by flooding the legal education *market* with money.
>
> (HappyAlumnus 2015)

Assuming that this is a real student, he or she shows unusual sophistication in pointing out that while legal education should work as a well-functioning market, it presently cannot with the safety net of unlimited federal student loan availability. Once again, their language naturalizes the "market-ness" of the field and even goes further in suggesting that the private sector as such is a solution to the dilemma of public finance.

The online environment has democratized criticism and commentary across much of social and economic life. This has been especially true of legal education, where students are extremely savvy in online communications and written advocacy. This section has illustrated some of the ways people use online sites to critique or comment on the current situation in legal education: some are student activists who remain involved after graduation, others are current students just commenting. In doing this, they frequently adopt market talk uncritically, though in some cases they do so with cynicism about the sector.

Law Scholars

Finally, occurrence of product talk among legal academics in scholarly commentary is primarily identified first by its appearance in legal academic journals. The work published in these outlets is edited not by scholars but by students, though presumably this only increases the academic freedom to criticize existing legal education structures. Student editors are likely not personally invested in those structures in the way potential faculty editors might be. Scholarly commentary also appears outside formal journals in more and more public fora such as blogs, social media, and the like. This section considers written utterances by full-time faculty in either domain.

Perhaps because of the availability of both kinds of fora, and the relative ease of publication in both, certain commentators have gained considerable professional traction using this discourse. One is Deborah Merritt of the Ohio State University, who advocates extensively for law school marketization. In an article reviewing Brian Tamanaha's 2012 *Failing Law Schools*, Merritt argues that Tamanaha did not go far enough in his deregulatory argument.[23]

> If we are going to protect students, new lawyers, employers, clients, and the legal system itself, we need to unleash *market* forces in legal education. This will require changing accreditation standards, altering the process for setting those standards, and limiting the government's blank-check support of legal education. But we need to go even further. In this essay, we build upon Professor Tamanaha's analysis by highlighting an even more important force that drives the spiraling cost of legal education: trade restraints on law practice. To reduce the unbearable price of legal education, improve the quality of that training, and deliver affordable services to clients, we need to unleash *market* forces in law practice itself.
>
> (Merritt and Merritt 2012, 2)

Here again, law school has been insufficiently marketized, and the best way to rectify this is to unfetter the market not only in legal education but also in legal profession. Merritt and Merritt goes on to say that law faculty alone may not be creative enough to foster the kind of service differentiation clients need.

> They may recognize the demand for a "Holiday Inn-type law school" to supplement the "Ritz-Carleton" mode. Faculty, however, are less likely to recognize that clients want an entirely different service, such as campgrounds or bowling alleys. Open *markets* are the most efficient way to channel information from *consumers* to *producers.*
>
> (Merritt and Merritt 2012, 14)[24]

23 Professor Deborah Merritt is a rare example of a law teacher with a long and respected track record of empirical work on the legal academy. See e.g. Merritt and Merritt (2012). See also, Merritt, Hargens, and Reskin (2001).

24 The authors continue that, "The market would generate approaches that we can't even imagine—approaches that are unlikely to originate from the crabbed creativity of law

Analogizing the market in legal education with the market in legal services, Merritt and Merritt takes for granted that clients want something "entirely different." As in the last section, this raises a question whether that difference is a *type* of- or *quality* of service.

A second question is whether differentiated law faculty would be able to separate these two things. For now, law professors retain a unitary profession in part to maintain, at least aspirationally, a unitary professional quality. With this in mind, can it be that marketization might compromise the latter?

> Will deregulation allow untrained, unscrupulous hacks to prey upon unsuspecting consumers? Of course it will, but no more so than the current system of regulation. Scholars have repeatedly complained that courts and bar committees do a poor job of disciplining incompetent or dishonest lawyers. Disciplinary authorities are reluctant to penalize colleagues within their own guild; judges, similarly, resist malpractice actions against fellow lawyers. An *open market* for legal services would not abandon all regulation; it would replace self-interested guild regulation with all of the anti-fraud and consumer protection laws available in our legal system.
>
> (Merritt, Hargens, and Reskin 2001, 15).

But if marketization would not be able to improve upon use of law as, in the words of Saskia Sassen (2017), a "predatory formation," then why would we make the shift given all the other uncertainties it would bring with it? One answer may be that we should do so because a law school "market" better matches the dominant ideology of the moment. From this point of view, the market may not be better at servicing the legal consumer, it may not promote greater social citizenship among lawyers, but it allows at least for more extensive economic citizenship. This argument is influential, but it may not take adequate account of the ideological—the speciously emancipatory character—of the market as contrasted with regulation.

Pepperdine tax professor Paul Caron is another influential writer. Curator of the widely read Tax Profs Blog, Caron has often been named "one of the most influential names in legal education" (Thisdell 2017). He was writing about "differentiation" before many had heard the term applied in this context; his writings also embrace the emancipatory promise of markets.[25] Writing in 2004 about the emergence of the case method in the early 1900s, Caron and Gely explained how its slow initial uptake allowed for different approaches to legal education. Though some schools embraced it,

> [o]ther law schools ... were skeptical of the usefulness of the case method, opting instead to rely on other forms of delivery of legal instruction such as reading courses, lectures on jurisprudence, and work in legal-aid practice. Law

faculties preparing students for a unitary profession" (Merritt, Hargens, and Reskin 2001, 15).

25 As with the quote from Merritt and Merritt above, Caron was pushing for law schools that differentiated how and what they taught depending on what kinds of jobs their students were likely to be getting.

> schools thus provided different "products" from which those aspiring to be lawyers could choose.
>
> (Caron and Gely 2004, 1504)

Naturalizing the legal education-as-product equivalence, this has the added significance of applying it retrospectively across legal history so that law schools around the turn of the century were, themselves also engaged in product differentiation. Here, a cultural historian or historical anthropologist might ask whether the actors and institutions themselves viewed it this way, or whether this may be a form of presentism—reading contemporary interpretation back into the historical record. The language of products and competition appears repeatedly in Caron and Gely's discussion of legal education's early North American history.[26] Once U.S. legal history is characterized in this fashion, it narrows the remaining options for critical approaches to the "market" metaphor in contemporary debates.

In a discussion over at the scholarly blog *ProfessorBainbridge.com* which was titled: "Want To Solve The Law School Scam? Expose Law Schools To A Market For Control," clinical professor Daniel Sokol wrote, "I would like to see more experimentation across schools and more *product* differentiation as to the type of skills a law school provides" (Sokol 2015). William Henderson, a supporter of better skills training and another "most influential" figure (Thisdell 2017), meanwhile characterizes this evolution in reform focus toward market skills as something recent. As if to confirm that this scholarly trend has itself been market driven, Henderson says:

> A focus on business factors is new for us. For the past two decades, the *market* for legal education has been seemingly defined by a rankings competition. We focused on rankings, or lamented their inaccuracies and limitations, because virtually no law school was feeling pressure on the three factors that make a law school financially viable. Now that the entry-level legal *market* has hit hard times, applicants are in much shorter supply.
>
> (Henderson 2013, 467)

Critics sometimes speak of regulatory capture to argue that regulation is inherently corruptible, and therefore inconsistent as a form of discipline. Henderson's note here suggests that legal education reformist thinking—what many might

26 See Caron and Gely (2004, 1506): "These rules required all law schools to provide a very similar type of product, with very little differentiation"; and Caron and Gely (2004, 1506–1507): "Before the creation and development of the AALS, the world of legal education was, albeit in its infancy, a competitive industry. Law schools competed in a number of dimensions in delivering their product. Although the measures of organizational success were constrained by the times and the absence of technology we take for granted today, law schools were able to identify winners and losers at least at a rudimentary level."

expect floats above material economic shifts—has itself been reacting to tightening markets.

Finally, Erwin Chemerinsky, another "most influential" commentator, has disputed the charge that legal education is in a contemporary crisis. In an interview with me for a project related to this one, Chemerinsky, echoing his own op-ed piece in *The New York Times* (Chemerinsky and Menkel-Meadow 2014), explained the dilemmas facing many lower-end law schools today as *not* a systematic crisis but rather a natural culling process given legal education's assumed reality as a market.

> I don't think there's a crisis in legal education. Undoubtedly, it's a very different reality depending on where schools are in the *U.S. News* tiers. There are schools that have experienced much greater decreases in applications or much greater financial problems than other schools. It's hard to generalize. Some *products* are doing worse than other *products*. That doesn't mean there's a crisis in that *market*. If a certain brand of car isn't selling as well as other cars, that doesn't mean there's a crisis in the auto industry.[27]

Chemerinsky is one of the most highly regarded law scholars and he has remained deeply committed to social justice and pro bono service. He nevertheless has been criticized as overly faithful toward elitism in legal education, and for setting up the UC Irvine School of Law on a "Cadillac" model rather than an economically affordable model more conducive to public interest post-graduate career choices (Zahorsky 2009). I cite his statement last as an example of where naturalization of the market through law school product talk has reached, by some accounts, the highest levels.

Thus we find in scholarly discussions a surprisingly uncritical acceptance of "product talk" and market ideology, despite scholars' usual habit of questioning and analyzing law and culture. Notably, scholars have naturalized the market metaphor both by claiming it goes back in history, and by describing it as new and desirable.

***

These foregoing paragraphs show diverse examples of what I have here termed "product talk" in legal education. Emanating from institutions, journalists, students and activists, and law scholars, they—with the rare exception of the noted negative treatments—support the conclusion that this form of discourse is widespread, deployed by figures of relative significance, and surprisingly consistent in the way it takes for granted the wisdom of "market" exchange in general, and its relevance to the law school context specifically. These examples do not prove that everyone is speaking in this way. But several do support the idea that broad adoption of this discourse is relatively novel.[28] They also underscore the ongoing importance of "product talk" and its precise underlying market ideology at a time

27 Interview with author, May 26, 2015.

28 Henderson (2013) and Merritt and Merritt (2012) both suggest this is *new* and should not be.

when legal education reform solutions could (and arguably should) draw from a wider base of ideological formations. Unquestioning adoption of the market metaphor begs the question whether legal education is a market through and through—and if so, does that leave room for the separate realm of social obligations? If law schools, employers, professors, and students are all to be viewed as players in a yet-to-be "unleashed" market, then are the norms that govern their interactions to be market-based only? Where would this leave law's important and longstanding social responsibilities?

Pros and Cons of the Market Metaphor in Legal Education

Although this chapter has focused on how law and the legal profession are susceptible to this problem, they are not unique. The problem—in which the economic aspects (exchangeability) of legal training are substituted for its social aspects (relationality,[29] justice goals, etc.)—is that of commodification more generally. Discursive treatment of the law school education or degree as a "product" in the evidence presented above begs for consultation of the extensive literature on commodities and commodity fetishism. Here, the lay terminology of "product" is roughly interchangeable with the more academic-sounding term "commodity." Both describe an object of value subject to exchange. Marx described hauntingly the way in which the commodity—the product of human labor and social relations—came to supersede those human relations such that the things of exchange would seem more independently important than the people exchanging them (Marx 1978).[30] This he aptly called "commodity fetishism."

But whereas certain objects of exchange like furniture or clothing could be easily viewed as *real* commodities because they were fungible and bore the clear traces of human labor, other objects could not. In *The Great Transformation*, Polanyi wrote of the process whereby *all* objects—not only "outputs" but also "inputs" of production—could be considered and treated as commodities (Polanyi 1968 [1944], 73, 132). Previously, at least up until the 19th century, a furniture product such as a table might have been severable from the human relations that produced it and therefore divisible and commodifiable, but the inputs that went into it—natural resources like wood, human resources like labor, or labor's reproducibility in things like family household care—were not. In the broad

29 In other words, the fact that developments in legal education have direct and relatively immediate impacts on the people it serves.

30 "There it is a definite social relation between men, that assumes, in their eyes, the fantastic form of a relation between men, that assumes, in their eyes, the fantastic form of a relation between things. In order, therefore, to find an analogy, we must have recourse to the mist-enveloped regions of the religious world. In that world the productions of the human brain appear as independent beings endowed with life, and entering into relation both with one another and the human race. So it is in the world of commodities with the products of men's hands. This I call the Fetishism which attaches itself to the products of labour, so soon as they are produced as commodities, and which is therefore inseparable form the production of commodities" (Marx 1978).

transformation from discrete markets to wholesale market *economy*, however, this distinction faded so that natural resources, labor, and care could suddenly also be bought and sold freely.[31] Polanyi called the process enabling the latter, all-encompassing, or socially disembedded markets "fictitious commodification."

For purposes of this chapter, I want to focus most upon the area of fictitious commodification that relates to "care." Nancy Fraser has described this arena as one of "social reproduction."

> [T]here is the strand pertaining to social reproduction, reflected in the growing strain, under neoliberalism, on what some call "care" or "affective labor," but what I understand more broadly as the human capacities available to create and maintain social bonds, which includes the work of socializing the young, building communities, of reproducing the shared meanings, affective dispositions, and horizons of value that underpin social cooperation.
>
> (Fraser 2012, 4)

This characterization, focused upon the "capacities available to create and maintain social bonds," is key to the application of fictitious commodification to the law school reform movement. The question it highlights is the following: In attempting to "solve" the current problems of U.S. legal education, ***are we going to envision law school training as an economic "input," an "output," or both?***

There are, it seems, very good reasons for treating it as both. On one hand the law degree, at least in theory, has clear value to its possessor in the form of potentially increased earning capacity, and potentially increased social prestige. On the other hand, it like all other educational degrees is only a symbol of a long arduous process of study, experience, and assessment. The purpose of that process is not simply to enable an individual to "practice law"; it is to enable the *competent* and *civically responsible* practice of law within the parameters of ethical and professional citizenship. It is to ensure that the professional uses of law remain socially reproductive rather than corrosive, so that the practice of law is an enterprise that supports rather than hinders social reproduction. This line of argument suggests that legal education might be viewed, even if

31 Fraser writes that there had been no formally separate "economy" and "society" but, "All that changed, however, with the invention of the utterly novel idea of a 'market economy'." Decisively rejecting all previous understandings, proponents of this idea envisioned a separate economic system, institutionally differentiated from the rest of society, and entirely directed and controlled by market mechanisms. In this system, all production would be organized for sale on price-setting markets, which would be governed immanently, by supply and demand. Not just luxury goods, not just ordinary goods, but all the inputs of production, including human labor, raw materials, and money credit, would be traded on such "self-regulating markets." Thus, the necessary conditions for commodity production would themselves become commodities. But that meant introducing the logic of market relations into virtually every aspect of social life. What was originally envisioned as a separate "economy" would inevitably colonize the surrounding society, remaking the latter in the image of the former. A "market economy" could only exist in a "market society"

(Fraser 2012, 6).

only in part, as a form of "input," subject to the disciplinary norms of society and not absolved of these by the unencumbered normativity of markets. Marketization of legal education through the linguistic puissance of product talk can be, I suggest therefore, a form of "fictitious commodification" of the kind Polanyi and Fraser describe.[32]

If that alone were not troubling, the added problem is that fictitious commodification in the legal education context is liable to produce the results Polanyi predicted it would have on the broader economy. Uncritical treatment of society as "commodities all the way down" (Fraser 2012, 6). would, he said, destabilize the social order and provoke crisis:

> To allow the market mechanism to be the sole director of the fate of human beings and their natural environment ... would result in the demolition of society. For the alleged commodity "labor power" cannot be shoved about, used indiscriminately, or even left unused without affecting the human being who happens to be [its] bearer ... . In disposing of a man's labor power the system would, incidentally, dispose of the physical, psychological, and moral entity "man" attached to the tag. Robbed of the protective covering of cultural institutions, human beings would perish from the effects of social exposure [and] social dislocation ... . Nature would be reduced to its elements, neighborhoods and landscapes defiled ... the power to produce food and raw materials destroyed. Finally, the market administration of purchasing power would periodically liquidate business enterprise, for shortages and surfeits of money would prove as disastrous to business as floods and droughts were in primitive society.
>
> (Polanyi 1968 [1944], 76)

Given all this, it is important to approach product talk cautiously as a solution to the contemporary legal education crisis.

In attempting to resolve its social dilemmas—moral hazard and limited access to justice—product talk assumes in part then that the *absence* of market discourse was a cause for those dilemmas in the first place. Evidence for this assumption is also apparent in broader reform efforts such as the "Law School Transparency" movement. There activists have demanded, organized, and disseminated greater and more accurate data about law graduate outcomes from accredited law schools, and pushed for better use of this data among prospective law students, accrediting bodies, and institutional marketing offices. As in the discursive shift toward

32 Polanyi uses the undifferentiated notion of "fictitious" to mean unnatural. Fraser calls this the *ontological* interpretation. She then criticizes this as deterministic and limited, arguing instead for a *structural* interpretation where the "fictitious" quality stems not from the underlying character of the object but the degenerative effect its commodification tends to have on the very underpinnings of productive "society." This is crucial she writes, because: "In the case of [the] social reproduction condition, what is at stake are the sociocultural processes that supply the solidary relations, affective dispositions and value horizons that underpin social cooperation, while also furnishing the appropriately socialized and skilled human beings who constitute 'labor'" (Fraser 2012, 7).

product talk, law school transparency has assumed that the solution to current problems is greater marketization.

Yet there is good evidence that commodification preceded the current crisis. Beginning in 1985, *U.S. News and World Report* began ranking law schools annually based on a variety of reputational indicators including selectivity rate, incoming scores, and a reputational survey. Several have said rankings of colleges and universities initiated the modern commodification of the undergraduate sector. A similar argument is plausible for its effect among law schools. Forcing schools to reduce their characteristics to a series of measurements, it also encouraged new students to view their choice of attendance as one of consumption among fungible offerings. Over time, critics charged that the rankings have forced a one-size-fits-all approach to program design.[33] Rather than succumbing to criticisms, rankings in the subsequent years became even more important, more robust, and more extensive. The story of their emergence and domination for both student applicants and law school administrations and business offices is a story about rapidly increasing commodification in the decades before the current "crisis."[34] This suggests that marketization in discourse may have contributed to what we now call the law school crisis.

Thus the literature on commodification warns of the dangers of adopting the market metaphor in efforts to improve legal education. Several responses are possible. One strand of possible counterarguments might assume that, in most cases, the widespread adoption of product talk is merely descriptive or recursive; it reproduces this language only because this corresponds to existing, circulating interpretations. "The law degree is a commodity," according to this kind of counterclaim, "not because *I* say it is but because everyone else treats it that way." Such an argument might point to the intense competition at almost every level of the process: from institutional recruitment, to student engagement and study, to job applications, to employer recruitment, and to faculty scholarship and self-promotion. It might also point to the lingering, documented "economic value" of the law degree itself (Simkovic and McIntyre 2014). To the extent we accept this approach, we can view law school attendance and completion as bringing a certain aggregated "cash value" to its successful participants.

One could also argue, again on descriptive grounds, that use of this language is merely describing how the world *is*, not how it *should* be; and that product talk only reflects this. However, this counterargument is problematic for several reasons. To begin with, there is palpable agreement that true markets must be "well-functioning," and that any putative existing market among law schools resists this adjective (Inside the Law School Scam 2012; Harper 2015; See, Jr. and Tamanaha 2013). The generally easy access to Title IV federal student loan money is only one reason for this: there is not true competition since pricing appears in present terms to be unlimited. Another difficulty is the longstanding problem of informational accuracy and accessibility—a

33 See e.g., Tamanaha (2012); Weyenberg (2009).

34 See e.g., Espeland and Sauder (2007).

problem that persists despite the growing transparency movement. Still another is the unequal bargaining power between academic institutions and would-be law students, particularly near the bottom of the *U.S. News* rankings and in certain geographic regions. For at least these reasons, defense of product talk on a descriptive basis remains weak. Legal education is not simply a "market" because it "behaves" like one if it does not, on close assessment, even behave like one.

A second set of possible counterarguments against the commodification critique might be normative; it would defend product talk because law schools and their various stakeholders *should* behave as if they were in a market. This is more plausible, in part because it requires so little evidence. Believers recognize the deficiencies just listed and mobilize these as reasons why *more* marketization—that is to say deregulation—is needed. Once "unleashed," the market would overcome the artificial insulation caused by Title IV, it would force the free flow of outcome information, and it would help place students on more equal footing in making enrollment and transfer choices between schools.

The normative "should" justification for market discourse has strong support from the approaches of Law-and-Economics. There, legal scholars steeped in the thinking of Vilfredo Pareto, Ronald Coase, and Gary Becker among others, have argued for legal solutions that promote efficiency, wealth maximization, human capital, and so forth.[35] Their language is itself a kind of product talk; it takes the discourse of economics and applies it to non-market (e.g. judicial) decision-making in the hopes of having a non-market social institution (e.g. law) simulate "the market." Normative users and defenders of product talk in legal education make the same move: applying a certain kind of economism (e.g. market fundamentalism) to what is only partially economic activity (e.g. higher education and law schooling). In both cases, there is an uncounted remainder: the many social aspects and relationality involved in professional training—especially for those headed into the legal profession. These social aspects are, I suggest, at the very foundation of law's legitimacy. Making law school a commodity "all the way down," some reformers would liquefy the social bedrock on which it stands, and which allows it to adapt to new social realities.

Still more possible counterarguments remain. Perhaps the refusal to marketize in the name of a romanticized "society" is *itself* elitist. Whereas market citizenship could arguably be democratic (albeit mediated through exchange), this vision of some underlying social relationality will always be prone to hegemony (minority cultural rule), nativism, and exclusivity. Garth's historical example of the Catholic and Jewish law programs is again illustrative (Garth 2013, 2).[36] Some might concede the imperfection of market reductionism, but suggest it at least is resistant to

35 See e.g. Posner (1983); Reynolds (2002).

36 Fraser lodged a similar complaint against Polanyi for reading "fictitious commodities" against "real" or ontological ones. "Conversely, the ontological reading occults the fact that struggles to protect nature and society from the market are often aimed at entrenching privilege and excluding 'outsiders.' Ignoring hierarchy and exclusion, it lends itself to a defensive project: protecting extant constructions of labor, land, and

capture in a way regulation is not.[37] They would likely also add that this social disembeddedness will better serve "the underserved."[38]

But if law school commodification preexisted contemporary problems—and may well have contributed to them—is it safe to put our faith in further commodification to resolve those problems? If not, the corrective today might not be to ignore legal education's market-like features but rather, following Marcel Mauss, to admit of the duality of this economy, regain what we would like to be its social underpinnings, and then continue to suggest reforms honoring separately but coherently both its market and non-market features. This approach most resembles Viviana Zelizer's "multiple markets" theory in which society remains un-subsumed by one monolithic "market" because it *consists* rather of many—each with differing moral constraints (Zelizer 2011, 344).

Conclusion

This chapter has demonstrated the use of "product talk" in legal education emanating from law school marketers, professional journalists, online activists, and legal scholars. Whereas many in these categories call for positive changes in the sector, they may be limited by an overarching uncritical use of the market metaphor to describe what law schools are doing in contemporary society. Evidence from this research that supports this description, as we've seen, includes marketers' overwhelmingly positive use of product talk to sell law school offerings, journalists' tendency to seek more product talk as a remedy for law school problems, online activists' similar usage calling for transparency to better serve the market, and legal scholars' tendency to naturalize the market qualities of legal education by conceptualizing its offerings as products in longer historical perspective. This chapter introduced an important critique of the commodification of law schools that results from use of the market metaphor and accompanying product talk, and went on to consider possible rejoinders to that critique, as well as reasons why

money, along with the domination inhering in them, from marketization" (Fraser 2012, 7).

37 See e.g. Merritt and Merritt (2012, 15): "We conclude by addressing two concerns frequently voiced about deregulation. First, will deregulation allow untrained, unscrupulous hacks to prey upon unsuspecting consumers? Of course it will, but no more so than the current system of regulation. Scholars have repeatedly complained that courts and bar committees do a poor job of disciplining incompetent or dishonest lawyers. Disciplinary authorities are reluctant to penalize colleagues within their own guild; judges, similarly, resist malpractice actions against fellow lawyers. An open market for legal services would not abandon all regulation; it would replace self-interested guild regulation with all of the anti-fraud and consumer protection laws available in our legal system."

38 "How will we provide legal services to the poor? Without the ideals of a protected profession, will any lawyers step forward to offer pro bono legal assistance? The answer to this question, sadly, is straightforward: Despite more than a century of economic protectionism, the American legal profession has never given low and middle-class Americans the affordable legal services they need" (Merritt and Merritt 2012, 16).

those rejoinders fail. In conclusion, I explore the power and possibility of adopting a differentiated approach to law schools' missions and markets—one that draws on sociocultural anthropology.

As a first step, we should differentiate between uses of "market" to describe the various key aspects of law school life such as: (1) student recruitment; (2) graduate employment; and (3) curricular and extracurricular activity. The first two of these are arguably the most overtly commercial in nature: they are clearly influenced by monetary value, driven by wider context, and so forth.[39] But curricular and extracurricular life—the parts of the cycle where students are students—should be shielded from marketization. It is during these years that students try out different possibilities, expand their comfort zones, and reevaluate their extant values. It is during these efforts that students develop their faculties not only to "slot" themselves into an existing economic role, but also to develop the tools needed for adapting themselves to varied new roles.

Like the Kula ring discussed by Malinowski and Mauss, it is possible that the law school rite of passage may partake of two different economies at once: one market-based, the other not. Given the sociocultural significance of Kula in reproducing Melanesian society, it seems to have shared with legal education the inculcation of strict norms. Instead of becoming a commodity "all the way down," legal education could be protected from market creep at its core, where norms are inculcated—in the crucial time "during the J.D." The problem with product talk in this chapter, then, is not its tendency to view any *one* thing as commodity, but to view *everything* as one.

If protecting this duality is important, what are potential alternatives to a market metaphor? If the language of commodity exchange is inadequate, are there even alternatives? Economists of education more generally have asked whether institution-based learning—particularly the kind supported by public finance moneys—should actually be treated as a "public good."[40] Higher education might be a public good in the important sense that everyone benefits from a more educated populace. Democratic processes work more "accurately" because voters can decide issues based on greater informational literacy; industries develop better because workers can bring more conceptual knowledge to product development and design; and social cohesion may be augmented by an increase in sociocultural tolerance brought about by increased—if only theoretical—familiarity with foreign ideas, places, and people.

But paradoxically, in one important alternative sense, collectively more higher education is a private *ill*. The more education everyone receives, the less the private, individualized value of an education is worth. Getting a college degree no

39 Recruitment for all but the top law schools is commercial in the sense that it relies on marketing and seeks to support, if not grow, operating budgets. See e.g. Tejani (2017) for examples of how student recruitment is directly tied to maintaining ambitious growth projections in one law school. Likewise, both Tamanaha (2012) and Campos (2012) have called for students to make enrollment decisions more directly based upon graduate outcomes, or "return on investment."

40 See e.g., Chattopadhyay (2012).

longer makes you valuable once everyone has the same, so now you are forced to attain a graduate degree as well—and on a private level, this costs more. Yet this alternative sense requires a significant shift of perspective from the "public" to the "private" perception of benefit. The two therefore coexist: you may be better off for living in a highly educated society, but you may also be worse off because your B.S. degree commands less in entry-level salary. Is the same true of legal education?

A society benefits from a well-trained cadre of attorneys made easily accessible to the greatest number of people. Present-day laments and proposals about the "justice gap" are a testament to this axiom. Law faculty regret the frenzied clustering of their graduates around six-figure salaried positions not simply because this leaves so many unemployed,[41] but also because it leaves underserved large swaths of the society in need of legal services—and because there is something about meeting those needs that is more than just an economic "opportunity" (Rhode 2015; Herrera 2014). It is, many feel, also a matter of civic responsibility.

The voices quoted in this chapter speak of legal education as a "market" for a certain kind of "product." Their choice is not, I want to emphasize, a mistake; but it is an accurate representation of the legal education experience only from a particular perspective: that of the individual student deciding whether or not the choice to attend is privately a good one. Certain legal education critics have advocated that more students should ask this question, because they believe it will better hold admissions and business offices to account in assessing tuition prices.[42] The lofty ideal of joining legal education as a "priceless" path toward social justice and community service, they say, has been a smokescreen for what law students have been really doing: entering a commercial transaction with an institution to hand over hundreds of thousands of dollars in publicly financed tuition in exchange for training in the skills to pass a bar exam and earn back that amount plus more over the career of a licensed attorney. So far this approach has been an important step toward accountability because it brought into question the longstanding myth that law faculty and administration—disproportionately trained in a handful of elite law schools focused on policy and philosophy—were somehow *not* part of a high stakes moral economy.

But this was only a first step. Because it destabilized the myth of institutional moral neutrality, the idea that law students should act simply as "rational" market actors, who are consuming a professional commodity, has been useful thus far. But it poses a danger if left unmodified by the next stage in the critique and reform effort. That stage, broached in this chapter, is to reclaim law school education as a *dual* process of skills *and* values training, and therefore of private *and* public good cultivation. This reconciliation effort must question the dominant metaphor that enabled the prior critique: that of law schools as a market trading in an educational commodity. Key to

41 This poses a problem if you have valued your tuition in the present based upon the majority attaining such positions.

42 See e.g. Tamanaha (2012).

taking this next step is understanding how the market-as-metaphor may crowd out attention to other important parts of law school education.

References

Block, Fred. 2008. Polanyi's Double Movement and the Reconstruction of Critical Theory. *Revue Inteventions Économiques* 38: 2–14.

Callinicos, Alex. 1999. *Social Theory: A Historical Introduction.* New York: NYU Press.

Callon, Michael. 2007. What Does It Mean to Say that Economics Is Performative? In *Do Economists Make Markets? On the Performativity of Economics*, ed. Donald MacKenzie, Fabian Muniesa, and Lucia Siu, 311–357. Princeton, NJ: Princeton University Press.

Campbell University School of Law. n.d. 10 Questions with Dean Leonard. http://law.campbell.edu/page.cfm?id=605 (accessed January 18, 2017).

Campos, Paul. 2012. *Don't Go to Law School (unless): A Law Professor's Inside Guide to Maximizing Opportunity and Minimizing Risk.* United States: CreateSpace Independent Publishing Platform.

Caron, Paul, and Rafael Gely. 2004. What Law Schools Can Learn from Billy Beane and the Oakland Athletics. *Texas Law Review* 82: 1483–1554.

Chattopadhyay, Saumen. 2012. Education as a Public Good. In Saumen Chattopadhyay, *Education and Economics: Disciplinary Evolution and Policy Discourse.* Oxford: Oxford University Press.

Chemerinsky, Erwin, and Carrie Menkel-Meadow. 2014. Don't Skimp on Legal Training. *The New York Times*, April 14.

Duina, Francesco. 2011. *Institutions and the Economy.* Cambridge: Polity Press.

Durkheim, Emile. 1982 [1895]. *The Rules of Sociological Method*, trans. W.D. Halls. New York: The Free Press.

DustyFeathers. 2017. Undergraduate Major Before Law School. *College Confidential*, January 23. http://talk.collegeconfidential.com/college-search-selection/1957955-undergraduate-major-before-law-school.html (accessed January 24, 2017).

Espeland, Wendy Nelson, and Michael Sauder. 2007. Rankings and Reactivity: How Public Measures Recreate Social Worlds. *American Journal of Sociology* 113: 1–40.

Fairclough, Norman. 1995. *Critical Discourse Analysis: The Critical Study of Language.* London: Longman Publishers.

Feldman, Noah. 2016. Commentary: Law Schools Should Have to be Really Honest. *Chicago Tribune*, March 8. www.chicagotribune.com/news/opinion/commentary/ct-law-schools-employment-graduates-20160308-story.html (accessed January 23, 2017).

Fordham University School of Law. n.d. Apprenticeship Program. www.fordham.edu/info/26384/apprenticeship_program (accessed January 18, 2017).

Frank, Robert H. 2009. The Invisible Hand, Trumped by Darwin? *The New York Times*, July 11.

Fraser, Nancy. 2012. *Can Society be Commodities All the Way Down? Polanyian Reflections on Capitalist Crisis.* FMSH-WP-2012–2018. https://halshs.archives-ouvertes.fr/halshs-00725060 (accessed August 8, 2019).

Fraser, Nancy. 2013. A Triple Movement? Parsing the Politics of Crisis after Polanyi. *New Left Review*June: 119–132.

Garth, Bryant. 2013. Crisis, Crisis Rhetoric, and Competition in Legal Education: A Sociological Perspective on the (Latest) Crisis of the Legal Profession and Legal Education. *Stanford Law and Policy Review* 24(2): 503–532.

Graeber, David. 2001. *Toward an Anthropological Theory of Value: The False Coin of Our Own Dreams.* New York: Palgrave.

Greenhouse, Carol. 2011. *The Paradox of Relevance.* Philadelphia: University of Pennsylvania Press.

Haney-Lopez, Ian F. 1994. The Social Construction of Race: Some Observations on Illusion, Fabrication, and Choice. *Harvard Civil Rights-Civil Liberties Law Review* 29: 1–62.

Hann, Chris, and Keith Hart. 2011. *Economic Anthropology: History, Ethnography, Critique.* Cambridge: Polity Press.

HappyAlumnus. 2015. NYT "Law School Debt Crisis." *College Confidential,* October 25. http://talk.collegeconfidential.com/discussion/comment/18898140#Comment_18898140 (accessed January 24, 2017).

Harper, Steven. 2015. Too Many Law Students, Too Few Legal Jobs. *The New York Times,* August 25.

Hart, Keith. 2016. The Anthropology of Debt. *The Journal of the Royal Anthropological Institute* 22(2): 415–421.

Harvey, David. 2005. *A Brief History of Neoliberalism.* Oxford: Oxford University Press.

Henderson, William. 2013. A Blueprint for Change. *Pepperdine Law Review* 40: 461–507.

Herrera, Luz. 2014. Educating Main Street Lawyers. *The Journal of Legal Education* 63: 189–210.

Ho, Karen. 2009. *Liquidated: An Ethnography of Wall Street.* Durham, NC: Duke University Press.

Horkheimer, Max, and Theodor Adorno. 2001 [1944]. *Dialectic of Enlightenment.* New York: Continuum Publishing.

Hymes, Dell. 2013. *Foundations in Sociolinguistics: An Ethnographic Approach.* London: Routledge.

Inside the Law School Scam. 2012. Market Failure. August 20. http://insidethelawschoolscam.blogspot.com/2012/08/market-failure.html (accessed May 29, 2017).

Kitroeff, Natalie. 2015. Five Charts that Show You Should Apply to Law School this Year. *Bloomberg News,* April 22. www.bloomberg.com/news/articles/2015-04-22/five-charts-that-show-you-should-apply-to-law-school-this-year (accessed January 26, 2017).

Lakoff, George, and Mark Johnson. 2003. *Metaphors We Live By.* Chicago: University of Chicago Press.

Malinowski, Bronislaw. 2002 [1922]. *Argonauts of the Western Pacific: An Account of Native Enterprise and Adventure in the Archipelagoes of Melanesian New Guinea.* London: Routledge.

Marx, Karl. 1978. *The Marx-Engels Reader* 2d. Ed., ed. Robert Tucker. New York: W.W. Norton & Company.

Maurer, Bill. 2005. *Mutual Life, Limited: Islamic Banking, Alternative Currencies, Lateral Reason.* Princeton, NJ: Princeton University Press.

Mauss, Marcel. 1970 [1954]. *The Gift: Forms and Functions of Exchange in Archaic Societies.* London: Cohen & West.

McEntee, Kyle. 2013. What's Driving Change in Legal Education and Why You Should Care. *Law School Café,* May 30. www.lawschoolcafe.org/2013/05/30/whats-driving-change-in-legal-education-and-why-you-should-care/ (accessed January 23, 2017).

Merritt, Deborah Jones, and Daniel C. Merritt. 2012. Unleashing Market Forces in Legal Education and the Legal Profession. *Georgetown Journal of Legal Ethics* 26: 367–386.

Merritt, Deborah, Lowell Hargens, and Barbara Reskin. 2001. Raising the Bar: A Social Science Critique of Recent Increases to Passing Scores on the Bar Exam. *University of Cincinnati Law Review* 69: 929–968.

Mertz, Elizabeth. 2000. Teaching Lawyers the Language of Law: Legal and Anthropological Translations. *John Marshall Law Review* 34: 91–117.

Mertz, Elizabeth. 2007. *The Language of Law School: Learning to "Think Like a Lawyer"*. Oxford: Oxford University Press.

Mitchell Hamline School of Law. 2016. Minnesota Lawyer: Mitchell Hamline Builds "Dream Law School" With Career Focus. News and Events, September 16. http://mitchellhamline.edu/news/2016/09/16/minnesota-lawyer-mitchell-hamline-builds-dream-law-school-with-career-focus/ (accessed January 18, 2017).

Moliterno, James. 2013. A Way Forward for an Ailing Legal Education Model. *Chapman Law Review* 17: 73–88.

Muller, Derek. 2013. Legal Education is Innovating by Educating More non-JD Students. *Excess of Democracy*, November 8. http://excessofdemocracy.com/blog/2013/11/legal-education-is-innovating-by-educating-more-non-jd-students (accessed January 25, 2017).

Olson, Elizabeth. 2014. Law School Is Buyers' Market, With Top Students in Demand. *The New York Times*, December 1. https://dealbook.nytimes.com/2014/12/01/law-school-becomes-buyers-market-as-competition-for-best-students-increases/ (accessed January 23, 2017).

Patrice, Joe. 2013. The ABA Is Coming Around on Reforming Legal Education. *Above the Law*, February 11, 2013. https://abovethelaw.com/2013/02/the-aba-is-coming-around-on-reforming-legal-education/ (accessed January 25, 2016).

Polanyi, Karl. 1968 [1944]. *The Great Transformation*. Boston, MA: Beacon Press.

Posner, Richard. 1983. *The Economics of Justice*. Cambridge, MA: Harvard University Press.

Pound, Roscoe. 1946. What is Law? In Roscoe Pound, *Social Control through Law*. New Brunswick, NJ: Transaction Publishers.

Reynolds, Noel B. 2002. Pareto Optimality and the Rule of Law. In *Method and Morals in Constitutional Economics: Essays in Honor of James M. Buchanan* (Studies in Economic Ethics and Philosophy), ed. G. Brennan, H. Kliemt, and R.D. Tollison, 237–252. Berlin: Springer.

Rhode, Deborah. 2015. *Access to Justice*. Oxford: Oxford University Press.

Riles, Annelise. 2004. Property as Legal Knowledge: Means and Ends. *Journal of the Royal Anthropological Institute* 10: 775–795.

Rosen, Lawrence. 2006. *Law as Culture: An Invitation*. Princeton, NJ: Princeton University Press.

Sarat, Austin, and William L.F. Felstiner. 1995. Law and Social Relations: Vocabularies of Motive in Lawyer/Client Interaction. In *The Law and Society Reader*, ed. Richard Abel, 403–430. New York: NYU Press.

Sassen, Saskia. 2017. Predatory Formations Dressed in Wall Street Suits and Algorithmic Math. *Science, Technology & Society* 22(1): 1–15.

SeeJr., Harold F., and Brian Z. Tamanaha. 2013. Are American Law Schools Failing?: An Exchange Between Brian Tamanaha & Harold See. *Engage* 14(3), October. www.fed-soc.org/publications/detail/are-american-law-schools-failing-an-exchange-between-brian-tamanaha-harold-see (accessed May 29, 2017).

Segal, David. 2011a. Is Law School a Losing Game? *The New York Times*, January 8. www.nytimes.com/2011/01/09/business/09law.html (accessed February 10, 2017).

Segal, David. 2011b. Law School Economics: Ka-Ching! *The New York Times*, July 16. www.nytimes.com/2011/07/17/business/law-school-economics-job-market-weakens-tuition-rises.html (accessed January 23, 2017).

Simkovic, Michael, and Frank McIntyre. 2014. The Economic Value of the Law Degree. *The Journal of Legal Studies* 43(2): 249–289.

Sokol, Daniel. 2015. RE: Want to Solve the Law School Scam? Expose Law Schools to A Market for Control. *ProfessorBainbridge.com*, January 25. www.professorbainbridge.com/professorbainbridgecom/2015/01/want-to-solve-the-law-school-scam-expose-law-schools-to-a-market-for-control.html (accessed January 25, 2017).

Sunstein, Cass, and Richard Thaler. 2008. *Nudge: Improving Decisions about Health, Wealth, and Happiness.* Chicago, IL: University of Chicago Press.

Tamanaha, Brian. 2012. *Failing Law Schools.* Chicago, IL: University of Chicago Press.

Tejani, Riaz. 2016. Efficiency Unbound: Processual Deterrence for a New Legal Realism. *U.C. Irvine Law Review* 6(2): 207–242.

Tejani, Riaz. 2017. *Law Mart: Justice, Access and For Profit Law Schools.* Stanford, CA: Stanford University Press.

Tham, Alex. 2017. The Financial Crisis and Moral Accountability: Translating Practices of Risk, Profit, and Uncertainty. In *The New Legal Realism: Translating Law-and-Society for Today's Legal Practice*, ed. Elizabeth Mertz, Stewart Macaulay, and Thomas W. Mitchell, 223–243. Cambridge: Cambridge University Press.

Thisdell, Katie. 2017. Most Influential People in Legal Education 2016. *The National Jurist*, Winter: 18–19.

University of Nebraska-Lincoln. n.d. Roscoe Pound: Influences of the University of Nebraska's Golden Age. http://unlhistory.unl.edu/exhibits/show/pound-influences/pound-influences (accessed August 3, 2019).

Urciouli, Bonnie. 2010. Neoliberal Education: Preparing Students for the New Workplace. In *Ethnographies of Neoliberalism*, ed. Carol Greenhouse, 162–176. Philadelphia: University of Pennsylvania Press.

Wahlberg, Adam. 2015. Why William Mitchell and Hamline Law Had to Merge. *Minnesota Post*, February 18. www.minnpost.com/education/2015/02/why-william-mitchell-and-hamline-law-had-merge (accessed January 18, 2017).

Wake Forest University School of Law. n.d. Master of Studies in Law Degree Featured in Wall Street Journal Article, in News and Events. http://news.law.wf.edu/2013/05/master-of-studies-in-law-degree-featured-in-wall-street-journal-article/ (accessed January 18, 2017).

Weiner, Annette. 1992. *Inalienable Possessions: The Paradox of Keeping-While-Giving.* Berkeley: University of California Press.

Weyenberg, Michelle. 2009. *U.S. News and World Report* Seriously Considers Proposed Changes to Their Law School Ranking. *The National Jurist*, May 28.

Wtracing. 2008. RE: Life After T4. *Law School Discussion*, January 16. www.lawschooldiscussion.org/index.php?topic=100280.msg2545652#msg2545652 (accessed January 24, 2017).

Zagursky, Erin. 2010. Meese and Stafford Team Up to Teach Law and Economics. William and Mary Law School, News Archive, May 7. http://law.wm.edu/newsstories/2010/professors-team-up-to-teach-law-and-economics-courses.php (accessed January 18, 2017).

Zahorsky, Rachel. 2009. Irvine by Erwin. *ABA Journal*, August 20. www.abajournal.com/magazine /article/irvine_by_erwin/ (accessed February 10, 2017).

Zelizer, Viviana. 2011. *Economic Lives: How Culture Shapes the Economy.* Princeton, NJ: Princeton University Press.

Part III

Invisible Processes and Images in Legal Training

7 Language, Culture, and the Culture of Language

International JD students in U.S. Law Schools

Swethaa Ballakrishnen and Carole Silver[*]

Higher education in the United States has witnessed an increasing trend of international student enrollment and just in the last three decades, international students have more than doubled in enrollment, both in terms of actual numbers and as a rate of proportionate representation within the larger student population.[1] Yet, situated in context, these numbers encompass more specific and nuanced institutional trajectories. For instance, international students comprise a more significant proportion of graduate-level enrollment than they do of students enrolled in all academic levels combined, but this graduate enrollment is not constant across programs.[2] Specifically, these students are more likely to pursue – or, rather, more likely to be admitted to – master's level (often self-funded)[3] programs rather than (often more selective and

* This research was supported by the Northwestern University Pritzker School of Law Faculty Research Program (Silver) and the AccessLex Visiting Scholarship in Legal and Higher Education at the American Bar Foundation (Ballakrishnen). For invaluable research assistance, we thank Northwestern Law graduates Shinong Wang and Injune Park and Laura Castillo at UC Irvine School of Law. We are indebted to the law schools that supported our work by facilitating access to their students, and to unnamed key informants at those and other law schools; in addition, we are especially grateful to the students and graduate alumni who shared their experiences so generously with us. For comments on earlier versions of this work, we thank Steven Boutcher, Bryant Garth, Sida Liu, Beth Mertz, Gregory Shaffer, and the participants at Legal Ethics Schmooze (June 2019), Law & Society Annual Meetings (June 2017, 2018), The Globalization of Legal Education: A Critical Study (September 2017), Legal Education in Crisis? (March 2017), After the JD and Future Research (November 2016), Metrics, Diversity and Law (May 2016), International Legal Ethics Conference (July 2016), University of Wisconsin East Asian Legal Studies Center (Feb. 2016), and the Global Legal Skills Conference (May 2015).

1 International students accounted for approximately 5.5% of all enrolled students in U.S. higher education in 2017–18, when 1,094,792 students came to the U.S. for their studies. In contrast, three decades earlier in 1987–88, 481,280 international students came to the U.S. for higher education and accounted for 2.8% of all enrolled students (IIE 2018).

2 In 2016–17, for instance, international students comprised 5.3% of all enrolled students (IIE 2017), and about 13% of all enrolled graduate students (IIE 2017; National Center for Education Statistics 2017).

3 According to research focused on international students studying in Australia, "most international students are self-funded and seek a return on investment in the form of graduate employment in the host country" (Gribble, Rahimi, and Blackmore 2017, 16).

institutionally funded) doctoral programs.[4] Moreover, enrollment in professional degree programs is even more limited than in other graduate programs, with international students accounting for only approximately 1% of professional degree students.[5] While these are not insignificant numbers, seen this way, these percentages reflect what we know about the push and pull factors that ground the transnational processes of human capital flow more generally: shorter and specialized graduate programs that are universally transferable have more institutional resources, incentive and support to attract international students. In contrast, professional programs that are jurisdiction-bound have more circumscribed "legs" and much less appeal for investment by international students.

To some extent, law schools mirror these larger national patterns, with higher international enrollment in graduate programs than in their core professional program, the JD. Indeed, in many law schools the trend is more pronounced than the national figures, with international students comprising all or at least the lion's share of students in LLM – equivalent to a master's degree – and SJD programs – equivalent to a PhD in law (Hupper 2015, 2007). But although a much smaller proportion of the main professional degree program (the JD) is international, the last decade has witnessed a new growth spurt of international students even within this program. This is because, despite the JD traditionally being considered a "domestic" and mainstream law degree (ABA n.d.), it offers a more plausible route into the U.S. legal labor market for those who seek it. This shift in focus is in no way to suggest that programs tailored for international students are losing popularity. In fact, significant numbers of international students continue to be admitted to U.S. law schools in such programs (Adams 2017; Muller 2016; National Jurist 2014). However, this trend – especially in elite law schools – has continued alongside the rising entry of international students into JD degree programs.

These demographics have shaped the scholarship that has emerged around international law students. Over the last few decades, the robust research on legal education in the U.S. has expanded to include narratives about international student participation and experience (Lazarus-Black 2017; Garth 2015; Lazarus-Black and Globokar 2015; Ballakrishnen 2012; Silver 2012a; Silver 2010; Spanbauer 2007; Goldhaber 2005; Silver 2002) but this has almost exclusively focused on students in international-friendly (and, often, international-specific) programs like the one-year master's level LLM[6] or the research-

4 More than 20% of all international student enrollment was centered in master's degree programs (225,883 students in 2017–18), compared to approximately 11% in doctoral programs (123,500 students) and only approximately 1% in professional degree programs (13,020 students) (IIE 2016/2017).

5 The Institute of International Education (IIE) reported 13,020 students in professional degree programs (IIE 2016/2017).

6 We refer to all post-graduate master's-level degrees earned by graduates of foreign law degrees as an "LLM" here, although there are other names for this degree; the

focused doctorate in law, the SJD. There are indications in this research about why interest may be shifting to the JD among some international students. Specifically, unlike the one-year "capstone" style program of the LLM (which has varying levels of credibility in U.S. and international labor markets (Silver 2010; Ballakrishnen 2012) and the more academically oriented SJD degree (used almost only by students interested in academic job markets, typically in their home countries), the JD promises a more immersive U.S. experience and a path into the legal market based in the U.S. Indeed, this path even extends to foreign legal markets like China and Korea where U.S. law firms exert a significant influence. However, despite these factors that might make the JD more attractive to these students, there still is very little that is known about their experiences, and how these experiences compare to those of students in more traditionally internationally focused programs. Our research seeks to bridge this gap.

To understand how being international matters in a "mainstream" law school setting, this chapter draws from interviews with 58 international JD students to shed light on student perspectives across three distinct levels of analysis. We *first* address the importance of studying these students by mapping the historic rise of international students in law school, especially in contrast to other trends in higher education. In doing so, we explore the supply side dynamics that feed into this situated context and argue that this increase might be attributed to the technical – rather than perceived – limitations of the more traditional international tracks in these schools. *Second*, we consider the ways in which interactions with classmates, faculty and others in the law school buffer students' experiences in law school. Specifically, our focus here is on interactions around language and culture that include and exclude students in different contexts and constellations of law school participants. We suggest that language and, beyond literal language, the cultural extensions of language are particularly significant in determining students' senses of identity and belonging. *Finally*, we draw on the ways in which international students and their interactions are embedded within institutional pressures and contexts. Shedding light on the variations in this experience, we show that the backgrounds of students might affect their identity and experience, but it is within the context of the structures they are embedded in that valorization is afforded to them. Altogether we argue that the language of law school privileges a certain kind of ideal student and this expectation has implications for schools as well as the various actors that increasingly have to navigate them.

University of Michigan, for example, offers a Master in Comparative Law degree (MCL) that requires fewer credits than does its LLM degree. At the same time, certain law schools offer an LLM degree that requires two years rather than one; see, e.g., Georgetown Two-Year (describing a two-year LLM with a Certificate in Legal English). Additional variation on the basic degree framework goes beyond these, too; see, for example, Stanford SPILS, which is a one-year or longer program to prepare foreign lawyers to apply for an SJD.

Trends of International Students in U.S. JD Programs

International students in law schools are a fraction of the enrollment for international students in fields like engineering and business that are seen as more transportable than law.[7] Even so, at many law schools, graduate programs host a higher proportion of international students than the 13% that international students represent in graduate level enrollment in the U.S. overall (IIE 2016/2017; NCES Digest n.d.). For at least two decades, a significant proportion of U.S. law schools have offered postgraduate master's-level degree programs (typically leading to an LLM degree) specifically for international law graduates – meaning students who earned their first degree in law from a school situated outside of the U.S. The popularity of the LLM for international law graduates is reflected in the growth in the proportion of law schools offering them: in the mid-2000s, approximately 40% of all American Bar Association (ABA)-approved law schools offered at least one LLM program open to international law graduates (Silver 2006); today, this has increased to more than 75% of all ABA-approved law schools.[8] Information about the proportion of LLM students who are international is not easy to determine because it is not required to be reported by law schools, but application information for LLM programs suggests that as many as three-quarters of U.S. LLM applicants are international law graduates.[9] Moreover, even specialist LLM programs like tax, which used to require a U.S. JD as a condition to entry, now openly embrace international law graduates in their application and marketing materials (Georgetown Law 2018; Northwestern Law 2018; University of Florida 2018). Overall, LLM programs generate important revenue for law schools in light of the decline in JD enrollment in the last several years, and importantly they do this without affecting the *U.S. News* ranking of the law schools. Today, LLM and other post- and non-JD degree programs account for a larger proportion of law school enrollment compared to the JD (ABA 2017), and in this way, the students contribute to internationalizing their law schools.

In contrast to these graduate programs, a much smaller percentage of students in JD programs in U.S. law schools is international. Still, as we show in recent work, this percentage is rising and emerging to be crucial, especially when compared to other

7 On enrollment by international students in these areas, see IIE (2014–2016) (reporting that the three most popular fields of study for international students studying in the U.S. are (i) engineering (216,932 international students), (ii) business and management (200,312 international students) and (iii) math and computer science (141,651 international students)).

8 The 75% figure is based on data reported by the ABA Section of Legal Education and Admissions to the Bar regarding law schools with post-JD and non-JD programs, and a review of the websites of listed law schools. As per these data, 154 U.S. law schools supported at least one LLM or other postgraduate program open to international law graduates.

9 The Law School Admissions Council (LSAC) reported that 7,194 of 8,601 LLM applicants as of August 2015 were graduates of non-U.S. law schools (LSAC 2015). Note, however, that these LSAC data likely do not represent all applicants to all U.S. LLM programs because certain schools allow applicants to bypass the LSAC credentialing service.

minority populations, particularly in elite law schools (Ballakrishnen and Silver 2019). Some of this rise is the historic context of this emergence: U.S. law schools struggled to maintain enrollment after 2008 (Sloan 2018), leading to a nurtured interest from international applicants and a subsequent rise in their enrollment. Arguably as a result, in the same period, international enrollment increased more significantly compared to other kinds of domestic minority student enrollment (Ballakrishnen and Silver 2019). In 2017, for example, international students (defined by the law schools in terms of their non-resident alien status)[10] accounted for 3.32% of JD enrollment, still the smallest segment compared to Asian/Asian American students (6.20%), Black students (8.42%), Latina/o students (12.60%) and white students (60.83%) (ABA Standard 509 Requirement Disclosures 2017, see ABA 2011–2017). But these figures belie the growth spurt: the percentage of international students enrolled in JD programs grew by nearly 87% from 2011 to 2017, compared to the increase for Latina/o students (slightly more than 37%) and Black students (nearly 18%) during the same period (Ballakrishnen and Silver 2019). Perhaps equally important, the growth of international enrollment in JD programs was more pronounced at schools in the highest positions of the *U.S. News* ranking, where these students accounted for nearly 8% of the JD population in 2017, up from just over 4% in 2011 (ABA 2011–2017). We argue that this growing significance of international students in JD programs calls for some urgency in understanding their experiences, both as an important research insight to their navigation of these processes, as well as a broader lens for gaining a more nuanced view of the experiences of other populations of diverse students.

Particularly, these rising demographics of international students reflect a range of interrelated mechanisms at play. For instance, at least some of these shifts can be explained more generally by the internationalization of higher education (IIE 2016). The shift to the JD specifically reflects certain overseas legal markets becoming anesthetized to the U.S. LLM (Silver and Ballakrishnen 2018). At the same time, declining enrollment in law school also has been crucial in directing schools to embrace and seek out new applicant pools (Sloan 2017; McEvers 2016; Douglas-Gabriel 2015; Hansen 2015; Olson and Segal 2014; Silver 2012b; Tamanaha 2012). For example, international applicants may experience law schools' shift to embracing the GRE in admissions as increasing accessibility. Moreover, it is possible that law school leaders perceive that being international is necessary in order to maintain their schools' reputations as elite organizations, just as this phenomenon has characterized law and other professional service firms. And from the perspective of international applicants, the change of course towards the JD might reflect students' seeking superior returns from their law degree in the United States, seeing a U.S. job as an important step in their careers.

In this chapter, our analysis takes shape from the interaction of these institutional perspectives with students' actual experiences and choices. Navigating the JD is

10 See Ballakrishnen and Silver (2019) for a discussion of the ways in which international identity compares to immigration status.

complicated by expectations of faculty and administrators, classmates and even prospective employers. These challenges often are discussed under the umbrella of "language" difficulties, but as we show below, language involves considerably more than technical syntax and vocabulary. In highlighting this role of language and the way it intersects with students' actual lived experiences, this research extends other work on the role of different kinds of legal language and culture in reproducing hierarchy (e.g. Mertz 2007; Kennedy 1982) to this new and increasingly relevant demographic.

Data and Methods

In order to study international students, it was necessary to come to some understanding of what it means to be international for purposes of U.S. legal education. Essentially, we could not pursue this research simply by obtaining a law school list of its "international" students.[11] Instead, we pursued a two-pronged approach to generate as diverse a sample as possible in terms of law school attended, home country, gender, year in school and path to the JD program. On one hand, we invited students identified as non-resident aliens by their law schools to participate in the research,[12] and on the other hand we used a snowball sample method by asking each interviewee to identify other students who they thought would be interested in participating, who we then invited to an interview. Approximately one-third of the interviewees were obtained through snowball sampling, with the rest coming from law schools' direct or indirect outreach to their students

11 The starting point for this was learning that U.S. law schools categorize students according to their visa status, so that "international" students are those individuals classified as non-resident aliens according to immigration regulations. This is the basis for law schools' reporting to the ABA and is reflected in their enrollment reports. But non-resident alien status is only one way to identify who is international, and in order to avoid inadvertently reproducing the judgment of law school administrators, faculty or students about what it means to be international, we explored the symbolic notion of being international directly in our research (Dezalay and Garth 1995, 31). In this way, we are able to explore the seeming cohesiveness of the category as well as how students select themselves and are sorted into more nuanced subsets.

12 Two law schools provided Silver with the contact information of every non-resident alien JD. One of these schools had fewer than 10 such students, and Silver invited each of the students to participate through an interview; approximately 75% of these students participated in the research. The other school enrolled approximately 50 non-resident alien students in its JD program, and Silver selected students from this list in order to balance the general interview pool that was developing simultaneously. To that end, first-year students and students from particular home countries were excluded because of a concern that these populations were over-represented in the existing sample. Approximately 75% of students who were solicited at this second school participated in the research. Three other law schools facilitated the research by indirect means. At one of these schools, the administration emailed its non-resident alien students about the research and directed interested students to contact Silver directly. Another school included a message about the research in a student newsletter, indicating students should contact Silver. The third school arranged for Silver to meet with a group of seven non-resident alien students.

(together, these conversations with 58 JD students are referred to here as "interviews").[13]

The interviewees attended a set of 17 distinct law schools that are diverse in terms of ranking, size and affiliation.[14] Thirty-eight percent of the interviewees were enrolled in one law school, while 28% graduated from eight different law schools at which between two and seven interviewees were enrolled. The remaining interviewees each graduated from a different law school.[15] The interviewees also came to their JD programs by way of varied paths, which we have discussed in more detail in other work (Silver and Ballakrishnen 2018). Sixteen students earned a first degree in law outside of the U.S., and half of these earned a U.S. LLM before beginning the JD.[16] Twenty-one interviewees earned a U.S. undergraduate degree,[17] and three earned a non-law master's degree in the U.S. before matriculating in the JD. Three students were in a JD-MBA program. In addition, certain students varied in their paths based on transferring within the JD program,[18] or spending fewer than 3 years in the JD program.[19] Each of these distinctions might exert an important influence on students' experiences in the JD program. Of the interviewees enrolled in a three-year JD program (including transfers), 13 were 1Ls when we interviewed them, 15 were 2Ls and 16 were 3Ls. Four students had graduated the year before their interview.

Women comprised approximately 60% of the interviewees, and students claimed citizenship in a total of 17 countries. Chinese citizens accounted for approximately 45% of the interviewees. While a smaller segment of the sample, citizens of South

13 As a complement to this research, Silver also conducted individual interviews with 12 international LLM students or recent LLM graduates; all but one of these students earned their LLM at a single law school that also enrolled certain of the international JDs who participated in this research.

14 Of the 17 law schools represented among the interviewees, seven schools were rated by *U.S. News* within the top 14 spots in 2014, which was the year when most interviewees were considering and applying to law school. Half of the remaining schools were in the 15–50 ranked positions, and the other half of the schools were in the 51– unranked positions.

15 Four of the law schools that our interviewees attended or graduated from are part of public universities. Forty-seven of the interviewees attended a law school situated in the Midwest. All but five of the law schools included in the study are located in major metropolitan areas. Schools ranged in the size of their student bodies: 11 schools enrolled between 500 and 1000 JD students; five were larger and one was smaller. Each of the schools also enrolled post-JD students (including LLMs).

16 Half of the LLM graduates and half of those who earned a first degree in law in their home country enrolled in a top-14 ranked law school for their JD program.

17 Citizenship for interviewees who earned a U.S. undergraduate degree includes Korean (five), China (five), U.S. (four) and one each in Canada (dual citizenship with another country), England (dual), Hong Kong (dual), Japan, Poland, Viet Nam and a small Eastern European county.

18 Six interviewees transferred from one law school to another within the JD program.

19 Ten interviewees spent fewer than 3 years in their JD program, either because they received advance standing on the basis of earning a U.S. LLM or because the program otherwise was abbreviated in recognition of their earlier legal studies.

Korea and Canada also represented significant segments of our interviewees (16% and 10% respectively). It is not possible to determine whether this break-out reflects the general population of international JD students because law schools are not required to report students' home countries in their ABA reports. Nevertheless, in extrapolating from two sources that provide some insight into this issue of sending countries, our sample is generally reflective of the significance of China, South Korea and Canada as the three largest sending countries for JD students,[20] although in our sample, students from China are over-represented. In addition to China, South Korea and Canada, multiple interviewees also claimed citizenship in Mexico (three interviewees, one of whom held citizenship in two other countries, including the U.S.), Hong Kong (two, in each case holding dual citizenship) and the U.S. (five interviewees, one of whom held citizenship in two other countries). In addition, four interviewees either held or anticipated obtaining permanent residency status in the U.S. in the immediate future.

The interviews were conducted either in person or through a video call platform (Skype or FaceTime) by Silver, with the exception of three interviews that were conducted by her trained research assistant, who also was an international JD student at the time. The interviews were open-ended and semi-structured. Interviews were recorded (with the exception of two, for which detailed notes were taken), and recordings were transcribed and coded using a scheme of 174 codes. Both authors were involved in developing the interview questions, determining the coding scheme and in the analysis of the interview data. Interviewees here are referred to by a pseudonym derived from published information about common given and family names in the home countries of our interviewees. Certain interviewees used American names, and for these we followed this pattern and assigned American names to them.[21]

Interactional Identities of Being an International JD Student

Law schools categorize students as being international based upon their immigration status as non-resident aliens, and this also serves as the basis for their reporting international student enrollment to the ABA.[22] But immigration status, as we

20 The two sources are data from the Law School Admissions Council and data on visa approvals for students studying law in the U.S. in a doctoral level program (which is categorized to include the JD), according to immigration records for the years 2008–2012. These are discussed fully in Ballakrishnen and Silver (2019). Our research sample is more heavily weighted toward China than either of these comparison groups.

21 Interviews are cited by reference to a numerical code in the format of "I1501," where "I" refers to interviews conducted with a single interviewee, "G" to those conducted in a small group, "15" or "16" refers to the year when the interview was conducted (2015 or 2016) and the last two digits reflect the numerical code for the particular respondent (e.g., "01"). Page references to interview transcripts are indicated following a comma, where relevant.

22 See ABA (n.d.), "Guide to Data" (describing that under the heading "JD Enrollment and Ethnicity" the "spreadsheet reports on the gender, race, ethnicity, and non-resident status of the study body as a whole and of the first-year class").

have demonstrated in recent research, does not always coincide with students' self-perception of their identities (Ballakrishnen and Silver 2019). Instead, our data reveal that being international is a more fluid category that depends on experience at least as much as on formal status. For example, while technical status certainly had its advantages, for many students in our study who were born in the U.S. or who later obtained citizenship or permanent residency, status was not determinative of their sense of identity.

For example, Daisha Robinson, who was born in the U.S. but grew up in another country, returning only for college at age 18 (I1535), described herself as both technically an American student and yet very much also identifying as an international student. Similarly, Robert Silva, who held U.S. citizenship (based upon his father being a U.S. citizen) as well as passports in two other countries described himself as not feeling entirely at home in the United States, despite his citizenship. Robert's sense of flexible identity is striking in the way he describes his first visits to the U.S.:

> I consider myself an immigrant, even though I have the citizenship, and I'm not a … immigrant, but some things are similar to an immigrant, where the networks in your family and the people there to help you out when you first arrive is very important.
>
> (I1542, p. 12)

Other students with permanent residency status also identified as being international. It was common for such students to describe themselves as having a "dual-identity." Among those who referred to this notion was Daniel Tao, a third-year student from China, who described that "most of the time, I just consider myself both ['Chinese or to be more Chinese American or Asian American'], as one package, if that makes any sense" (I1528, p. 5).

In this meaning making around their international identity, language was a predominant moderator for many students. Seohyun Lee, for example, was a U.S. permanent resident who had moved to the U.S. with her family from South Korea when she was 10. During our interview, she described how introducing herself to American peers always included interactional discomfort because she had to navigate saying her name in ways that felt easy or comfortable to people who did not speak Korean. She admits that although she now pronounces it just as she "would say it to other Korean friends," historically she tried to pronounce her name "the way Americans do" but never "felt comfortable" doing so and "always hated ice-breakers" because she'd have to say her name (I1533, p. 16). Similarly, for Michael Choi, who was in the process of getting his green card (based on his wife's citizenship status), language continued to operate as a constant reminder of his outsider status. He spent his high school and college years in the U.S., but despite having "spent a good amount of time in the U.S.," he admitted that the fact that English was not his "mother tongue" was "always in the back of his mind," affecting his confidence in law school, particularly when he was on call in the classroom and had to speak in front of his peers (I1524, pp. 6–7).

These examples illustrate that even for students with the right to remain permanently in the U.S., their international status and identities were moderated by a range of abilities and expectations about language. Of course, as we show in other work (Ballakrishnen and Silver 2019), beyond technical classifications, not all students felt they fit within the one fixed category of "international student," and for a few – especially those that had spent a lot of time in the U.S. or were native English speakers for other reasons – being international was more a logistical annoyance than an unbridgeable cultural hurdle.[23] Instead, identity was mediated through a range of personal and professional interactions that students navigated in law school. Across different settings, while formal and informal status remained pertinent, so too did perceptions about identity and the ways in which they were differently signaled and received in interactions (Ballakrishnen and Silver 2019).

At the same time, for a number of students in our study, their choice of the JD program as opposed to the more traditionally international LLM or SJD degree programs, reflected an important signal of both their professional ambition as well as their desire to distinguish themselves from other kinds of international identities within the law school. Interviewees described core advantages of the JD program, even if there were steep costs associated with it. For example, Yu Wei, a 1L from China, explained, "If I want to stay in United States, of course I will choose JD. Even though it's, like, three years program, you need to put efforts and time in it, but it's worth it" (I1517, p. 12). And several students emphasized the JD as the best option for those who intend to make their careers in the U.S. Liang Min, another 1L from China, commented:

> But for law students, especially LLM students, Chinese LLM students, most of them will go back to China. Yeah, especially for all the students that just graduate from China and they come to U.S. They don't have any working experience. It's very hard for them to get job here.
>
> (I1507, p. 17)[24]

Relatedly, interviewees also described the advantages of the JD as including more time in law school (three years versus the LLM's nine months), the credibility on the job market and the overall feeling that their legal training was more solid.

23 A classic example of this was David Zamora, a non-resident alien according to his law school's categorization but someone who did not consider himself international. David, when approached, declined to participate in the study, explaining: "I'm not exactly your target audience. I have lived in the U.S. since I was 7, so I feel more American than international. The only respects in which I've had a different experience have been with visa issues/concerns" (I1557).

24 Another interviewee commented on the differences between LLM and JD graduates: "I have some LLM fr- … students and they are my friends. And they come back … They came back to China and they applied job. … They say their … the … the hiring manager, look, their resume, they think their LLM is not … It's not … JD. … If you have a JD program in your resume, it's better to apply to job in China" (I1512, p. 47).

Some of them even – despite not knowing the exact extensions of the LLM degree – felt that they were better prepared to take a bar exam if they went through the JD program (I1517, p. 11).

Yet, over and above these rational, logical distinctions, international students viewed the JD program as offering other soft advantages. In particular, it provided an opportunity to divorce themselves from the normal routes pursued by international students – that is, the LLM or SJD – and gave them a chance to unstick themselves from what felt like an "othering" identity, a chance to avoid "seeming like LLMs." This distancing from what was considered a less than ideal status often was framed in terms that included a reference to language. For example, Victoria Zeng, a Canadian student of Chinese descent, explained why students – especially those whose first language was not English – would want to signal that they are *not* LLM candidates, that their international status ought not to be the singular thing that defined them:

> I do feel like people whose, let's just say if English isn't their first language and they sound like they may be an LLM or they're international I feel like there is a bias kind of that people don't necessarily want to work with them.
>
> (I1539, p. 12)

Victoria was not including herself in this at-risk group; she felt that she fit in in her law school for the most part (she explained that "I feel like … people generally don't even realize that I'm international … . I've been told I sound like I'm from California" (I1539, pp. 11–12)), so her comment reflected her perception of *other* international JDs rather than a revelation about how her peers responded to her. Similar to Victoria, Adam Marquez, a student from Mexico, also put himself in a different category from international LLMs. Adam was pursuing a joint JD-MBA degree, but his reasons for why the LLM category was a non-ideal one went beyond language:

> [F]or some reason I've seen a lot of negative comments, I hear them all the time from JDs about LLMs. And I think a lot of it has to do with the language barrier and sometimes LLMs don't know how to express themselves very good in class and so it slows down the class or … . And some people criticize the LLM, like [they] think that many LLMs don't take studying as seriously, like they're more here or some of them are just here for a year and they go back to the law firm and they're more like having a good time and they're not going to be as prepared for class. And some people get upset about that, things like that.
>
> (I1525, p. 17)

In Adam's description, the unattractive association of the LLM category went over and above just sounding foreign. Instead, it consolidated his desire to disassociate from stereotypical characteristics about international students that he had internalized from his interactions with classmates (e.g. that LLMs might be read as transitory, less hard working and generally not fully committed to the program). Of course, not all students chose to distance themselves from their LLM peers and some – especially if they were otherwise able to distinguish themselves as cosmopolitan – sought the community of LLM students who shared other kinds of cultural identities with them like a common language or country of origin.[25]

Still, despite this meaning making that prompted students to invest in the JD degree, the shift in academic programs alone often was not enough for them to necessarily reap the corresponding anticipated benefits of identity they so desired. Sometimes, their awareness of this seemed almost to unfold during our conversation, especially when they spoke about their ability to access resources within the law school from their position as JD students. For example, Yu Wei, a 3L student, described her disappointment with her career advisor: "Like career service, I got an advisor. She – I don't think she, like, she showed much interest in my background … when we talked about my Chinese background" (I1517, p. 11). Other students described their career advisor as helpful but uninformed about the particular needs of international JDs, especially around international placements and visa policies of hiring firms (I1518, pp. 34–35). In other contexts, too, international JDs experienced the consequences of institutional conflation of being international with the LLM degree program. For example, Victoria, mentioned earlier, recognized that the distinction between LLM and JD students could work against her and other international JDs in the way that the university – in this case, the International Office – identified "international" as equivalent to "LLM" in the context of the law school, resulting in her feeling overlooked by an orientation presentation allegedly aimed at all international students but perceived as being pitched to the particular problems of LLMs.[26]

25 For example, Emily Ye, a 3L who held passports in Canada and Hong Kong, commented: "I was asked to speak on a panel about marginalized voices on campus … where they brought in marginalized voices … one of the voices that they brought in was an LLM student from the Caribbean, and she was speaking about the foreign student and LLM student experience. I think having her on the panel that I was a part of really brought in another layer of marginalized voices, because she was bringing forth to all the professors the fact that there are students from different places who have a different perspective to bring into the classroom, that sometimes aren't invited to bring it, so they feel awkward, or they feel like it's unnecessary, and so they just don't say anything. So, I've seen it through other people. I don't necessarily know where I've been put in that situation, except for I'm taking a seminar right now on nationalism and cultural identity, which I love. It's amazing. Everyone there is like me and has these weird mixed identities" (I1545, p. 17).

26 "[D]uring orientation week there was this panel for international students hosted by the IO, the International Office. And a lot of international JD students walked away from it feeling really unsatisfied because although it was marketed as a panel for all international students the focus was really on the LLMs. They talked about all the issues that the LLMs were faced and for the JDs we felt like we had to raise our hands and be like, wait a minute, what about us? What do we do in this situation? And it just seemed like IO wasn't very concerned about the JDs" (I1539, p. 24).

Alongside each other, these interactions signal the perception that international JDs still remained "different" from the average ideal student in the law school. For these international students, the "fit" with their respective environments, notwithstanding their possible intention to assimilate, still was an uncomfortable compromise between their actual and imagined identities.

Language, Culture, and the Culture of Language

A significant context for being perceived as an international student was the law school classroom, and although the reasons varied across respondents, it was a particularly grueling space for many interviewees. Broadly, the culture of the classroom posed a milieu of hurdles for the average international student, including trouble with expressing their opinions, participation and, especially if they were not (or, worse, not seen to be) native English speakers, language. It is worth noting that the international JD students in our sample (and generally) did not suffer because of the absence of language proficiency per se. They satisfactorily completed the LSAT exam as an entrance requirement, and many graduated from English-speaking programs (in or outside of the U.S.) in college and even high school. Notwithstanding this, language operated as more a coded cultural term – used by the students, their peers, faculty and staff for what it meant to communicate in the law school classroom. Violet Min's description of the classroom space she navigated as a language outsider summed up the classic obstacles that many students whose first language was not English felt about the hardship of keeping track of their foreign surroundings:

> I think in law school there are basically two things that struggle me. … One is the language problem. … And I have to pay more attention to … the class. And sometimes I … have to sit in the front row. … And I can listen clearly. And … I'm trying to be more involved in class 'cause I noticed that some other American people, they answer the question frequently and carefully, but most of Chinese people won't answer the questions, even though they know the answer, they don't want to hands up and answer that … . And the second … thing is about the … way you think. … Just like what I talk about, about the legal system, and the different teaching method that you should get used to that. … I think this semester is getting better. … Last semester it just … even though I read, I finished my reading, I did not understand it. … So I cannot do great job during class and answer the question.
>
> (I1511, pp. 41–42)

Violet's description of her setback in the classroom is not unlike other accounts of international students in American higher education (Newsome and Cooper 2016; Helal 2013; Terui 2012; Lefstein and Snell 2011; Wa et al. 1992). But a few things make what seems like a standard case of "language trouble" extra pertinent. For one, unlike other graduate programs where language might be incidental,[27] law and the legal profession are constructed in ways that emphatically privilege language. We have to wonder how different these students' experiences are because they are studying law. Specifically, it raises the question whether the way law is taught and studied in the U.S., with the heavy emphasis on verbal skills and absence of particular prerequisites, is responsible for the divide that many of the interviewees described. Insight was offered by several interviewees who also had experience in another higher education program in the U.S., whether business school or an engineering program (notably, both of which are among the fields that draw in most international students). These students described law school, in comparison, as more segregated and generally less international. But it is, perhaps, the emphasis on language in the law school culture as well as curriculum that is a significant distinction. Michael Choi contrasted law school to his college engineering studies:

> One thing that I wanted to mention is that being an international student as an engineer [his undergraduate major] in college … it's just very different, because in engineering, especially, more than half the students were all international and predominantly Asians in the class. So when I first came to law school, my first classes, that was very strikingly different. And also a lot of words instead of numbers, so that's also different.
>
> (I1524, p. 11)

Similarly, Timothy Cho, a JD-MBA student, drew distinctions between the typical law and business student, among other things:

> [A]t the law school you can see a lot of the American students will hang out with the American students and, like, the LLM students hang out the LLM students, like international students hang out with themselves. … But we don't really see that at [the business school] because everybody is so international both in terms of perception and experience … somehow they [i.e., those in the business school] get by, I think. Because if half the students don't speak English fluently, I mean don't quote me on this but, I mean, if half the students aren't as fluent in English as, like, the American JD students here, then it kind of becomes normal and they really don't, you know, have a problem at all. And people who don't speak fluently don't feel uncomfortable at all. Whereas, if you think about it, the American JD students here are really very, very bright students who are very well spoken even among, like, the Americans, right? They talk very fast, they're very eloquent, they're very quick and smart, so, it could be pretty difficult for someone who don't speak English very well to socialize with them, I think.
>
> (I1521, pp. 29–30)

27 In fact, the fields that draw in most international students are the more language-agnostic fields of engineering, business and management, and math and computer science. See IIE (2014–2016, n. 7 supra).

Together, these comments indicate that it was not just the lack of technical language skills, or law as a field, that made Violet feel inadequate in the classroom – it was also her cultural praxis that held her back from being in sync with what she saw as the rest of the class, or, in some sense, her view of the ideal student. In Violet's terms, she might not put up her hand to answer a question "even though she knows the answer" and "unlike some other American people" who, as she says "answer the question frequently and carefully." This learned pattern of how to be present in an American classroom no doubt comes from a cultural expectation around exchange and communication that goes beyond technical ability. Hui Qiao, another Chinese student, similarly identified the combination of English being her second language and the U.S. law classroom dynamics where she felt misunderstood and unheard as leading to her sense of frustration with being invisible in class:

> Sometimes I need to speak out. Like, I need to tell my other U.S. classmate my … my thought. They maybe don't consider what I'm thinking … . Because they cannot understand what your position, what's your difficulties when you study. So I hope my classmates will understand me and just give me a chance to express my opinions. Because sometimes … some classmate, they are very talkative.
>
> (I1512, p. 56)

While we use Violet and Hui Qiao to make the case about invisibility and presence in communication, their position of feeling like they could not articulate their thoughts because of lapses in language was not shared by all of our respondents. The layered relationship with communication was common among many students for whom English was not a first language, but most students in our sample did not report experiencing direct language barriers. Instead, they described feeling more subtle barriers that marked the hesitation in interactions: an accent, for example, or a confidence lapse in specific interactions, or culturally specific affect in conversations (Ballakrishnen and Silver 2019). And while the challenge of invisibility loomed against many – if not most – of the students in our sample, this was addressed differently by different students. Zhang Wei, for example, a second-year male student from China who had earned a master's degree in finance in a different U.S. university before beginning law school, described gaining confidence from watching the interactions of other international students in class:

> In the beginning, … I was feared of talking out loud and this weird accent. But then you get used to it and just what really matters is your confidence. So I think even those LLMs from Spain, they talk really even weirder accent, just my personal opinion. And they're confident … . They are expressing their opinions, their thoughts, and that's good for the community. They bring different aspects, they bring their knowledge from Spain. So that's good and I could do the same … . And I think I get more time to prepare

> for each class, I felt more, I think, more about class for each subject so I talk more in class. And that feel good.
>
> (I1510, pp. 18–19)

This account of Zhang's sounds much like any law student who might be intimidated by a U.S. law classroom – language then, was much more about, as Zhang puts it, "confidence," than it was about language itself. Still, at the same time, while it was certainly a good ideal, many students never gained the sort of comfort that Zhang described. Some considered the risk of embarrassment at being an obvious "other" too high, like Minsoo Lee, a 3L from Korea:

> And I'm, you know, frankly speaking, I'm … I'm always afraid to make mistakes in front of American students who are in class. Then I'll get really embarrassed. So I try not to speak when I know that it's … when I'm not too confident with grammar. I only speak in class when I'm confident enough that I won't make any grammar mistakes. So even though my English … even though I can communicate and I'm capable of conveying my thoughts in … in English, I'm always self-conscious about the fact that my English … isn't perfect.
>
> (I1518, p. 30)

Minsoo's comments were all the more significant because it was unlikely that someone could have determined his identity based just on his accent. But it also reminds us how pertinent extensions of language such as accent, cultural assumptions about clarity and confidence – rather than technical language itself – were critical in making students feel like they were accepted within these environments. Another Korean student, Jennifer Shin, also was acutely aware of language as a distancing factor, and here she goes further than Minsoo in describing how she had borne the brunt of comments she perceived as critical regarding the perfection of her spoken English. Jennifer had been in the U.S. since high school; in fact, even earlier through summer camp experiences. Nevertheless, her interactions with her American law school classmates were colored by anxiety about those characteristics that most clearly identified her as international:

> Koreans are very diligent and disciplined, and … so they try their best, but I guess that happens to everyone in law school. But international students have to take another additional step to be on the same level as other people. Some people make fun of my grammatical mistakes or talk to others that, oh, she makes a lot of grammatical errors, and it just – not all of them, but there are some people who will do that. That could hurt my dignity. But I don't think this person would generalize the U.S. students.
>
> (I1519, p. 31)

Interactions with faculty in the classroom context also contributed to international students feeling ignored or specifically targeted. Often this was not related to a professor intentionally trying to exclude or include the student. Rather, the palpable difference came from a failure to acknowledge that this new type of law student needed some adjustment in the classroom. Minsoo Lee, for example, relayed an experience when his professor intentionally refused to acknowledge that his international background might implicate distinct challenges:

> I actually asked my professor once that I want to record his class, because … because English is not my first language. He, and he actually refused, saying if, if you're a JD student, and if you're here, I don't think you will have any problem. And so he was very respectful in, in his refusing my request. But that was his … response … . I accepted it, and I, you know, sink or swim.
>
> (I1518, pp. 21–22)

Minsoo's disheartened acceptance of the "sink or swim" response from a faculty member demands attention not because faculty ought to mollycoddle students (although allowing someone to tape in a classroom can hardly be considered "mollycoddling"), but rather because the silencing of Minsoo's problem comes from making him invisible within a more cohesive category of what it means to fall within the ideal type of a JD student.[28] If the ideal – or, worse, the only – type of JD student is one who "will not have a problem" understanding English, then making an exception for Minsoo seems unnecessary and impossible. Yet, this rejection, which Minsoo had no choice but to accept, signals a rejection by faculty of the reality of a more diverse student body. Given the rising demographic of international students in these classrooms – many of whom are not native English speakers – the construct of the ideal JD student may itself need to shift. Essentially, if law professors are to best serve all of their students, they may have to re-imagine who comes within their vision of the "ideal" or even the "typical" JD student.

In another aberration from this ideal type of American law student, a Korean student, Seohyun Lee, relayed an experience she had in class where she felt singled out for different treatment for reasons related to her international identity:

> So I had one professor who cold called everybody by their first names, but I don't blame him at all, I think it's natural, but he referred to me and this other Korean JD MBA by our last names because it was easier. I wasn't offended by it, but it just feels more distant. That's one. And I'm not sure if this … if professors also think about this consciously, but I never get cold called in the

28 It also is worth noting that many students, for a range of reasons, could have made a similar request to tape a lecture and yet the request was denied not because of a standard policy against recordings in the classroom, but, rather, on the specific grounds of Minsoo being an international that once "here" should not "have any problem" understanding him.

> beginning of the semester. And I like to think that it's because my name is not … When you're looking at the seating chart it's not the first thing that pops up. It's not the easiest I think for professors to say, that's my guess.
>
> (I1533, p. 21)

Seohyun here related events that made her feel uncomfortable – first her exclusion from a normal classroom exchange (i.e., at not being "called on" – an important part of law school life in the United States) and then her expressly primed minority status (i.e. of being referred to by her last name while others were not). However, she explained these as unintentional slights – done merely for the professor's convenience and therefore, relatively in-offensive to her personally. And recall, Seohyun's comment earlier about her own discomfort with pronouncing her name in a way that aligned with American expectations and the Korean language. These comments remind us that exclusion need not stem – and most often does *not* stem – from an intention to target or exclude a specific student. Nevertheless, even unintentional exclusion still may have salient repercussions. Li Min, for example, a Chinese 1L, told us about her professor referring in class to the television show, *The Simpsons*, and calling her out as the only student in the class who "doesn't not know [The] Simpson[s]." She described this as the "worst experience, but … [the] only one bad experience in law school" (I1507, pp. 21–22). Language, then, is not just about words used, but, rather, interactional contexts conflated with popular culture that may be inclusive or isolating to different students. One can imagine that Li Min's professor was only trying to make the class more relatable, but it sets up one more way in which language is not just language, but its extensions within the confines of a very specific cultural context that can add further alienation.

These examples of exclusion and express inclusion highlight two important things to consider in increasingly diverse classrooms. First, students might, even when professors do not intend it, feel alienated if they are in classrooms where they are expressly treated differently because they are not part of the dominant group (in this case, not being seen as domestic students). Second, students might be under-reporting or, as in Seohyun's case, explaining away with logic, actions that might alienate others and even themselves. As researchers who study these newly diverse environments, we have to pay attention both to the position and the relative standing of international students as they navigate these terrains. After all, even targeted alienation, in the eyes of a student who has structurally less power, can seem "just another quirk." In addition, this alienation might escape being flagged as problematic by the students because, in addition to having less power in these situations, students have incentive to pay less (rather than more) attention to these divisive classroom dynamics; from their vantage point, after having worked so hard at trying to fit in, who would want to make a scene about how they are expressly being made to stand out?

Further, and in addition to these direct interactions, were the perceptions informed by informal interactions and observations that are central to framing the impressions of international students in the eyes of other JDs. In the context of relaying his own experiences as an international JD, James Wilson, a 2L from Canada, also explained typical preconceptions about certain international students that limited the potential for meaningful interaction:

> I think particularly toward international students from East Asian, East and Southeast Asia there's a presumption among many American students that their English ability will be limited or that their cultural understanding will be limited. That may not always be true, and that presumption can actually hinder what could otherwise be fruitful discussions … . Never anything quite so overt as rolling eyes, but cutting conversations short early because of a slight language barrier or conversations among westerns where people just sort of express an attitude of like, what's the point of talking to that person or like referring to someone as like some random Asian chick or whatever … . I mean I've had those interactions where I'm at an event and it might be a loud, crowded event and someone tries to have a conversation with me and I just literally can't understand what they're saying. And I'm like, I don't want to be dismissive, but I just cannot understand between the noise and the accent and the vocabulary.
>
> (I1540, pp. 9–10)

Crucial to this explanation is the difference between what *actually* marks a student's identity (their language, cultural references) and what is *seen* as marking their identity. These kinds of differences (here, for example, between what a student is *seen* as versus the way they actually identify) can foreclose any chance of communication or exchange with international students, thereby reinforcing a social gap that might already be at play in these interactions. As James highlights above, there *are* cases where the language gap is real, but assuming that it always exists just comes in the way of "what could otherwise be fruitful discussions."

Yet even as these examples of language-related hurdles in the classroom were widely prevalent, they were only one more form of distancing that international students described encountering in the classroom. Of course, not all international students were similarly disadvantaged. And as we show in other work (Ballakrishnen and Silver 2019), certain students experienced these environments very differently, whether because of their English proficiency or *perceived* English proficiency. But among the students who could not "pass," the disadvantage was real and students seemed to understand that language was not just about whether they could speak English but, rather, a more layered cultural expectation.

In fact, for many students in our study, one of the anticipated benefits of the JD program was a chance to be part of an environment that could socialize them more completely into an American law school, as well as into the wider American culture, both of the legal profession and generally. But the bias these students experienced in interactions with peers, particularly in class, was a powerful, if indirect, exclusionary force. As a consequence, for many students, their social interactions did not integrate them to a wider network of friends and, in some cases, even further distanced them from being part of these new social circles. Particularly in interaction with peers, there still was a bias against international students, one that many perceived in indirect – but no less powerful – ways from their environment. Consider the description by Hillary Han, a 3L who earned her undergraduate degree at a Big Ten university and was enrolled in a law school at another Big Ten school, of how excluded she felt in her first-year Civil Procedure course – a required class for most first-year JD students. Her description of both feeling like she did not know what was going on *and* that she did not feel comfortable enough in her surroundings to ask for clarifications, sets up exactly the kind of hostile environment that many international students have to endure:

> So for the Civil Pro class – I had never taken any law class before, because we don't have a law degree in the U.S. And I never had any legal background. … And then I find out that I had a problem understanding what the professor is talking about in Civil Pro. And I felt so awkward to ask questions, because I feel everybody else around me knows what is going on, except myself. And I still remember one day one of my classmates asked me a question. I have no idea what she's talking about. And she gave me a really dirty look … it just feels so hard.
>
> (G1659, p. 7)

Similarly, Ya-ting (Anna) Chang, a Taiwanese 3L student, echoed Hillary's comment: "When there is class discussion and when I am paired with other people, and when I talk, people don't have eye contact with me. I wonder why. And then I tend to not like those classes with class discussions" (I1655, p. 6). These examples point at ways in which students may self-select themselves out of classes when they feel like they are not seen or heard ("I tend to not like those classes with class discussions") – actions that may both further isolate these students but also give schools a convenient excuse to suggest that such isolation is of the students' own accord.

Navigating Law School: Peer Networks and Career Goals

In this section, we highlight two additional themes in these interactions that moderated the status of being international. As we saw earlier, identity creation for most students was a complicated process that was motivated by a variety of reasons. Student identity and experiences were shaped by technical markers like citizenship and language proficiency, but they similarly were shaped by more subtle motivations (e.g. the need to signal that they were not a certain kind of "international"). Particularly, interactional factors were crucial and international students had to face a range of hurdles in classroom interactions and more diffuse peer interactions that distanced them from peers and colleagues both because of the ways in which they communicated as well as the ways in which they did not – or could not – communicate. But language and culture also had effects beyond general perception and reception of these students to determine more particularly the kinds of groups, networks and cliques that students were part of in these institutions. Of course, who their friends were depended on these preceding two mechanisms and yet, at the same time, their friendship groups set up an extended reflection of how they saw their environments. Similarly, these law school experiences contributed to students focusing on different kinds of activities and coursework in law schools, choices that had implications for their career goals and trajectories. Our data does not afford us complete information about either these networks or their future career choices more generally,[29] but the kinds of choices students in our study were making allude to several interrelated and iterative processes that defined the ways in which international student experience in law schools may impact their early careers more generally. Together, then, these mechanisms offer an interactional tapestry that buoyed each student's particular fit within their surroundings.

Friends Networks, Cliques, Study Groups and Others

Not all students spoke about isolation or exclusion in the same ways. In contrast to students who told us that they were not seen or heard, several described themselves as having acquaintances who found their international experiences interesting. And for some of our (for example, Canadian) respondents who felt assimilated in terms of language and culture, the JD offered a much more cohesive law student experience. Still, the perspective of being perceived as different was not far beneath the surface for most of the students we interviewed, even if they could and did easily interact with American students on a superficial level (Ballakrishnen and Silver 2019). An example was Andrea Diaz, a Latin American student who was close friends with American students yet still felt like they did not "get her." Her interactions only further accentuated their differences, as she explains in this discussion about humor:

> [I] n general, [Americans] have a really different sense of humor from what Latinos have, for example. ... So a lot of times what happens to me is that I make jokes ... . It's not the same sense of humor. I find that's like a really big barrier because then I have to keep explaining myself all the time when I make jokes that they will never understand. They think I'm being serious. And some of them feel offended ... . And I just find that happens in general with a lot of Americans. They just don't get me.
>
> (I1534, p. 6)

29 In separate forthcoming research, we are exploring the relationships and networks of law students, including international JDs and LLMs. In addition, future research is focused on understanding the career trajectories of international JD graduates and the ways in which being international is perceived as a factor.

Like humor, cultural references to things like sports and television shows often were used as ways to establish a comfortable rapport. But unlike Li Min, mentioned earlier, who felt badly because she was called out as having no context for understanding *The Simpsons*, other students recognized these cultural references as mechanisms of assimilation, even as they felt disassociated with it themselves. Seungmin Suh, for example, a Korean 3L student, described learning about local sports teams as a way to have a common topic of conversation with law firm lawyers during recruiting. He explained:

> Where you're from leads to, for guys especially … leads to sports … . Sports is a pretty quintessential topic of conversation. I was having this conversation … , so it just dawned on me, there's professional sports and college sports, and I was getting a lecture that those are really different things. Professional sports is just light, but college sports is where you're from. Even though I went to college in the U.S., you don't really have the sense of belonging. And I think of that, a lot of my friends went to college in Korea, and this is not just about guys and sports teams. It's hard not to feel isolated when you're not really immersed in the community. And being knowledgeable enough about sports, and faking it, it's like a get-out-of-jail free card in conversations. If you're not saying anything about sports, people might think of you as a little aloof, awkward. So even though I'm not interested, I make a conscious effort to keep up. I don't really care about the Cubs, but I try to watch them and learn their names.
>
> (I1520, p. 51)

Thus, even in this intentional effort to fit in by investing in learning a topic that was assured to draw in American classmates and others in the legal profession in the U.S., international students experienced a sense of difference. And for those who felt that they were not part of the in-group of English speaking, mostly domestic students, their networks remained quite homogenous, comprised generally of other students from their home country or region. John Oh, for example, who graduated from a Big Ten university and also had spent time in the U.S. during elementary school, explained that his close friends are Korean,[30] and described that "being Korean" in this context:

> means that they speak fluent Korean, they have a Korean culture that really matches with me. And I'll give you an example in the law school even. Some students would say they're Korean, but the way they act and the way they interact with people they're just completely Americans. Because Korean culture has this kind of hierarchy by age so you're supposed to respect your elders.
>
> (I1526, p. 4)

30 In Oh's definition, "Korean" does not include American students of the same ethnic heritage. He described a gulf even between interactions with such students. For example, in describing the students who were active in an Asian American student association at his law school, he perceived a "wall between Asian-American versus national Asian" students (I1526, p. 14).

Of course, friendship networks – and their homogeneity – also depended on who else was in the law school. Minsoo Lee reflected on this when describing the different experiences he had in his 1L year and after transferring to a new law school. His second and third years were spent in a law school with quite a large Korean student population, and he explained this as leading to him retreating from interacting with American students:

> I think more Korean students there are, then your interaction with American students actually become less because you, you know, hang out with Korean students and there's so ... there's a lot. So it's ki- ... I guess it's kinda like a self-segregation ... . 'Cause I mean, if there were no Korean students at all, then you would have to, you know, make friends with Americans, unless you wanna be alone. And that might force you to, you know, go to, like ... like social gatherings and events and ... and try to make friends that way. But when ... When there's ... there are so many Koreans, you don't really ... You try to remain in your comfort zone. So that actually is, you know, makes less interaction with ... with Americans, I think.
>
> (I1518, p. 45)

Even apart from the transfer experience, interviewees described their interactions and friends shifting over the course of their three years in the JD program. Recall Michael Choi, a Korean 3L who attended high school and college in the U.S.

> So when I first came to law school I wanted to hang out with as diverse group of people, friends as possible. So I tried that for a little bit, but then just naturally it happened such that the remaining friends that are close to me are Asian-Americans. And that seems to be a two-way street too. It's interesting.
>
> (I1524, p. 9)

Andrea Diaz, described earlier, explained these changes as working in two directions – being more willing to engage in small talk with Americans, and at the same time, shifting her friendship relationships towards more students from her home country region:

> if anything I've just met more Latinos and I hang out with more Latinos than I did in my 1L year. I mean, I do, like, say hi to more people in the corridors, with more Americans, I'm like, "Hi," or, "Hi, how are you doing?" It is just a minute or two of small talk and that's all there is. There is more of that than when I started, but actually being friends with people, I'm friends with more Latinos now then I was at the beginning.
>
> (I1534, p. 7)

As these students describe, the friendship groups of international JDs are quite focused on classmates from the same home country or region – including even for Canadians, who tended to bond with other Canadians while also easily relating to

American students.[31] These challenges are not unique to law schools or to the international JD population (Silver 2013, 474–475; Gribble, Rahimi and Blackmore 2017, 26). But as a result, the social networks described by our interviewees were even less international and more homogenous than the social networks of even many international LLMs who, despite their limited interaction with U.S. JD students, had more culturally diverse cohorts and interactions because of the international nature of their degree program.

Effects of Institutional Identity on Career Goals and Growth

Law students generally focus on how their coursework will lead to a particular career path. For international JDs, this implicates decisions about where students anticipate living and working once they graduate. In speaking about these decisions, uncertainty was a constant refrain, but this went well beyond the norm for their American peers. International students – assimilated and non-assimilated alike – were uncertain about finding a job in the U.S. because of their international status. Most faced uncertainty related to their immigration status and whether they could obtain a long-term visa, even if their firm or employer would sponsor them (much less pay for these costs). But even for those with citizenship or permanent residency, students voiced concern with other transnational issues of belonging and attachment. Many could not predict their feelings of wanting to be near family when they began their own families or as their parents aged. And similarly, many expressed the hope of contributing to their home countries through their professional roles in the future. In fact, for most of the students in our study, the idea of returning home percolated throughout their law school experience and reflected interrelated considerations, from personal and family concerns to immigration status, opportunities and transportability.

These considerations combine to frame the ways in which students viewed and pursued their legal education. Even if they sought to begin their careers in the United States, these factors suggested a more global career trajectory. And, among other things, how they approached and pursued law school reflected their thinking about how to make their degree and early practice experience portable to their home countries. Many interviewees reflected about moving back to their home country and they generally thought that it would be easier for them to use their practice experience and legal education at home in a transactional, corporate-focused context, rather than in one where their practice focused on litigation. For instance, Liwei Jiang, a Chinese 3L, explained:

> being an international student influences the courses I take and my career path. I can't say for sure that I would practice litigation and took more litigation courses in law school if I am a native, but I would at least considered

31 As Victoria Zeng explained, "I only know a few other international students because the Canadians tend to talk, so those are the people I know. But outside of that all my friends are American" (I1539, p. 9).

> that option and perhaps tried it myself. As an international student, I never seriously considered being a litigator. Almost all other international students around me are in corporate practice, this was how they get employed. I think this message was to me that only international students have to focus on transactional practice … . The chance of not being able to stay in the U.S. is a big concern for me, and that really convinced me to practice corporate law. If I practice litigation, and had to return to China because I didn't get the visa, my litigation skills won't be very helpful in Chinese legal market. On the other hand, corporate skills are much more transferrable. I think this probably explains why almost no international JD students became litigators in the U.S.
>
> (I1549, pp. 4, 7)

Similarly, Kenneth Luo explained that he did not want to limit his choice to practicing law in the U.S. He discussed his plans of keeping open the option of returning to China, his home country. As a result, when deciding upon which practice area he would focus in his job search, he "tried to look for practices that would allow [him] to work overseas if [he] wanted to." Because "corporate is a little bit more international than litigation in that aspect," he eventually chose to pursue a career in corporate law, as opposed to a litigation practice (I1541, p. 9).

Only rarely did an interviewee describe intentionally ignoring this portability consideration in order to pursue a course of study and first career step that might not transfer to home in the event he decided to move. Richard Jin was that rare international JD, who described himself in just those terms, as "exceptional" with regard to his determination to take litigation-related courses, and this was aligned with his determination to pursue a career in litigation:[32]

> Let's start with courses. Again, I'm exceptional. My view is that I'm here to learn American law, so I'm gonna do litigation or really American law courses. But, most of my Chinese friends, they are taking something useful to them after going back to China, so they are mostly taking commercial law, corporate law, … that kind of thing. But, for me, it's more litigation or criminal, things like nobody takes.
>
> (I1554, p. 6)

32 Richard's explanation for his focus was, however, substantive and not geography centric. As he explains: "I am interested in practicing litigation. I am interested in litigating a lot, and my first choice is constitutional litigation, which is not that common. Otherwise, I'm really interested in something like white collar crime, or probably just general litigation. I don't know. Those areas are not common or, not common at all to international JDs, because litigators tend to probably require better language skills or a better understanding of the culture. I don't know, there's more strategy involved in litigation than transaction. For most international JDs, I would say they definitely prefer transaction, I guess. Another reason is that, if you are going back to your country sometime after your practice here, it's a lot easier and more fluid to take those transactional experiences back to your country. I mean, M&A in China and the U.S. is not that different. But, litigation is just really like two worlds" (I1554, p. 10).

At the same time, going home – or interacting with their home country – did not always involve a physical move. It also framed the interest of certain international JDs in creating careers that allowed them to make a positive difference in ways intrinsic to their identities. As Daisha Robinson reflected:

> I have these long-term goals that are not necessarily set in stone, but they still kind of exist in my mind to contribute to my country and region in a certain way. Like whether that means I'm physically there or whether that means I am here and building better connections and networks for my country for business people or for non-profit organizations there.
>
> (I1535, p. 24)

In addition to these portability considerations about being able to utilize their legal expertise if they returned home or worked to benefit their home country, however, international students described their international backgrounds as framing decisions about what they did during law school, including which law school classes to take. A JD degree signals a certain breadth of exposure to American legal education that includes first-year courses, a particular pedagogical approach, and topics that illuminate the ways in which law matters and is used in everyday U.S. society. These common law-school experiences distinguish JDs from LLMs, too. But in addition to being structured in ways that alienated international students (as illustrated by the Taiwanese student who felt alienated in classes with heavy peer discussions), many courses deeply implicate American history and political culture, and these presented challenges for international students who had not grown up in the U.S. and/or immersed in its popular and civic culture. So interviewees described carefully selecting courses to ensure that they would minimize what Seungmin Suh described as "playing catch-up":

> I think Asian students, or at least Korean students, have a general sense of, they generally want to avoid classes that involve a more fundamental, like abstract understanding of the U.S. court system and the government system. So for example, classes like Constitutional Law, Federal Jurisdiction and Administrative Law, I think those classes are ones that we tend to avoid because, especially because if you are … in a curved [grading] situation, your, my thought is that … . I was really worried that I would be … having to play a catch-up game with other students who were, you know, born and raised in an environment where they were constantly getting news updates, they would read the papers and they would just have a more, like, a fundamentally solid knowledge of the system to begin with … . I generally want to avoid playing that catch-up game. I don't want to … have to … go out of my way to, you know, just be at the same level … as where a lot of the native-born people here are. So … that kind of ties into … class selection … . I might have incredibly enjoyed Federal Jurisdiction or … Criminal Procedure, those classes … . But I think that

> being an international student kind of affects that judgment in that way, because you know for a fact, at least for yourself, that you're not at a … equal level of understanding as … most of the other peers who have really first-hand experience with the system here … . But I can get a job just fine by not really, like, sinking my teeth deep into the system here. And like, so that's, I think, something I wanted to mention.
>
> (I1520, p. 46)

A similar comment was made by a Canadian student about the double-burden that international students faced while choosing to take a course like Constitutional Law, which beyond being a foundational law school class, also was thoroughly imbued with the background of American society.

> I feel the same way about Con Law, too … it's something about not being raised with these issues in mind, that you feel like a disconnect with them. And you feel like you're learning a lot of stuff for the first time, too. So whilst I feel like a lot of my peers have like this advantage of being … of having the historical context and understanding what this country has been through, you're sort of trying to learn that whilst also talk about this in a complex legal manner. Which is a barrier in itself. I mean, because you're learning two things versus one.
>
> (G1656, p. 5)

These patterns illustrate how the international backgrounds of these students intersected with the schools' various institutional factors to shape not just experiences, but also agentic choices. Law school grading curves were combined with competitiveness, choices about enrolling in important law school classes came enmeshed with the worry that these students might never escape their status, or that their lack of cultural familiarity and comfort might inevitably lead to their detriment. While students navigated their identities for themselves, they also had to continually struggle to navigate them against set perceptions and institutional patterns that were established without them in mind. And it is within this context that many international students were forced to acknowledge their otherness of not being an ideal student.

Conclusion

This chapter highlights the importance of taking into account a range of supply-side narratives as the demographics of U.S. legal education start to change. International students are no longer just specialized actors outside the "mainstream" logics of the U.S. law school. Their parallel admission and graduation trajectories can no longer be explained away as different from what the "regular" law student does or wants. Instead, these rising trends within the JD program signal a need to rethink what these notions of "regular" and "mainstream" can mean for students and schools alike. While our research is by no means comprehensive in its ability to report on the varied experiences of international law students, it highlights the fact of variation and the ways in which this interacts with the individual and institutional characteristics and contexts to shape the experience of international students, as well as that of their environments and its other participants. As we repeatedly suggest, there is not one kind of international law student or experience that is most reflective of this collective whole. But as law schools admit more international students, it is useful to consider the ways in which inclusion may still remain exclusive to a specific kind of law student. Further still, schools might gain from considering their part in creating and fostering this inequity of access.

A central pattern in our research, as we elaborate in this chapter, is the importance of language to the international student experience. At first appraisal, it might seem like a straightforward extension – language is an obvious hurdle in any educational setting and international students who are non-native English speakers are most poised to have to deal with it. However, as we show, language is seldom just technical language. Rather, in the construction of this more layered interactional language, culture and the cultural connotations of language were key. Other scholars have argued evocatively for a reconsideration of the institutional effects of this kind of "language" in the law school. Beth Mertz (2007), for example, argues that language, operating in terms of a set of institutionalized thought and speech processes that translate into trusting the ability of learned legal analysis in the law school context, functions to reproduce race and privilege under the guise of meritocracy. Similarly, other research shows that the kinds of cultures that law schools breed have important implications for isolating certain kinds of students and faculty alike (Deo 2019; Young 2018; Pan 2017). Research on language and international students more generally recommends that with increasing numbers, rethinking pedagogy and assimilatory strategies for students is key (Wu 2015; Unruh 2014). Silence and speech across contexts might not have the same meanings (Brista 2011) for example, and without being able to unpack this, we might be seemingly welcoming to new entrants at the institutional level without being substantively inclusive. Our research confirms that for many international students the language of law school is obfuscated for reasons beyond syntax and grammar. It complicates and challenges relationships with classmates, faculty and staff, and shapes perceptions in ways that extend well beyond individual choices and experiences.

From the student's standpoint, the fact that English is a hurdle that many of them will face remains an important, but altogether expected and unchangeable part of the system. Those accessing professional educational systems in the United States do so knowing that language proficiency is one that they will have to encounter, much like it might be for an English proficient if they chose to study in a country were the medium of instruction was *not* English.[33] But the struggle with

33 Law school application requirements include TOEFL scores or other indicia of fluency for non-English speaking applicants to the LLM program, but schools may not demand such evidence of fluency from international applicants to the JD program because they rely on the LSAT as a filter for language proficiency. See, e.g., Columbia University Law School's International Student FAQ, available at www.law.columbia.edu/admissions/jd/apply/faq/international (explaining that TOEFL is not required for JD admissions).

language in the traditional law classroom is not just about student capability. In fundamental ways, language – understood broadly as described in this chapter – implicates the policies and embedded structure of law schools in nurturing students' development of their professional identities, and this continues as students strategize about their early careers.

The implications reach beyond the international student population. For instance, a predominant theory to understand why women and under-represented minorities are consistently treated unfairly in organizations (even, that is, as they make spirited gains at admission) is that organizations are constructed around an "ideal" often white, male worker and aberrations (i.e. women and minorities) are rationally seen as "bad" or deviant from the norm (Acker 1990; Thornton 2013). What is true for organizations extends theoretically for understanding the minority experience within the American law school as well. If schools are set up to cater to a certain kind of "ideal" student – that is, one who does not need to record notes in a classroom, one who is confident in interactions, one whose learned behavior reflects a commitment to being – or, at least seeming – American, then of course everyone who does not look, sound, prep, socialize or learn in ways that conform to the standard must seem like deserved outsiders. But one can imagine that this "ideal" category is not just about being "American" and each process of such exclusion – whether it be on the basis of gender, race, national identity – can be problematic and lead to persistent inequalities in their own ways. Similarly dangerous are characteristics like participating vocally in class that seem neutral but instead can unfairly disadvantage new entrants and minorities (Guinier, Fine, and Balin 1994).

From the school's standpoint, the increase of international JD enrollment likely challenges existing policies and approaches. A recent article describing the decline in international enrollment overall in the U.S. highlighted this issue, recalling a "backlash from American students who complained that their international classmates changed the campus environment, from parents who worried that there would be fewer spots for their children, and from professors who struggled to cope with the newcomers' different learning styles" (Fischer 2019). For law schools, the common approach thus far has been to think about the challenges international students face as an *international student cost* or *problem for the international students*, which helps schools disassociate from thinking about the hurdle as a shared one. In many law schools, faculty have not had to come to terms with what the changing demographics of their law school student body means for what is required to be an effective teacher. Law schools do not privilege teaching generally, and policies that schools developed to purportedly support international students enrolled in LLM programs may have isolated and segregated those international students into particular internationally identifiable classes, thereby enabling certain faculty to bypass these students. These separation policies may have been seen as supportive for students, but they also removed the challenge of teaching classes with broadly diverse students. The rise of international enrollment in JD programs makes this "solution" untenable. Moreover, international students also require support outside of classrooms, too, including career strategizing and preparation. This might take the form of discussions aimed at contingency planning around the risks associated with visa uncertainties, for example, or of developing expertise around law firm policies that support the sort of mobility implicated in international legal education and careers. At this point, international students may develop this expertise outside of the law school's resources, but this is an incomplete, inefficient and temporary solution. The evidence in this chapter suggests that beyond these quick fixes, it might be time to reconsider our established notions of an ideal student – or at least time to recognize that committing to such an ideal type does a disservice to the equal opportunity we purport to inhabit as educators. Schools cannot just include new kinds of diverse entrants without including a substantive and cohesive commitment to rethinking what we valorize as actors within this institution. Adhering to objective criteria of merit without critically considering the kinds of inequality such meritocracy masks can only further reinforce existing inequalities.

While still only a small proportion of the law student population, international students are no longer the aberrant other that we can continue to ignore. In fact, as we compare them to other kinds of under-represented "domestic" minorities, the salience of this group becomes even more prominent – they become a sort of "other" diversity that demands attention in the context of a more general endeavor to make the law school more inclusive. But while international students serve as an important lens into dissecting the experiences of all under-represented minorities in these settings, they also are deserving of this attention on their own, reflecting the increasingly global worlds that *all* institutions and actors must now navigate. Our research begins to address these challenges, but research alone is insufficient. As this important group grows and begins to take root, it is going to need not just scholarly thoughtfulness but a deeper institutional commitment to managing these students' flexible – but still very vulnerable – academic citizenship.

References

American Bar Association (ABA). 2011–2017 (2011, 2012, 2013, 2014, 2015, 2016, 2017). Section of Legal Education. 509 Required Disclosures. Compilation All Schools Data. www.abarequireddisclosures.org (accessed April 29, 2019).

ABA. 2017. Statistics, JD and Non-JD Enrollment Data, Fall 2017. www.americanbar.org/groups/legal_education/resources/statistics.html (accessed April 29, 2019).

ABA. n.d. American Bar Association Guide to Compilation – All Schools' Data ABA Standard 509 Information Report Spreadsheets. http://abarequireddisclosures.org/Disclosure509.aspx (accessed April 29, 2019).

Acker, Joan. 1990. Hierarchies, Jobs, Bodies: A Theory of Gendered Organizations. *Gender and Society* 4(2): 139–158.

Adams, William. 2017. Speech presented at Association of American Law Schools Annual Meeting, International Legal Exchange and Post-Graduate Legal Education Joint Breakfast, San Francisco, California, January 5, 2017 (transcript in authors' possession).

Ballakrishnen, Swethaa S. 2012. Homeward Bound: What Does a Global Legal Education Offer the Indian Returnees? *Fordham Law Review* 80(6): 2441–2480.

Ballakrishnen, Swethaa S., and Carole Silver. 2019. A New Minority? International JD Students in US Law Schools. *Law and Social Inquiry* 44(3): 647–678.

Brista, Krishna. 2011. Why Some International Students are Silent in the U.S. Classroom. *Faculty Focus*, June 23. www.facultyfocus.com/articles/teaching-and-learning/a-first-person-explanation-of-why-some-international-students-are-silent-in-the-u-s-classroom/ (accessed April 29, 2019).

Deo, Meera. 2019. *Unequal Profession: Race and Gender in Legal Academia*. Stanford, CA: Stanford University Press.

Dezalay, Yves, and Bryant Garth. 1995. Merchants of Law as Moral Entrepreneurs: Constructing International Justice from the Competition for Transnational Business Disputes. *Law & Society Review* 29(1): 27–64.

Douglas-Gabriel, Danielle. 2015. Why Law Schools Are Losing Relevance – and How They're Trying to Win it Back. *The Washington Post*, April 20. www.washingtonpost.com/business/economy/why-law-schools-are-losing-relevance–and-how-theyre-trying-to-win-it-back/2015/04/20/ca0ae7fe-cf07–11e4-a2a7–9517a3a70506_story.html?utm_term=.5e10f7fc2756 (accessed April 29, 2019).

Fischer, Karin. 2019. How International Education's Golden Age Lost Its Sheen. *The Chronicle of Higher Education*, March 28. www.chronicle.com/interactives/2019–03–28-golden-age (accessed April 29, 2019).

Garth, Bryant. 2015. Notes Toward an Understanding of the U.S. Market in Foreign LL.M. Students: From the British Empire and the Inns of Court to the U.S. LL.M. *Indiana Journal of Global Legal Studies* 22: 67–79.

Georgetown Law. 2018. Taxation LL.M. Georgetown Law Center. www.law.georgetown.edu/academics/academic-programs/graduateprograms/degree-programs/taxation/ (accessed May 12, 2018).

Goldhaber, Michael D. 2005. They Rule the World. *The American Lawyer*, September 1. www.law.com/americanlawyer/almID/1125392710528/?hubtype=Inside&id=1125392710528/&slreturn=20190706073504 (accessed August 5, 2019).

Gribble, Cate, Mark Rahimi, and Jill Blackmore. 2017. International Students and Post-study Employment: The Impact of University and Host Community Engagement on the Employment Outcomes of International Students in Australia. In *International Student Connectedness and Identity*, eds. Ly Thi Tran and Catherine Gomes, 15–39. Singapore: Springer Science+Business Media.

Guinier, Lani, Michelle Fine, and Jane Balin. 1994. Becoming Gentlemen: Women's Experiences at One Ivy League Law School. *University of Pennsylvania Law Review* 143(1): 1–110.

Hansen, Mark. 2015. As Law School Enrollment Drops, Experts Disagree on Whether the Bottom is in Sight. *ABA Journal*, March 1. www.abajournal.com/magazine/article/as_law_school_enrollment_drops_experts_disagree_on_whether_the_bottom (accessed April 29, 2019).

Helal, Fethi. 2013. Discourse and Intercultural Academic Rhetoric. *Open Journal of Modern Linguistics* 3(2): 149–156.

Hupper, Gail J. 2007. The Rise of an Academic Doctorate in Law: Origins Through World War II. *American Journal of Legal History* 49(1): 1–60.

Hupper, Gail J. 2015. Educational Ambivalence: The Rise of a Foreign-Student Doctorate in Law. *New England Law Review* 49(3): 319–449.

Institute of International Education (IIE). 2014–2016. Fields of Study. www.iie.org/Research-and-Insights/Open-Doors/Data/International-Students/Fields-of-Study (accessed July 6, 2017).

IIE. 2016. Open Doors 2016, Executive Summary. www.iie.org/Why-IIE/Announcements/2016-11-14-Open-Doors-Executive-Summary (accessed April 29, 2019).

IIE. 2016/2017. Open Doors, Academic Level 2016/2017. www.iie.org/Research-and-Insights/Open-Doors/Data/InternationalStudents/Academic-Level (accessed May 3, 2018).

IIE. 2017. Open Doors 2017, Fast Facts. www.iie.org/Research-and-Insights/Open-Doors/Fact-Sheets-and Infographics/Fast-Facts (accessed May 3, 2018).

IIE. 2018. Open Doors 2018, Infographics International Student Data Graphics. www.iie.org/Research-and-Insights/Open-Doors/Fact-Sheets-and-Infographics/Infographics/International-Student-Data (accessed April 29, 2019).

Kennedy, Duncan. 1982. Legal Education and the Reproduction of Hierarchy. *Journal of Legal Education* 32(4): 591–615.

Lazarus-Black, Mindie. 2017. The Voice of the Stranger: Foreign LL.M. Students' Experiences of Culture, Law and Pedagogy in US Law Schools. In *Handbook on Comparative Law and Anthropology*, ed. James A.R. Nafziger, 462–488. Cheltenham: Edward Elgar Publishing.

Lazarus-Black, Mindie, and Julie Globokar, 2015. Foreign Attorneys in U.S. LL.M. Programs: Who's In, Who's Out, and Who they Are. *Indiana Journal of Global Legal Studies* 22(1): 3–65.

Law School Admission Council (LSAC). 2015. Applicants as of 17 August 2015 (Country of First Law Degree). www.lsac.org/search-results?action=results&q=2015%20llm-applicants20150817&num=10&in=Public_CMS (site no longer active).

Lefstein, Adam, and Julia Snell. 2011. Promises and Problems of Teaching with Popular Culture: A Linguistic Ethnographic Analysis of Discourse Genre Mixing in a Literacy Lesson. *Reading Research Quarterly* 46(1): 40–69.

McEvers, Kelly. 2016. As Law School Applicant Pool Shrinks, Student Bodies Diversify. *NPR*, April 26. www.npr.org/2016/04/26/475773282/nations-top-law-schools-face-near-record-enrollment-decline (accessed April 29, 2019).

Mertz, Elizabeth. 2007. *The Language of Law School: Learning to "Think like a Lawyer"*. Oxford: Oxford University Press.

Muller, Derek. 2016. The Coming Reckoning for Non-JD Legal Education. *Excess of Democracy*, November 14. http://excessofdemocracy.com/blog/2016/11/the-coming-reckoning-for-non-jd-legal-education?rq=post-JD (accessed April 29, 2019).

National Center for Education Statistics. 2017. Post-baccalaureate Enrollment. https://nces.ed.gov/programs/coe/indicator_chb.asp# (accessed May 11, 2018).

National Center for Education Statistics (NCES Digest). n.d. Digest of Education Statistics, Table 303.80. https://nces.ed.gov/programs/digest/d17/tables/dt17_303.80.asp (accessed March 18, 2019).

National Jurist. 2014. Why are U.S. LL.M. Programs so Popular? *The National Jurist*, November 19. www.nationaljurist.com/national-jurist-magazine/why-are-us-llm-programs-so-popular (accessed April 29, 2019).

Newsome, Linda K., and Paul Cooper. 2016. International Students' Cultural and Social Experiences in a British University: "Such a hard life [it] is here". *Journal of International Students* 6(6): 195–215. https://files.eric.ed.gov/fulltext/EJ1083255.pdf

Northwestern Law. 2018. *Tax Program*. www.law.northwestern.edu/academics/degreeprograms/llms/tax/documents/Tax-Brochure-2016-Final.pdf (accessed May 12, 2018).

Olson, Elizabeth, and David Segal. 2014. A Steep Slide in Law School Enrollment Accelerates. *New York Times*, December 17. https://dealbook.nytimes.com/2014/12/17/law-school-enrollment-falls-to-lowest-level-since-1987/ (accessed April 29, 2019).

Pan, Diana. 2017. *Incidental Racialization: Performative Assimilation in Law School.* Philadelphia, PA: Temple University Press.

Silver, Carole. 2002. The Case of the Foreign Lawyer: Internationalizing the US Legal Profession. *Fordham International Law Journal* 25(5): 1039–1084.

Silver, Carole. 2006. Internationalizing U.S. Legal Education: A Report on the Education of Transnational Lawyers. *Cardozo Journal of International & Comparative Law* 14: 143–175.

Silver, Carole. 2010. The Variable Value of US Legal Education in the Global Legal Services Market. *Georgetown Journal of Legal Ethics* 24(1): 1–57.

Silver, Carole. 2012a. States Side Story: "I like to be in America": Career Paths of International LLM Students. *Fordham Law Review* 80(6): 2383–2440.

Silver, Carole. 2012b. Coping with the Consequences of "Too Many Lawyers": Securing the Place of International Graduate Law Students. *International Journal of the Legal Profession* 19: 227–245.

Silver, Carole. 2013. Getting Real about Globalization and Legal Education: Potential and Perspectives for the U.S. *Stanford Law & Policy Review* 24(2): 457–501.

Silver, Carole, and Swethaa S. Ballakrishnen. 2018. Sticky Floors, Springboards, Stairways & Slow Escalators: Mobility Pathways and Preferences of International Students in U.S. Law Schools. *University of California Irvine Journal of International, Transnational, and Comparative Law* 3: 39–70.

Sloan, Karen. 2017. Number of LSAT Takers is Up, But Law School Applications Are Down. *Law.com*, April 7. www.law.com/sites/almstaff/2017/04/07/number-of-lsat-takers-is-up-but-law-school-applications-are-down/ (accessed April 29, 2019).

Sloan, Karen. 2018. Law Schools See First Real Enrollment Gains Since 2010. *Law.com*, December 14. www.law.com/2018/12/14/law-schools-see-first-real-enrollment-gains-since-2010/ (accessed April 29, 2019)

Spanbauer, Julie. 2007. Lost in Translation in the Law School Classroom: Assessing Required Coursework in LL.M. Programs for International Students. *International Journal of Legal Information* 35: 396–446.

Tamanaha, Brian Z. 2012. *Failing Law Schools.* Chicago, IL: University of Chicago Press.

Terui, Sachiko. 2012. Second Language Learners' Coping Strategy in Conversation with Native Speakers. *Journal of International Students* 2(2): 168–183.

Thornton, Margaret. 2013. The Mirage of Merit: Reconstituting the Ideal Academic. *Australian Feminist Studies* 26(76): 127–143.

University of Florida Levin College of Law (University of Florida). 2018. LL.M. in Taxation, Admissions. www.law.ufl.edu/areas-of-study/degreeprograms/ll-m-in-taxation (accessed May 12, 2018).

Unruh, Susan. 2014. Struggling International Students in the United States: Do University Faculty Know How to Help? *Athens Journal of Education* 2(2): 99–110.

U.S. News & World Report (U.S. News). 2011–2017. Best Law Schools. www.usnews.com/best-graduate-schools/top-law-schools/lawrankings?int=9c0f08 (site no longer active for years other than current year).

Wa, The-yuan, et al. 1992. Academic Stress of International Students Attending U.S. Universities. *Research in Higher Education* 33(5): 607–623.

Wu, Hsiao-ping, Esther Garza, and Norma Guzman. 2015. International Student's Challenge and Adjustment to College. *Education Research International* 2015: 1–9.

Young, Kathryne M. 2018. *How To Be Sort of Happy In Law School.* Stanford, CA: Stanford University Press.

8 How the Law School Admission Process Marginalizes Black Aspiring Lawyers

Aaron N. Taylor[*]

Introduction

In his landmark book, *The Souls of Black Folk*, American sociologist, W.E.B. Du Bois poses the question: "Why did God make me an outcast and a stranger in mine own house?" (1903, 3). The question pertained to the social and psychic conflicts facing Black Americans, nominally freed from enslavement, but hampered by an imposed second-class citizenship. Du Bois was describing a group of people living a marginalized existence, prevented from fully integrating into larger society and, therefore, unable to realize the full extent of their theoretical freedoms. The analytical framework that Du Bois introduced in *Souls* to describe the experiences of Black Americans has been the foundation of the robust concept of marginalization, the multifaceted process through which marginality – or the condition of being marginal – occurs.

This chapter argues that Black people who aspire to be lawyers endure marginalized existences in the law school admission process. The manner in which the Law School Admission Test (LSAT) drives the vetting of law school applications ensures that Black applicants face steep disadvantages in gaining admission. In 2015–16, it took about 1,786 Black applicants to yield 1,000 offers of admission, compared to only 1,176 among White applicants and 1,315 overall.[1] These trends are explained in large part by racial and ethnic disparities in average LSAT scores. The average score for Black test-takers is 142 – eleven points lower than the average for White and Asian test-takers of 153 (Dalessandro, Anthony, and Reese 2012).[2] Therefore, for large proportions of Black law school applicants – 44

* Executive Director, AccessLex Institute Center for Legal Education Excellence; Professor, Saint Louis University School of Law. B.A., North Carolina A&T State University; J.D., Howard University School of Law; Ed.D., Vanderbilt University. I thank the staff at the Law School Survey of Student Engagement for assistance with data analysis; and, most importantly, the more than 16,000 law students who shared insights about their experiences via the LSSSE Survey in 2016. Any errors or misstatements are my own.

1 Compare LSAC (2017), (listing admitted applicant stats by race and ethnicity) (on file with author), with *Applicants by Ethnic and Gender Group* (listing applicant stats by race and ethnicity) (on file with author).

2 Latino/a test-takers score an average of 146 (Dalessandro, Anthony, and Reese 2012).

percent in 2015–16 – their marginalization in the admissions process ends in outright exclusion (LSAC 2017).

This exclusion, however, is of questionable legitimacy. The LSAT is designed to be a partial predictor of first-year grades. But law schools commonly couch admission in the broader context of a student's potential as a lawyer – as they should. Law schools exist to produce successful lawyers and leaders. The first year of law school is merely one step, albeit one of inflated importance, on the path from layperson to lawyer. The fundamental goals of legal education are longer term; but the LSAT does not predict one's chances of attaining these goals well, surely not well enough to be the primary admission criterion.

For example, Texas Tech recently found that the LSAT explained just 13 percent of variance in bar exam scores of its law graduates (Austin, Christopher, and Dickerson 2017, 766). The University of Cincinnati found that among its law graduates the "LSAT score does not correlate with Ohio bar exam performance" (Chanvisanuruk 2016). Two professors from the University of California Berkeley found that the LSAT had very weak (or no) value in predicting lawyering skills among its law graduates (Shultz and Zedeck 2008, 53). In a letter seeking to correct inflated claims about the LSAT's power, LSAC stated that test scores were not appropriate tools for assessing things like bar passage risk (Bernstine 2015). Nonetheless, the LSAT is used by law schools in ways that systematically exclude Black people to extents experienced by no other racial or ethnic group – using justifications that merit much suspicion.

Unfortunately, for Black applicants who do receive offers of admission, the marginalization process continues. This is the group on which this chapter focuses. Part I of the chapter introduces the concept of marginalization. Part II explains how the law school admission process funnels Black students into schools with the least favorable outcomes. Part III discusses how law school scholarship policies contribute to higher student loan debt among Black students. In the end, Black aspiring lawyers often attend law school under the least favorable conditions, a form of marginalization called adverse incorporation.

What is Marginalization

The origins of marginalization as a research framework are typically said to be within sociology, most notably, in an article titled, "Human Migration and the Marginal Man." The article, written in 1928 by American sociologist Robert Park (Dunne 2005, 11),[3] presents the concept of "the marginal man," a person who, due to societal upheaval,[4] is torn between the "warm [but limiting] security" of

3 *Also see* Jenkins (2005, 54) (asserting that the marginal man concept arose out of previous research in other academic fields, including cultural anthropology and psychology).

4 Park framed this upheaval in the context of his "catastrophic theory of progress," which posits that progress is most forcefully advanced through territorial and cultural conquests and the "collisions, conflicts, and fusions of people and cultures" that often accompany these phenomena (Park 1928, 882n9).

his cultural origins and the "cold freedom" of the larger, changing world (Park 1928, 892). Park was describing a person essentially on the margins of two societies or cultures because of circumstances thrust upon him. But Park's focus on the psychic effects of marginality seems to render the framework as much a psychological concept as a sociological one (Park 1928).

Park was not the first person to conceive of marginality as a condition. In *Souls*, W.E.B. Du Bois writes about the "double-consciousness" of being an "American Negro." This duality captured the psychic and social conflicts facing Black Americans, the descendants of enslaved Africans.[5] In *Souls*, written a quarter-century before *Human Migration*, Du Bois describes individuals split between their country of nominal citizenship and the land of their not-too-distant heritage. The latter was particularly significant given the stigma associated with darker skin and given the distinctive culture spawned by the endurance of African customs among people enslaved in America.[6] Elementally, Du Bois was describing people torn between two conflicting existences: "an American, a Negro; two souls, two thoughts, two unreconciled strivings; two warring ideals in one dark body" (Du Bois 1903, 4). This was the fundamental basis of the theory of marginalization.

Defining Terms and Framing Concepts

Marginalization frameworks have been adapted to many academic traditions, including sociology, psychology, geography, economics, political science, anthropology, and ecology. This diffusion has spawned a plethora of conceptions and definitions of relevant terms. Thus, clarity regarding the meaning and scope of important terms is essential (Dennis 2005, 8).

The terms *marginalization* and its lexical cousin, *marginality*, are both derivatives of the word *marginal*. Thus, the meanings and conceptions of *marginalization* and *marginality* descend from how *marginal* is defined. The Oxford Dictionary defines *marginal* as "Relating to or situated at the edge or margin of something" (Oxford Dictionaries n.d.). Therefore, *marginal* is a relative construct denoting deviation or distance from some notion of normality, center, or power (Cullen and Pretes 2000, 216).[7] Building on this basic conception, *marginality* has been conceived as a "complex condition of disadvantage" (Mehretu, Pigozzi, and Sommers 2000, 90); "the temporary state of having been put aside" (Gurung and Kollmair 2005, 10); and "an involuntary position and condition" of existing at the margins (von Braun and Gatzweiler 2014, 3). *Marginalization* has been defined as "a process of becoming peripheral" (Trudeau and McMorran 2011, 438), representing the "convergence of political, cultural, economic, and environmental

5 Stonequist (1935, 4) noted that slavery "deprived the Negro of his African cultural heritage and forced him to accept the American culture and its values."

6 An example of this merging of culture, according to Du Bois, was the black church, which he described as "the social center of Negro life in the United States, and the most characteristic expression of African character" (Du Bois 1903, 120).

7 "Deviants from a standard or norm are deemed 'marginal,' just as those people who differ from Western society are deemed 'primitive'" (Cullen and Pretes 2000, 216).

problems" (Mehretu et al. 2000, 90). In essence, research frameworks centered on marginalization attempt to describe and explain the multifaceted processes that cause marginality. The multidisciplinary and interdisciplinary nature of the frameworks reflect the nature of the processes being studied. Von Braun and Gatzweiler asserted that marginalization frameworks integrate "poverty, discrimination, and social exclusion; the degradation of ecosystem function; and access to services, markets, and technology" (von Braun and Gatzweiler 2014, 14).

Informed by the relevant literature, essential terms are defined thus:

- *Marginal* is defined as *Relating to incomplete assimilation or adverse incorporation into dominant cultures or centers of power, resulting in deficient power in relevant contexts.*
- *Marginality* is the multidimensional condition of being marginal.
- *Marginalization* is the multifaceted process through which marginality occurs.

Marginality as Adverse Incorporation

Adverse incorporation is essentially inclusion on disadvantageous terms. Park (1914) illustrated this type of marginality in a strikingly, if not unsettlingly, romanticized account of slavery. He asserted that slavery fostered the assimilation of enslaved Africans into "their masters' families" (Park 1914, 612). This assimilation was characterized by the adoption of certain "manners and customs" (Park 1928, 612) The completeness of the assimilation, according to Park, depended on the level of "close and intimate contact" between the enslaved and their enslavers (Park 1928, 614). Therefore, the enslaved person who toiled in the "patriarchal big house" (Du Bois 1903, 103) was more assimilated than "the Negro field hand" (Park 1928, 612). Du Bois made a similar point in *Souls* when he lamented the post-American Civil War decline in the "bonds of intimacy, affection, and sometimes blood relationship" between "domestic servants" and their enslavers (Du Bois 1903, 114).

The significance of these illustrations lies mainly in how they highlight the often one-sided nature of the assimilation process. For marginal people, assimilation means embracing dominant culture. They may be technically assimilated, but are rarely considered equal in a substantive sense. So while Park and Du Bois waxed nostalgic about "kindly relations of master and slave" (Park 1928, 613), those relationships were rooted in power asymmetries that left the enslaved assimilated, but on disadvantageous terms.

An adversely incorporated student could be one who enrolls in a school with unfavorable outcomes, due to few, if any, other options. A student who enrolls without the benefit of a scholarship, resulting in higher student loan debt at graduation, is another example. In both scenarios, the students are enrolled and, therefore, incorporated, but under unfavorable, or adverse, circumstances. Marginalization through adverse incorporation is the primary focus of this chapter.

Marginalization and the Admission Process

In 2015–16, only 56 percent of Black law school applicants received at least one offer of admission. This was the lowest proportion among all racial and ethnic groups. As explained earlier, score disparities on the LSAT are the primary explanation for these trends; but these differences do not fully explain the high level of exclusion among Black applicants. Compared to White applicants and overall, Black applicants are admitted at lower rates irrespective of LSAT score. For example, 20 percent of Black applicants with LSAT scores between 135 and 139 received at least one offer of admission, compared to 27 percent of White applicants and 25 percent of applicants overall (LSAC 2017).[8] At the other end of the distribution, 85 percent of Black applicants with scores of 165 or higher received at least one offer, compared to 91 percent of White applicants and 90 percent of all applicants.[9]

The latter trend truly highlights the marginalized condition of Black law school applicants. Scores of 165 or higher are rare – only 13 percent of the entire 2015–16 applicant pool scored at this level.[10] Among Black applicants, scores at this level are *exceedingly* rare. There were only 156 Black applicants nationwide who scored 165 or higher, a miniscule three-tenths of one percent of the national applicant pool.[11] These applicants are the proverbial unicorns of law school applicants; yet, almost two-in-ten did not receive even one offer of admission.[12]

The trends at lower points in the distribution are also noteworthy. They contradict the conventional wisdom that Black applicants with lower LSAT scores have advantages over White applicants with similar or even higher scores. Regrettably, the opposite seems to be true. White law school applicants with scores below 150 were more likely to gain admission than Black applicants. Sixty-four percent of White applicants with scores between 135 and 149 received at least one offer, compared to half of Black applicants within the same range.[13] It is noteworthy that the entire range falls well below the average LSAT score for White test-takers (153) and straddles the average for Black test-takers (142). Even if the range is narrowed to 135–144, the lower limits of what even "access" schools would consider theoretically acceptable, White applicants were more likely than

8 An LSAT range of 135–139 means that a test-taker answered 32–39 questions correctly out of 100. Law School Admission Council, *Law School Admission Test; Computing Your Score*, www.lsac.org/free-sample-test/computing-your-score.asp.

9 Overall: 90 percent (6,547/7,240); Black: 85 percent (132/156); White: 91 percent (4,847/5,333) (LSAC 2017).

10 There were 7,240 test-takers with scores at this level and 56,479 test-takers overall (LSAC 2017).

11 There were 156 test-takers with scores at this level and 56,479 test-takers overall (LSAC 2017).

12 This trend is very curious, in that the rarity of these applicants seems to suggest that they would have many options for law school. The likeliest explanation for this trend rests with where the applicants applied and when they applied. Many of these applicants likely applied later in the cycle to schools with very competitive admission processes. The timing of the application is particularly important at these schools.

13 Black: 50 percent (2,692/5,181); White: 64 percent (5,791/8,981) (LSAC 2017).

Blacks to receive at least one offer of admission – 46 percent to 37 percent (LSAC 2017). The trends suggest that to the extent factors other than the LSAT bear upon admission decisions, it is to the detriment of Black applicants.

Applicants are assessed based on an ostensibly uniform application of standards. The downside of this uniformity is that it assumes equality of opportunity and too often ignores the unequal backgrounds from which applicants come. In an article titled "Reimagining Merit as Achievement," I argued that law schools should consider the credentials and accomplishments of applicants in the context of "what could have reasonably been expected, given their background" (Taylor 2014, 6). This type of contextualization is the only fair way to assess merit. Otherwise, you get the continued propagation of a system that rewards privilege under the guise of meritocracy.

There are a few "non-merit" factors, ostensibly within the control of the applicant, that can influence whether an applicant is admitted to law school. Where an applicant applies and when an applicant applies are two such factors. If an applicant only applies to schools with low admit rates, she is less likely to receive an offer of admission, irrespective of her credentials, than if she also applied to at least one "safety" school. The number of applications submitted matters too. More than 95 percent of applicants who applied to ten or more law schools received at least one offer compared to 56 percent of applicants who applied to only one law school (LSAC 2014).

The timing of application submission is important as well. Most law schools use a "rolling" admissions framework, in which they consider applications roughly in the order they are received. Applicants who apply later in the cycle are often less likely to gain admission, due to fewer available seats remaining in the entering class. It is likely that at most law schools more than half of entering class seats are accounted for before the application deadline passes. As supply dwindles, competition increases. An applicant who could have been a shoo-in for admission in November could be waitlisted or outright denied in March.

The decisions of where and when to apply rest with the applicant; but they are influenced by many factors, including access to information. There are more than 200 ABA-approved law schools. It is virtually impossible to acquire substantive information about all of them, and it may be needless to do so. But information is critical to developing an application strategy. Applicants who have access to pre-law advisors and others who can effectively assist in the development of an application strategy tend to fare best. Unfortunately, students who attend non-selective colleges, the types of institutions Black students are most likely to attend,[14] have less access to advisors. As one group of researchers asserted, high student-to-advisor ratios at these schools mean that advisors "rarely have time to engage in long-term education planning, discuss career goals, or provide comprehensive support" to students (Karp, Kalamkarian, Klempin, and Fletcher 2016, 4). Therefore, students at these schools tend to have less support in pursuing graduate and professional school, including in developing strategies for applying to law school.

14 *See e.g.*, Baylor (2016).

Financial resources also loom large in the decisions of when and where to apply. Applying to law school can be an expensive endeavor (LSAC n.d.). Application fees at individual schools can be as high as $100.[15] The LSAT costs $180 (LSAC n.d.). Applicants must also have their academic transcripts and letters of recommendation processed by the Law School Admission Council (LSAC) Credential Assembly Service (CAS) – another $185. Then the cost of having the CAS report sent to law schools is $35 each. Applicants who apply to ten or more schools have the best chances of receiving at least one offer, but the cost of submitting ten applications can be upwards of $1,300.[16] LSAC offers need-based fee waivers, and many law schools will grant application fee waivers. But these waivers do not cover all the expenses of applying,[17] and some applicants likely do not know about the waivers. Lack of money can force some applicants to limit the number of schools to which they apply or delay applications until sufficient funds are acquired. Thus, while the decisions of where to apply and when to apply do indeed rest with the applicant, they are nonetheless influenced by factors that disproportionately disadvantage some applicants, especially Black applicants.

Racial Stratification as Marginalization

Exclusion is the most extreme form of marginalization, and as the data point out, Black aspiring lawyers are excluded from legal education to the largest extents. And while an offer of admission spares Black aspiring lawyers from being excluded, it does not spare them from marginalization. In fact, an offer of admission can begin a longer marginalization process that begins as adverse incorporation. Black admitted applicants are granted access to legal education, but often on disadvantageous terms. Racial and ethnic stratification in legal education provides a compelling example.

The 2010–11 admission cycle represented a boon for law schools, with record numbers of first-year students enrolling that fall.[18] But the manner in which law schools packed their classes that year was a harbinger of vast declines in applications and enrollments that would take hold once it became clear that the recessionary legal job market could not support the volume of graduates that law schools were producing. Law school admissions have become more selective in this climate.[19] Less has been written about the extent to which these trends have made it harder for Black law students to gain admission to schools with the most favorable outcomes.

15 *See, e.g.*, Stanford Law School, *JD Application Process*, https://law.stanford.edu/apply/how-to-apply/jd-application-process/ (listing an application fee of $100).

16 Ten applications at an average fee of $60 ($600) + the cost of one LSAT administration ($180) + the cost of sending CAS and sending ten CAS reports to law schools ($185 + $350) is $1,315.

17 The LSAC fee waiver covers two LSAT administrations and four CAS reports sent to law schools. Applicants must self-fund LSAT administrations beyond two, and any CAS reports beyond four (LSAC 2017–2018). Also, some law schools may grant application fee waivers only in extreme cases. *See e.g.*, Stanford Law School, *JD Application Process* ("The [application] fee may be waived in cases of extreme personal hardship").

18 A record 52,488 first-year students enrolled that year (ABA n.d.)

19 *See e.g.*, Taylor (2015a).

In previous research, I divided law schools into five groups based on their 2010–11 median LSAT score. The median LSAT was used as a proxy for factors such as institutional wealth, factors that are associated with a school's ability to invest heavily in the success of its students.[20] Compared to schools with the lowest median LSAT scores, schools with the highest scores had lower student-faculty ratios,[21] almost double the number of advanced courses offered,[22] much lower student attrition,[23] higher bar passage rates,[24] and higher employment rates among their graduates[25] on the market. These schools typically have ample financial resources and often enjoy lofty standing within legal education and, therefore, are best positioned to foster not only diversity, but also wide-ranging success among diverse groups of students. Unfortunately, these schools are doing little to foster diversity, and even less now than they were before the application downturn.

In fall 2015, Black first-year students were less likely to be enrolled in schools with the highest LSAT medians and most favorable student outcomes than they were in the record-breaking fall 2011. In the earlier year, 33 percent of Black first-year students were enrolled in the schools in the two highest median LSAT groupings. In 2015, that proportion had declined to 29 percent. On the other hand, White and Asian first-year students were more likely to attend these schools. In fall 2011, 39 percent of White first-year students were enrolled in these schools; that proportion increased to 47 percent in 2015. The increase among Asian first-year students was even more dramatic, from 52 percent to 64 percent.

These trends reflect an intense urgency among these schools to protect their LSAT profiles, in a climate of not only fewer applications, but of particularly intense declines among applicants with high LSAT scores.[26] In other words, when forced to choose between fostering diversity and maintaining a symbol of status,

20 Of the thirty-six law schools in this grouping, thirty-three were affiliated with a university that had an endowment of more than one billion dollars (Taylor 2015a, 357) (listing schools in grouping).

21 Schools with the highest median LSAT scores had median student-faculty ratio of 11:1, compared to 15.5:1 among schools with the lowest median LSAT scores. Calculations by author.

22 Schools with the highest median LSAT scores had median number of advanced courses of 193, compared to 104 among schools with the lowest median LSAT scores. Calculations by author.

23 Schools with the highest median LSAT scores had median attrition rate of 3 percent, compared to 17 percent among schools with the lowest median LSAT scores. Calculations by author.

24 Schools with the highest medians had median differential between their bar exam passage rate and that of their relevant jurisdictions of plus-10 percent, compared to minus-5 percent among schools with the lowest median LSAT scores. Calculations by author.

25 Schools with the highest median LSAT scores had median full-time employment of 91 percent, compared to 67 percent among schools with the lowest median LSAT scores. Calculations by author.

26 As of February 3, 2017, the number of applicants with LSAT scores of 165 or higher declined 9 percent, from 6,265 at the same point in 2016 to 5,704. The number of applicants with scores below 165 increased 1 percent to 25,738 from 25,440. (Data from LSAC. Report on file with author)

these schools have chosen the latter. The result is higher proportions of Black law students being funneled into law schools with fewer resources and less favorable outcomes. This form of adverse incorporation increases the risks of legal education for Black law students. They are granted access to legal education, but on less favorable terms.

Marginalization and Scholarships

As the pressure to attract students with high LSAT scores and undergraduate GPAs has increased in legal education, merit aid has grown as the predominant form of tuition discounting (Arewa, Morriss, and Henderson 2014, 965). According to the ABA, merit scholarship funding increased 68 percent among public law schools and 53 percent among private schools between 2005 and 2010 (ABA 2015). Need-based funding – the most equitable form of tuition discounting – remained essentially flat (ABA 2015). Funding for so-called "need-plus" scholarships increased 68 percent and 59 percent at public and private law schools respectively (ABA 2015). (Law schools purport to consider both financial need and notions of merit in awarding these "need-plus" scholarships.) Indirect trends, however, suggest these scholarships have little equitable impact, operating as merit scholarships by another name.

Law schools are highly tuition-dependent. In 2013, tuition payments accounted for an average of 69 percent of law school revenue. A quarter of law schools (about fifty) received 88 percent or more of their revenue from tuition. This financial structure has direct implications on scholarship policy. For schools that are highly tuition-dependent, tuition discounts to some students are funded in large part by tuition revenue from other students. Therefore, students who pay full tuition (or close to it) subsidize the attendance of their peers receiving scholarships.

The LSAT-driven nature of scholarship awarding ensures that tuition discounts will flow most lucratively to students from privileged backgrounds (Taylor and Christensen 2017). Disadvantaged students are then required to pay higher proportions of the tuition rate in order to account for the discounted rates of their privileged peers. While this method of cost-shifting is pervasive throughout legal education, the wealthiest institutions tend to rely less on tuition revenue in funding scholarships. For instance, Ivy League law schools award based predominantly on financial need (Powell 2018). But because Black students are less likely to attend the wealthiest schools, they are disproportionately funding the attendance of their often more well-off peers. These trends, in turn, contribute to higher student loan debt among Black law students.

Scholarship Awarding Trends

The data underlying this section is taken from the 2016 administration of the Law School Survey of Student Engagement (LSSSE). LSSSE is a roughly 100-item annual survey of the effects of legal education on law students. LSSSE is rooted in the concept of student engagement, which is based on the simple, yet powerful observation that the more engrossing the educational experience, the more students will gain from it. Student engagement is a holistic concept, capturing the intricate web of individual and institutional processes and actions that contribute to desired student outcomes (McCormick, Kinzie, and Gonyea 2013, 51).

In 2016, 16,424 students from 67 U.S. law schools accredited by the American Bar Association responded to the survey. The demographics of LSSSE respondents tends to reflect those of all law students, giving the Survey immense descriptive value as a means of investigating legal education trends.

Below is the racial and ethnic breakdown of LSSSE respondents:

Race and ethnicity

- American Indian or Native American: 0.6% (98)
- Asian, Asian American or Pacific Islander: 6.1% (1,007)
- Black or African American: 7.8% (1,290)
- Hispanic or Latino/a: 9.2% (1,519)
- Multiracial: 2.5% (404)
- Other/Unknown: 9.5% (1,572)
- White: 62.5% (10,275)
- International or Foreign National: 1.6% (259)N=16,424

The racial and ethnic demographics of LSSSE respondents align closely with those of the 111,881 law students enrolled in Juris Doctor programs nationwide during the 2015–16 school year.[27] The four largest racial and ethnic groups comprised the following proportions of all law students: Asian: 6.6 percent (7,409); Black: 8.8 percent (9,894); Latino/a: 10.2 percent (11,402); White: 62.3 percent (69,870).

Law schools profess to use an array of criteria to select scholarship recipients, and to an extent most do. Factors such as undergraduate grades, leadership ability, diversity, and even financial need can impact scholarship awarding decisions.[28] But this theoretical holism cannot shield an incontrovertible reality: the LSAT is the primary driver of scholarship awards. In this way, the scholarship awarding process is an almost seamless extension of the admissions process. Applicants with advantages in the admissions process tend to benefit from the same advantages when scholarships are awarded.

Most law students receive scholarships. Seventy-one percent of LSSSE respondents reported receiving scholarships or grants during the 2015–16 school year.[29] As a means of rough comparison, among all law students, almost

27 These numbers come from the Access database and reflect the 201 law schools in the U.S., excluding the three law schools in PR.

28 For example, the University of the District of Columbia School of Law lists the following criteria: academic record, LSAT score, career goals, overcoming adversity or obstacles, extensive community involvement, military participation, range of employment and life experiences, DC residency, quality of written documents, diversity, and commitment to public service (University of the District of Columbia 2017).

29 10,844 of 15,278 respondents received scholarships.

64 percent received scholarships or grants during the 2014–15 school year (the latest data available);[30] this figure was up from 49 percent just four years earlier.[31] The increased awarding is driven mostly by the need to fill classes in a very challenging environment. Historic application and enrollment declines have forced most law schools to increasingly discount tuition to attract students (Phipps 2012).

By LSAT score

LSAT pressures have intensified the stakes. Not only do many schools need to attract students, but they want to attract students with very competitive LSAT scores. The application declines have been most intense among high LSAT-scorers,[32] so the battles for the remaining applicants have increased in pitch, often prompting outright bidding wars among law schools (Brown 2015). The resulting bounty, ostensibly a favorable development for students, has not been spread evenly or equitably. The aid has tended to flow most generously to students most likely to come from privileged backgrounds.

Merit scholarships are, by far, the most prominent type of tuition discount awarded by law schools. Seventy-nine percent of the scholarships awarded to LSSSE respondents were merit-based.[33] The manners in which awarding patterns tracked LSAT scores were unsurprising, yet stark. Respondents with higher LSAT scores were most likely to have received merit scholarships. Table 8.1 charts the trends.

Respondents in the highest LSAT band (166–180) were almost six times more likely to report receiving a merit scholarship than respondents in the lowest band (140 and under). But the disparities among closer bands tell an even more unmistakable story. In lockstep fashion, a higher LSAT band was associated with a higher chance of having received a merit scholarship. Eighteen percentage-points separated the 156–160 band from the 151–155. It is difficult to imagine that differences on

Table 8.1 Scholarship Chances by LSAT Score Band

LSAT band	*140 or less*	*141–145*	*146–150*	*151–155*	*156–160*	*161–165*	*166–180*
Scholarship	16%	36%	45%	57%	75%	87%	90%
N=	28/176	365/ 1023	1111/ 2495	1966/ 3420	2135/ 2857	1567/ 1803	504/ 558

30 74,949/118,012, AccessLex, *Analytix* (Calculations by author, using 2016 "Financial Aid" dataset).

31 73,187/148,401, AccessLex, *Analytix* (Calculations by author, using 2012 "Financial" dataset).

32 As of February 3, 2017, the number of applicants with LSAT scores of 165 or higher declined 9 percent, from 6,265 at the same point in 2016 to 5,704. The number of applicants with scores below 165 increased 1 percent to 25,738 from 25,440. (Data from LSAC. Report on file with author.)

33 8,823 of the 11,208 scholarships awarded were merit-based.

other factors would be so stark among these respondents to justify such a profound difference in merit scholarship chances. Differences in average undergraduate GPAs trended higher across the ranges, but never exceeded one-tenth of one point between adjoining ranges.[34] But in spite of the small size of these differences, it is possible that variation in UGPAs contributed to the trends as well.

Even when scores were analyzed individually, the trends were remarkable. Over the 21-point span of 140–161, a span within which 84 percent of LSSSE respondents scored,[35] scholarship chances ranged from 13 percent at the lowest extreme to 86 percent at the highest. There were only five instances over the span where a group of respondents with a certain LSAT score received merit scholarships at a lower rate than a group with the next lower score.

By Race/Ethnicity

Disparities in LSAT scores had predictable racial and ethnic impacts among LSSSE respondents. As a threshold matter, within each demographic group, receipt of a merit scholarship was associated with a higher LSAT score (see Table 8.2).

Overall, Black respondents had both the lowest average LSAT score and the lowest chance of receiving a merit scholarship (see Table 8.3).

These trends are tangible reflections of the marginalization of Black aspiring lawyers. Black applicants are least likely to gain admission. Even when offered admission, they are least likely to attend law schools with the most favorable outcomes and least likely to receive financial aid that reduces their costs of attendance. This latter form of adverse incorporation contributes to another hallmark of marginalization among Black aspiring lawyers: higher student loan debt.

Table 8.2 Average LSAT Score by Merit Scholarship Recipience, by Race

	Asian		*Black*		*Latino/a*		*White*	
Scholarship?	Yes	No	Yes	No	Yes	No	Yes	No
Average LSAT	156	152	150	146	154	150	157	152

Table 8.3 Scholarship Chances and Average LSAT Score, by Race

	Asian		*Black*		*Latino/a*		*White*	
Scholarship chances	61%	705/1162	48%	498/1045	52%	779/1507	66%	5858/8897
Avg. LSAT	154		148		152		155	

34 Average UGPAs for each LSAT band: 140 or less: 3.04; 141–145: 3.1; 146–150: 3.18; 151–155: 3.25; 156–160: 3.35; 161–165: 3.42; 166–180: 3.45.

35 10,375 of 12,332 LSSSE respondents

Marginalization and Student Loan Debt

Student loan debt trends are a manifestation of the adverse incorporation that Black law students disproportionately endure. In their most common form, scholarships are tuition discounts. Schools leverage these discounts for different reasons, but most commonly as enrollment incentives. For many students, a tuition discount has direct implications for the amount of money borrowed for law school. Therefore, a law school's decision to grant or not grant a discount to a particular student has far-reaching implications for that student.

About 83 percent of LSSSE respondents incurred or expected to incur student loan debt from law school. This high level of usage[36] along with the high costs of legal education render law graduates a highly indebted group. In 2012, the average debt for graduates of private law schools was $127,000; the average for public law school graduates was $88,000 (The Institute for College Access & Success 2018). These figures, which are surely higher today, place the typical law graduate in the top 3–4 percent of student loan indebtedness.[37]

As with all things, student loan reliance and indebtedness are not distributed evenly. Blacks and Latino/as have the highest rates of borrowing and the highest expected student loan balances.[38] On the LSSSE Survey, 95 percent of Black respondents and 92 percent of Latino/as reported relying on student loans to cover the costs of law school. Reliance among Asian and White respondents was high as well; but at 77 percent and 81 percent respectively, they are tangibly lower than their counterparts.

LSSSE asks respondents to estimate how much law school debt they expect to incur by graduation (see Table 8.4). Forty percent of Black respondents expected to owe more than $120,000 in law school debt; only Latino/as had a higher proportion (43 percent). The respective rates for White and Asian respondents were 27 percent and 30 percent. At the other end, Black respondents were least likely to expect no law school debt (5 percent).

Taken together, the trends discussed in this section appear to highlight the impact of inequitable merit scholarship policies on student debt. With less of their tuition discounted, legal education is more expensive for Black and Latino/a students.[39] And because these students are less likely to have access to other sources of funds, they must rely more heavily on loans. The implications of these inequities are vast and long-lasting, and represent textbook marginalization.

36 As a means of comparison, 68 percent of college graduates incurred student loan debt during their course of study (The Institute for College Access & Success 2018).

37 Student loan debtors owing more than $100,000 comprise 4 percent of all student loan debtors (Weeden 2015).

38 Disparities in student loan debt based on the socioeconomic, racial, and ethnic backgrounds of students persist throughout higher education. *See e.g.*, Baum and Steele (2010).

39 In another piece, I called the higher education costs paid by first-generation law students with lower LSAT scores a "merit surtax" (Taylor 2015b).

Table 8.4 Expected Debt by Race

	N=	$0	$1–$40K	$40,001–$80K	$80,001–$120K	$120,001–$160K	$160,001–$200K	> $200K
All	14,137	17%	11%	20%	22%	14%	10%	6%
Asian	832	23%	10%	16%	17%	15%	10%	9%
Black	1,045	5%	7%	22%	27%	20%	12%	8%
Latino/a	1,290	8%	8%	16%	25%	19%	15%	9%
White	8,937	19%	12%	21%	22%	13%	9%	5%

Conclusion

Black people who aspire to be lawyers endure marginalized existences as they seek admission to law school. For those who are not excluded altogether by a denial of admission, this marginalization takes the predominant form of adverse incorporation. These aspiring lawyers are offered admission, but disproportionately to schools with unfavorable outcomes and often without the benefit of tuition discounts or other forms of financial aid. The end result is a risky undertaking with adverse impacts that span the law school admission process through the matriculation process and into the scrum for post-law school jobs and beyond. This marginalization contributes to the enduring underrepresentation of Black law students and lawyers. If legal education is to serve as a robust pipeline into the profession among people from underrepresented backgrounds, law schools must adopt methods of selecting and rewarding students that are rooted in equity, fairness, and legitimacy.

References

American Bar Association (ABA). n.d. *Enrollment and Degrees Awarded 1963–2012 Academic Years.* www.americanbar.org/content/dam/aba/administrative/legal_education_and_admissions_to_the_bar/statistics/enrollment_degrees_awarded.authcheckdam.pdf (accessed May 13, 2019).

American Bar Association (ABA). 2015. *Task Force on the Financing of Legal Education.* June 17. www.americanbar.org/content/dam/aba/administrative/legal_education_and_admissions_to_the_bar/reports/2015_june_report_of_the_aba_task_force_on_the_financing_of_legal_education.authcheckdam.pdf (accessed May 13, 2019).

Arewa, Olufunmilayo, Andrew Morriss, and William Henderson. 2014. Enduring Hierarchies in American Legal Education. *Indiana Law Journal* 89(3): 941–1068.

Austin, Katherine A., Catherine Martin Christopher, and Darby Dickerson. 2017. Will I Pass the Bar Exam?: Predicting Student Success Using LSAT Scores and Law School Performance. *Hofstra Law Review* 45(3): 753–784.

Baum, Sandy, and Patricia Steele. 2010. *Who Borrows Most? Bachelor's Degree Recipients with High Levels of Student Debt.* College Board. https://trends.collegeboard.org/sites/default/files/trends-2010-who-borrows-most-brief.pdf (accessed May 13, 2019).

Baylor, Elizabeth. 2016. Closed Doors: Black and Latino Students Are Excluded from Top Public Universities. Center for American Progress, October 13. www.americanprogress.org/issues/education/reports/2016/10/13/145098/closed-doors-black-and-latino-students-are-excluded-from-top-public-universities/ (accessed May 13, 2019).

Bernstine, Daniel O. 2015. *Why LSAT Scores Should Not Be Used to Label Law Schools and Their Students.* Law School Admission Council. www.lsac.org/sites/default/files/media/lsac-statement-dec-1-final_0.pdf (accessed May 13, 2019).

Brown, Dorothy. 2015. Law Schools Are in a Death Spiral. Maybe Now They'll Finally Change. *The Washington Post*, March 9. www.washingtonpost.com/posteverything/wp/2015/03/09/law-schools-are-in-a-death-spiral-maybe-now-theyll-finally-change/ (accessed May 13, 2019).

Chanvisanuruk, Joel. 2016. *The Import and Application of Detailed Bar Exam Score Reports in Tailoring Bar Preparation Outreach to Law Students.* University of Cincinnati College of Law (powerpoint slides on file with author).

Cullen, Bradley T., and Michael Pretes. 2000. The Meaning of Marginality: Interpretations and Perceptions in Social Science. *The Social Science Journal* 37(2): 215–229.

Dalessandro, Susan P., Lisa C. Anthony, and Lynda M. Reese. 2012. *LSAT Technical Report Series: LSAT Performance with Regional, Gender, and Racial/Ethnic Breakdowns: 2005–2006 Through 2011–2012 Testing Years.* Law School Admission Council. http://citeseerx.ist.psu.edu/viewdoc/download?doi=10.1.1.258.4820&rep=rep1&type=pdf (accessed May 13, 2019).

Dennis, Rutledge M. 2005. The Age of Marginality. In *Marginality, Power, and Social Structure: Issues in Race, Class, and Gender*, ed. Rutledge M. Dennis, 3–8. Amsterdam: Elsevier.

Du Bois, W.E.B. 1903. *The Souls of Black Folk.* Chicago: A.C. McClurg & Co.

Dunne, Robert. 2005. Marginality: A Conceptual Extension. In *Marginality, Power, and Social Structure: Issues in Race, Class, and Gender*, ed. Rutledge M. Dennis, 11–28. Amsterdam: Elsevier.

Gurung, Ghana S., and Michael Kollmair. 2005. *Marginality: Concepts and Their Limitations* (IP6 Working Paper No. 4). www.nccr-pakistan.org/wp-content/uploads/2018/09/Marginality.pdf (accessed May 13, 2019).

The Institute for College Access & Success. 2018. Project on Student Debt. http://ticas.org/posd/map-state-data (accessed May 13, 2019).

Jenkins, Thomas. 2005. The Marginal Man: Evolution of a Concept. In *Marginality, Power, and Social Structure: Issues in Race, Class, and Gender*, ed. Rutledge M. Dennis, 49–69. Amsterdam: Elsevier.

Karp, Melinda M., Hoori Santikian Kalamkarian, Serena Klempin, and Jeffrey Fletcher. 2016. How Colleges Use Integrated Planning and Advising for Student Success (iPASS) to Transform Student Support (CCRC Working Paper No. 89). https://ccrc.tc.columbia.edu/media/k2/attachments/how-colleges-use-ipass-transform-student-support.pdf (accessed May 13, 2019).

Law School Admission Council (LSAC). 2014. *Cautionary Policies Concerning LSAT Scores and Related Services.* www.lsac.org/sites/default/files/media/lsat-score-cautionary-policies_0.pdf (accessed May 13, 2019).

Law School Admission Council (LSAC). 2017. *U.S. National Decision Profiles.* www.luc.edu/media/lucedu/career/pdfs/guideshandouts/Law%20School%20national-decision-profiles-2016.pdf (accessed May 13, 2019).

Law School Admission Council (LSAC). 2017–2018. LSAC Fee Waiver Program: Instructions for Fee Waiver Applicants. www.lsac.org/lsat/lsat-dates-deadlines-score-release-dates/lsat-cas-fees-and-refunds/fee-waivers-lsat-credential (accessed August 13, 2019).

Law School Admission Council (LSAC). n.d. LSAT & Credential Assembly Service (CAS) Fees. www.lsac.org/jd/applying-to-law-school/lsat-cas-fees (accessed May 13, 2019).

McCormick, Alexander C., Jillian Kinzie, and Robert M. Gonyea. 2013. Student Engagement: Bridging Research and Practice to Improve the Quality of Undergraduate

Education. In *Higher Education: Handbook of Theory and Research*, vol. 28, ed. M.B. Paulsen, 47–92. Dordrecht: Springer.

Mehretu, Assefa, Bruce Wm. Pigozzi, and Lawrence M. Sommers. 2000. Concepts in Social and Spatial Marginality. *Geografiska Annaler. Series B, Human Geography* 82(2): 89–101.

Oxford Dictionaries. n.d. Definition of marginal in English. www.oxforddictionaries.com/us/definition/american_english/marginal (accessed May 28, 2016).

Park, Robert E. 1914. Racial Assimilation in Secondary Groups with Particular Reference to the Negro. *American Journal of Sociology* 19(5): 606–623.

Park, Robert E. 1928. Human Migration and the Marginal Man. *American Journal of Sociology* 33(6): 881–893.

Phipps, Chelsea. 2012. More Law Schools Haggle on Scholarships. *The Wall Street Journal*, July 29. www.wsj.com/articles/SB10000872396390444130304577557182667927226 (accessed May 13, 2019).

Powell, Farran. 2018. 10 Things to Know About Merit Aid Scholarships. *U.S. News & World Report*, February 12. www.usnews.com/education/best-colleges/paying-for-college/slideshows/10-things-to-know-about-merit-aid-scholarships (accessed May 13, 2019).

Shultz, Marjorie M., and Sheldon Zedeck. 2008. *Identification, Development, and Validation of Predictors for Successful Lawyering*. www.law.berkeley.edu/files/LSACREPORTfinal-12.pdf (accessed May 13, 2019).

Stanford Law School. n.d. JD Application Process. https://law.stanford.edu/apply/how-to-apply/jd-application-process/ (accessed May 13, 2019).

Stonequist, Everett. 1935. The Problem of the Marginal Man. *American Journal of Sociology* 41(1): 1–12.

Taylor, Aaron N. 2014. Reimaging Merit as Achievement. *New Mexico Law Review* 44: 1–47.

Taylor, Aaron N. 2015a. Diversity as a Law School Survival Strategy. *St. Louis University Law Journal* 59: 321–383.

Taylor, Aaron N. 2015b. Law School Scholarships Foist Surtax on Neediest. *The National Law Journal*, July 13. www.nationallawjournal.com/id=1202731858541/OpEd-Law-School-cholarships-Foist-Surtax-on-Neediest (accessed May 13, 2019).

Taylor, Aaron N., and C. Christensen. (2017. *Law School Scholarship Policies: Engines of Inequity (LSSSE Annual Results 2016)*. Bloomington: Indiana University Center for Postsecondary Research.

Trudeau, Dan, and Chris McMorran. 2011. The Geographies of Marginalization. In *A Companion to Social and Cultural Geography*, eds. Vincent J.Del Casino, Jr., Mary E. Thomas, Paul Cloke, and Ruth Panelli, 437–453. Malden, MA: Blackwell Publishing.

University of the District of Columbia, David A. Clarke School of Law. 2017. Scholarships for Entering Students. www.law.udc.edu/?page=FinAidScholarships (accessed May 13, 2019).

von Braun, Joachim, and Franz Gatzweiler. 2014. Marginality – An Overview and Implications for Policy. In *Marginality: Addressing the Nexus of Poverty, Exclusion, and Ecology*, eds. Joachim von Braun and Franz W. Gatzweiler, 1–23. Dordrecht: Springer.

Weeden, Dustin. 2015. *Hot Topics in Higher Education: Student Loan Debt*. www.ncsl.org/Portals/1/Documents/educ/StudentLoanDebtBrief.pdf (accessed May 13, 2019).

9 The Culture of "raceXgender" Bias in Legal Academia

Meera E. Deo

Natalie is a tenured law professor, one of the exceptionally few multiracial women in legal academia. She recalls that a decade ago, when she was "the first woman of color to go up for tenure" at her law school, her colleagues "made it very difficult." Although she is "always the one they trot out for sample classes and speeches [when they need a diverse and] dynamic professor," this does not mean that she is "a beloved professor." Since its founding, her school has been steeped in what she calls "huge gender-race" issues, and Natalie has been "tortured by those standards," both by students and colleagues. Natalie knows that her students of color appreciate having a woman of color professor while many of their classmates, who are "happy, liberal white people, young [and] outspoken," agreed enough to recently award Natalie a teaching award. She was shocked when the news was announced, recalling, "I was like, 'Are you guys kidding? You guys don't like me!'" Her confusion stemmed from enduring many "disrespectful things" in the classroom, including "physical intimidation, mouthing off, and [biased] student evaluations running the gamut from, 'Why doesn't she wear her wedding ring? Is she trying to tease us?,' to 'She thinks she's so smart, [but really she isn't].'" Similarly, she has one primary ally on the faculty, also a person of color; together, they are labeled "the two troublemakers," simply "because we say things like, 'We should have a diverse appointment pool,' [and] 'Give out scholarships [to] people from diverse backgrounds.'" At best, Natalie's colleagues toe the line, thinly lamenting a lack of diversity by saying, "'We've tried, but you know we just can't get those qualified people of color.'" At worst, they purposefully perpetuate a disappointing dearth of diversity while alienating the few professors of color already on the faculty. Either way, their actions feed into an academic culture of law school that maintains an unequal status quo.

Natalie's experience encapsulates many of the challenges facing women of color law faculty, who not only remain a significant minority of all law teachers but also are at the losing end of both visible and invisible power structures that perpetuate inequality in legal academia. The Association of American Law Schools (AALS) reports that while a full 46.4% of law faculty members are white men, only 7.0% are women of color.[1] The American Bar Association (ABA) has released similar figures, noting 9.6% women of color faculty as compared to 47.9% white men.[2] Natalie's narrative highlights the ways in which women of color remain outside the norm not only in terms of numbers, but also in how they are received—silenced, disrespected, and presumed incompetent by students and faculty alike.

This chapter draws from original quantitative and qualitative data collected from participants in the Diversity in Legal Academia (DLA) study, the first formal empirical study of law professors in the U.S. utilizing an intersectional lens to investigate the experiences of law faculty from all walks of life and all stages of the profession. Empirical findings from the DLA data reveal various intersectional challenges facing women of color faculty, as well as individual and structural approaches to improve faculty inclusion. Improving the qualitative experience for women of color faculty would not only give these traditionally underrepresented faculty a greater sense of belonging and inclusion, but could improve legal education overall.

A focus on raceXgender—the compound of effects of devaluation based on both race and gender—provides an opportunity to study a largely ignored and invisible group of traditionally underrepresented faculty who remain in the minority in legal academia: women of color.[3] Intersectionality holds that various identity characteristics meld together to affect outcomes, such that the experiences of women are shaped not only by their sex or gender, but also "by other dimensions of their identities, such as race and class" (Crenshaw 1990–1991, 1242).[4] When the identity of an individual is comprised of intersecting "sites of oppression," there are multiple opportunities for devaluing that identity in a compound way (Delgado and Stefancic 2001, 51–55). This concept is firmly grounded in Critical Race Theory, which gives voice to oppressed groups and utilizes storytelling to reveal complex theories and real experiences alike (Bell 1992).

This chapter and this research build on the expanding field of "eCRT"—empirical methods merged with Critical Race Theory (CRT).[5] Intersectionality is especially useful to frame formal empirical research, particularly when qualitative data is used to compare the processes and outcomes of study participants from

1 Because data from the AALS includes many non-tenure-track positions, it is over-inclusive when considering the tenure- or tenure-track, non-clinical/legal writing/library faculty participants in the DLA study presented here. AALS data is no longer available online, but Tables and analysis can be found in previously published articles relying on Diversity in Legal Academia (DLA) data, including Deo (2015, 962).

2 The data presented here is from 2013, the year that data was collected for the empirical study guiding this chapter. American Bar Association (ABA) statistics are available online at: www.americanbar.org/content/dam/aba/administrative/legal_education_and_admissions_to_the_bar/statistics/2017_fall_1l_enrollment_gender_minority.xlsx (also on file with author).

3 While 62% of law professors are men and at least 71% are white, women of color comprise only 7% of all legal academics. AALS statistics are included in previously published Tables, including Deo (2015, 962, Table 4).

4 See also Collins (2000); Glenn (2002); Crenshaw (1989).

5 See Obasogie (2013). See also Mertz (this volume).

various combinations of identity intersections. Together, combining quantitative or qualitative data with a narrative style from CRT, eCRT seeks to utilize data to further the goals of highlighting inequities, turning theory into praxis, and giving voice to the marginalized.[6]

One of the earliest articles introducing intersectionality focused on the ways in which the combination of devalued identity characteristic resulted in unique outcomes for affected groups (Crenshaw 1989). We learned then that while African Americans could sue for employment discrimination and women could sue for employment discrimination, neither courts nor the relevant legal doctrine were equipped to handle discrimination claims filed by African American women who endured bias based on both race and gender (Crenshaw 1989). Focusing on intersectionality, and the compound effects of what this project terms raceXgender, provides an opportunity to highlight experiences that are specific to women of color faculty in an environment centered around and focused on white men.

Additionally, there are many ways in which the gendered bias pervasive in law school creates shared experiences between women of color and white women faculty; racial bias also ties together the experiences of men of color and women of color. Including comparative samples from different racial/ethnic and gender backgrounds therefore allows for similarities and differences based on race and gender to shine through, while also highlighting the unique circumstances of women of color faculty who are often doubly devalued.

Dozens of narratives over the years have indicated that there are ongoing disparities in the experiences of law faculty depending on the race or gender of the professor. Scholars studying gender in legal academia have highlighted the myriad challenges associated with women working in a male-dominated workspace.[7] Early empirical research on the experiences of law faculty of color found that they faced "discrimination in hiring and promotion, alienation among their colleagues, hostility from students, and a lack of support," (Deo 2014 citing Delgado and Bell 1989, 369–370) with little expectation that law schools would intervene to improve the situation (Delgado and Bell 1989). This dismal prediction has been confirmed in contemporary empirical research by scholars Katherine Barnes and (this volume's co-editor and contributing author) Elizabeth Mertz who report that "despite significant progress toward more [numerical] diversity, women and scholars of color face continued difficulties" (Barnes and Mertz 2012, 511). While their research is directly in conversation with raceXgender-based disparities involving tenure, their data also reveal "[c]ommon negative themes [that] center on the effects of implicit bias in the tenure process, and differential impacts on women and on scholars of color of the law school's pre-tenure institutional structures and cultures" (Barnes and Mertz 2012, 522–523).[8]

6 See Crenshaw et al. (1996).

7 See, e.g., Angel (2000a); Angel (2000b); Angel (1988); Guinier et al. (1994, 3); Moran (1986, 508); Merritt and Reskin (1992, 2356–2357); Resnik (2003).

8 There are also disparities in job satisfaction after tenure, following established patterns of racialXgender bias. See Katherine Barnes and Elizabeth Mertz, *Law School Climates: Job Satisfaction among Tenured U.S. Law Professors* (2018).

Building on this literature, this chapter begins with a brief introduction to the DLA project, which is the first formal empirical study to investigate the personal and professional lives of legal academics throughout the U.S., across the professional trajectory, and with a purposeful lens of examining challenges and opportunities based on race and gender identity. Next, the chapter shares empirical findings from the DLA study, exploring how the academic culture and power structures of legal academia serve as barriers to the professional success of women of color faculty who are 1) presumed incompetent by students and colleagues alike, and 2) expected to be caretakers for both law students and fellow faculty. The subsequent section proposes data-driven individual strategies and structural solutions to improve the experiences of non-traditional faculty, and thereby advance legal education overall. The Conclusion considers the theoretical implications of this research, emphasizing that only a true commitment to diversity and inclusion will move us beyond the status quo to ameliorate raceXgender bias in our unequal profession.

The Diversity in Legal Academia Study

The DLA project investigates the causes of the intersectional raceXgender disparity in law teaching by empirically examining how the compound effects of racial and gender differences affect experiences and outcomes among law faculty. DLA research centers on a core sample of 63 women of color, including those who are Black, Latina, Asian American, Native American, Multiracial, and Middle Eastern. A comparative sample of 30 white men, white women, and men of color explores similarities and differences based on race and gender.

Through a novel target sampling technique, participants were carefully selected to ensure diversity across various domains, including: race/ethnicity, gender, region, tenure status, leadership status, and school selectivity. Target sampling is a variant of snowball sampling, wherein a seed group of participants nominates other possible research subjects (Goodman 1961). While snowball sampling has been criticized for allowing potential bias in the sample—as representation is not assured when all nominated subjects are added to the study—target sampling recognizes this potential for bias and works to ameliorate it. Target sampling begins with a seed group of participants that are diverse among recognized domains; additional participants are then carefully selected from among those nominated to ensure ongoing representation (Watters and Biernacki 1989). To maximize broad representation in the DLA study, diversity among participants was rigorously maintained with regard to: race, gender, tenure status, leadership status, school selectivity, school region, and more. For instance, if the sample already included three Black women from the Midwest (both tenured and untenured; leaders as well as non-leaders; from elite as well as less-selective schools) no additional Black women from the Midwest would be included; instead, additional Black women added to the study would be from the South or West Coast or East Coast while those from the Midwest might be Asian American men or white women. This painstaking process yielded the 93 participants in the final DLA sample.

Each participant completed an online survey in advance of a 45–90 minute in-depth interview. The survey covered demographic, behavioral, and attitudinal questions (e.g., race/ethnicity; frequency of interaction with faculty from different backgrounds; likelihood of remaining in legal academia) while the interview allowed for detailed responses to queries regarding the participant's career trajectory, professional relationships, and work/life balance, among other topics.[9] Participants also proposed both individual strategies and structural solutions to combat race-and-gender-based challenges in legal academia.[10]

Expecting Incompetence and Academic Caretaking

Two poignant themes that draw from largely invisible power structures and discrimination in academic culture emerge from the DLA data.[11] While each stands apart, they are also interlocking and layered together to create complications for women of color law faculty. This section first discusses how women of color faculty are presumed incompetent by students and colleagues alike. Second, the chapter reviews how the expectation that women of color serve as caretakers at work serves as an additional barrier to their professional success.

A Presumption of Incompetence

The 2012 anthology *Presumed Incompetent* perfectly sets the stage for how women of color are viewed and treated in legal academia (Gutierrez y Muhs et al. 2012). In various chapters, that book discusses the experiences of women of color academics across the disciplines. While some authors draw from a narrative tradition and others employ empirical methods, one overarching theme is that women of color are assumed to be incompetent: unqualified to teach, unprepared to research, and unsuited to succeed in academia.[12] Various power structures in institutions of higher learning bar the way for women of color to succeed as academics. Law faculty contributors in particular note the many challenges of navigating a hostile campus for those who are seen as intruders in the mostly-white and mostly-male bastion of legal education.[13] The very culture of law school, predominantly white and overwhelmingly male, perpetuates the understanding that women of color do not belong.

The remainder of the chapter includes anonymized qualitative data in the form of verbatim excerpts from DLA participant interviews, allowing professors from

9 The actual survey instrument and interview protocol used in data collection are included in the Appendix of Deo (2019).

10 For more on the data and methods used in the DLA study, see Deo (2014, 375–382) and the Appendix of Deo (2019).

11 For more on academic culture and inchoate power, see Lazarus-Black (this volume).

12 For instance, see Arriola (2012) (discussing her personal challenges as a woman of color at an unsupportive predominantly white institution). For more discussion on these themes from *Presumed Incompetent* and on the relevant literature generally, see Deo (2014, 371–375).

13 See, e.g., Lazos (2012, 167); Onwuachi-Willig (2012, 148); and Wing (2012, 359–60)

underrepresented backgrounds to speak for themselves about their experiences while giving voice to those who are traditionally marginalized in legal academia. Qualitative DLA data and accompanying analysis confirm ongoing hostility against women of color law faculty directly related to the cultural norms and power structures of law schools. The hostility faced by women of color faculty comes not only from their colleagues, but also from students who have never before been confronted with a woman of color authority figure and are not expecting a woman of color at the podium. The combination makes for a powerfully negative working environment. Since "both minorities and women are presumed to be incompetent as soon as they walk in the door," women of color are doubly burdened by the presumption of incompetence (Lazos 2012, 177). This presumption leads to classroom confrontations, biased evaluations, faculty conflict, and silencing.

Classroom Confrontations

Though most students are respectful and cooperative in class, the few who create conflict demand the attention not only of the professor, but also of their classmates—thereby damaging the learning experience for everyone. Some confusion stems from the students' expectation that their professors will be white men—a reasonable assumption given that this demographic comprises almost half of all law professors.[14] When a woman of color is at the front of the room, some students are disappointed. Patricia, a Black law professor, notes, "Their image is the white male professor who scares them, and that's just not a model that I can follow. Not being a white male, and not really being privileged enough to be able to scare them." Similarly, a multiracial professor named Emma has clearly noticed how students' expectations are dashed when they see her at the podium instead of the white male they were expecting; this leads to "push back." She says:

> They don't necessarily appreciate somebody in my position, as a new professor, as a woman, and as a person of color, having power over them. So I got a lot of push back particularly from male students about, "Do you know your stuff?" "Are you a credible source of authority?" "Why should I listen to this stuff from you?"

On Susan's first day of class, she immediately registered the distraught looks on her students' faces connected to their disappointment at being assigned who they assumed was, in her words, "the dud professor." She could tell from their expressions what they were thinking: "'Oh my god, we got the Black lady teaching us and [the other lucky section] got the white guy?!'" It was clear that they felt both entitled to have a white male professor and cheated out of that preferable experience when confronted with Susan as their professor.

14 At least 71% of all law professors are white, 62% are men, and a full 46% are white men—compared to just 7% of women of color. AALS statistics are included in previously published Tables, including Deo (2015, 962, see Table 4).

When DLA participants were asked to share common characteristics of those few students initiating confrontations, most agree with a Black professor named Patrice who notes that "they're primarily white men." Armida, a Latina professor, teaches classes where the problem students "tend to sit together" and be "white, male, [and] arrogant." In talking with colleagues, these women of color faculty realize that while the presumption of incompetence hounds them constantly, these confrontations are rare for others. For instance, a Middle Eastern professor named Zahra recently had faculty colleagues conducting observations in her classroom. Afterwards, they confided to her, "Wow, I can't believe that so-and-so guy said this to you in class. Like, they would have never done that to X-male colleague."

Students of color, on the other hand, tend to be appreciative and enthusiastic about the few faculty of color teaching their courses. When Alexandra, a Black professor, first started her academic career, she remembers, "I got inundated with requests [which] says that these students aren't feeling as supported as they could." Likely because there were few other faculty of color on campus to share the load, she recalls, "as soon as I got here, I was asked to be an advisor on several student Notes; I've been asked to be the faculty advisor for BLSA; I've been asked to coach trial teams." Alexandra knows that "from the student perspective, they are just so excited that I'm here," and she recognizes that "they need involvement from a young woman of color professor."[15] Because students of color are also underrepresented in law schools, the disappointment that their white male students display towards women of color faculty may take precedent.

Biased Evaluations

Though many women receive plenty of positive comments on student evaluations, the presumption of incompetence is also on open display. Some students tend to focus their observations on the personal style of the woman of color professor over her course content or pedagogical approach, while aggressive and even hostile comments are also not uncommon.

To be sure, the vast majority of student evaluations include complimentary comments about professors, whether male, female, white, or faculty of color. Most women of color enjoy high numerical scores on their evaluations as well as positive comments. Aisha, an Asian American professor, enjoys excellent rapport with the vast majority of her students, noting, "I have my groupies and they follow me from class to class," taking every elective she offers. Grace, a multiracial professor, notes, "My relationship with students pretty much across the board at every

15 She continues, "From my perspective it's just been very difficult to give them that energy," with young children at home and with a focus on producing the scholarship necessary to attain tenure. The accessibility of many women of color professors creates additional service obligations, especially when coupled with "other-mother" expectations discussed later in the chapter.

institution that I taught has been really wonderful." Her evaluations "have been fabulous," though even she will occasionally "get the random comment from students [on evaluations, asserting], 'Professor Grace doesn't like white people.'" Grace's example shows that even when women of color faculty are respected and revered overall, intersectional bias still occasionally rears its ugly head.

Just a few negative, biased, irrelevant comments can be used to thwart the tenure dreams of junior faculty or focus attention away from teaching excellence. Even when evaluation comments are not horrendous, they often still draw from raceX-gender bias and offer little constructive feedback, focusing on the woman of color professor's physical appearance or personal style over her teaching effectiveness. Annie, an Asian American professor, has received "a lot of comments about my appearance. I think women tend to get that more than guys." Black women are subject to particular scrutiny for their looks. Trisha's evaluations also include "inappropriate personal comments about my appearance." June's students seemed obsessed with her personal style even during class time; she once had a student who wrote in an evaluation nothing about the course material or what she learned, but simply, "'I came to class [because] I wanted to see what you were going to wear.'"

Anonymous evaluation comments can go beyond nonsense or irrelevance into open hostility. June suffered attacks on her personal style, but also "remember[s] this statement: 'I know we have to have affirmative action, but do we have to have this woman?'" Here, the student managed to weave the presumption of incompetence directly into the evaluation comment, suggesting that June was unqualified but hired solely based on her race and gender through affirmative action, and that she fell short of even the low expectations the student held for affirmative action hires. Danielle once "got an evaluation that [read], 'She's Black, enough said.' So I'm being evaluated based upon things that have nothing to do with my teaching, like my skin color." When skin color is used as a proxy for incompetence, it becomes almost impossible to surmount the associated burdens. Marybeth, a white professor, "never read the evaluations" from a particularly challenging course because she knew they would be "horrible," after "every bad thing that could happen in a law school class happened to me in that classroom."

Faculty Conflict

When asked about their relationships with fellow professors, the vast majority of participants in the DLA sample begin by noting the "collegiality" and "civility" of their peers. Hannah, a multiracial professor, notes of her colleagues, "Everyone gets along [and] is just very nice and very kind in general." Melanie, a Latina professor, sees faculty relationships as "generally very positive," and the faculty as a whole as "pretty collegial." She notes that "one of the great pleasures" of her job is to be "very well-supported by my colleagues." Although others initially mention the collegiality of their faculty, their responses to probing questions and requests for details frequently reveal that many colleagues wear a "mask of collegiality" hiding deep-seated indifference, distrust, and even hostility.

The presumption of incompetence that students project onto women of color professors is reflected in the actions of some faculty colleagues. In her first semester teaching, a Latina professor named Alicia encountered a "very hostile" white male student who quickly voiced his complaints about her to "a white male faculty member." That colleague could have made clear to the student that he strongly supported Alicia; he could have approached Alicia to discuss the student with an open mind; instead, he "assumed that of course the student was correct in his complaints" and met with Alicia to advocate for the student. Once he took "the student's side, [that] empowered the student to act out even more," and encouraged other students to follow suit. Ultimately, Alicia had "a little cabal of problematic students that I then had to manage," thanks to her colleague's intervention.

Cindy, an Asian American professor, knew soon after she was hired that her law school had deep-seated problems involving discrimination, including "a lot of stuff based on race and gender." Though a white male professor was hired at the same time, "there was a major difference in how he was treated and how I was treated." Cindy "was treated like the 'dumb one,' sort of an affirmative action hire in the worst sense of the word [meaning that I was unqualified, but hired because of my race and gender,] and he was the 'real one.'" As a new professor, and because she witnessed "a lot of favoritism towards him from particular faculty members," Cindy internalized her colleagues' intersectional discrimination until she too "felt like he was the real deal, and I'm not." Ironically, "as it turned out, it was kind of opposite," with Cindy outperforming her colleagues' expectations and the white male hire falling flat.

Sonia, a Latina who is now a professor and administrator, was the first woman of color hired at her law school many decades ago. When her colleagues essentially shunned her, and the institution withheld even basic support, Sonia recalls, "I just thought it was humiliating." She also fought against "the presumption … that I didn't have it and that I would never write," all with a backdrop of gossiping colleagues. Fighting through it did not quell the presumption of incompetence entirely. She recalls:

> Even after I was in the midst of writing, I remember someone coming up and saying, "There's a rumor that you're paralyzed and can't write." "Well," I said, "I don't know why, because I have several pieces, and they're coming out."

This belief that she could not write is a direct result of the presumption of incompetence—with the added insult of a colleague telling Sonia directly that other faculty had low expectations of her success.

Silencing

Silencing takes many forms in legal academia, including male colleagues overtly voicing the expectation that women stay mute, subtly suggesting that women should keep their opinions to themselves, or ignoring the contributions of women speakers. This gender-based power imbalance obscures even race-based bias, affecting white women and women of color alike. Isabella, a white scholar, recalls speaking up at one of the first faculty meetings she attended a decade ago when she "didn't realize women were meant to be seen and not heard." Afterward, a white male colleague exclaimed his surprise at her contribution, noting, "'Wow! You're really articulate!'" Rather than taking pride in his supposed compliment, Isabella remembers that the comment "stunned me because I thought all of us on the law faculty would be articulate," quickly learning that women were usually silent. Zahra, an untenured professor, and her "junior female colleagues" have been "shown over and over [that] our voice doesn't matter when we express opinions." Undeterred, they continue making efforts to speak out, but are "not heard [or] understood" by colleagues who expect little from them.

Whether taking the form of hepeating, mansplaining, or whitesplaining, female faculty members are frequently reminded to stay silent. The unfortunately widespread and common experience of *hepeating* occurs when a woman's contributions are ignored, while a man is praised for simply repeating her ideas as his own (Dodgson 2017). Perhaps worse, men sometimes explain to women things that are within the women's own sphere of knowledge, assuming that as men they know more than the expert herself. This is *mansplaining*, when a woman's "expertise [is] instantly dismissed because of the lady-shaped package it came in" (Lewis 2014). People of color also suffer through *whitesplaining*, when their ideas are dismissed or ignored—largely because they are presumed incompetent—until co-signed by a white person speaking out in agreement (Deo 2015, 976–978).

Elaine, an Asian American professor, has experienced hepeating first-hand; early in her career, she would try to contribute by "saying things at a faculty meeting, and no one paid attention to it; and then a man would say it, and then everyone would pay attention to it." The same thing happened to Carla, a Latina, who asserts, "I've counted over 10 times on my faculty where I've said something and [nobody has responded; then] a male faculty has repeated it and another male colleague has said, 'Good idea!'" When women are presumed incompetent, their words are not expected to carry weight or be worthy of response (Resnik 2003, 570–571).

Mansplaining is another frequent complaint among women faculty. Even before they get to the evidence supporting their case, women must first fight "simply for the right to speak, to have ideas, to be acknowledged to be in possession of facts and truth, to have value, to be a human being" (Solnit 2008).[16] Stacey, a Black professor, recalls that after a white male colleague engaged in a racially charged incident, her dean got involved to explain why Stacey should get over it instead of speaking out, saying, "He just feels so bad. And he's gay. And he doesn't understand how he could've said something racist if he's gay. I kid you not. [The dean] basically told me he couldn't have said something racist because he's gay." As a scholar of race and identity, as well as a Black woman, Stacey is well versed in ways in which intersectionality creates divisions even

16 See, e.g., Valenti (2014).

among those with overlapping identity characteristics; yet, her white dean and white colleague thought they knew better and attempted to educate her on her own area of expertise and personal identity.

Smita has also experienced both mansplaining and whitesplaining as an Asian American professor. She speaks up regularly at faculty meetings, but believes that what she says "would carry more weight with the faculty if it were being said by white people," regardless of whether the content involves "the importance of diversity or whatever else." The power structure of law school is one that recognizes and rewards the words of white men. When Smita's white colleagues remain silent on hot button racial issues, she and the few other people of color faculty carry the burden of speaking out, though they are largely ignored by a law school culture that adheres to the myth of equality in legal education. Ironically, because whitesplaining is so entrenched, Smita needs white faculty to be more outspoken or the issues themselves are ignored along with the people of color raising them. While "there is a sense of your voice being discounted in a lot of respects," Smita wants to ensure important issues are still discussed. Whether pushing for diverse hires, championing nontraditional faculty applications for tenure, or supporting women in leadership, Smita does not "hear it enough from my white colleagues, even those who consider themselves progressive." Women of color—subject to bias based on their race and gender—thus have unique interactions with hepeating, mansplaining, and whitesplaining all happening concurrently and consistently.[17] These traditional outsiders to legal academia are given a clear signal that they do not belong, and should remain silent.[18] The cost-benefit analysis of speaking up—where a woman must fight against the expectation that she remain silent, only to have her words ignored, hepeated, mansplained, or whiteplained—"keeps women from speaking up and from being heard when they dare [or] crushes young women into silence by indicating … that this is not their world" (Solnit 2008).

Expected Caretakers

In the midst of this hostility, women of color and white women faculty alike frequently play a caretaking role at work.[19] Both as other-mothers with students and while taking care of the academic family for colleagues, women of color faculty carry the bulk of the burden of getting things done.

17 For more on how intersectionality creates not only additive but cumulative effects, see Delgado and Stefancic (2001, 51–55).

18 In fact, it seems prevalent throughout academia generally, given that there is a website dedicated to academic mansplaining, *Academic Men Explain Things To Me, Where Women Recount Their Experiences of Being Mansplained, in Academia and Elsewhere*, http://mansplained.tumblr.com (last visited February 2, 2015).

19 For more on the work/life balance challenges facing women of color faculty who balance increased caretaking expectations not only at work but also at home, see Chapter 6 in Deo (2019).

Other-Mothers

Empirical research has highlighted how white students and students of color alike view female faculty of color as especially approachable and accessible.[20] DLA data confirm that many women of color law professors enjoy close mentoring relationships with students. Martha, a Latina professor, says that students are "the best part of the job really." For Zahra too, "the best thing about the school is the students." Grace gushes, "I love my students as a general matter. I always have." A Native American named Laura agrees, stating, "Oh well, of course, your relationship with students is one of the best parts about the job."

Students seek out female faculty from all backgrounds not only for clarification on substantive course material, but also for a host of other educational, professional, and even personal matters. Madison, a white junior scholar, says:

> I find it easy to interact with our students and I do have a couple each semester that I end up connecting with on a deeper professional development level because they are not hesitant to come into the office or to send an email and ask a question about being a lawyer and not just class.

Hannah frequently entertains students "asking for advice" on everything from "what to do with their lives, or if they have difficulty in a particular *other* class how to prepare for that, or what courses I might recommend," or even those who "cry in my office because of personal issues." While many women faculty willingly and earnestly engage in these personal interactions with students, they nevertheless endeavor to maintain some professional distance from the students who seek them out.

The "ethic of caring" that many female faculty of color display at work often results in their being mistaken for *other-mothers* (Guiffrida 2005, 701–703). While students may share personal matters with white women faculty, they tend to respect their boundaries. For instance, a white professor named Ava recalls that when she started teaching, "I was one of the few women in the building and certainly the only young one and I got surrounded by students all the time and they just wanted my attention." Yet, students may demand pedagogical changes or display other open forms of entitlement with their women professors of color. This role expectation follows in a long tradition of women of color as caretakers, or "mammies," such that even a female professional is "categorized as a service worker, here to provide instead of guide" (Whitaker 2013). Collectively, these female faculty of color are devalued in the academic culture of law school, seen not "as leaders with positions of power, but instead as caretakers," whose purpose is to cater to the needs of others (Hill-Brisbane 2005). Male faculty are rarely expected to provide similar functions, which explains in part why there are a "myriad of demands" facing women of color and white female faculty that are

20 Deo, Vue, and Woodruff (2010) (citing empirical findings indicating that students find nontraditional faculty more accessible and approachable).

rarely applied to men (Brooks 1986, 420). As a Black law professor named Kayla says, "I definitely feel I bear the disproportionate impact—the brunt—of service to students of color."

Often, female faculty of color appreciate these opportunities to serve. Gabrielle, a Black professor, enjoys "the opportunity here to mentor African American students [on the Frederick Douglas] Moot Court and [other] things [that] are personally rewarding for me." Yet, her deep attention to students comes at a cost since there are few rewards and little recognition for this work, which also takes her away from her scholarly priorities. During Bianca's "very first semester" as a law professor, a student came to meet her in office hours; she remembers that he approached her as if "he thought he was maybe doing me a favor [by] saying, 'I'm just not used to someone who teaches like you,'" and then suggesting her pedagogical approach could be improved by catering to his preferred style. Bianca was likely this student's first Latina professor, at least in law school.[21] The raceXgender power dynamic at play in their interaction—a white male challenging a Latina—overrode what may be considered a dominant power dynamic in law school, of professor over student. The student's perception of Bianca as an other-mother also clearly played a role in his expectation that she would change her approach to accommodate his request.

Taking Care of the Academic Family

Broader service to the institution also garners little appreciation from administration, takes time away from other priorities, and is a mainstay of the professional lives of women of color academics. Alexandra, a junior faculty member, notes that "scholarship and teaching" are what the institution expects faculty to prioritize and what senior colleagues reward come time for tenure. A mentor constantly prompts Alexandra "to say no" to extra service duties by reminding her, "'You are not going to *not* get tenure over service.'"[22] While demonstrated effectiveness in teaching, scholarship, and service are the three common requirements to achieve tenure, they are rarely if ever weighted equally.[23] A lackluster publication record or sub-par teaching evaluations are frequently cited as reasons for tenure denials—while the high levels of service that women of color faculty provide tend to far exceed the nominal requirements.

21 Latinas comprise just 1.3% of American law professors—including not only tenured and tenure-track faculty, but also visitors, contract, legal writing, library, and other faculty members. With just 138 Latinas out of 10,965 law faculty members total, this particular student would likely never encounter a professor who looked like Bianca again (Deo 2015, 962) (citing AALS statistics in Table 4).

22 Tenure-related challenges associated with the caretaking roles and overload service characterizing the experience of many female faculty of color are included in Deo (2018).

23 The common adage "publish or perish," highlighting the primary importance of scholarship over all other professional academic duties, comes to mind.

Research on the division of service has found that "women faculty perform more service than male faculty in academia," and are especially invested in jobs that directly serve the institution, including student mentoring and committee work; even at work, women are "taking care of the academic family" (Guarino and Borden 2017). Brianna, a senior Black scholar and administrator, understands that "disparate 'housekeeping' requirements" contribute to women of color carrying "extra burdens of service." Carla's research leave was rescinded just weeks prior to it starting, when an administrator "called me and said, 'You can't go on research leave. You have to Chair [a particular] committee.'" Carla was neither flattered nor impressed with being selected, noting, "I've been in this long enough to know that's not really a compliment; that means someone needs to stay and clean the house [and] it's going to be you." Carla and many other women of color have said yes to these demands far more often than they should need to—and more often than their colleagues—as they continue in their caretaker role, even at work (Guarino and Borden 2017). Although white women also struggle to balance the demands of academic caretaking with their scholarly work and teaching loads, many recognize how women of color have even more to juggle; for instance, a white female professor named Jordan notes that her women of color colleagues are "unduly put upon" at her school, expected to "be on every diversity committee and do this and do that and constantly mentoring and talking to students." She recognizes that these colleagues "are doing a lot of additional committee work and it's not that they're aren't into it, but they are doing twice as much" as everyone else, with no extra reward or compensation.

Sharing Best Practices and Structural Solutions

The penultimate question in the DLA interviews asked participants for their suggestions to improve diversity in legal academia. Most respondents provided thoughtful personal strategies for combatting the intersectional challenges they face at work. This section begins with individual tactics, in the hopes that these best practices can be utilized and useful to other non-traditional faculty facing similar issues. Yet, as structural solutions must be part of the answer for these systemic problems in the academic culture and power structure of law school, these are explored as well.

Individual Strategies

Women of color have come up with many creative responses to combat the presumption of incompetence and expectations of caretaking that confront them in legal academia. Three particular strategies recurred frequently in the data: preparation (especially for the expected emotional labor of academia), education, and keeping the big picture in mind.[24]

24 Emotional labor "includes 'the management of feeling to create a publicly observable facial and bodily display,' where women of color faculty regulate their true 'emotions to comply with [workplace] norms,'" which can result not only in extra work but even in negative health consequences (Deo 2019). See also Brooks (1986).

First and foremost is preparation, beyond mastering the substantive material to managing their emotions in the classroom and navigating challenging colleagues. Keeping a big picture in mind—instead of obsessing about little issues—also helps women of color overcome both a presumption of incompetence and the expectation that they will be caretakers at home and at work.

Annalisa, an Asian American professor, knew before she started that she would "have to overcome this perception that a woman and a person of color is not as smart as [a white man.] You know, not a fraud, basically." To combat the presumption of incompetence, she says, "There's always a [pressure] on my side to over-prepare." Brianna reminds us that while all professors "have to know [the] material," women of color law faculty also must "exude a confidence [through] a classroom persona," or risk confronting "students [who] sense vulnerability [and] will devour you." Armida suggests "credentializing yourself" with the students, "incorporating in the conversation [past] experience [which] impresses them [and] gives them a value in me. [They think,] 'Sullivan & Cromwell, that means that she's smart,'" working directly against the presumption of incompetence which assumes she is not.

Nontraditional faculty must employ different strategies to overcome negative presumptions from colleagues. Elaine adopted a multi-pronged strategy to be heard by her colleagues. She always "thought carefully before I said things, but once I decided to say something, I said it emphatically—not like dramatically, but with a lot of conviction." Also, she took her time making comments because "if you talk a little longer," people listen. She would not "just blurt it out," but would state her case, then "give an example, and then maybe relate it back" to what she had said earlier. Finally, Elaine and many others strategically organize "groups of people who seemed to listen to each other" into "coalitions" so that they are primed when they hear her "good idea [in a faculty meeting] to say, 'Oh, I agree with what she said,'" thereby validating the speaker while voicing support for her idea.[25]

In addition to advance preparation, education is key. A white male professor named Joe knows that his faculty has "hired people who look like themselves," which he sees as something that "institutions tend to do." Yet, examining the actual reasons for our actions will help reveal patterns for mismatches between our purported beliefs and our actions. These mismatches will sometimes be indicators that bias is at play. Implicit bias can be difficult to uncover. But achieving greater equality in legal academia will require us to act purposefully toward this goal, even when doing so makes us uncomfortable; this discomfort is often caused by our stretching beyond what are often seen as acceptable or at least accepted law school cultural norms—a necessity if we are to discover a new normal of greater equality. Recall how Alicia's white male colleague approached her on her white male student's behalf, exacerbating the ongoing conflict in Alicia's classroom and creating a new faculty challenge for Alicia. Rather than ignore her colleague's intervention

25 One recent article highlights Obama-era women "amplifying" one another's perspectives to claim them for the original female speaker (Goff 2016).

and accept the resulting complications as expected, Alicia "decided he was educable and [that] I had enough of a relationship with him that he could hear me." So Alicia approached him directly:

> I said, "We need to talk about what happens in the classroom to women of color and I need you to read this article [on the topic]." And he did. And we had a conversation about it. And he was open to understanding what had gone on [including] what he had done in terms of making the situation worse for me by reacting as he did, by not immediately standing up for me.

Alicia's colleague took the time to learn about the experiences of women of color faculty by reading a relevant article; he was open to hearing about his own role in perpetuating the presumption of incompetence; and he reached an understanding about how he could be more supportive going forward.[26]

Finally, many women of color consciously remind themselves to keep the big picture in mind, rather than being bogged down by immediate challenges. Marjorie, a senior Black scholar, reminds herself of the early female "pioneers," many of whom survived in legal academia without any support. On her difficult days, she tells herself, "'You think you have it tough, girly? What about [if there were just] one of us? [At least now] there are about four of us. You can have dinner [together] at this table.'" Annalisa faces numerous challenges with work/life balance, expected to manage her household while putting in extra service duties on campus. She "used to feel guilty [because] the kids are in school all day, and now I have a babysitter picking them up. And I only see them at dinner." With young children at home, demanding teaching and service duties, and a passion for scholarship, she also knew she "couldn't be the best mom … and be with them all the time, and [also] be good at what I did at school, so something had to give." Over time, her solution has been to create different expectations between the academic year and the summer, so that when her teaching load is heavy, "I'm doing more work and less mothering," but then in the summer, "the kids go to summer camp from about to 9 to 2pm and then I pick them up and we hang out together afterwards."

Structural Solutions

While personal strategies certainly can help individual professors facing the presumption of incompetence and the expectation of caretaking, only structural solutions can truly ameliorate what this data reveal to be systemic raceXgender

26 While many women of color personally use education as an individual strategy, it is also important that the administration address this as a structural concern—themselves bringing up ways to educate faculty, staff, and students on implicit bias, intersectionality, privilege, and other mechanisms that maintain an unequal status quo in legal education.

bias. Allies in the administration must champion women of color faculty, purposefully showing their strong support for non-traditional professors. Collectively, each of us can also do more, by examining our own biases and working purposefully to improve diversity in legal academia.

Administrative Allies

Instead of expecting women of color to take care of the academic family, a Native American professor named Melissa recommends "recognition for all the many roles often women of color play in the law school; the advising and the retaining students role is completely undervalued." This would give women of color credit for "taking care of the academic family" (Guarino and Borden 2017). Michelle, a Black professor and administrator, suggests that to prevent overwhelming service burdens from detracting from teaching and scholarship priorities for women of color, administrators should "protect them from themselves. Many women of color, people of color, have a very [deep obligation to] service that can hurt them." By reminding women of color to equalize priorities—and by equalizing the service workload—administrators would improve diversity in legal academia.

Understanding the presumption of incompetence and the caretaker role could help administrators and colleagues alike recognize and respond appropriately to intersectional challenges facing women of color in legal academia. Armed with that knowledge, when students complain about women of color professors, a Latina professor named Marisol believes colleagues might "recognize that students may be pushing you in a different way because you're a female or you're a person of color or you're both." When reviewing negative evaluations, she suggests that senior faculty and administrators ponder the following: "'Do your evaluations suck because you suck as a teacher, or is there something else going on?'"

Do More

The burden of improving diversity in legal academia cannot rest with administrators alone. Each of us can do more. This includes hiring more candidates who come from diverse backgrounds, as well as creating an environment conducive to their success. Fermin, a Latino professor, notes that administrators must "be on the lookout all the time" for potential candidates from diverse backgrounds; following the standard hiring procedures are more likely to result in maintaining an unequal status quo rather than yield more diverse hires.

Gabrielle knows that increasing diversity not only provides career opportunities for people currently underrepresented in legal academia, but could improve legal education overall, and even enhance her own experience. After all, "it might make it seem more normal for me to be at the head of the classroom if there were more people [of color law faculty]." Thus, a deep commitment to equality, diversity, and inclusion is needed. As a Black faculty member named Ryan notes:

> [I]f you would like a woman of color on your faculty, then you have to go and hire a woman of color. You can't not give it the full attention that it deserves and hope a woman of color comes your way. [Instead, t]o make diversity work you have to be serious and committed to making diversity work.

Vivian, an Asian American professor, reminds us that for women of color to overcome intersectional obstacles, other "people have to deal with their own institutional bias and their own subconscious bias." She has seen colleagues reconstruct reality to explain "why the white guy hasn't written as much as opposed to the African American" candidate, including "completely different narratives, like, 'Oh he's been so busy developing his economic theories' [for the white candidate,] as opposed to, 'I don't think he's capable to do the level of work' [for the African American]." She believes that if we all were to help colleagues realize that they may be looking "for people like themselves subconsciously," they may become more open-minded in considering candidates from different paths.[27] Aisha has also seen colleagues "finding reasons to ***not*** hire" candidates of color though they simultaneously "find reasons *to hire* white people." To do this, they "give alibis to the deficiencies of white people but ... look for the holes in [a person of color's] record to keep [them] down." Instead, she urges faculty to work against automatic or implicit bias[28] as well as purposeful discrimination; pushing back against this unconscious discrimination will allow those who "want to increase the number of women in academia [to simply] hire them, obviously." She is correct that "there's not a dearth of applicants out there," as the pool of qualified applicants is not the problem.[29] What is lacking is simply "a commitment to do it. It's not rocket science." A Latina law professor named Lola is similarly direct:

> I think you always hear administrators say it's so hard to find a woman of color or minorities and I think that's a bunch of bullshit. I think they purposely don't look for candidates. It's easier to say there aren't any. ... I would say if you really are interested in improving diversity, then do it instead of saying it's hard. I think a lot of it is just lip service.

Surya is also straightforward, asserting, "Well, I honestly don't think the problem is that administrators don't know what they can do." Instead, as a Black professor named April asserts, "I think there's so few women in legal academia because white people won't hire them. [They] feel for some reason that we can't take a

27 Vivian's observations are borne out in the research, which confirms that implicit bias "leaks into everyday behaviors such as whom we befriend, whose work we value, and whom we favor" (Kang and Lane 2010, 467–468).

28 Implicit bias includes behaviors that "affect social judgments but operate without conscious awareness or conscious control" (Kang and Lane 2010, 467) For more on implicit bias, see Mertz's chapter in this volume.

29 For a thorough discussion of why a lack of qualified applicants cannot explain the current lack of diversity in legal academia, see Deo (2014, 359–364).

'risk' on someone who doesn't fit [the standard] profile," even if the candidate has numerous other markers of success. A true commitment could go a long way.

Conclusion

With an academic culture that both perpetuates race and gender disparities and maintains an unequal status quo regarding power and privilege, legal academia is the perfect environment to view from the lens of intersectionality. Using this framework from Critical Race Theory allows us to investigate how raceXgender—the compound combination of two devalued identity characteristics—affects the lived experiences of law faculty from various backgrounds.

The combination of empirical data with Critical Race Theory in this chapter also contributes to the field of eCRT. Drawing directly from intersectionality, projects explicitly steeped in raceXgender explore the particular ways in which the compound effects of discrimination based on both race and gender affect women of color in legal academia. This chapter is thus an example and a building block of eCRT, merging qualitative data from the DLA study—from women of color, white women, men of color, and white men—with both the narrative style of CRT and the broader goals of putting theory into practice and amplifying the voices of the traditionally silenced minority.

Empirical data from the DLA study do bolster the importance of intersectionality, revealing that women of color face unique obstacles with regard to a presumption of incompetence and the expectation of caretaking. Yet, gender permeates the entire power structure of law school. Male students push back against female faculty. Male colleagues use silencing, mansplaining, and hepeating to enforce an academic culture where white women and women of color alike are expected to contribute little aside from academic caretaking. While intersectionality is useful in this context at the margins to reveal variations in how women from different racial backgrounds endure discrimination, the gender bias in legal academia is so pervasive as to transcend racial differences between women and highlight ongoing barriers preventing women of all backgrounds from achieving their maximum potential.

Conversely, intersectional differences do emerge strongly around a double paradox faced by women professors of color regarding faculty–student interactions. On the one hand, women of color faculty appreciate and enjoy building strong relationships with students, many reflecting that this is the best part of the job. On the other hand, these strong relationships result in women of color becoming more overburdened by service than their white women colleagues, with little reward or recognition given for carrying these extra burdens. Even more problematic are the few (usually white male) students who push back against the authority of women of color faculty, doubting their competence and testing their ability to manage the classroom. The double paradox can be simplified in the following ways: 1) women of color appreciate and enjoy interactions with students overall, though they are overburdened by student demands on their time; also, 2) though the vast majority of student–faculty interactions are positive, including those involving women of color faculty, the few confrontational students in the classroom who also express bias in student evaluations create a negative environment overall that requires significant energy and investment to overcome and detracts from the learning of all students. These negative raceXgender effects are thereby doubled for professors who face bias on both gendered and raced dimensions.

In addition to these theoretical contributions, DLA data confirm that schools, administrators, and individual faculty members who truly seek to increase the number of traditionally underrepresented faculty and improve their workplace experiences must make a strong commitment to diversity in legal academia and act accordingly. A surface commitment to diversity will not yield results; a core commitment is necessary.[30] Those who do share a core commitment to faculty diversity must do more than simply follow established guidelines on sexual harassment or nondiscrimination. Following established patterns and norms will likely lead to more of the same—perpetuating the myth of equality in legal education, ongoing power inequities based on raceXgender bias, and an academic culture that heightens gender and racial disparities.

A core commitment begins with educating ourselves, our colleagues, and our administrators to understand the experience of traditional outsiders who join legal academia. Part of educating ourselves involves examining our own biases, to recognize overt or even subtle ways in which we contribute to tarnishing the application process for new or lateral hires or otherwise perpetuate systems of inequality in law school culture.

Though many have played this role at their institutions, female faculty of color should not bear the burden of individually educating each of their colleagues; allies who provide a listening ear or sympathetic shoulder should always make their intentions known and voice their support for more marginalized faculty. When a white senior scholar named Abigail was a junior professor years ago, she remembers that any time there was a meeting "and we needed a note taker there would be the turning of all eyes to whichever female was in the room and she would become the note-taker." After this pattern became obvious to one of Abigail's white male colleagues, "he would say, 'Hey, why are we all looking at the [women faculty]? I'll take notes [today]. Next time, John, you can take notes.'" His speaking up moved women from a menial caretaking role closer to an equal faculty position. Sometimes hostility is more entrenched. Scarlett, a white professor, knows that improving her school's faculty diversity is "an uphill battle" because the white male administrators "are really holding on to their positions of power," which includes "trying to bring in people like them." Few DLA participants discussed "diversity training" or other opportunities on campus to examine their own biases and learn how to move past them for everyone's benefit. A multiracial professor named Sofia initiated a "session on gender in the classroom" herself, after

30 Lee (2010, 479–480) (discussing "surface" versus "core" diversity ideals in the workplace).

realizing that few of her colleagues recognized their own privilege or were "really thinking about [how] gender affected what you can do in the classroom."

White male allies must point out inequities in the system, challenging those aspects that prefer and benefit them directly based on race and gender. Instead of placing the burden on individual faculty who themselves are burdened by the presumption of incompetence, administrators and white allies should champion these efforts—signaling both their trust in the data and the need for all faculty to work past stereotypes. In Madison's first semester of teaching, a "notoriously difficult" student "made the day-to-day class more challenging." Yet, with "the full support of the faculty," including gentle intervention by an administrator who addressed the problem student, her classroom become "easier to manage" and she also learned to lean on and trust her colleagues.

Once educated, individual faculty members and administrators must work actively both to hire diverse candidates and create a welcoming atmosphere for those who accept and join legal academia. Once non-traditional faculty are hired, administrators must also follow Marisol's advice to "put systems in place to make sure that person is going to succeed." Melissa reminds us that "there definitely has to be recognition for all the many roles often women of color play in the law school; the advising and the retaining students role is completely undervalued." Overall, valuing diversity and the unique benefits of a diverse faculty are key. As Grace suggests:

> Value [women of color] the way you value the white male colleagues. Treat them in that same way, give them the space to do scholarship versus spend all this time to do service. Understand evaluations ... are subjective and affected by race, gender, [and] sexual orientation.

With a commitment to diversity and equality in place, we can work together to move beyond our contemporary unequal academic culture toward one where power is distributed more equitably, and we ultimately leave behind raceXgender barriers to instead celebrate diversity as a predictor of success.

References

Angel, Marina. 1988. Women in Legal Education: What It's Like to Be Part of a Perpetual First Wave or the Case of the Disappearing Women. *Temple Law Review* 61: 799–846.

Angel, Marina. 2000a. Comments in Reply: It's Becoming a Glass House. *Journal of Legal Education* 50: 454–456.

Angel, Marina. 2000b. The Glass Ceiling for Women in Legal Education: Contract Positions and the Death of Tenure. *Journal of Legal Education* 50(1): 1–15.

Arriola, Elvia R. 2012. "No hay mal que por bien no venga": A Journey to Healing as a Latina, Lesbian Law Professor. In *Presumed Incompetent: The Intersections of Race and Class for Women in Academia*, eds. Gabriella Gutierrez y Muhs, Yolanda Flores Neimann, Carmen G. Gonzalez, and Angela P. Harris, 372–392. Boulder: University Press of Colorado.

Barnes, Katherine, and Elizabeth Mertz. 2012. Is It Fair? Law Professors' Perceptions of Tenure. *Journal of Legal Education* 61(4): 511–539.

Barnes, Katherine, and Elizabeth Mertz. 2018. Law School Climates: Job Satisfaction among Tenured U.S. Professors. *Law & Social Inquiry* 43(2): 441–467.

Bell, Derrick. 1992. *Faces at the Bottom of the Well: The Permanence of Racism*. New York: Basic Books.

Brooks, Roy L. 1986. Life After Tenure: Can Minority Law Professors Avoid the Clyde Ferguson Syndrome? *University of San Francisco Law Review* 20: 419–427.

Collins, Patricia Hill. 2000. *Black Feminist Thought: Knowledge, Consciousness, and the Politics of Empowerment*, 2nd edition. New York: Routledge.

Crenshaw, Kimberlé. 1989. Demarginalizing the Intersection of Race and Sex: A Black Feminist Critique of Antidiscrimination Doctrine, Feminist Theory and Antiracist Politics. *University of Chicago Legal Forum* 1989: 139–167.

Crenshaw, Kimberlé. 1990–1991. Mapping the Margins: Intersectionality, Identity Politics, and Violence Against Women of Color. *Stanford Law Review* 43(6): 1241–1299.

Crenshaw, Kimberlé, Neil Gotanda, Gary Peller, and Kendall Thomas, eds. 1996. *Critical Race Theory: The Key Writings that Formed the Movement*. New York: The New Press.

Delgado, Richard, and Derrick Bell. 1989. Minority Law Professors' Lives: The Bell–Delgado Survey. *Harvard Civil Rights-Civil Liberties Law Review* 24(2): 349–392.

Delgado, Richard, and Jean Stefancic. 2001. *Critical Race Theory: An Introduction*. New York: New York University Press.

Deo, Meera E. 2014. Looking Forward to Diversity in Legal Academia. *Berkeley Journal of Gender, Law, & Justice* 29(2): 352–387.

Deo, Meera E. 2015. The Ugly Truth about Legal Academia. *Brooklyn Law Review* 80(3): 943–1014.

Deo, Meera E. 2018. Intersectional Barriers to Tenure. *U.C. Davis Law Review* 51(3): 997–1038.

Deo, Meera E. 2019. *Unequal Profession: Race and Gender in Legal Academia*. Palo Alto, CA: Stanford University Press.

Deo, Meera E., Rican Vue, and Maria Woodruff. 2010. Paint by Number? How the Race & Gender of Law School Faculty Affect the First Year Curriculum. *Chicana/o-Latina/o Law Review* 29(1): 1–42.

Dodgson, Lindsay. 2017. Men Are Getting the Credit for Women's Work through Something Called "Hepeating". *Business Insider*, September 26. www.businessinsider.com/what-is-hepeating-2017–9 (accessed May 20, 2019).

Glenn, Evelyn Nakano. 2002. *Unequal Freedom: How Race and Gender Shaped American Citizenship and Labor*. Cambridge, MA: Harvard University Press.

Goff, Keli. 2016. How the Women of the Obama White House Fought Gender Inequality—and We Can Too. *Daily Beast*, September 23. www.thedailybeast.com/how-the-women-of-the-obama-white-house-fought-gender-inequalityand-we-can-too (accessed May 20, 2019).

Goodman, Leo A. 1961. Snowball Sampling. *The Annals of Mathematical Statistics* 32(1): 148–170.

Guarino, Cassandra M., and Victor M.H. Borden. 2017. Faculty Service Loads and Gender: Are Women Taking Care of the Academic Family? *Research in Higher Education* 58(6): 672–694.

Guiffrida, Douglas A. 2005. Othermothering as a Framework for Understanding African American Students Definitions of Student-Centered Faculty. *The Journal of Higher Education* 76(6): 701–723.

Guinier, Lani, Michelle Fine, and Jane Balin with Ann Barrow and Deborah Lee Stachel. 1994. Becoming Gentlewomen: Women's Experiences at One Ivy League Law School. *University of Pennsylvania Law Review* 143(1): 1–110.

Gutierrez y Muhs, Gabriella, Yolanda Flores Niemann, Carmen G. Gonzalez, and Angela P. Harris, eds. 2012. *Presumed Incompetent: The Intersections of Race and Class for Women in Academia*. Boulder: University Press of Colorado.

Hill-Brisbane, Djanna A. 2005. Black Women Teacher Educators, Race Uplift, and the Academic Other-Mother Identity. *Advancing Women in Leadership* 19. www.advancingwomen.com/awl/fall2005/19_5.html (accessed May 20, 2019).

Kang, Jerry, and Kristin Lane. 2010. Seeing Through Colorblindness: Implicit Bias and the Law. *UCLA Law Review* 58(2): 465–520.

Lazos, Sylvia. 2012. Are Student Teaching Evaluations Holding Back Women and Minorities?: The Perils of "Doing" Gender and Race in the Classroom. In *Presumed Incompetent: The Intersections of Race and Class for Women in Academia*, eds. Gabriella Gutierrez y Muhs, Yolanda Flores Neimann, Carmen G. Gonzalez, and Angela P. Harris, 164–185. Boulder: University Press of Colorado.

Lee, Rebecca K. 2010. Core Diversity. *Temple Political & Civil Rights Law Review* 19(2): 477–514.

Lewis, Helen. 2014. The Essay that Launched the Term "Mansplaining". *New Republic*, July 4. www.newrepublic.com/article/118555/rebecca-solnits-men-explain-things-me-scourge-mansplaining (accessed May 20, 2019).

Merritt, Deborah J., and Barbara F. Reskin. 1992. The Double Minority: Empirical Evidence of a Double Standard in Law School Hiring of Minority Women. *Southern California Law Review* 65(5): 2299–2360.

Moran, Rachel F. 1986. Commentary: The Implications of Being a Society of One. *University of San Francisco Law Review* 20(3): 503–514.

Obasogie, Osagie. 2013. Foreword: Critical Race Theory and Empirical Methods. *U.C. Irvine Law Review* 3: 183–186.

Onwuachi-Willig, Angela. 2012. Silence of the Lambs. In *Presumed Incompetent: The Intersections of Race and Class for Women in Academia*, eds. Gabriella Gutierrez y Muhs, Yolanda Flores Neimann, Carmen G. Gonzalez, and Angela P. Harris, 142–151. Boulder: University Press of Colorado.

Resnik, Judith. 2003. A Continuous Body: Ongoing Conversations About Women and Legal Education. *Journal of Legal Education* 53(4): 564–577.

Solnit, Rebecca. 2008. Tomgram: Rebecca Solnit, The Archipelago of Arrogance. *TomDispatch.com*, April 13. www.tomdispatch.com/post/174918 (accessed May 20, 2019).

Valenti, Jessica. 2014. Mansplaining, Explained: "Just Ask an Expert. Who is Not a Lady". *Guardian*, June 6. www.theguardian.com/commentisfree/2014/jun/06/mansplaining-explained-expert-women (accessed May 20, 2019).

Watters, John K., and Patrick Biernacki. 1989. Targeted Sampling: Options and Considerations for the Study of Hidden Populations. *Social Problems* 36(4): 416–430.

Whitaker, Manya. 2013. The Color of Teaching: Expectations of Mammy in the Classroom. *Feminist Wire*, November 6. https://thefeministwire.com/2013/11/the-color-of-teaching-expectations-of-mammy-in-the-classroom (accessed May 20, 2019).

Wing, Adrien Katherine. 2012. Lessons from a Portrait: Keep Calm and Carry On. In *Presumed Incompetent: The Intersections of Race and Class for Women in Academia*, eds. Gabriella Gutierrez y Muhs, Yolanda Flores Neimann, Carmen G. Gonzalez, and Angela P. Harris, 356–371. Boulder: University Press of Colorado.

10 Canaries in the Mines of the U.S. Legal Academy

Elizabeth Mertz

Introduction: Imperfect Empirical Information

> Race, for us, is like the miner's canary. Miners often carried a canary into the mine alongside them. The canary's more fragile respiratory system would cause it to collapse from noxious gases long before humans were affected, thus alerting the miners to danger. The canary's distress signaled that it was time to get out of the mine because the air was becoming too poisonous to breathe.
>
> Those who are racially marginalized are like the miner's canary: their distress is the first sign of a danger that threatens us all. It is easy enough to think that when we sacrifice this canary, the only harm is to communities of color. Yet others ignore problems that converge around racial minorities at their own peril, for these problems are symptoms warning us that we are all at risk.
>
> (Guinier and Torres 2002, 11)

Despite this warning, and many others like it, recent empirical research points to a continued problem of marginalization for men and women of color, and for white women, within the U.S. legal academy. How can it be that one of the most educated and politically aware professions has had such difficulty overcoming these problems? This chapter takes up that question, reviewing what we know, delving into literatures that provide perspectives on this continuing problem, and suggesting that law schools take a serious look at forms of inchoate and largely invisible bias that remain entrenched within their walls.

In the quotation above, Lani Guinier and Gerald Torres compare the miner's canary to communities of color in the United States, making the case that attention to the marginalized and vulnerable is important not only for its own sake, but also because those communities may be wiser than others about looming problems facing everyone. There is a fine line between this prescriptive argument and what Derrick Bell described as "interest convergence" – that is, the paradox created when marginalized people only receive attention to the extent that their concerns overlap with those of powerful members of society (Bell 1980).[1] This is

1 Bell later described the U.S. Supreme Court's subsequent approach to approving affirmative action as a quintessential example of the interest-convergence paradox, inasmuch as "no matter how much harm blacks were suffering because of racial hostility and discrimination, we could not obtain meaningful relief until policymakers perceived

obviously a major concern because playing to the powerful, by using an argument based in interest convergence, forever condemns one part of society to matter only insomuch as it can serve and benefit another part. It is important, however, to pay attention to the fine line here, because Guinier and Torres illuminate a different point. The point, also powerfully made by W.E.B. Du Bois years ago (1990 [1903]), is that the dominant members of society should pay attention to the marginalized not only because to do so is morally correct but also because, on many issues, the disempowered can generate superior knowledge. On crucial issues, those at the margins may have better information than the powerful, generating a truer vision of the larger picture of the societies in which they live (see Matsuda 1987).

Ironically, the scholarship that bears a tag indicating its association with marginalized perspectives is often discounted as "biased" in favor of particular groups – feminist and/or women's studies, critical race theory of many kinds, class crits, queer theory – perhaps to a lesser extent, area studies. This is unfortunately aided by our tendency to unconsciously read language content from linguistic form (see Mertz and Weissbourd 1985; Silverstein 1985). So, for example, if the language format describing a kind of theory includes an adjective like "feminist" – as in "feminist legal theory" – then speakers may accept without questioning that the content of the theory does not pertain equally to everyone.[2] This linguistic mistake can also lead us to accept another myth, still powerful although it has been dispelled many times: that the field traditionally called "legal theory," unadorned by adjectives, *does* equally pertain to everyone. Instead – and entirely predictably – traditional "legal theory," unmarked as to gender or race, tends to reflect majority culture and dominant elite perspectives. This means that it regularly misses important parts of what is going on throughout law and society, while imagining itself able to theorize the entire field of law.[3]

One goal of this chapter is to join other scholarly writings in pointing out what should be an obvious truth, though it is often overlooked: taking account of traditionally excluded perspectives, when generating hypotheses for social science study, will allow us to be more – not less – objective. Similarly, if legal theory considered a larger range of conceptualizations of law and justice, it would likely gain a fuller understanding, rather than a diminished one. We've known for some

that the relief blacks sought furthered interests or resolved issues of more primary concern," and that such relief "minimize[d] the importance of race while offering maximum protection to whites" (Bell 2003, 1624; Bell 2005, 151).

2 Indeed, some may discount the theory altogether as biased, based on such labels.

3 To take just one example – this one from the growing literature on implicit bias – unacknowledged dynamics surrounding racial prejudice (more likely to be completely invisible to members of the dominant race) exact epistemic costs for everyone, not just members of the racial group that experiences domination (Gendler 2011, 33–63). An additional note here is that the field of "jurisprudence" (a term that is in some ways coterminous with unmarked "legal theory," in some way not) has been especially resistant to any self-critique or even mild wonderment about its persistent focus on a very small segment of the polity (arguably partially leading to an extreme lack of diversity among its practitioners).

time that mainstream perspectives, uncorrected, fail in important ways to provide a superior ground for social science understandings – or for normative legal theorizing. Social science disciplines such as anthropology have long spelled this out. Perhaps that is why they've remained the most marginalized of social science disciplines in the legal academy: they challenge received wisdom at a fundamental level. It is far easier to give the viewpoints identified with minority groups a somewhat condescending position at the margins than to accept their wisdom into the heart of legal scholarship.[4]

There is a risk in drawing attention to this phenomenon, despite its solid base in scholarship. The risk is that *any* attempt to challenge the partial (in two senses) vision of "unmarked" dominant perspectives will itself be deemed to be "political" or "unscientific." But if we reject challenges arising from marginalized perspectives *a priori*, we dismiss hypotheses or ideas simply because they've been generated by one group of people as opposed to another. That would be a very subjective, biased reason for ruling out concepts and perspectives. To decide before investigation that one hypothesis is "political," and therefore should not be seriously entertained, is actually to inject politics into the very heart of objective inquiry. Instead, as we are finding out more and more, allowing creative insights and new perspectives to be explored and tested only deepens our knowledge.

In similar fashion to research by traditionally excluded scholars, the field of anthropology has for some time been working to develop empirical methods that allow us to discover and analyze perspectives from outside of dominant groups and paradigms. This chapter argues that more attention to these kinds of methods would allow scholars from law (and, indeed, from some social sciences) to systematically explore important – but under-recognized – new ideas. This in turn might open the door to empirically sound insights which could help in addressing problems that have remained oddly resistant to change. It would also help researchers identify the flaws in generally accepted approaches that have emerged from "mainstream" scholarship whose parameters have too often been defined by people who occupy privileged positions in society.

An important case in point is the stubborn persistence of race and gender disparities within the professions – including the legal profession and the academy – despite many years of avowed efforts to create equal playing fields. As study after study is now showing us, even professions with high professed standards for

4 I do not claim superiority for anthropology as a field in terms of its inclusiveness, for it certainly bears the imprint of its roots in the academy of the global north, as well as of its colonial roots (see, e.g., Asad 1973). But the methods of anthropology, and the field's goals in producing knowledge, arguably provide some better tools for these purposes than do those of other similarly located social science fields. While I focus on anthropology in this chapter, certainly other fields such as qualitative sociology have also developed methods for incorporating non-dominant groups' experience into the basic frame used for research, rather than using an exclusively majority group perspective. And, at the same time, all of these fields need to exercise more continuous scrutiny to guard against the reproduction of irrational social hierarchies within their theories, methodologies, ways of framing and selecting research questions, and disciplinary practices.

fairness and egalitarianism continue to reproduce unfair social hierarchies (see, e.g., ABA Commission on Women in the Profession 2006, 2013; Files et al. 2017; Jacobi and Schweers 2017). In many cases, academic professions, which are supposed to have superior access to the best knowledge (presumably including on sources of bias and how to correct them), seem embarrassingly impotent in efforts to overcome old limitations. Indeed, some scholars writing about the academy either fail to consider the existence of an unequal playing field there, or assume that any inequalities have been adequately addressed (see, e.g., Bonica et al. 2018; Cassidy 2012). The continued invisibility of inequality within the legal profession and the legal academy creates problems that branch out further, because lawyers and law professors play an important role not only within their own professional communities but in wider U.S. society. How can professionals who are unaware of their own implicit biases – of their own acquiescence in unfair workplace inequalities – successfully contribute to wider law reforms aimed at ending discrimination and at promoting fair and equal access to all kinds of societal institutions and benefits?[5]

I suggest that the professions and the academy in general – and the legal academy in particular – have suffered from imperfect information generated by biased presuppositions that hinder them from achieving superior knowledge – what some would label better "objectivity."[6] That superior knowledge, along with fuller

5 Deo makes a similar point about the special position of the legal academy: "In a sense, if things are unfair, inequitable, or biased in legal academia, what hope do we have for other professions, academic institutions, workplaces and campuses?" (2015, 956). She bases this in part on the idea that there should theoretically be less overt discrimination (discrimination that would violate the law) in a workplace (the law school) where the workers should theoretically have more knowledge of – and concern with – the law than in other workplaces (2015, 956). Of course, both Deo and I acknowledge the research-based finding that there is more than just an intellectual problem here – but facing that intellectual problem might be a useful step in then attempting to remedy more deeply structural aspects of inequality.

6 I use the term "objectivity" here to draw attention to the fact that the form of knowledge indicated here would be superior in terms of standards that those aiming toward more "objective," complete, and "scientific" knowledge in the social sciences espouse. The more complete epistemological foundation provided by the approach described here does in fact offer a more sophisticated approach to generating knowledge that takes into account the social conditions under which that knowledge is generated – an issue explored more thoroughly in some social sciences than others (see, e. g., the discussion in Carbado and Roithmayr (2014) of Horkheimer's famous critique). For social science, this is the equivalent of instrument calibration in the natural sciences; it is a way of detecting sources of bias in the way information is collected. Another important step, which is aided by the use of theory to guide method, is an assessment of the limitations of any particular instrument or method – as no method captures everything. Precision thus requires that we specify and actually take account of what our method can NOT capture – a step that is all-too-often skipped over lightly by legal academics (mis-)using social science methods. I readily admit the limitations of a language of "objectivity" in terms of what we now know about the social foundations of human knowledge (explored in depth by STS scholars in recent years) – but also am unwilling to cede the ground of "objectivity," to the extent it is possible, to those who wield it most frequently (and often unthinkingly). I thank Devon Carbado for pushing me to clarify this point.

information and the power it offers for productive change, requires an epistemological openness – an openness that challenges blindness resulting from partial (and therefore often biased) perspectives. The argument in this chapter also poses a challenge to legal scholars and law schools who are embracing a particular form of "Empirical Legal Studies" (ELS) that prioritizes statistics and forms of quantitative research lacking any serious grounding in qualitative, theoretical, and/or critical perspectives.[7] For those ELS scholars who dive into quantitative analyses without obtaining fuller information on the social and cultural contexts surrounding the phenomena they enumerate, there remain serious risks that the numbers produced will be misleading (see e.g., Zuberi and Bonilla-Silva 2008; Merry 2016; Merry et al. 2016). On the other hand, those same numbers, when they emanate from studies informed by more sophisticated contextual empirical analysis (usually qualitative), can also be extremely useful. The best empiricism, then, draws on all methods and seeks actively to question received frameworks in order to better study and grasp what is actually happening. It is especially important to exercise this kind of quality control when using empirical studies of any kind to inform decisions about justice.[8]

If mainstream scholarship and reform efforts within the legal academy have been slow to focus on their own and others' continued bias, they have also paid insufficient attention to the now well-established empirical effects of intersectionality – despite the fact that the term intersectionality itself originated in the legal academy. Professor Kimberlé Crenshaw's germinal article (1991) posed a sharp challenge to legal research that failed to examine the combined effects of identities such as gender and race – a crucial example of which is provided by women of color. Note that this is not an argument for biased research but for accurate research: research that achieves better precision by examining a phenomenon often elided in studies that only considered the separate effects of race or of gender. The question often remained invisible, beneath the radar, in part because the researchers proceeded from unfounded assumptions based in their own presuppositions about how to study inequality. It fell to women scholars of color – and also to social sciences whose methods permitted a fuller consideration of what was happening with gender and race – to push this question into the consciousness of supposedly objective scholars whose vision (like everyone's) was partial. Here we see how ignoring the insights generated by traditionally marginalized scholars can delay progress toward deeper and more empirically accurate understandings.

This chapter begins by reviewing early scholarship on race and gender dynamics within U.S. law faculties, as a precursor to discussions of the recent *After Tenure* and *Diversity in Legal Education* studies. Given those studies' findings, the chapter

7 I hasten to add that not all who participate in empirical legal studies fall prey to this error; there are some ELS scholars who proceed more carefully from foundations in social science theories from various disciplines, and who remain open to mixed methods selected to match the questions asked.

8 In this regard, social science experts in multiple methodologies have made the case for "triangulation" of results reached using different methods as the most reliable way of achieving accuracy (see, e.g., Fielding 2012; Tashakkori and Teddlie 2003).

then proceeds to ask what is known about possible sources of bias in institutions like the U.S. legal academy. After brief overviews of work in psychology, anthropology, and critical race scholarship, the chapter concludes with a discussion of how largely invisible forms of power can continue to distort knowledge within the legal academy, following work by anthropologist Mindie Lazarus-Black. Coming full circle, the conclusion considers what the miners' canaries in legal education teach us about overall defects in the system today.

Empirical Information on Race and Gender Dynamics among U.S. Law Faculty

Although research on diversity issues within U.S. law faculties dates back at least to the work of Donna Fossum at the American Bar Foundation, our information today is nonetheless surprisingly meager. Using AALS data[9] from the mid-1970s, Fossum (1980) reported that 96% of full-time law professors were white, and 93% were male. It was already the case that recruitment to the ranks of tenured faculty strongly favored graduates of elite institutions. Using data collected a decade later, Richard Chused (1988) reported that by the academic year 1986–87, 15.9% of tenured or tenure-track law professors were women (a larger, 20% proportion of full-time faculty were women, but this included non-tenure-track professors). Chused also identified some small, slow progress toward racial integration, with 3.7% Black faculty, 0.7% Latino/a faculty, and 1.0% faculty members from other minority groups.[10] Using a sample from the AALS 1988–89 Directory, Robert Borthwick and Jordan Schau (1991–1992) confirmed a 20% figure for full-time women faculty at that time. While these quantitative studies provided valuable information, they could not fill in details regarding law school cultures and practices that qualitative research would yield.

9 AALS data are collected annually by the American Association of Law Schools, a national U.S. organization of law schools that largely overlaps with the American Bar Association's group of accredited law schools (although each organization has traditionally performed its own separate accreditation procedure – but often undertaken in jointly organized visits to each law school). The AALS Directory of Law Teachers, issued annually, provides information on each faculty member at accredited law schools, using an instrument that is generally filled out and verified by the administration at each school. Fossum excluded part-time faculty, and wound up with 3,850 faculty from 160 law schools.

10 Chused circulated a survey that asked at least one faculty member at each AALS member law school to provide information on faculty at his or her law school; he received responses giving demographic information for 149 law schools, which represented over 85% of AALS law schools at the time. His figures excepted African-American faculty at traditionally black law schools and Latino/a faculty at law schools in Puerto Rico so as not to exaggerate progress in integrating the bulk of U.S. law schools, which have been traditionally dominated by whites. Thus these numbers are lower than those reported by the AALS at the same time. Figures that included all full-time faculty at U.S. law schools in the school year 1985–86 reported that 6.5% of U.S. law faculty were minorities (Brooks 1987: 5, citing 1986 AALS Memorandum 86–57 from AALS Executive Director to Deans of Member Schools).

It was at that point in the mid-1980s that minority professors began to be more vocal about the difficulties they faced in U.S. law schools, pointing to differentially high turnover among scholars of color as well as egregious examples of open disrespect (see, e.g., Bell 1986; Brooks 1987; Chused 1988; Delgado 1988). In 1986–88, law professors Richard Delgado and Derrick Bell conducted a two-part study of minority law professors, combining a survey and 50 interviews. Having received survey responses from 35% of the identified minority professors then teaching in U.S. law schools, they noted that "[t]he most cautious interpretation would be that the survey data describe, in qualitative terms, the life experiences of the 106 professors who responded" (Delgado and Bell 1989, 354).

On an optimistic note, a high percentage (86%) of the minority professors who responded to the Bell–Delgado study indicated that they did not feel pressure to avoid controversial topics (such as civil rights) in their scholarship (1989, 357). Despite many qualitative comments that revealed continuing race-based difficulties, 80% of the respondents expressed themselves to be very or somewhat satisfied with their work situations (1989, 391). As the authors themselves pointed out, we can't generalize from these findings without further analysis of possible response bias; it's possible that these survey respondents were not typical of the group as a whole. Another difficulty is that a study including only professors of color doesn't allow us to compare their responses with their white counterparts; these generally positive results from survey respondents might still be significantly lower than whites' responses.[11] Nonetheless, taken more as qualitative evidence, we know from the survey that many minority law professors had positive experiences in their work environments, reporting warm, supportive institutional climates and relations with both colleagues and students (1989, 390). At the same time, a substantial number reported differentially negative race-based experiences in terms of (1) interactions with faculty and students, (2) fair assessments and possibilities for upward mobility, and (3) extra workloads and stress resulting from the fact that there were so few professors of color in their institutions.

Anticipating Guinier and Torres's account of the law professor of color as miner's canary, Bell noted (in his Introduction to the article reporting findings from the study):

> I do not think it detracts from the seriousness of this study's message to report that in my two decades as law teacher and dean, I have witnessed a great deal of outright discrimination against whites, males as well as females. Whites, as well as minorities, with impressive success in practice, are rejected for teaching openings if they did not attend the "right" law schools, did not earn top grades, hold law review editorships, or serve clerkships for prestigious judges.
>
> (Delgado and Bell 1989, 350)

11 For example, as the authors point out, it is hard to interpret results indicating high levels of time pressure among law professors of color without knowing the comparable figures for white law professors (1989, 356, 378). It is important, however, to pay attention to information received from 1/3 of the population at the time, because even if the results weren't typical of everyone, they nonetheless reported experiences from a substantial number of professors of color that indicated non-trivial ongoing problems.

And, according to Bell, many white faculty as well as faculty of color were negatively affected by the vague standards applied during law school hiring, promotion, and tenure processes, which often allowed controversial candidates to be excluded based on even a few expressions of vague disquiet about how those candidates might not "fit in" (Delgado and Bell 1989, 350). Just as the current studies cited above are demonstrating that racial and gender integration do not proceed in one-way, upward directions, writings and research in the mid-1980s mourned the apparent backsliding of the progress achieved during the foregoing decade.

During the 1990s, important research by Deborah Jones Merritt and Barbara Reskin tracked the experiences of women faculty and faculty of color, paying more attention to the effects of intersectionality than was found in earlier work (see, e.g. Merritt and Reskin 1992, 1997). Merritt and Reskin uncovered "empirical evidence of a double standard in law school hiring of minority women" (1992, 2299). They found that women of color were doubly disadvantaged by prejudices that accumulated against them because of the combined effects of their race and gender identities. Merritt and Reskin also demonstrated that both race and gender had significantly negative effects on the likelihood that a professor would be hired by an elite law school. And a study from the early to the mid-1990s by White for the AALS Committee on the Recruitment and Retention of Minorities (2004) found that both the hiring and the tenure gap between whites and minorities had actually widened during that time period.

The After Tenure *Study*

After the turn of the millennium, I launched the *After Tenure* study at the American Bar Foundation in collaboration with a number of other scholars, in an effort to shed light on an understudied part of the legal profession: law professors.[12] We also sought to remedy the dearth of information about the large part of these professors' careers that occurred after they were tenured – that is, the time period that constituted the bulk of their professional lives. Understandable concern about the effects of the tenure process had caused researchers to focus more on the pipeline leading from hiring to tenure than on what happens afterwards. In a sense, this reflects a widespread presumption that any race and/or gender problems that caused unfair difficulties (whether in hiring or at tenure) would abate once tenure was achieved – or that faculty who had survived those difficulties could continue to succeed in similar fashion after tenure. Our study provided an opportunity to test these assumptions.

The *After Tenure* study, the first of its kind, examines the post-tenure experiences of U.S. law professors, and has proceeded in three phases. Phase I pioneered the first

12 Professor Katherine Barnes has served as Co-PI with me for much of the time the project has been running, and Dr. Frances Tung has ably led as Project Manager. Earlier in the project, Provost Wamucii Njogu was Co-PI, and Molly Heiler was Project Manager; Dr. Joanne Martin played an important role during early data collection and analysis. For a full accounting of the research team involved in this project, see Mertz et al. (2011).

survey of U.S. law professors to employ a random national sample, stratified by gender and with an oversample for race. This allows Phase I to provide findings that are generalizable in keeping with standard statistical approaches. The survey instrument asked about multiple aspects of professors' job situations (including law school culture, job satisfaction, career trajectory, and personal characteristics). In order to provide a better qualitative context for these quantitative findings, Phase II involved over 100 interviews with a subset of respondents to the Phase I survey, yielding in-depth explorations of topics relating to how supportive (or not) the workplace was, the general culture and climate of the law school, and issues of equity and fairness. Phase III, currently ongoing, digs still deeper into professors' work contexts employing an innovative mix of linguistic and ethnographic methods.

Thus this is a unique data set for studying U.S. law professors, providing an opportunity to combine survey results from a randomly selected national sample of the full population of post-tenure professors with in-depth interviews from a smaller purposive sample selected from respondents to that original national study.[13] We focused on the period after tenure, in order to shed light on what happens once that important threshold has been crossed.

As noted, the Phase I survey was sent to a national sample of law professors drawn randomly from the AALS Directory of U.S. law professors, stratified on gender with an oversample for minority professors; it obtained a response rate of 63.1%.[14] Phase II of the project involved a purposive sample of 102 follow-up interviews conducted with a subset of the survey respondents; participants were chosen to provide a range of experiences, with target numbers for satisfaction level (as expressed in survey responses), experience (time in job), gender, race, geography, and relative ranking of law school.[15] Two coders analyzed transcripts of these interviews using Atlas.ti, tracking themes that emerged from the interviewees' own words and preoccupations.

13 A purposive sample is targeted based on the specific questions asked in a study. In this case, we selected among the professors who responded to our survey so that we would include equal numbers of target interviews from each of three reported satisfaction levels (very satisfied, neutral, very dissatisfied), as well as from different U.S. regions, different levels of seniority in teaching, and each of four demographic groups defined by intersectionality (women of color, white women, men of color, white men).

14 Especially in light of falling response rates in recent decades, this is an excellent rate of response – particularly given that we were working with professionals (Holbrook et al. 2008, 515–516). For details on survey methodology and analysis, see Mertz et al. 2011. Stratification by gender and oversampling for race permitted us to obtain enough respondents of color and enough female respondents to achieve acceptable levels for statistically valid analysis of gender and race dynamics. Results were weighted to account for this sampling approach as well as for identified patterns of non-response.

15 A subset of transcripts was coded by both coders to check on intercoder reliability; the remaining transcripts were coded by one of the coders and then checked by the other coder. The PI also oversaw the development of codes and the coding process, and met regularly with coders to review all coding issues or decisions. Because the results of this part of the study are interpreted qualitatively, the coding serves primarily as a guide to core themes that emerged from interviews, and as a check on the imposition of the researchers' own priorities in interpreting the interview data.

In a pair of articles from the project, my current co-PI Katherine Barnes and I found – using a combination of quantitative and qualitative results – that traditional outsiders on U.S. law school faculties were having differentially difficult times both with the tenure process and in terms of overall satisfaction with their work situations (Barnes and Mertz 2012, 2018; see also Mertz and Barnes 2016).[16] Women of color reported facing more challenges than did men of color or white women, in part because of their intersectional identity status: "Well, I think I've had to work harder in my teaching because, um, as an African-American woman, for many of my students, I'm the first time they've ever had such a person uh, as a teacher."[17] The continuing problems often took very subtle forms. Scholars of color commented, for example, that continued bias could be invisible to their white colleagues, given that individual white colleagues believed themselves to be free of racism. If the sum of individual attitudes creates institutional climates, such colleagues would reason, then how could the institutional climate be racist? After all, these white colleagues could see no visible evidence of continued racial bias among the individual professors who made up their law faculties. As one of our interviewees, a male professor of color, noted:

> And so my point is that it's – it's – racism is still alive and well and … and it's still alive and well within the – within academia – even though, you know, you might approach a – a white person and that per – person'll say, "Well, I'm not racist." You know? But that's – that – that's not the point. The point is that, institutionally speaking, there is this in- there's an institutional uh, uh, context and construct of – of racism within which we – we have to work. And so that – that's just something that um, I think we'll have to live with for – for the foreseeable future.[18]

In interview after interview, scholars of color gave examples of ongoing bias – sometimes subtle, sometimes fairly obvious (although they reported that even more obvious forms were still often invisible to most of their white colleagues). Similarly, women gave examples of gender-based bias in how they were treated and evaluated on law school faculties – again noting that their male colleagues often seemed unaware of the problems (Mertz and Barnes 2016; Barnes and Mertz 2018). Sometimes this lack of awareness had to do with the fact the bias took very subtle forms and seemed to operate outside of individuals'

16 As noted above, combining qualitative and quantitative research in this way allows for more reliable results, yielding depth and contextualized detail while also giving precise information on generalizability.

17 Interview 6132, African-American woman professor, elite law school, 10–19 years experience, high reported satisfaction. This section primarily summarizes results from other publications where those results are reported with more ethnographic detail. See Mertz and Barnes 2016 and Barnes and Mertz 2012, 2018 for discussions and examples of the extra burdens faced by women of color.

18 Interview 4180, Latino male professor, non-elite law school, 10–19 years experience, high reported satisfaction.

consciousness. At other times the lack of awareness stemmed from the fact that bias emanated from institutional structures that had differential impacts on scholars of color and women.

The Diversity in Legal Academia *Project*

Thus the *After Tenure* study documented continuing difficulties for women and professors of color in the legal academy – with women of color suffering the double burden created by their intersectional position. That study also located forms of implicit bias and institutional structure as important sources of ongoing inequality. These are both difficult sources to address and correct, given how deeply rooted they become over time in cultures, societies, and institutions. Some time has passed since Phase I of the study, however. Have the patterns identified thus far in the *After Tenure* study data continued after the first decade of the new millennium, or have they been eradicated?

Fortunately, Professor Meera Deo conducted the *Diversity in Legal Academia* (*DLA*) study during the second decade of the new millennium (2014, 2015, this volume). The *DLA* included pre-tenure as well as post-tenure professors. This research employed a novel intersectional framework to examine in particular the experiences of women professors of color, both pre- and post-tenure, with some smaller comparison interview groups of white women, men of color, and white men.[19] The *DLA* national target sample provides excellent recent information on the continued difficulties facing women of color and other traditional outsiders in the legal academy, and documents continuing patterns of implicit (as well as sometimes explicit) bias (Deo 2015). It is striking that the *DLA* and the *After Tenure* studies, although they were conducted independently using somewhat different approaches, nonetheless converge on quite similar results.

The qualitative findings from *DLA* indicate that several patterns remain the same. First, Deo notes that, in general, the faculty of color whom she interviewed reported "collegial interactions with colleagues," including Black faculty who describe their law schools as "very civil" and as places where faculty "genuinely like each other" and "are happy to see each other" (Deo 2015, 968). This parallels the *After Tenure* finding that mean satisfaction levels for all demographic groups remained relatively high, ranging from 3.8 to 4.3 on a five-point scale (Barnes and Mertz 2018, 11–12). On the other hand, women of color in the *DLA* study had differentially negative stories about discrimination, which were echoed to varying degrees in the stories of some men of color and white women (Deo 2015, 964–1001). Barnes and Mertz also found striking differences, with white male professors showing significantly higher levels of satisfaction than other groups (2018, 13). Deo's work importantly documents the roots of these differences in satisfaction through detailed and subtle qualitative analyses.

19 There were 93 total interviews in the *DLA* study, 64 of which were with women of color.

Thus Deo tracks a number of themes within her respondents' interviews. In terms of relationships with colleagues, the *DLA* collected qualitative data on law professors' feelings about levels of collegiality. One set of themes that emerged from these data dealt with the uncomfortable ways in which some women of color experienced a "mask of collegiality" with white, frequently male, colleagues within their home law schools (Deo 2015, 968–974). In some cases, these women were made to feel that they were more guests or exceptions than real members of the faculty, despite the show of collegiality that others on their faculties put forth. For example, these respondents received subtle – and not so subtle – cues that they were inferior and less intellectually able than their white male colleagues (Deo 2015, 970). These women also described receiving misleading advice from white male colleagues, who posed as supportive and friendly while simultaneously participating in negative gossip that had damaging effects. This kind of phenomenon would obviously diminish trust and comfort, and indeed many women of color in the *DLA* described distancing from their more powerful white male colleagues:

> while faculty are cordial with one another, this civility masks underlying distrust and distance. Of notable exception are the close relationships female faculty of color have with one another and other underrepresented and often marginalized faculty members at their institutions whom they draw on for support.
> (Deo 2015, 974)

The *After Tenure* results, along similar lines, showed that law faculty of color are more likely to turn to support groups and colleagues outside of their law schools than are white scholars (Mertz et al. 2011, 40–41, 45; re outsider professors generally, see Barnes and Mertz 2018, 15–19).

Another set of themes regarding collegial interactions identified by the *DLA* is even more congruent with the *After Tenure* findings, in that they focus on invisibility/silencing (Deo 2015, 974–985; on respect/voice, see Barnes and Mertz 2018, 455–457). Along with invisibility/silencing in Deo's findings were reported instances of sexual harassment, a problem that also emerged in the *After Tenure* qualitative results. Qualitative research is especially helpful in identifying problems that interviewees might find difficult to divulge in more impersonal surveys – and in highlighting connections among themes that emerge from interviews. Those kinds of themes typically work in a web of cultural and institutional logics that are not easily mapped quantitatively – although again, quantitative approaches are helpful in mapping the distribution and extent of some of these phenomena within communities and institutions (and wider societies).

The *DLA* results specified a number of particular issues involving invisibility and silencing of traditional outsiders within U.S. law faculties – issues that are sadly familiar from general literatures on race and gender bias (see above; Deo 2015, 975; and see Barnes and Mertz 2012: 512). For example, respondents described making comments that were ignored, only to be validated when white male colleagues later repeated the same points; similarly, some respondents noted that after years on their law faculties, some male colleagues still failed to greet or recognize them (Deo 2015, 276). Respondents also described high levels of stress caused by being dismissed or systematically undervalued in their work environments. These difficulties were patterned along lines that would be predicted by a number of different social science and scholarly traditions, as we will see below. Thus the *DLA* research unfortunately gives credence to the proposition that the problems of race and gender bias located by earlier research, while they might have abated in some times and places, still continue at a sufficiently high level to merit ongoing concern.

A Profession of Ideas? Deep Culture and Slow Institutional Change

Having reviewed research that indicates the existence of continuing problems surrounding diversity within the legal academy, we return to our opening question: why would a set of institutions nominally committed to justice and steeped in academic knowledge practices continue to face such stubborn problems surrounding diversity? As noted, existing studies point to implicit bias and institutional structures as key sources of these continuing difficulties. But why would legal academics, versed in analyzing problems and marshalling intellectual resources, be so often unable to discern or remedy those difficulties?[20] Here I draw on three kinds of scholarship to make sense of the empirical findings on inequality among U.S. law professors: psychological, anthropological, and critical. The first tradition, from psychology, is probably familiar to many legal academics (although that does not mean it has been widely accepted). The second tradition derives from anthropology – which despite its long-standing identity as one of the major social sciences in Western academic traditions, has yet to receive any serious consideration within the mainstream of legal scholarship. The third set of traditions, encompassing critical race, feminist, intersectionality, and other approaches grounded in critical perspectives on mainstream society, has deep roots within the legal academy despite the fact that it has yet to be broadly recognized and incorporated by the mainstream legal academy. These three together point in the same direction, and provide tools that might aid parts of the legal academy still struggling to achieve true racial and gender integration.

Psychological Approaches: The Problem of Implicit Bias

Psychological research on implicit bias began to receive serious attention in the legal academy in the 1990s, when Linda Hamilton Krieger (1995) published an article on the topic in the *Stanford Law Review*.[21] Krieger sounded an alarm about the state of employment discrimination law in the U.S., arguing

20 Of course, some individual professors may be unperturbed at the idea that race and gender problems persist within their institutions – but the institutions themselves typically at least pay lip service to a contrary aspiration – one of a fair playing field for all.

21 This heightened attention likely owed much to the at least partially successful deployment of relevant psychological research by Susan Fiske and others in the case of *Price Waterhouse v. Hopkins* (1989) (Fiske and Borgiga 2008).

that it rested primarily on an outdated model of the psychology behind discrimination. She explained how, in employment discrimination cases relying on claims of "disparate treatment," U.S. law essentially required that plaintiffs be able to point to "bad actors" who had intentionally discriminated – or required that any alleged stereotyping of plaintiffs be evident at the precise moment of an employment decision. With very few exceptions, courts did not take seriously the idea that racial discrimination could result from unconscious bias that operated pervasively to affect the environment in which decisions were made (Krieger 1995, 1170). But, by contrast with the courts' approach, psychological science had by that time uncovered myriad ways in which racial bias could operate at unconscious levels, beyond individual awareness; research had also indicated that the bias was often pervasive, so that "the distinction between stereotype-revealing comments made during decisionmaking and before decisionmaking utterly breaks down" (1995, 1185).

Krieger's article reviewed a lengthy history of psychological research reaching from the 1950s to the 1990s – research that had documented with increasing specificity that "[s]tereotypes, when they function as implicit prototypes or schemas, operate beyond the reach of decisionmaker self-awareness," that "people's access to their own cognitive processes is in fact poor," and that therefore "cognitive bias may well be both unintentional and unconscious" (1995, 1188).[22] In that same year, social psychologists Anthony Greenwald and Mahzarin Banaji provided a comprehensive overview of research on implicit social cognition, examining aspects such as implicit attitudes, stereotypes, self-esteem, and self-concept (1995). Since that time there have been numerous writings about the psychological science on implicit bias in law reviews, with a comprehensive overview by Professor Jerry Kang appearing in the *Harvard Law Review* in 2005.[23] Kang summarized the mounting psychological evidence demonstrating the ways our brains create shortcuts to navigate the vast array of sensory inputs we receive in making our way through an average day: we have to gather visual inputs into categories (that object is a "chair" not a "table") that then guide our actions (I can sit on it, or I can't) (Kang

22 Krieger cites research by a wide range of empirical scholars, from Jerome Bruner and Henri Tajfel in the 1950s and 60s, through Reid Hastie, Shelley Taylor, and Jennifer Crocker in the 1970s and 80s (1995, 1186–1194). As other examples, Krieger reviews the work of Patricia Linville, Edward Jones, and Susan Fiske on distortions in person perception as well as research by Loren and Jean Chapman, David Hamilton, and Robert Gifford on illusory correlation in the formation of stereotyping (1995, 1195–1198). In providing this review, Krieger brought decades of psychological research to a legal audience that was struggling with how best to understand discrimination – with the aid of a highly visible publication forum in the *Stanford Law Review*. The point was to underscore the degree to which unconscious stereotyping and accompanying racial discrimination is a predictable part of everyday mental processing and remembering (1995, 1199–1211).

23 Kang's website characterizes this 2005 paper as "the first major treatment in the law reviews." See http://jerrykang.net/2011/03/13/getting-up-to-speed-on-implicit-bias/ (last accessed 1/29/2018).

2005, 1498–1499).[24] Whether one thinks of these as schemas or metaphors or conceptual associations, it is clear that a great deal of background work is going on to organize what we perceive into manageable categories and groupings. Kang's article discusses how this applies to racial schemas: "Through law and culture, society provides us … with a set of racial categories into which we map an individual human being" – and once this categorization happens, our brains quickly bring to bear a wealth of associations, many of them unconscious (Kang 2005, 1499).

From here it is a short trip to both cognitions and emotions that can carry implicit bias, with important behavioral consequences. And, as those concerned with intersectionality could have told us, our brains are simultaneously picking up cues about everything from gender to role (doctor, police officer) to social class as they work to streamline how we take information in and how we respond (see Fiske and Taylor 1991, 121–145). Thus, to quote Greenwald and Banaji, the process that produces implicit bias is inevitably reliant on social contexts, and is accordingly quite variable: "Social experience histories are presumed to vary among people, producing attitudes, stereotypes, and self-concepts that differ among persons" – thus "variations in the mental structures result[] from the differing past histories of social experiences" (2017, 869). This kind of research in psychology highlights the social roots of implicit bias inasmuch as that bias relies on socially produced stereotypes and associations – but it is also important to look at entire institutions and social structures to see how they might both rest upon and reproduce those kinds of biases. Levinson and Smith note that bias seeps into institutions not only via "processes and people" but also through the cultural "underpinnings of the entire system" (2017, 407).

Social psychology, then, has increasingly produced research that demonstrates how individuals internalize social patterns and stigma in ways of which they are likely to be unaware. If law students have unconsciously internalized the expectation that authority figures in law are white males – be they law professors, lawyers, or judges – then these studies suggest that law professors from traditionally excluded groups might be subject to extra scrutiny. More recent work further stresses the ways that these prejudices might be incorporated into entire institutions, but psychology has not generally specialized in analyzing institutional and social structural levels. By contrast, social sciences like anthropology have been studying this phenomenon for some time.

Culture, Institutional Structures, and Anthropological Approaches: The Importance of Humility in Social Science Methodologies

Social science methods always involve trade-offs: anthropological methods are among the best available at preserving "external validity" – at capturing the way things actually occur in people's lives, with minimal alteration by the observer.

24 This is not news; social psychologists and psychological anthropologists have been demonstrating that these kinds of shortcuts are in operation for a long time.

Anthropologists typically immerse themselves in the settings they study, living alongside their research subjects for a year or more, learning the language, and doing their best to stay in the background. Importantly, they are also trained to continually confront and question their own assumptions, practicing a form of methodological humility in an effort to minimize imposition of their own ideas on those they study. Contrast with this a method very far removed from people's everyday practices – like bringing students into a lab and having them respond to experimental conditions. You will be able to capture the effects of changes introduced into the experiment very well, but will have altered the setting to the point that it doesn't resemble anything in the experimental subjects' normal everyday lives. The experimental method maximizes "internal validity" (Macaulay, Friedman, and Mertz 2007, 156). Even the format of a standardized interview risks imposing the interviewer's categories on the interview subject – who might be forced to answer questions that do not capture much about the interviewee's own categories of understanding (Briggs 1986). In the process, you will have held constant the prompt given to each person, which can produce useful information across a group of people, but you may miss what the people themselves find interesting. More open-ended interviews have a better chance of allowing interviewees' own views to emerge, but are harder to compare with one another.

To achieve a still more open-ended inquiry, full-blown anthropological fieldwork requires researchers to spend long periods of time (traditionally, a year or more) among the people they are studying. They must work in the local language and do their best to discover the priorities and assumptions of the people they're studying. They observe naturally occurring interaction within group settings – and those groups are not created by the anthropologist (as opposed to groups in experimental studies, for example),[25] but are groups that formed and existed prior to the research.[26] Fieldworkers are trained to use field notes, diaries, and other techniques to examine their perceptions critically, as they work to put aside their own cultural frameworks and to develop a maximally accurate understanding of the cultures they are studying on those cultures' own terms. Part of this involves keeping an eye on the limitations of their own research method – as no social science method is suited to answering every possible research question. As noted above, this careful reflexivity about one's own method is another form of humility, and it is the opposite of methods that try to claim absolute certainty about the totality of what they study, despite the fact that they inevitably produce only a partial vision (whether it is generated through statistics, economic modeling, fieldwork, interviewing, psychological experiments, or any other method).

25 These experiments, as I've noted, have other strengths. And not all psychological studies follow this protocol; some social psychologists use approaches that come close to tapping the actual social group at issue. For example, some social psychologists studying juries select their experimental subjects from the same jury pool that is the source of actual juries, thus closely replicating the social process by which real juries are created.

26 On fieldwork conventions generally, see Bernard (2006); Kenny and Smillie (2015); Moore (2012).

Of course, anthropology itself has had its own struggles to escape implicit assumptions imported from the colonial societies of the global north, from whose ranks the founders of the discipline were drawn. For example, the culture concept has long been identified with anthropology, which since its earliest days has worked to understand the very different shared group understandings and ways of life that can be found across diverse groups of people around the world.[27] Despite this professed goal, anthropologists made serious errors based on "ethnocentrism" – on a belief in the superiority of their own sociocultural system, based in deeply racist beliefs.[28] For example, at one point in time, anthropologists posited that there was an evolutionary scheme under which societies in general "advanced" until reaching a pinnacle in (of course) their own Western societies.[29] Early anthropological analyses also failed to consider how colonialism had affected the very societies being studied, despite the fact that massive, often negative, changes were underway in response to so-called "civilized" peoples' intrusions on the cultures being studied (Asad 1973; Said 1978). Over time, anthropologists worked to develop methods that required a more stringent humility in order to bracket off their own cultural assumptions more effectively, with varying effects (Harrison 1995).[30]

Although early anthropology developed a conception of culture that failed to consider issues of power and bias, the second half of the twentieth century saw some

27 Because of limited space, I cannot begin to do justice to the anthropological contributions to this kind of analysis, but I provide a very brief outline of them as a way of illustrating the potential advantages of this approach. Histories of the culture concept in Anglo-American anthropology commonly point to the work of Tylor 2016 [1871] as an important touchstone, but from there the myriad debates and definitions take off in complex directions (Bohannon and Glazer 1988; Moore 2012; and see for example Benedict 2005 [1934]; Douglas 1966; Geertz 1973; Greenhouse 1996; Ortner 1996; Silverstein 1985). Sociology also has extensive literatures on how institutions implicitly incorporate bias and social hierarchy – and the field of law-and-society pays particular attention to how this happens in legal institutions.

28 Franz Boas and his students employed forms of cultural relativism as an antidote to ethnocentrism, pushing ethnographers to examine other cultures' customs and beliefs as a whole, as ways of life that make sense only in relation to one another (Boas 1963 [1911]; Mead 2001 [1928]; Benedict 2005 [1934]).

29 Along with this self-serving teleological vision came mistaken historical assumptions, with "the Europeans imagining that so-called primitive peoples resembled what their own ancestors had been like in the past" (as if those peoples had not had their own histories leading up to their lives in current times – but instead existed out of regular time, in a sense, representing an earlier era) (Kenny and Smillie 2015, xiii).

30 A new generation of anthropologists is demanding more of the discipline, pushing for still deeper thinking about ongoing implicit forms of racism and bias within anthropological thinking and practice (see, e.g., Todd 2016; Pandian 2018). While I argue here that anthropological methods have more potential than some other social science methods for broadening epistemological frames, this is a possibility that depends on the same openness for which this chapter pushes in other forms of research – one which includes the voices and perspectives of the subjects of research, and of scholars from traditionally excluded groups. Unfortunately, there are very few disciplines, including anthropology, that can afford to take for granted that they've succeeded in this regard.

improvement. For example, in earlier days it was common to contrast the way *meaning* is organized in *cultures* with the way *behavior* is organized in *social structures*, but in time anthropologists developed conceptions of *sociocultural* systems that combined consideration of cultural systems of meaning with the study of power and material life (Kuklick 2008; and see Selby and Basso 1976). This was partially a recognition of the artificial nature of any separation between what we believe and what we do – a recognition that the institutions that shape our behaviors are also bearers of cultural beliefs. Earlier sharp divisions between economic anthropology and symbolic anthropology began to soften as anthropologists developed ways of showing how each part of a sociocultural whole was imbricated in the other parts. Religions are affected by economics; business firms have cultures. Anthropologists also moved on to contextualize the study of culture and power within historical contexts, and to ask about the complex dynamics through which people resist the imposition of power (Starr and Collier 1989; Lazarus-Black and Hirsch 1994).

Anthropological research, then, can uncover how shared cultural conceptions and social patterns of behavior shape people's views of each other. Those conceptions and behaviors are group-level phenomena; they emerge from histories of people interacting with one another in particular ways, using particular speech patterns, accepting certain divisions of power and measures of worth, sharing background orientations that may never be consciously acknowledged. For example, ideas about what women are like and how they should act are rooted in social and cultural patterns that make some behaviors seem "natural" and others not. And these ideas are not the same in all places or times. There is nothing inevitable about any particular configuration, although our own sociocultural configuration tends to feel natural (while others are perceived as "strange").[31] Where psychologists talk of implicit bias, anthropologists speak of deep sociocultural patterning that can leave lingering assumptions in place despite overt efforts to change those beliefs. Increasingly, they also speak of the way power relations inform and reinforce some of that patterning.[32] A great deal of recent work in anthropology tracks the imposition of colonial and neoliberal power on

31 One way of framing the anthropological enterprise is that its goal is to make things that seem strange more familiar, while also challenging us to see that what we take for granted in our own everyday lives can also be viewed as strange. Under this vision, the goal is not to understand "the other," but to use our encounters with people we perceive as "others" to develop more critical edges in understanding ourselves (see Lazarus-Black 2017 for a telling example of this approach from a study of "foreign" law students in U.S. law schools). This way of describing the field has its own perils however, as it assumes a shared hegemonic identity under "us" and classifies everyone who is not a white Westerner as "other." As anthropology itself became more diverse and more aware of this problem, unproblematized references to "the other" have become appropriately suspect.

32 In recent decades, anthropologists have drawn on social theorists like Bourdieu and Foucault in developing their theoretical frameworks for understanding the power dimensions circumscribing culture. As this is far beyond what I can develop in this short summary, I would simply point out that the examination of inequality and power in cultural patterning fits well with efforts to "de-naturalize" shared understandings that may well reflect more about established relations of power within institutions and societies than anything else.

societies around the world, all the while struggling with the fact that anthropology was itself formed (along with the other social science disciplines) in and through these very forms of power.

To understand how deeply held assumptions about traditional outsiders might be impacting their experiences in institutions, then, anthropological researchers would examine the small, subtle cues built into everyday norms and behaviors. How people look, or don't look, at women who speak up in meetings; what language and tone of voice is used; seating arrangements; the history and current makeup of the institution – all these and more give the ethnographer clues about the implicit cultural norms at work in groups. Something that is almost invisible – someone shifts in a seat or frowns, another violates cultural norms by interrupting someone deemed her superior – can hold clues to the very subtle ways institutional culture is maintained or is changing.

Linguistic anthropologists have paid special attention to the way structures of linguistic interaction play a role. For example, very subtle aspects of dinner-table conversations in middle-class U.S. families reinforce the natural-seeming idea that fathers are the heads of these households (Ochs and Taylor 2001). In seemingly inconsequential playground games, children use language to discipline other children and reinforce class and racial hierarchies (Goodwin 2006). Linguistic anthropologists studying legal systems find the very same dynamics at work. For example, small details of linguistic interchanges provide the matrix through which women mobilized in Kenyan Islamic courts to shift gendered power dynamics (Hirsch 1998). Sophisticated litigants representing businesses in U.S. small claims courts use "powerful" forms of language that give them an invisible advantage – while the individuals for whom small claims courts were designed lack this advantage (Conley and O'Barr 1990). Law reformers have tried to protect rape victims in U.S. courts using formal "rape shield" laws (limiting overt references to the victims' prior sexual conduct), but failed to consider the vast arsenal of subtle linguistic and physical cues through which implicit bias toward women could be mobilized (Matoesian 2001). And efforts to create courts that respect indigenous peoples' own law can at the same time use procedures that fundamentally violate the precepts of that law – and of the communities from which it emerged – in part because of how language is deployed (Richland 2008).

Through anthropological techniques that train observers to hold their own presumptions in abeyance to the highest degree possible (while remaining aware that this is always partial), we can start to examine tacit structures and assumptions that underlie social institutions. Like the therapist trained to listen without imposing his own viewpoint – but at a larger sociocultural level – the anthropologist does her best work when she practices humility. Like the lab scientist who must give up cherished hypotheses if her data do not support them, the ethnographer carefully tracks and lets go of cherished assumptions based in his own sociocultural background, allowing the worldviews of ethnographic subjects to challenge those deeply embedded beliefs. This challenge to his own implicit beliefs, based in the science of anthropological method, yields new insights not only about the culture being studied – but about the ethnographer's own society.

Thus anthropological insights teach us that dominant cultures in institutions such as law schools are likely to reproduce social hierarchies in hidden ways that appear "natural" to those inhabiting those institutions. Standards of "excellence" may incorporate deeply situated assumptions that actually reflect the way institutions grew in the hands of one group in society, but without the kind of searching examination afforded by anthropological (and other similar) methods, the continuing exclusion of newcomers will appear to result from "inferiority" rather than social dominance. Another important scholarly tradition that has the capacity to uncover such hidden patterning is the critical scholarship of outsiders to the academy – who like anthropologists, occupy a place from which the taken-for-granted assumptions of dominant societies can be questioned.

Critical Race, Feminist, and Intersectional Approaches: Invisibility and Silence

It is important to note that at least from the time of renowned sociologist W.E.B. Du Bois until the present, scholars of color have led the way in their use of empirical research to document forms of racism missed by mainstream scholarship. In addition, the development of ethnic and women's studies programs in U.S. universities during the 1960s and 70s gave scholars of race and gender added voice and visibility in close contact with many of the social sciences (see Zuberi 2011). As explained above, social science research improves when it widens the range of questions and ideas it entertains, either through permitting researchers from diverse backgrounds to participate, or through methods that tap and respect the experiences of people beyond the academy (Zuberi and Bonilla-Silva 2008). While anthropologists have used observation and cultural analysis to step outside of untested assumptions built into the dominant culture, critical scholars of race, gender, and sexuality additionally draw upon new forms of analysis and on their own "outsider" experiences.

Long before conceptions of implicit bias based in cognitive psychology became au courant in legal scholarship, Professor Charles Lawrence III had already powerfully pointed to unconscious bias as a serious, continuing problem facing any realistic legal efforts to confront discrimination:

> decisions about racial matters are influenced in large part by factors that can be characterized as neither intentional – in the sense that the outcomes are self-consciously sought – nor unintentional – in the sense that the outcomes are random, fortuitous, and uninfluenced by the decisionmaker's beliefs, desires, and wishes.
>
> (1987, 322)[33]

33 As Krieger (1995, 1164n.11) noted, Lawrence drew primarily on psychoanalytical theory that focused on motives, and thus differed from the newer generation of scholars who focused more on cognitive aspects of unconscious bias. However, as Krieger also observes, Lawrence did also mention cognitive bias and in general anticipated a great deal of the work of a subsequent generation in his concern with the unconscious dimensions of bias as they affect legal practice, doctrine, and professions.

As Lawrence goes on to explain, a shared national cultural history of racism in the United States has created a belief system, largely taken for granted, that unconsciously biases decision-making at many levels. This is a phenomenon, as noted above, that has been thoroughly documented by anthropologists and other social scientists. Lawrence also correctly argues that the phenomenon of unconscious racism cannot be addressed adequately at the level of individual actors:

> Understanding the cultural source of our racism obviates the need for fault, as traditionally conceived, without denying our collective responsibility for racism's eradication. We cannot be individually blamed for unconsciously harboring attitudes that are inescapable in a culture permeated with racism.
> (Lawrence 1987, 325–326)

Thirty years later, it is somewhat depressing to note that this very insight is now being treated as news in many quarters. To be sure, cognitive psychology has been providing vivid demonstrations of how the phenomenon of implicit bias operates, and this is a welcome addition to the general field of knowledge in the area. But the way institutional structures and cultural beliefs continue old patterns of this kind is hardly news to anyone versed in writings by scholars of color and other social scientists who have long studied how sociocultural systems work over time.

In terms of the legal academy, law professors were early leaders within the scholarly movement of Critical Race Theory. And indeed the critical race scholarship on this topic, as it pertains to law schools in particular, is so voluminous that it cannot be adequately reviewed within the scope of this chapter. Classic writings by law professors such as Derrick Bell, Patricia Williams, Richard Delgado, and many others spelled out the contours of the persistent problem of unconscious bias within the legal academy years ago, while younger generations of law professors now chart its continuing course within today's law schools (as well as within the university as a whole, and beyond universities within wider arenas pertinent to law).[34] Derrick Bell's 1993 article on diversity and academic freedom in law schools spelled out a number of the mechanisms that perpetuated racial inequality on those faculties – mechanisms still reported by law professors today.

34 Patricia Williams' laser-sharp description of implicit bias within the legal academy remains disturbingly accurate in 2018, according to the recent studies cited above (Williams 1991, 3–15, 80–97). In the 1980s, Richard Delgado described a form of implicit bias that operated in the citation practices of presumably well-intentioned civil rights law scholars, who kept citing white men to the exclusion of scholars of color, even when liberal law professors wrote on the subject of racism (1984). In 1992, Delgado updated his earlier article, noting a set of "second generation" problems, including some continued exclusion of minority and female scholars, but often more subtle marginalizing moves (adding names of outsider scholars at the end of a string cite while discussing theories of white male scholars in the text, mentioning outsider scholars briefly or dismissively in the text, citing the same one article by an outsider scholar over and over, recasting more radical analyses in tamer forms, and more) (1992, 1356–1368). Crenshaw (1994) offered suggestions for improving legal pedagogy to be more inclusive.

To take one example, rules that were applied to exclude minority hires by some law schools were then waived for white prospects, with no apparent conscious awareness of the disparities (Bell 1993, 375–376). As Bell pointed out, "the major opposition here is more than simple prejudice" because it likely operates through a seemingly non-racist preference for keeping things the same: "no group is more satisfied with the status quo than those law teachers who oppose any departure from traditional hiring procedures" (Bell 1993, 374–376).[35] Of course, those hiring traditions were shaped in times when there were strong limits of gender and race within law schools' cultures, but like members of any culture, many law professors internalized the traditional way as best, as natural, as the way it should be. In the end, Bell argued, adherence to past norms has actually hindered quality in legal education, because inclusion of diverse scholars and practitioners in new ways within U.S. law schools would raise standards for professors – requiring them to respond at higher levels to the changing needs of their students and of the legal system itself in today's world. These insights from Bell's article drew strength from the interview study with law professors conducted by Richard Delgado, with support from Bell (Delgado and Bell 1989).

In a similar vein, Taunya Lovell Banks wrote that integrating law faculties is important intellectually, because "excluded or devalued life experiences raise legal, social, and moral issues that … should be addressed by legal scholars because they reflect law as it operates" (Banks 1990, 48–49). She also highlighted the importance of intersectional identity, noting that "Black women academics/intellectuals … occupy a precarious position in legal education. We are misfits, not fully accepted by the Black or White community, and as women, we still are not full members of the feminist community" (Banks 1990, 48). Banks had conducted early empirical research on law teaching, completing one of the pioneering studies in that area as part of her exploration of race and gender dynamics in legal education (1988, 1990). The study used survey research to tap the views of students from 14 private and public law schools across the U.S. The results pointed to differentially negative experiences on the part of students of color, except when they attended historically black law schools.

In 2012, over 40 women academics – mostly scholars of color – and a small number of men worked together to produce a volume called *Presumed Incompetent: The Intersections of Race and Class for Women in Academia* (Gutiérrez y Muhs et al. 2012). The volume included first-person reflections as well as summaries and reports of empirical research. Over a quarter of the writers were law professors, including two of the four editors – who also authored the Introduction. Continuing their strong contribution to uncovering inequities in academic workplaces, a number of these law professors recounted their own and others' experiences in law

35 Bell's comment sheds more light on why law schools might not take the steps needed to create more friendly contexts for diversity, despite overt protestations to the contrary: doing things the way they've always been done just seems right, and feels more comfortable. This is supported by research in sociology demonstrating that people often feel more comfortable with others who are similar to them – a preference characterized as "homophily" (McPherson et al. 2001)

schools, identifying numerous examples of continuing bias facing women of color (see, e.g., Kupenda 2012; Onwuachi-Willig 2012; Arriola 2012).

Because they stood at multiple intersections, authors in this volume could speak to the distinct impacts of gender, race, and class bias – along with some discussion of sexual preference bias as well. In this sense, their insights reach to others who are experiencing racial or gender or class discrimination, while setting these experiences in a broader intersectional context. Their essays draw on empirical research as well as on their personal observations and theoretical analyses, demonstrating the fruitful scholarly synergy that emerges when social science is set in conversation with grounded analyses and narratives. For example, Armstrong and Wildman (2012) combine citations to empirical research with a narrative that gives readers a way to bring that research into grounded focus, explicating racial dynamics within workplaces. Sylvia Lazos (2012) provides a deep review of empirical studies pertinent to dynamics surrounding implicit bias in teaching evaluations, while also drawing on first-hand accounts of minority professors struggling with this phenomenon.

In recent years, a movement that explicitly marries empirical research and Critical Race Theory has developed under the aegis of empirical Critical Race Theory (eCRT). A key founder of this movement, Osagie Obasogie, points to eCRT working groups meetings in 2010 and 2011 as important launching moments, but he also notes that scholarship in this vein had been developing for some time (see, e.g. Gómez 2008; Obasogie 2006; Parks 2008). While CRT has generated new insights into structural inequalities that continually regenerate implicit bias, eCRT scholars believe that these insights "could be strengthened by increased reliance on social science methods" of both quantitative and qualitative varieties (Paul-Emile 2015, 2957). At the same time, these scholars "contend that social scientific research on race and identity could profit from the adoption of [CRT] theoretical frameworks that are more sophisticated than those that currently animate empirical methods" (Paul-Emile 2015, 2957).[36]

As Obasogie points out, however, the goal of eCRT goes beyond this mutual improvement effort to a fundamental rethinking of race scholarship "by eschewing theoretical and methodological silos in pursuit of deepening our understanding of race and racism to advance racial justice" (2013, 186). In this sense, like sociolegal studies, eCRT offers us an arena within which theoretical and empirical approaches that do not usually meet can enter into a more serious dialogue than is usually found in brief interdisciplinary encounters or conferences. In their article surveying the terrain of eCRT for the *Annual Review of Law and Social Science*,

36 Paul-Emile notes that eCRT has brought legal scholarship together with research in "sociology, social psychology, anthropology, economics, psychology, business, and political science" that draws on a range of methods and data to address theoretical, doctrinal and normative issues (2015, 2957). In remaining receptive in this way to social science empirical methods and findings, eCRT exemplifies the best of what New Legal Realism has urged in advocating for translation of a broad range of social science in service of studying law (see, e.g., Erlanger et al. 2005; Atuahene 2016; Dagan et al., 2018)

Carbado and Roithmayr similarly envision collaborations in which social science and critical race theory take each side's contribution seriously, without yielding tenets crucial to either:

> CRT and social science scholars can keep working from within the frameworks of their respective disciplines and at the same time transform disciplinary practices through their engagement with the other field. Just as social science should not dismiss CRT's commitment to the critique of neutrality, the critique of neutrality or objectivity should not prevent CRT from collaborating with fully engaged social science.
>
> (2014, 162)

The authors are at pains to stress that they do not argue that "critical race theorists should cherry-pick social science scholarship, citing the scholarship that supports their normative commitments and ignoring the scholarship that does not" (2014, 162). Rather, the CRT critique of purported objectivity and neutrality, along with other critical approaches, pushes the social sciences to acknowledge their limitations and to consider the ways in which scholars' own unexamined assumptions might limit their efforts.[37] In a telling example of how this can work, Carbado and his colleague Mitu Gulati (2013) published a recent book that tracked the complexities of intra-racial identity in professional settings, opening up myriad questions in need of further exploration before those professions are likely to be able to create truly fair working environments for traditional outsiders.

Law schools, of course, are formative professional settings that stand to benefit from more of the kind of searching inquiry that has emerged from Critical Race, empirical Critical Race, feminist, and other forms of "outsider" scholarship. These fields provide ways of framing research questions that can move beyond the taken-for-granted (and thus deeply unscientific) assumptions embedded in some scholarly writings on legal education. From early on, critical scholarship has shone a spotlight quite specifically on dynamics in U.S. legal education, raising concerns that have yet to be addressed effectively.

Conclusion: Inchoate Power and the Miner's Canary

This chapter began by reviewing recent studies that indicate continuing problems faced by "traditional outsider" law professors on U.S. faculties, who are still experiencing forms of marginalization based on race and gender. It then reviewed research from psychology, anthropology, and critical race studies, all of which supported those recent findings in that they had for some time documented how

37 In *Impure Science*, for example, Steven Epstein details how AIDS activists working with scientists were able to generate more effective research results than could the scientists alone, because they had not thought about some aspects of the problem they were studying which were obvious to members of the affected community (Epstein 1996).

difficult it is to change subterranean cultural and institutional patterns that categorize and marginalize certain socially defined groups; we focused in particular on the issue of race in our review of eCRT. All of this leaves us with a possibly discouraging conclusion: that despite generations of research from all corners of the academy – including law schools, it remains very difficult to get the academics who shape and control these workplaces to incorporate the changes which are, according to that research, necessary in order to improve diversity in legal education. Perhaps, then, the newer results from the study which I have helped to direct for some years – the *After Tenure* study housed at the American Bar Foundation – are similarly destined to fall on deaf ears.

If so, then empirical efforts to shed light on the legal academy will increasingly bring into sharp relief Lazarus-Black's observations about the effects of inchoate power in academic institutions. As she notes, this power operates largely below the radar, yet it is a crucial part of how those institutions internalize and recreate social inequality under a thick veneer of stated good intentions (see also Lazarus-Black and Globokar 2015). The mainstream legal academy's lack of attention to scholarship authored by scholars of color is yet another example of a distorting process, founded in social power relations, that affects even academics, who are ostensibly pledged to an intellectual life in which the weight of scholarly evidence matters more than the social positioning of the author. Of course, the psychological literature on implicit bias fully supports the possibility that academics could be affected by invisible assumptions that would cause them to ignore or dismiss solid evidence about the problematic character of some their own practices. On the other hand, as Lazarus-Black argues, paying attention to race, gender, class, international status, and other similar foundations for marginalization within the academy could help in challenging accepted – but mistaken – wisdom (Lazarus-Black in this volume, p. 66, also citing Moran 2000, 2329). This would not only permit institutions like law schools to live up to stated ideals of inclusion and fairness, but would enrich the knowledge base from which future scholarship could proceed. In the absence of such progress, the quiet exclusion described by professors of color and women professors in recent studies of law schools seems likely to persist.

Thus we return to the critical race scholarship with which we began, and to Guinier and Torres's warning about the hidden hegemonies that lie within traditional U.S. legal pedagogies – and indeed, within law itself. In recent years, flaring tensions around continuing bias have appeared at even the most elite law schools, which have more resources than other schools to address these issues.[38] This failure to eradicate old biases, as Guinier and Torres have warned, should function as a warning of toxic atmospheres that will undercut legal education in general; the distress of traditional outsider professors "is the first sign of a danger that threatens

38 See, e.g., www.chicagomaroon.com/article/2019/3/5/racism-thrives-law-school/, www.washingtonpost.com/news/grade-point/wp/2015/11/19/defacing-of-black-harvard-professor-portraits-investigated-as-hate-crime/?utm_term=.efc5b079e38c; see also Rahim (in press) on continued difficulties in addressing racial issues faced by Black students in U.S. law schools.

us all." If law schools cannot lead in the pursuit of justice within their own halls, there is little hope they can provide the leadership that they owe to the wider profession. A first step would be simply for those who hold power in these institutions to consider the possibility that the legal academy is not immune from implicit bias. There are more than enough resources available to scholarly institutions, once that first step is taken, to guide them in taking productive steps forward. Some of the leading scholars of race, gender, and many kinds of intersectional identities are law professors. Perhaps it is time their voices moved from the periphery to the center of legal scholarship and law school reform efforts.

References

ABA Commission on Women in the Profession. 2006. *Visible Invisibility: Women of Color in Law Firms.* Chicago, IL: American Bar Association.

ABA Commission on Women in the Profession. 2013. *Visible Invisibility: Women of Color in Fortune 500 Legal Departments.* Chicago, IL: American Bar Association.

Armstrong, Margalynne J., and Stephanie M. Wildman. 2012. Working across Racial Lines in a Not-So-Post-Racial World. In *Presumed Incompetent: The Intersections of Race and Class for Women in Academia*, eds. Gabriella Gutiérrez y Muhs, Yolanda Flores Niemann, Carmen G. González, and Angela P. Harris, 224–241. Boulder: University of Colorado Press.

Arriola, Elvia R. 2012. "No hay mal que por bien no venga": A Journey to Healing as a Latina, Lesbian, Law Professor. In *Presumed Incompetent: The Intersections of Race and Class for Women in Academia*, eds. Gabriella Gutiérrez y Muhs, Yolanda Flores Niemann, Carmen G. González, and Angela P. Harris, 372–392. Boulder: University of Colorado Press.

Asad, Talal, ed. 1973. *Anthropology and the Colonial Encounter.* Atlantic Highlands, NJ: Humanities Press.

Atuahene, Bernadette. 2016. Takings as a Sociolegal Concept: An Interdisciplinary Examination of Involuntary Property Loss. *Annual Review of Law and Social Science* 12: 171–197.

Banks, Taunya Lovell. 1988. Gender Bias in the Classroom. *Journal of Legal Education* 38: 137–146.

Banks, Taunya Lovell. 1990. Two Life Stories: Reflections of One Black Woman Law Professor. *Berkeley Women's Law Journal* 6: 46–56.

Barnes, Katherine, and Elizabeth Mertz. 2012. Is It Fair? Law Professors' Perceptions of Tenure. *Journal of Legal Education* 61(4): 511–539.

Barnes, Katherine, and Elizabeth Mertz. 2018. Law School Climates: Job Satisfaction among Tenured U.S. Professors. *Law & Social Inquiry* 43(2): 441–467.

Bell, Derrick. 1980. Brown v. Board of Education and the Interest-Convergence Dilemma. *Harvard Law Review* 93: 518–533.

Bell, Derrick. 1986. The Price and Pain of Racial Perspective. *Stanford Law School Journal.* Reprinted in Michael A. Olivas, *The Law and Higher Education: Cases and Materials on Colleges in Court*, 1122–1125 (2nd ed. 1997). Durham, NC: Carolina Academic Press.

Bell, Derrick. 1993. Diversity and Academic Freedom. *Journal of Legal Education* 43(3): 371–379.

Bell, Derrick. 2003. Diversity's Distractions. *Columbia Law Review* 103: 1622–1633.

Bell, Derrick. 2005. *Silent Covenants: Brown V. Board of Education and the Unfulfilled Hopes for Racial Reform.* Oxford: Oxford University Press.

Benedict, Ruth. 2005 [1934]. *Patterns of Culture*. New York: Houghton Mifflin Harcourt Publishing Co.

Bernard, H.Russell. 2006. *Research Methods in Anthropology*. Lanham, MD: Altamira Press.

Boas, Franz. 1963 [1911]. *The Mind of Primitive Man*. New York: Free Press.

Bohannon, Paul, and Mark Glazer. 1988. *High Points in Anthropology*, 2nd ed. New York: McGraw-Hill.

Bonica, Adam, Adam S. Chilton, Kyle Rozema, and Maya Sen. 2018. The Legal Academy's Ideological Uniformity. *Journal of Legal Studies* 47(1): 1–43.

Borthwick, Robert, and Jordan Schau. 1991–1992. Gatekeepers of the Profession: An Empirical Profile of the Nation's Law Professors. *University of Michigan Journal of Law Reform* 24: 191–238.

Briggs, Charles. 1986. *Learning How to Ask: A Sociolinguistic Appraisal of the Role of the Interview in Social Science Research*. Cambridge: Cambridge University Press.

Brooks, Roy. 1987. Anti-Minority Mindset in the Law School Personnel Process: Toward an Understanding of Racial Mindsets. *Law & Inequality: A Journal of Theory and Practice* 5(1): 1–31.

Carbado, Devon, and Mitu Gulati. 2013. *Acting White? Rethinking Race in "Post-Racial" America*. New York: Oxford University Press.

Carbado, Devon, and Daria Roithmayr. 2014. Critical Race Theory Meets Social Science. *Annual Review of Law and Social Science* 10: 149–167.

Cassidy, R. Michael. 2012. Beyond Practical Skills: Nine Steps for Improving Legal Education Now. *Boston College Law Review* 53(4): 1515–1532.

Chused, Richard. 1988. The Hiring and Retention of Minorities and Women on American Law School Faculties. *University of Pennsylvania Law Review* 137: 537–569.

Conley, John, and William O'Barr. 1990. *Rules versus Relationships: The Ethnography of Legal Discourse*. Chicago, IL: The University of Chicago Press.

Crenshaw, Kimberlé. 1991. Mapping the Margins: Intersectionality, Identity Politics, and Violence against Women of Color. *Stanford Law Review* 43(6): 1241–1299.

Crenshaw, Kimberlé. 1994. Foreword: Toward a Race-Conscious Pedagogy in Legal Education. *Southern California Review of Law and Women's Studies* 4: 33–52.

Dagan, Hanoch, Roy Kreitner, and Tamar Kricheli-Katz. 2018. Legal Theory for Legal Empiricists. *Law & Social Inquiry* 43: 292–318.

Delgado, Richard. 1984. The Imperial Scholar: Reflections on a Review of Civil Rights Literature. *University of Pennsylvania Law Review* 132: 561–578.

Delgado, Richard. 1988. Derrick Bell and the Ideology of Racial Reform: Will We Ever be Saved? *Yale Law Journal* 9: 923–948.

Delgado, Richard. 1992. The Imperial Scholar Revisited: How to Marginalize Outsider Writing, Ten Years Later. *University of Pennsylvania Law Review* 140: 1349–1372.

Delgado, Richard, and Derrick Bell. 1989. Minority Law Professors' Lives: The Bell–Delgado Survey. *Harvard Civil Rights – Civil Liberties Law Review* 24: 349–392.

Deo, Meera. 2014. Looking Forward to Diversity in Legal Academia. *Berkeley Journal of Gender, Law & Justice* 29(2): 352–387.

Deo, Meera. 2015. The Ugly Truth about Legal Academia. *Brooklyn Law Review* 80: 943–1014.

Douglas, Mary. 1966. *Purity and Danger: An Analysis of the Concept of Pollution and Taboo*. London: Routledge and Kegan Paul.

Du Bois, W.E.B. 1990 [1903]. *The Souls of Black Folk*. New York: Vintage Books.

Epstein, Steven. 1996. *Impure Science: AIDS, Activism, and the Politics of Knowledge*. Berkeley: University of California Press.

Erlanger, Howard, Bryant Garth, Jane Larson, Elizabeth Mertz, Victoria Nourse, and David Wilkins. 2005. Forward: Is It Time for a New Legal Realism? *Wisconsin Law Review* 2005: 335–363.

Fielding, Nigel G. 2012. Triangulation and Mixed Methods Designs: Data Integration With New Research Technologies. *Journal of Mixed Methods Research* 6(2): 124–136.

Files, Julia A., Anita P. Mayer, Marcia G. Ko, Patricia Friedrich, Marjorie Jenkins, Michael J. Bryan, Suneela Vegunta, Christopher M. Wittich, Melissa A. Lyle, Ryan Melikian, Trevor Duston, Yu-Hui H. Chang, and Sharonne N. Hayes. 2017. Speaker Introductions at Internal Medicine Grand Rounds: Forms of Address Reveal Gender Bias. *Journal of Women's Health* 26(5): 413–419.

Fiske, Susan T., and Eugene Borgiga. 2008. Providing Expert Knowledge in an Adversarial Context: Social Cognitive Science in Employment Discrimination Cases. *Annual Review of Law and Social Science* 4(1): 123–148.

Fiske, Susan T., and Shelley E. Taylor. 1991. *Social Cognition*, 2nd ed. New York: McGraw-Hill.

Fossum, Donna. 1980. Women Law Professors. *Law and Social Inquiry* 1980: 903–914.

Geertz, Clifford. 1973. *The Interpretation of Cultures.* New York: Basic Books.

Gendler, Tamar. 2011. On the Epistemic Costs of Implicit Bias. *Philosophical Studies* 156(1): 33–63.

Gómez, Laura. 2008. A Tale of Two Genres: On the Real and Ideal Links Between Law and Society and Critical Race Theory. In *The Blackwell Companion to Law and Society*, ed. Austin Sarat, 453–470. Malden, MA: Blackwell Publishing.

Goodwin, Marjorie H. 2006. *The Hidden Life of Girls: Games of Stance, Status and Exclusion.* Oxford: Blackwell.

Greenhouse, Carol. 1996. *A Moment's Notice: Time Politics across Cultures.* Ithaca, NY: Cornell University Press.

Greenwald, Anthony, and Mahzarin Banaji. 1995. Implicit Social Cognition: Attitudes, Self-Esteem, and Stereotypes. *Psychological Review* 102: 4–27.

Greenwald, Anthony, and Mahzarin Banaji. 2017. The Implicit Revolution: Reconceiving the Relation Between Conscious and Unconscious. *American Psychologist* 72(9): 861–871.

Guinier, Lani, and Gerald Torres. 2002. *The Miner's Canary: Enlisting Race, Resisting Power, Transforming Democracy.* Cambridge, MA: Harvard University Press.

Gutiérrez y Muhs, Gabriella, Yolanda Flores Niemann, Carmen G. González, and Angela P. Harris, eds. 2012. *Presumed Incompetent: The Intersections of Race and Class for Women in Academia.* Boulder: University of Colorado Press.

Harrison, Faye. 1995. The Persistent Power of "Race" in the Cultural and Political Economy of Racism. *Annual Review of Anthropology* 24: 47–74.

Hirsch, Susan. 1998. *Pronouncing and Persevering: Gender and the Discourses of Disputing in an African Islamic Court.* Chicago, IL: University of Chicago Press.

Holbrook, Allyson, Jon Krosnick, and Alison Pfent. 2008. The Causes and Consequences of Response Rates in Surveys by the News Media and Government Contractor Survey Research Firms. In *Advances in Telephone Survey Methodology*, eds. James Lepkowski, Clyde Tucker, J. Michael Brick, Edith de Leeuw, Lilli Japec, Paul Lavrakas, Michael Link, and Roberta Sangster, 499–528. Hoboken, NJ: John Wiley & Sons.

Jacobi, Tonja, and Dylan Schweers. 2017. Justice, Interrupted: The Effect of Gender, Ideology, and Seniority at Supreme Court Oral Arguments. *Virginia Law Review* 103: 1379–1496.

Kang, Jerry. 2005. Trojan Horses of Race. *Harvard Law Review* 118: 1489–1593.

Kenny, Michael, and Kirsten Smillie. 2015. *Stories of Culture and Place: An Introduction to Anthropology.* Toronto: University of Toronto Press.

Krieger, Linda Hamilton. 1995. The Content of Our Categories: A Cognitive Bias Approach to Discrimination and Equal Employment Opportunity. *Stanford Law Review* 47: 1161–1248.

Kuklick, Henrika, ed. 2008. *A New History of Anthropology*. Malden, MA: Blackwell.

Kupenda, Angela M. 2012. Facing Down the Spooks. In *Presumed Incompetent: The Intersections of Race and Class for Women in Academia*, eds. Gabriella Gutiérrez y Muhs, Yolanda Flores Niemann, Carmen G. González, and Angela P. Harris, 20–28. Boulder: University of Colorado Press.

Lawrence, Charles R.III. 1987. The Id, the Ego, and Equal Protection: Reckoning with Unconscious Racism. *Stanford Law Review* 39(2): 317–388.

Lazarus-Black, Mindie. 2017. The Voice of the Stranger: Foreign LL.M. Students' Experiences of Culture, Law, and Pedagogy in US Law Schools. In *Comparative Law and Anthropology*, ed. James A.R. Nafziger, 462–488. Cheltenham: Edward Elgar.

Lazarus-Black, Mindie, and Julie Globokar. 2015. Foreign Attorneys in U.S. LL.M. Programs: Who's In, Who's Out, and Who They Are. *Indiana Journal of Global Legal Studies*, 22(1):3–65.

Lazarus-Black, Mindie, and Susan Hirsch, eds. 1994. *Contested States: Law, Hegemony, and Resistance*. New York: Routledge.

Lazos, Sylvia. 2012. Are Student Teaching Evaluations Holding Back Women and Minorities?: The Perils of "Doing" Gender and Race in the Classroom. In *Presumed Incompetent: The Intersections of Race and Class for Women in Academia*, eds. Gabriella Gutiérrez y Muhs, Yolanda Flores Niemann, Carmen G. González, and Angela P. Harris, 164–185. Boulder: University of Colorado Press.

Levinson, Justin, and Robert J. Smith. 2017. Systemic Implicit Bias. *The Yale Law Journal Forum* 126: 406–416.

Macaulay, Stewart, Lawrence Friedman, and Elizabeth Mertz. 2007. *Law in Action: A Socio-Legal Reader*. New York: Foundation Press.

Matoesian, Gregory. 2001. *Law and the Language of Identity: Discourse in the William Kennedy Smith Rape Trial*. Oxford: Oxford University Press.

Matsuda, Mari. 1987. Looking to the Bottom: Critical Legal Studies and Reparations. *Harvard Civil Rights – Civil Liberties Law Review* 22: 323–399.

McPherson, Miller, Lynn Smith-Lovin, and James Cook. 2001. Birds of a Feather: Homophily in Social Networks. *Annual Review of Sociology* 27: 415–444.

Mead, Margaret. 2001 [1928]. *Coming of Age in Samoa: A Psychological Study of Primitive Youth for Western Civilization*. New York: HarperCollins Publishers.

Merritt, Deborah, and Barbara Reskin. 1992. The Double Minority: Empirical Evidence of a Double Standard in Law School Hiring of Minority Women. *Southern California Law Review* 65: 2299–2359.

Merritt, Deborah, and Barbara Reskin. 1997. Sex, Race, and Credentials: The Truth about Affirmative Action in Law School Hiring. *Columbia University Law Review* 97: 199–311.

Merry, Sally Engle. 2016. *The Seductions of Quantification: Measuring Human Rights, Gender Violence, and Sex Trafficking*. Chicago, IL: University of Chicago Press.

Merry, Sally Engle, Kevin E. Davis, and Benedict Kingsbury, eds. 2015. *The Quiet Power of Indicators: Measuring Governance, Corruption, and the Rule of Law*. New York: Cambridge University Press.

Mertz, Elizabeth, and Katherine Barnes. 2016. Combining Methods for a New Synthesis in Law and Empirical Research. In *The New Legal Realism: Translating Law-and-Society for Today's Legal Practice*, eds. Stewart Macaulay, Elizabeth Mertz, and Thomas W. Mitchell, 180–200. New York: Cambridge University Press.

Mertz, Elizabeth, and Bernard Weissbourd. 1985. Legal Ideology and Linguistic Theory: Variability and Its Limits. In *Semiotic Mediation: Sociocultural and Psychological Perspectives*, eds. Elizabeth Mertz and Richard Parmentier, 261–285. Orlando, FL: Academic Press.

Mertz, Elizabeth, Frances Tung, Katherine Barnes, Wamucii Njogu, Molly Heiler, and Joanne Martin. 2011. *After Tenure: Post-Tenure Law Professors in the United States* [Project Report]. Chicago, IL: American Bar Foundation (available at www.americanbarfoundation.org/publications/367; modified version available at LSAC).

Moore, Jerry. 2012. *Visions of Culture: An Introduction to Anthropological Theories and Theorists*, 4th ed. Lanham, MD: AltaMira Press.

Moran, Rachel. 2000. Diversity and its Discontents: The End of Affirmative Action at Boalt Hall. *California Law Review* 88: 2241–2352.

Obasogie, Osagie K. 2006. Race in Law and Society: A Critique. In *Race, Law and Society*, ed. Ian Haney Lopez, 445–464. Florence: Taylor and Francis.

Obasogie, Osagie K. 2013. Foreword: Critical Race Theory and Empirical Methods. *University of California Irvine Law Review* 3: 183–186.

Ochs, Elinor, and Carolyn Taylor. 2001. The "Father Knows Best" Dynamic in Dinnertime Narratives. In *Linguistic Anthropology: A Reader*, ed. Alessandro Duranti, 431–449. Malden, MA: Blackwell.

Onwuachi-Willig, Angela. 2012. Silence of the Lambs. In *Presumed Incompetent: The Intersections of Race and Class for Women in Academia*, eds. Gabriella Gutiérrez y Muhs, Yolanda Flores Niemann, Carmen G. González, and Angela P. Harris, 142–151. Boulder: University of Colorado Press.

Ortner, Sherry B. 1996. *Making Gender: The Politics and Erotics of Culture*. Boston, MA: Beacon Press.

Pandian, Anand. 2018. Open Access, Open Minds. *Cultural Anthropology*. https://culanth.org/fieldsights/1455-open-access-open-minds (accessed December 1, 2018).

Parks, Gregory Scott. 2008. Toward a Critical Race Realism. *Cornell Journal of Law & Public Policy* 17: 683–745.

Paul-Emile, Kimani. 2015. Foreword: Critical Race Theory and Empirical Methods Conference. *Fordham Law Review* 83(6): 2953–2960.

Rahim, Asad. In press. Race as Unintellectual. *UCLA Law Review*.

Richland, Justin. 2008. *Arguing with Tradition: The Language of Law in Hopi Tribal Court*. Chicago, IL: University of Chicago Press.

Said, Edward. 1978. *Orientalism*. New York: Pantheon Books.

Selby, Henry, and Keith Basso, eds. 1976. *Meaning in Anthropology*. Albuquerque: University of New Mexico Press.

Silverstein, Michael. 1985. Language and the Culture of Gender: At the Intersection of Structure, Usage, and Ideology. In *Semiotic Mediation: Sociocultural and Psychological Perspectives*, ed. Elizabeth Mertz and Richard Parmentier, 219–259. Orlando, FL: Academic Press.

Starr, June, and Jane Collier, eds. 1989. *History and Power in the Study of Law: New Directions in Legal Anthropology*. Ithaca, NY: Cornell University Press.

Tashakkori, Abbas, and Teddlie, Charles. 2003. The Past and Future of Mixed Methods Research: From Data Triangulation to Mixed Model Designs. In *Handbook of Mixed Methods in Social and Behavioral Research*, eds. Abbas Tashakkori and Charles Teddlie, 671–702. Thousand Oaks, CA: Sage.

Todd, Zoe. 2016. An Indigenous Feminist's Take on the Ontological Turn: "Ontology" is Just Another Word for Colonialism. *Journal of Historical Sociology* 29(1): 4–22.

Tylor, Edward Burnett. 2016 [1871]. *Primitive Culture Vol. I*. Mineola, NY: Dover Publications

White, Richard A. 2004. *The Promotion, Retention, and Tenuring of Law School Faculty: Comparing Faculty Hired in 1990 and 1991 to Faculty Hired in 1996 and 1997*. American Association of Law Schools. [Report on file with the author.]

Williams, Patricia. 1991. *The Alchemy of Race and Rights*. Cambridge, MA: Harvard University Press.

Zuberi, Tukufu. 2011. Critical Race Theory of Society. *Connecticut Law Review* 43(5): 1573–1591.

Zuberi, Tufuku, and Eduardo Bonilla-Silva, eds. 2008. *White Logic, White Methods: Racism and Methodology*. Lanham, MD: Rowman, & Littlefield Publishers.

Cases Cited

Price Waterhouse v. Hopkins (1989) 490 U.S. 228.

Index

www.ingramcontent.com/pod-product-compliance
Lightning Source LLC
LaVergne TN
LVHW011115300926
849160LV00008B/390
* 9 7 8 1 0 3 2 2 4 0 1 2 1 *